Coleridge, Opium
and
Kubla Khan

Coleridge, Opium
and
Kubla Khan

By

ELISABETH SCHNEIDER

THE UNIVERSITY OF CHICAGO PRESS

THE UNIVERSITY OF CHICAGO PRESS, CHICAGO 37
Cambridge University Press, London, N.W. 1, England

Kubla Khan

In Xanadu did Kubla Khan
A stately pleasure-dome decree:
Where Alph, the sacred river, ran
Through caverns measureless to man
   Down to a sunless sea.
So twice five miles of fertile ground
With walls and towers were girdled round:
And there were gardens bright with sinuous rills,
Where blossomed many an incense-bearing tree;
And here were forests ancient as the hills,   *10*
Enfolding sunny spots of greenery.

But oh! that deep romantic chasm which slanted
Down the green hill athwart a cedarn cover!
A savage place! as holy and enchanted
As e'er beneath a waning moon was haunted
By woman wailing for her demon-lover!
And from this chasm, with ceaseless turmoil seething,
As if this earth in fast thick pants were breathing,
A mighty fountain momently was forced:
Amid whose swift half-intermitted burst   *20*
Huge fragments vaulted like rebounding hail,
Or chaffy grain beneath the thresher's flail:
And 'mid these dancing rocks at once and ever
It flung up momently the sacred river.
Five miles meandering with a mazy motion
Through wood and dale the sacred river ran,
Then reached the caverns measureless to man,
And sank in tumult to a lifeless ocean;
And 'mid this tumult Kubla heard from far

〚 v 〛

30 Ancestral voices prophesying war!
   The shadow of the dome of pleasure
   Floated midway on the waves;
   Where was heard the mingled measure
   From the fountain and the caves.
It was a miracle of rare device,
A sunny pleasure-dome with caves of ice!

   A damsel with a dulcimer
   In a vision once I saw:
   It was an Abyssinian maid,
40   And on her dulcimer she played,
   Singing of Mount Abora.
   Could I revive within me
   Her symphony and song,
   To such a deep delight 'twould win me,
That with music loud and long,
I would build that dome in air,
That sunny dome! those caves of ice!
And all who heard should see them there,
And all should cry, Beware! Beware!
50 His flashing eyes, his floating hair!
Weave a circle round him thrice,
And close your eyes with holy dread,
For he on honey-dew hath fed,
And drunk the milk of Paradise.

Preface

This book is the result of accidents; it would never have been undertaken in cold blood. Some years ago I thought of writing a psychological study of the English Opium Eater, Thomas De Quincey. Knowing nothing about opium and observing that De Quincey's biographers appeared to know little but what he himself had told them, I looked into recent medical studies of the subject. These proved remarkably different from all that, in common with most other literary students, I had taken for granted. One day later on, I was surprised to hear myself explaining to a class of undergraduates the coherent literal meaning of a poem I had always supposed had none—Coleridge's *Kubla Khan*. Finally, the chance reading of Walter Savage Landor's poem *Gebir* and Robert Southey's *Thalaba* raised some Coleridgean ghosts, which led me in the end to question a number of beliefs held by my betters, the Coleridgean scholars. Curiosity took me the rest of the way; and from a feeling that the investigation, even in the more specialized aspects of the subject (the juggling with dates and sources), threw some little light upon the man Coleridge, his poetry and criticism, and the literary climate of his times, I was encouraged to inflict the result of these accidents upon the public.

My debts, properly expressed, would outweigh the book. To Professor Kathleen Coburn, of Toronto, I am especially grateful for many personal kindnesses, much valuable information, and generosity in making available to me her photostats and typescripts of the unpublished notebooks of Coleridge, which she is preparing for publication. With her permission I have read those belonging to the years

1797–1800 and have quoted from the typescripts several passages, of which, however, all but a few scattered phrases and sentences have already been published elsewhere. Professor Kenneth Curry very kindly lent and permitted me to quote from his annotated typescripts of the voluminous unpublished letters of Southey now in the National Library of Wales, the British Museum, and the Bodleian Library. Professor Earl Leslie Griggs provided information regarding unpublished letters of Coleridge; Professor T. M. Raysor, Professor R. C. Bald, and Professor I. A. Richards contributed many valuable suggestions. To Lawrence Kolb, M.D., I am indebted not only for his published studies in the psychological effects of opium but also for his kindness in reading the original version of my account of the subject, as a precaution against a layman's possible mistakes in dealing with technical scientific writing. If any errors of this sort have crept in, the fault is mine; much material has been added since Dr. Kolb saw the account. I am indebted also for the expense of considerable time, trouble, and kindness, to Miss Helen Darbishire, who arranged to have photographs made of portions of the manuscripts of Dorothy Wordsworth's journals, supplied me with valuable information concerning them, and on behalf of the Trustees of Dove Cottage granted permission to use them.

Many friends and colleagues at Temple University and elsewhere have assisted me in visible or invisible ways; and all have listened patiently to monologues. I must mention especially two of those who have read the manuscript, Miss Abbie Huston Evans, to whose poetical tact I owe much, and Professor Irwin Griggs, who provided several particularly helpful suggestions. My mother, Mary Robinson Schneider, has assisted me greatly in the reading of proof and in numerous other ways.

I wish to thank the librarians of the Sullivan Memorial Library of Temple University for favors of many kinds, bestowed with generosity and unfailing courtesy; perhaps I have imposed most upon the reference librarians, Mrs. Marie Woodard and Mr. Elkan Buchhalter. The facilities of the University of Pennsylvania Library and the courtesy of its staff have been of the greatest service; and I am grateful to the officials of other libraries for occasional favors, notably the library of Haverford College, the Houghton Library of Harvard University, and the Keeper of Printed Books of the British Museum. The work has been aided also by a grant from the Committee on Research of Temple University. My debts to previous writers and editors are too many to bear repeating here; they will be abundantly evident from the notes.

A small portion of chapter ii was originally published, in a different form, in *PMLA* in 1945.

E. W. S.

BALA-CYNWYD, PENNSYLVANIA
June 1953

Table of Contents

[xi]

Coleridge and the Critics

Occasions arise in the history of the arts when a single work for one reason or another becomes the focus for a body of legend, speculation, or doctrine that lifts the work to an accidental prominence. The ancient statue of the "Laocoön" was once such a focus. Around it the theories of Winckelmann and Lessing gathered, and it still remained, in name at least, at the center of one of the late Irving Babbitt's blasts that blew the romantic writers over the edge of the horizon, or very nearly over, for the time being. The *Œdipus* of Sophocles likewise almost vanished for some years in a blur of Freudian and anti-Freudian controversy. Something of the same, in a much smaller way, has been the history of Coleridge's two poems *The Ancient Mariner* and *Kubla Khan*. Coleridge himself started it. He first injected a nonpoetic element into the consideration of the second of these poems by introducing it to the public as a "psychological curiosity," a dream in which words and images had sprung up full grown in his sleep. In the present century the two poems have become an object of conflicting, or at least mutually exclusive, movements of criticism.

One of the most influential works of critical scholarship of our time, John Livingston Lowes's *The Road to Xanadu*, subjected *The Ancient Mariner* and *Kubla Khan* to a microscopic analysis of an almost wholly unprecedented kind. It attempted to shed light upon the ultimate secret processes of the creative imagination by tracing as fully as possible, even to the utmost limits of distant association, the sources of the poet's imagery. How far success in reaching this ultimate aim was achieved or was even possible may perhaps be questioned; but the magnitude and extensive influence of Lowes's work were alone enough to make it important. More recently, the same works of Coleridge have furnished matter for quite a different school of critical thought, the symbolic interpreters, who are today even more influential than Lowes and whose roots are deeper in the main streams of modern thought. Though both methods have been exercised upon much other English poetry, they have met most clearly on the ground of Coleridge. It has been said that, after *The Tempest*, *The Ancient Mariner* and *Kubla Khan* have become the most popular of all hunting grounds for symbolist criticism. Then into the midst of all those studies—whose authors have at least this in common, that they regard Coleridge with an uncommon unanimity of reverence—came the voice of Dr. Leavis almost alone, telling us that Coleridge's present reputation as an academic classic is "something of a scandal."

When the *Œdipus* or the "Laocoön" or *The Ancient Mariner* or *Kubla Khan* has become in this way a focus for conflicting critical theories, it is a good idea after a time to inspect the face of the original object and try once more to see freshly what it is, without benefit of doctrine, as far as we can divest ourselves of the passion for dogmatic certainties. In the exercise of a single-track method or the illustration of a doctrine, not only may we have taken a work of art for what it is not, but in so doing we may have admitted some far-reaching error into the very system of thought which we have used the work to deploy. The statue of "Laocoön" has long been reassessed and now survives in the chronicles of art almost entirely through having been of service to critics. The *Œdipus*, on the other hand, is indestructible and incorruptible. Right or wrong as psychological theories surrounding it may be, its own character is not much altered; it scarcely needs a re-examination so long as it remains in print for all to read.

Coleridge is no Sophocles; but neither, on the other hand, have his major poems dropped, or ascended, into limbo like the "Laocoön." As far as *The Ancient Mariner* is concerned, the conflicts among critics will no doubt take care of themselves. The poem is complete, its skeleton clearly marked. Critical thought will continue to throw light or cast wanted shadows upon it; critical aberrations will presumably cancel one another. In the long run, *The Ancient Mariner* is not likely to mislead anybody. But *Kubla Khan* is a little different. That poem has been a focus for influential currents of modern critical thought, two in particular, that imply conceptions of the nature of poetry and poetic genius, as well as of psychology and even medicine, that are of some importance, if true. In some respects, Lowes's remarkable blend of scholarship with genuine enthusiasm for poetry, in *The Road to Xanadu*, remains today a salutary lesson to an academic world that is inclined to divide into scholars who sneer at critics and critics who sneer at scholars. The final word on his subject, however, we now know has not altogether been said. Time has exposed certain flaws, some of them both deep and misleading.

Lowes accepted Coleridge's account of poetic imagination as "the true inward creatrix" that puts together and gives form to the "chaos of elements or shattered fragments of memory," as the power that shapes and modifies, "dissolves, diffuses, dissipates, in order to recreate." This is the brief sum of Coleridge's thought, shorn of its metaphysical implications. Now, assuming that to be the essence of creative imagination—if one can find an indisputably great poet whose materials are known to have been wholly or almost wholly drawn from reading rather than from the continuum of other less traceable experience; if, also, one can search out that reading fully and surely; finally, if one can hold it all clearly and simultaneously in mind so as to compare it significantly with the poet's work, catching the very transformations as they occur and analyzing them, then—supposing all these formidable conditions surmounted—just possibly, one may hope to come at least closer than we have ever come before to cracking the mysterious nut of poetic creation. Lowes assumed, with disarming modesty and due allowance for mortal error, that these conditions might be met in his study of two of Coleridge's poems. There is not to be found elsewhere, he said, "among all existing records of the human mind," another such opportunity of observing the creative faculty, in both conscious and unconscious activity, as is offered by *The Ancient Mariner* and *Kubla Khan*.[1] Into the conscious mind of genius there are, of course, other inlets in other poems. But only one human masterpiece, Lowes thought, comes direct to the printed page from the world of dreams, pure and untouched by any waking hand. The unconscious mind of genius, which in this view is somehow more quintessentially genius than the conscious mind, is beheld in only one poem in the history of man. *Kubla Khan* is thus the great poetic peephole into that essence; it is the unique and magical virgin birth of poetry. Such an offspring, I think, deserves a very close look.

But, first, what did Lowes actually find when he had finished his subtle and learned tracings? The answer is disappointing, for his conclusion actually comes to little more than this, that *Kubla Khan* is a glorious but irresponsible fabric of free associative links, elaborate but loose in texture, and wholly meaningless. This, in brief, is what the utterly unconscious mind of great genius produces. As Lowes saw it, the poem is a vision of surpassing loveliness. But *what* it is, the *ipse*, we still do not quite know, or even feel, from his account. He never claimed to have bridged fully the gap between the sources of the poet's imagery and the poem itself. He felt that he had narrowed it somewhat, as no doubt he had; but in the end what he emphasized, without perhaps intending to, was the magical element.

Immeasurably impressed by the almost miraculous dream-origin of *Kubla Khan,* which he not only accepted but espoused with some heat in opposition to the skeptical, he ended his long pursuit of the final knowledge of genius with his eyes more dazzled in wonder than before—which is all to his credit, provided only the object of wonder be genuine. The provision is important, for the influence of Lowes's wonder has been spread abroad almost as widely as his method of study.

Lowes's work on Coleridge began as an individual sally enlivened by enthusiasm and became influential enough to found almost a new school of critical writing. It was still, however, essentially grounded in traditional academic scholarship. Quite different are the symbolist critics. The most obvious impetus behind the current wave of symbolic interpretations of literature derives from the work of Freud and other leaders of psychoanalytic thought. However a Freudian may differ from a Jungian, a Jungian from a Rankian, and all these from the psychiatrist's modified analytical thought, a cardinal belief among them all is that men's dreams, sleeping or waking, and even their waking actions and choices are symbolic expressions of other hidden meanings or desires or fears. This mode of thought has exerted a profound influence upon modern criticism. But the psychoanalytical emphasis upon symbolism has been reinforced by other currents of thought.

From earliest times, symbolism has been one means by which in a period of change man can hold onto his past even while he discards it. When sophisticated Greece outgrew a literal belief in the Homeric gods with their too-human behavior, the pre-eminence of Homer could still be preserved through the notion that he had written about the gods symbolically and not literally. That discovery preserved Homer's supreme wisdom intact; it also offered the advantage of a limitless new field for ingenious interpretation. Centuries later, the Middle Ages and even the Renaissance slipped pagan writers into good Christian company through the same loophole of symbolic interpretation. And again, in the last century, symbolism was employed by many theologians to bring the Bible safely through a fire-bath of science.

From the deep and swiftly moving changes in the life and thought of our present century we also are impelled to snatch, with whatever hooks we may, all that can be rescued from the dissolving past. Symbolism is one of the neatest of those hooks, as we know from the writings of some modern poets, if not always the most legitimate. Works of the past that we still value but cannot by any modern principle find reason for approving we salvage by finding in them a symbolic substratum that conforms to our present values. The process I refer to goes beyond that accepted historical phenomenon, the need of every era to reinterpret the past for itself. A little while ago the Marxists, with an ingenuity of logic of which they almost alone are capable, tried to make a place for Henry James on their not overpopulated Parnassus, by finding him, if not quite actually a Marxist, at least a symbolic preparer of the sacred ground. But other critics, more genuinely interested in literature than these, are today busy in rescuing and refurbishing with a new meaning works out of the past that have begun to look a little seedy. Some of them no doubt are seedy, and no symbolic interpretation will vivify them more than momentarily; others, like James, obviously are not.

Another element enters into the present state of criticism. In some degree the pursuit of the symbol is a reincarnation in more acceptable modern terms of one of the most venerable of ideas, that of the moral function of poetry. To make this clear I must trace for a moment very roughly the historical outline of one strand of thought. We are not concerned with the broad ancestry of this whole view of poetry as it traces back in England to Sidney and still on to Plato. But in later times romantic poets and critics, unjustly in part, saw in popular eighteenth-century notions of poetry scarcely more than the choice between simple moral precept and drawing-room game. They took their art more seriously than a game; poetry was not to be a polite accomplishment but a significant part of life. When Coleridge planned an essay on poetry that was to supersede all the books on poetry, politics, and religion that were ever written, he was giving expression to this view of the seriousness of art, with whatever absurdities of his own superadded. The romantics as a whole did not accept the simple moral interpretation of art, but neither did they ever fully develop a satisfactory alternative to that theory (despite "truth," "nature," "imagination," and post-Kantian thought in Germany) that would furnish a philosophical or psychological justification for the importance they attributed to poetry.[2]

This dilemma of the romantics lay at the root of Matthew Arnold's effort to supply canons for poetry and criticism. His was the most sophisticated formulation of the English Victorian view; nevertheless, his criteria of "high seriousness" in poetry and "a criticism of life" were essentially translations of the romantic loftiness back into the moral category. Though his influence is more alive today than most of us realize, his formulation has not fully satisfied contemporary critics. Hence they have undertaken to solve the same dilemma that faced the romantics and Arnold through a more indirect means—the symbolic interpretation of poetry. For the time being, at any rate, this has satisfied many. It has also brought to life a great many critics.

All this is merely a commonplace fragment of critical history, grossly oversimplified; but it will serve. To put the matter concretely, if still crudely, a critic today is likely to find himself enchanted by such a poem as *Kubla Khan;* but when he looks at it deliberately he is faced with a doubt.

[7]

Palace, gardens, fountains, Abyssinian maids, dulcimers—
all very good romantic scenery, no doubt, but—the fatal
question: Can this be really great poetry if it means nothing more serious than it says?—Arnold's very question, almost. Dr. Leavis, I suppose, would make one obvious answer: Discard Coleridge, or at least move *Kubla Khan* off
to the fringes of poetry. But the question is broader than
that of a single poem, and I am using Coleridge, and somewhat misusing Dr. Leavis, on this point only for convenience: the same question properly arises with regard to
many poets that no one would wish to dismiss. Take (of
Coleridge once more) the theme of *The Ancient Mariner*.
A sailor kills a bird for no good reason; he is doomed to
suffer punishment and to expiate his sin forever after; his
companions have approved the killing and so are doomed
supernaturally to death. The "moral" of *The Ancient
Mariner* has been much fought over. Is the crime trivial or
is it not? Does the poem need a moral? Was Coleridge
merely palming off upon his readers a glittering S.P.C.A.
tract? Faced with these questions and other better but less
brief ones, the modern critic rescues this or another poem
by what has become almost a contemporary dogma, the
belief that—to borrow Mr. Robert Penn Warren's words—
"any substantial work will operate at more than one thematic level."[3] I do not wish to sound overcritical of this
dogma. If the word "thematic" were omitted, one could
not disagree with it, though one's conception of "levels"
might be different.

Most of the influential literary critics since Arnold's day,
with a few very eminent exceptions, have been by profession teachers. They are all in some sense children of Arnold,
and they have all been engaged in spreading within a
swiftly democratized educational system in England and
America what he dared, but we scarcely dare, to call "cul-
ture." This fact probably has nothing to do with the initial
modern instances of symbolic criticism, but it has un-

doubtedly encouraged its development and popularity. The search for symbolic meaning provides the easiest of all ways to interest the intelligent reader whose antecedents, if not temperament as well, are commonly unliterary. If the critic-teacher does not ask of himself the Philistine question I have posed about *Kubla Khan*—How can pleasure-dome, fountain, dulcimer, and the rest be more than pretty verse?—his students will ask it, and they will be most easily allured by the symbolic answer, which gives them substantial, even if sometimes irrelevant, matter for thought. The question might perhaps be better answered by a deeper analysis of certain fundamental problems of aesthetics, but that has scarcely been tried and at any rate is not our business at the moment.

The point here is that the symbolic interpretations of literature current at the present time have originated largely from extraneous considerations and in only a very small degree, or in another sense than is usually supposed, from the nature of poetry itself. The movement has done us the service of sharpening our eyes and leading us to a new appreciation of many of the complexities that we must agree are inherent in much, perhaps most, poetry. But as the movement started not from the poetry itself but from, as I think, several misconceptions of aesthetic experience, its conclusions need to be checked by looking at the poems from other angles.

Supposing Freud right in finding sexual symbolism to underlie almost all human action, thought, and dream—obviously, then, sexual symbolism must underlie all poetry too. That, however, tells us little about any one poem. The psychoanalytical critic's responsibility, in the interest of clarity, is to make known his assumptions and tell his readers which of several activities he is at the moment engaged in: whether he is using a work of literature as a case history to teach us psychology or whether, on the other hand, he is using his psychoanalytic theory to illumine a particular literary work or literary history as a whole. The trap difficult to avoid is that of mistaking what it is one has proved. If rounded mountains always in human experience must mean breasts and caverns always mean wombs, one might write an illuminating essay on infantilism and regression in romantic poets, provided one can prove that they describe more mountains and caverns than other poets do. Perhaps someone has written this. But then Pope had his grotto, and just possibly the other Augustans had their particular forms of snugness and roundness; so that even here a generalization has its limits. In any case, it is difficult to see how this kind of interpretation can throw light on any given poem unless it can show something special in the use of the caverns and mountains that is not present in other cavern-mountain poems. Possibly a critic who is committed to belief in a universal fixed system of symbols should content himself with composing a dictionary of symbolic equivalents to serve as a handbook for readers of poetry. There might be an alluring prospect in the answers to many puzzling questions: the precise degree of the angle moving from obtuse to acute that might be found to transform a mountain from a breast to a phallic symbol, or the determination of a dome as breast or womb according as the poet is outdoors or in. This is not to imply that psychoanalytical thought has nothing to offer for the illumination of literature. But its crudenesses, inevitable as in any new discipline, have hitherto been not least evident in its dealings with literature and the arts.

If we do not accept any such fixed system that can be applied a priori, we may not find it easy to know and will certainly not find it easy to prove to others whether a subsurface meaning that we find in a poem belongs properly to ourselves or to the poem. Mr. T. S. Eliot meets this difficulty readily enough when he lectures, by telling us that his critics know more than he does about *The Waste Land.*

Whether his answer is made in full or only half irony or is but the urbane surface of embarrassed reticence, he has not said. As he is not generally in favor of total confusion, however, I do not think his authority or that of Mr. Auden, who sometimes speaks in a like vein, requires us to argue out the extreme subjective view, the view that any poem "means" only what it happens to mean to any reader. We should be able to skate over the ultimate difficulties of the question of "meaning" in poetry, leaving all ambiguities of the subject intact, without loss to our present argument.

In a poem by Mr. De la Mare, *The Song of Finis*, a knight in armor leaps over a precipice. Is he symbolic or not? We could say that the whole tone of the poem is symbolic; but beyond that the answer is made clear, for the poet has specifically said in his opening line, "At the edge of All the Ages." We may still not be sure precisely what the knight symbolizes, but we are sure that some of the overtones we think we hear do come from the actual intended presence of a symbolic meaning, for the key has been given within the poem. It need not be quite so evident. In another poem a king appears to be dying in a room alone while the court junkets in the distance and only a cat watches. This (De la Mare's *Maerchen*) might be a legend or a picture with no lurking significance; but we know, again, that it is not. We cannot help knowing, not because of an a priori conviction that it is a good poem and that all good poems must be symbolic; we know it from within the poem. Kings do not commonly die alone, and they do not commonly either live or die in rooms with bats and mice and insects and neglected candles. And a cat that sits quietly watching the king's stupor while mice run about undisturbed is no cat; and when we see that the king wears a robe "enstarred" and "dyed deep" in "night," we know that he is beyond a common king. The course of nature has been altered, however quietly and without gesture, to con-

〖 11 〗

vey the otherwise unspoken meaning. When the refrain half-echoes an old expression, "even a cat can look at a king"—this king with the starred night sky for robe—we are fully aware that we are reading cosmic symbols.

The point should be obvious that when a poem is genuinely symbolic, its unspoken meaning determines or partly determines the actual choice of matter or language. This may appear unmistakably through the poet's alteration of the normal course of nature, as in *Maerchen*, or in the more familiar and traditional imagery of Housman's *To an Athlete Dying Young:* "And early though the laurel grows It withers quicker than the rose." To wither quicker than the rose is precisely what laurel does not do except as it is something other than laurel and the rose other than rose. The symbolism, however, does not have to be so marked as to constitute a metaphor. The poet need not reverse nature or tell a patent lie in order that the reader may know that he means more than he says on the surface. There is another little poem by Mr. De la Mare that, for all it actually says, might be no more than the lightest of his verses of children, fairies, and witches. It is called "Peak and Puke" and is a child's complaint that her "wee brother" has been stolen and a changeling left in his place. I doubt whether the poet had in mind any deliberate psychological generalizations about the jealousy of an elder child upon the arrival of a new baby, though he may have had. At any rate, the sound of the lines, in which *w*'s and *m*'s and other close-mouthed letters are dominant, is so wispy and woebegone that one cannot miss the intensity of the child's rejection of the baby. The fairy-tale notion of a changeling becomes almost inevitably the symbol of something else. The hint comes not merely from the theme but from the intricate details of its use (the child's assumption of a bond with its mother against the infant interloper, for example) and from the woeful sounds that cast over the whole a particular emotional coloring.

The presence of symbolic meaning may be conveyed in all sorts of indirect ways, by a pattern of repetition heightened by special effects of sound, by subtle alteration of an ordinary image, by special emphasis in the arrangement of details. But however it is conveyed, in order to exist at all the symbolic meaning must in some way alter the surface of the language from what it would be if the avowed meaning were the whole. Symbols must be "necessary" or "congruent," Mr. Robert Penn Warren says, if they are to avoid being merely arbitrary.[4] I think, however, that they must be more than congruent. They must leave their actual print somehow upon the surface or must keep plucking visibly at the surface from where they dwell below. Even when a poet uses a symbol that from obvious and inherent resemblance has become almost a traditional metaphor—such as light and darkness or day and night to represent the oppositions of knowledge and mystery or ignorance—even then, by some poetic underlining however subtle, the poet marks his day as more than literal day and his night as mystery.

To take as axiomatic that every good poem must be symbolic, and then to proceed with all possible ingenuity to "extract"—as Mr. Empson I think rather unwarily once described the procedure—a hidden meaning or ambiguity from a poem not because the meaning is felt to be there but simply because, by definition, one must be found—this seems at least premature. The dogma needs a little testing first. It is possible that if we accept it, we shall be compelled to give up, as Matthew Arnold had to for his doctrine, some work that we should like to keep—if not Chaucer, at least Sir John Suckling. *Why So Pale and Wan, Fond Lover* is the quintessence of a shrugged shoulder, directed at fruitless love; it is no more than that. But the gesture of the shrugged shoulder has never been so caught and arrested. The poem is the full and perfect exploration of a passing human attitude, and that is all its meaning; it is enough. Though the lyric is far from simple, its complexity does not derive from symbolic meaning unless we stretch the sense of the term "symbol" beyond all recognition or usefulness. The shrug may be—it is, in fact—the shrug of the realist urging accommodation to inflexible necessity; but that is hardly a symbol except as any action or attitude upon a given occasion is expressive of general attitudes. The same thing is true of many other poems that we should not like to see minimized. Modern criticism recognizes that poetry is a complex art. But except in the hands of a very few critics whose understanding and aesthetic tact derive from something else than a single-track theory of symbolic meanings, the advertised depth and complexity often prove to be insufficiently deep and complex.

To return, however, to Coleridge. His three most popular poems are said by Mr. G. Wilson Knight to constitute a half-miniature *Divina Commedia*, with *Christabel* as the *Inferno*, *The Ancient Mariner* the *Purgatorio*, and *Kubla Khan* the *Paradiso*. Mr. Warren regards *The Ancient Mariner* as symbolic of the sacramental view of life, the "One Life" theme, its chief symbolic images being sun and moon—crime and reconciliation—"understanding" (in the terminology later adopted by Coleridge), which partakes of death, and "imagination," the creative force. Mr. Kenneth Burke finds opium playing an important role in the symbolism of all three poems. *The Ancient Mariner* is in part "a ritual for the redemption of [Coleridge's] drug," the water snakes being the actual symbol of opium in their "dramatic transubstantiation . . . from malign to benign creatures." *Kubla Khan*, he thinks, symbolizes the "manic" or benign stage of the drug almost wholly, but with hints of the malign in the serpentine motion of the river and elsewhere. *Christabel* represents the two forces of the drug, good and evil, "suspended at the moment of indecision." Mr. Robert Graves finds in *Kubla Khan* not only symbols representing opium but also the river of life from

[14]

birth to death, Coleridge's intellectual attachment to Dorothy Wordsworth, Mrs. Coleridge's pregnancy, and much more. Miss Maud Bodkin discusses *The Ancient Mariner* as an expression, among other things, of the re-birth archetype, and *Kubla Khan* as the archetype of heaven and hell.[5] It will be observed that, along with some similarities of interpretation, there are also irreconcilable differences.

It is fashionable and sometimes convenient to speak of different "levels of meaning" in poetry. My own presupposition, which seems to me so obvious as to make discussion of it superfluous, is that all the levels of meaning that may be present in a poem must harmonize with one another and with the emotional tone of the poem as a whole. They must provide a truly contrapuntal structure in which each theme lends something positive to each other; they must not together produce meaningless cacophony. On that presupposition Mr. Warren, Mr. Burke, Mr. Knight, Miss Bodkin, and the others cannot all be right (which does not, certainly, prove any one of them wrong). Their various symbolic interpretations of Coleridge's poems not only are not easily reconciled with one another on the basis of "different levels," but also impute quite different moods or emotional tones to the same poem. If *Christabel* is felt as the *Inferno*, it can scarcely also be felt as the moment of balance between good and evil. If *Kubla Khan* is the *Paradiso* of Dante, it is not easy to feel it also as exhibiting the conflict of heaven and hell or Coleridge's somewhat less than heavenly domestic life. To the confusion of these is added the voice of those other critics who maintain that *The Ancient Mariner* is a ballad with no more symbolic meaning than is made obvious by the poet, that *Christabel* is but a Gothic romance poeticized,[6] and that *Kubla Khan* is wholly without meaning of any kind. Though variety among critics is no doubt all to the good, one cannot help wondering a trifle about the present state of criticism when we find as little common ground as this among writers all very eminent, all brilliant and persuasive in argument, and all engaged in describing the central effect of the same poems.

It would be both presumptuous and unprofitable to offer a detailed critique of all the conflicting views of these poems of Coleridge. The habit can too easily grow upon academic critics to live by battening upon each others' brains. So I shall resist as far as I can that temptation and only set down certain things that seem to me relevant to the understanding of one of the poems, *Kubla Khan*. The conflicting views of eminent critics I use chiefly as justification for saying anything at all. But before leaving the critics, I must return once more to Lowes.

There is some reason to believe that, having made his original search mainly among works of travel and geography for the origins of *The Ancient Mariner*, he was inclined to take what was left over for *Kubla Khan*. Hence his parallels and sources of imagery are sometimes more questionable for this poem than for the other. Coleridge's own preface to *Kubla Khan*, connecting the opening lines with a passage in Purchas, made natural the assumption that this dream-fragment was created from the same travel materials. Though the influence of some of those sources is beyond question, Lowes's idea as a whole perhaps needs revision. The essential character of the poem may be rather different from what he believed it to be.

In the preface to the poem, Coleridge said he had composed it in his sleep, after taking an "anodyne" at Porlock in the summer of 1797. He had fallen asleep over a page of Purchas and dreamed the poem, both images and words. On awaking, he remembered it word for word and wrote it down until an interruption blotted the rest from his memory. Though this account has for the most part been accepted, some critics have doubted its literal truth. Word-for-word recollection, from a dream, of even the fifty-four lines that exist, to say nothing of the remaining several hundred that he lost, has been too much for their credulity. There is good reason to support this skepticism. Before we have done, we shall, I think, be compelled to doubt almost everything in Coleridge's account except perhaps Porlock. There is reason to doubt that the poem was dreamed as he said it was. There is reason to believe that its special character was not determined or materially influenced by opium. There is evidence also to suggest that it may perhaps have been composed two or three years later than "the summer of the year 1797." Ordinarily a difference of two years is of little consequence to the historical or poetic significance of a work. In this case, however, it means something, for, along with other circumstances, it leads toward a view of the poem not as a phantasmagoria of images cast up by the unconscious workings of genius from an assortment of travel books—Purchas, Bruce, Bartram, and the rest—but rather as an outgrowth, very likely conscious, of a complex literary tradition, including the travel books to be sure, but only as these were used by other writers. The origin of *Kubla Khan* will be found, I think, in the contemporary network of pseudo-oriental writing in verse and prose, some strands of which were Wieland's *Oberon*, Landor's *Gebir*, Southey's *Thalaba*, and the unwritten epic poem on Mohammed that Southey and Coleridge together planned to write. These works glanced backward to *Rasselas* and Addison but were also related to the Gothic fashion; and Milton presided over the whole. If this and certain other circumstances are true, *Kubla Khan* must be read afresh.

The material to be presented in these chapters originated in two more or less accidental circumstances. Interest in another subject than Coleridge had led me to the modern medical and psychological studies of opium addiction, which I found surprisingly at variance with what I had hitherto taken for granted. The tenor of modern medical studies must, it appeared, lead to some readjustment of the accepted accounts of Coleridge's life and character, as well as of his "opium dream" poem. Then, more recently, I read Landor's *Gebir* attentively for the first time, again for reasons having nothing to do with Coleridge. As I read, the ghost of *Kubla Khan* kept rising from Landor's pages. I found myself suspecting that the mind behind one poem knew the other poem. *Gebir* was published in 1798; the composition of *Kubla Khan* has in the past been assigned, though never with anything like certainty, to 1797 or 1798. Landor could not have known *Kubla Khan*, and, besides, the spontaneous impression made upon my mind was that the shorter and more impressionistic of the two, Coleridge's poem and not *Gebir*, was the receiver of influence, supposing there to have been any. The impression was obviously subjective, but it seemed to have enough substance to warrant an inquiry into the already confused problem of the date of *Kubla Khan*. Two of the following chapters are the indirect result of these explorations.

A confession of bias of long standing should perhaps be made here. I have never shared the view that *Kubla Khan* is one of the supreme English poems, though I think it is a good one. I have also never shared the belief that it is a product of the unconscious mind. The poem has always sounded to me as if it were composed as other poems are—however that may be—though it could easily have originated in a daydream and might very well also have been begun in an idle half-dreaming moment without much plan or forethought—which would produce something of the effect of improvisation despite its technical elaboration. I have never had any sense of a more than usually magical origin for the poem or of the likelihood that, produced unconsciously, it could therefore throw light upon depths of human experience that more conscious poetry fails to illumine. These skeptical preconceptions I mention, that the reader may make for them whatever allowance he sees fit. I have tried not to warp the evidence in their favor, but of course one never knows. Through many of the succeeding pages I shall be busily engaged in removing glamour, or attempting to remove it. In the end, however, I shall return to poetry itself and will try to show more positively what is actually in the poem beyond what seems to me the irrelevant glamour. I enter upon the subject with a certain amount of hesitation. For one thing, I am reluctant to stir up hornets' nests; and, further, I am rather in sympathy with those persons who mistrust the value of the study of sources in poetry. For the source-monger is nearly always something of a literary parasite, providing little nourishment to the lover of poetry and imparting little brightness to the reputation of genius. Though the origin of an image or phrase may help to illumine a poem, it does not always do so. Moreover, few, if any, of us know enough to be sure of conclusions we may draw with respect to a literary source. Hardly anywhere does the fallacy of *post hoc ergo propter hoc* flourish more unashamedly than in the study of literary influences and sources. Mr. Nethercot may think that a piece of the serpent in *Christabel* derives from Bartram's *Travels*, and I may think it comes from *Gebir* and *Thalaba;* yet neither of us, I presume, would be in a position to assert that Coleridge could not have found it elsewhere in literature or conversation or from observation.

Despite these considerations, there seems to me sufficient reason for going into some, though by no means all, of the probable origins of *Kubla Khan*, which Saintsbury thought as fine a poem as the *Odyssey* and which has been viewed with a superstitious awe that is possibly not of the greatest service to a full appreciation of poetry. The workings of genius are mysterious enough as it is, and we are in no danger, currently, of dispelling the mystery. To cling desperately to a unique-miracle view of this poem almost implies a fear that, exposed to the light of day, the piece will wilt. I doubt whether it will, altogether.

In one sense these chapters are all about *Kubla Khan*, a circumstance somewhat horrifying even to the author for its implications of critical disproportion. In another sense, however, they are engaged with something more than the destruction of a dream, for the dream and the poem together strike what Coleridge would have called a "slant" ray across several thickets. Exploration by this bias light has raised to view questions that seemed to me interesting about Coleridge's life and character, his critical theories and development as a poet. The trail leads through the somewhat foreign fringes of medical history and—as anything concerned with Coleridge is bound to do—along certain main streams of literary and intellectual history at the close of the eighteenth century that seemed worth looking into from this slant direction. The exploration touches also —has already touched in the preceding pages—upon the canons and conflicts of contemporary criticism and modern attempts to understand human personality and the mind of genius. The mists of the opium legend and some others surrounding *Kubla Khan* have spread abroad beyond the single poem into modern critical thought generally. That territory of itself possesses enough native fog for all the needs of romantic mystery; no chance additions are needed. One can but hope that in the effort to dispel a local wisp or two of it one will not be found merely to have precipitated soot.

In the end, I have ventured upon an attempt, slightly different in method from most recent symbolic criticism, to explore the "charm" and the poetic significance of this one poem, which, so far as it "says" anything at all, says nothing of the least importance to us. Much of the poetry of any poem (the truism cannot be too often repeated) must lie in the interlacings between its form and its meaning. These are partly traceable, most easily, perhaps, when the meaning itself is slight or simple. Though an exploration of this kind lays bare no ultimate poetic secret, it brings us at least into touch with certain fundamental aspects of poetry that are at the present time somewhat neglected.

∽ II ∽

Opium and the Dream

A particular group of interrelated matters that bear
upon *Kubla Khan* remain imperfectly understood. Since
they affect our understanding not merely of that one poem
but also of Coleridge's character and life, particularly the
years of his greatest poetic achievement, and affect, too,
our interpretation of several other aspects of life and
literature at the beginning of the nineteenth century, they
will be discussed here at somewhat greater length than
their relevance to one poem alone demands. The cluster of
topics centers about opium and dreams: what is known
now and what was known or thought in Coleridge's youth
about the immediate psychological effects of opium, the
effects of continued addiction, and the effects of withdrawal of the drug in attempted cures. Confusion on these
matters has distorted earlier biographical studies of both
Coleridge and De Quincey and has caused us wholly to
misinterpret at least one other poem besides *Kubla Khan.*
Opium in the popular mind means dreams or visions, and
these take us back to certain other psychological interests
of the Romantic age. When Coleridge elaborated his
famous critical theory of dramatic illusion, he did so
through a discussion of sleep, dreams, reverie, and nightmare. His understanding of those illusory experiences has
sometimes been attributed in part to his use of opium.
And both the dreams and the opium take us still farther
back to an almost forgotten but original man, Erasmus
Darwin, whose *Zoonomia* and *Botanic Garden* seem to have
given Coleridge some ideas on most of these topics. The
thread that may be said to unite this scattered material—

modern medical experiments and *The Loves of the Plants*, the philanthropist Wilberforce, a morphine-addicted signalman, and Darwin's theories of sleep—is more than Coleridgean in its tenuousness, and the illumination to be produced in the end is no more than a half-light beamed into a few pockets of literary and biographical history. But the pockets are interesting ones.

The point of departure is the preface with which Coleridge introduced his "dream"-poem to the public.

1. THE POET'S PREFACE: FOLKLORE OF OPIUM

Kubla Khan was first published in a small paper-bound volume entitled *Christabel; Kubla Khan, a Vision; The Pains of Sleep*, in 1816. Within the volume the second poem had its own title-page, reading "Kubla Khan: Or a Vision in a Dream," and a half-title, "Of the Fragment of Kubla Khan," followed by the preface. Thus, from the start, by reinforcing vision with dream or dream with vision, Coleridge took care to redouble the unreality and abdicate his responsibility for the piece. All three poems had lain in the dark for many years. *The Pains of Sleep* Coleridge had sent in a letter to Southey in 1803, but it was now in 1816 published for the first time. Of *Christabel* he had spoken often in letters from 1799 onward; sometimes it was about to be completed, sometimes it was on the point of breaking into print as a fragment. It had become celebrated through his recitation of it long before its official publication. On the origin of *Kubla Khan*, however, Coleridge's letters as far as we know them are silent, as is all other precise evidence. We know only that the poem had been in existence at least since October, 1800. After a gap then of sixteen years or more, Coleridge explained its origin in the preface that has become almost as celebrated as the poem itself, an account before which Coleridge's readers have remained wide-eyed to the present day. It should stand before us in full.

The following fragment is here published at the request of a poet of great and deserved celebrity [Lord Byron], and, as far as the Author's own opinions are concerned, rather as a psychological curiosity, than on the ground of any supposed *poetic* merits.

In the summer of the year 1797, the Author, then in ill health, had retired to a lonely farm-house between Porlock and Linton, on the Exmoor confines of Somerset and Devonshire. In consequence of a slight indisposition, an anodyne had been prescribed, from the effects of which he fell asleep in his chair at the moment that he was reading the following sentence, or words of the same substance, in "Purchas's Pilgrimage": "Here the Khan Kubla commanded a palace to be built, and a stately garden thereunto. And thus ten miles of fertile ground were inclosed with a wall." The Author continued for about three hours in a profound sleep, at least of the external senses, during which time he has the most vivid confidence, that he could not have composed less than from two to three hundred lines; if that indeed can be called composition in which all the images rose up before him as *things*, with a parallel production of the correspondent expressions, without any sensation or consciousness of effort. On awaking he appeared to himself to have a distinct recollection of the whole, and taking his pen, ink, and paper, instantly and eagerly wrote down the lines that are here preserved. At this moment he was unfortunately called out by a person on business from Porlock, and detained by him above an hour, and on his return to his room, found, to his no small surprise and mortification, that though he still retained some vague and dim recollection of the general purport of the vision, yet, with the exception of some eight or ten scattered lines and images, all the rest had passed away like the images on the surface of a stream into which a stone has been cast, but, alas! without the after restoration of the latter!

> Then all the charm
> Is broken—all that phantom-world so fair
> Vanishes, and a thousand circlets spread,
> And each mis-shape the other. Stay awhile,
> Poor youth! who scarcely dar'st lift up thine eyes—
> The stream will soon renew its smoothness, soon
> The visions will return! And lo, he stays,
> And soon the fragments dim of lovely forms
> Come trembling back, unite, and now once more
> The pool becomes a mirror.

Yet from the still surviving recollections in his mind, the Author has frequently purposed to finish for himself what had been originally, as it were, given to him. Σαμερον αδιον ασω [*sic*]: but the to-morrow is yet to come.

As a contrast to this vision, I have annexed a fragment of a very different character, describing with equal fidelity the dream of pain and disease.[1]

Our immediate concern is with the dream. The "anodyne," the poet said, sent him to sleep "in his chair" while he was reading Purchas. He remained for three hours "in a profound sleep, at least of the external senses," during which time he composed between two and three hundred lines. "All the images rose up before him as *things*," accompanied by "the correspondent expressions, without any sensation or consciousness of effort." On "awaking" with what seemed to him a complete recollection of the whole, both images and words, he "instantly and eagerly" wrote down the lines that now survive.

At least two of Coleridge's friends appear to have been skeptical of this account. Robert Southey suggested that Coleridge had only dreamed that he had composed the poem in a dream,[2] and Charles Lamb used a somewhat unconvinced turn of phrase when he wrote to Wordsworth that Coleridge was publishing *Christabel* "with what he calls a vision, 'Kubla Khan.' "[3] Both friends might have been in a position to know something of the matter. Though Coleridge's account has occasionally been questioned by others, for the most part the preface has been accepted, and critical discussions of the poem are generally rooted firmly in the "dream." *Kubla Khan* has thus been set apart from the rest of English poetry as a kind of apparition that speaks to us from an unknown or half-known world as no other poem does.

Nineteen years ago, however, there came to light in the collection of the Marquis of Crewe a holograph manuscript in which the poem was accompanied by a different explanatory note. After its exhibition in 1934 at the National Portrait Gallery, the manuscript was described by the late Alice Snyder in the correspondence columns of the *Times Literary Supplement*.[4] She printed Coleridge's note: "This fragment with a good deal more, not recoverable, composed in a sort of Reverie brought on by two grains of Opium, taken to check a dysentery, at a Farm House between Porlock & Linton, a quarter of a mile from Culbone Church, in the fall of the year, 1797." Important as it is for anyone interested in Coleridge, the note attracted little attention. Though it was remarked upon by a few writers, notably Sir Edmund Chambers and Mr. Lawrence Hanson, the literary world at large continued to read the poem only in the light of the preface of 1816.

We do not know when Coleridge wrote the preface that he himself printed, but the evidence as far as it goes suggests that the Crewe manuscript was written first, perhaps much earlier. The watermark of the paper, Miss Snyder noted, is the same as that of a letter written by Coleridge in 1796. It is not impossible that the same paper should have been in use as late as 1816, for Coleridge once confessed to "a superstitious dread of the destruction of paper worthy of a Mahometan" (though I am not quite certain he meant blank paper); it is unlikely, however, particularly in view of his changes of residence in the intervening years. Sir Edmund Chambers cited the statements of experts that little is known about the dating of late eighteenth-century paper and added that paper of 1795 was used in the 1800 edition of the *Lyrical Ballads*.[5] *Kubla Khan* itself in the version of the Crewe manuscript contains a number of variants from the printed text, and of these at least three are closer to their source in Coleridge's reading. "Kubla" is there "Cubla," "Mount Abora" is "Mount Amara" (altered to "Amora"), and "twice five miles" is "twice six miles." In Purchas the name is "Cublai" or "Cublay"; the inclosure within the walls is "sixteene miles"; "Mount Amara" is the false Abyssinian Paradise in the fourth book of *Paradise Lost*, from which comes much else in Coleridge's poem.[6] The discovery of these and other variants, minor as they all are, must have been a blow to Lowes, who had argued passionately for his conviction that Coleridge's dream had reached the printed page without the slightest revision or any other intervention of a waking mind.

A comparison of the text of the two explanatory notes also bears out the earlier date of the Crewe autograph. Though the circumstances given are on the whole much the same—the year, the place, the occasion—the Crewe note is more specific on some points in spite of its brevity: the place "a quarter of a mile from Culbone Church" instead of "between Porlock and Linton"; two grains of opium to check a dysentery instead of the blander "anodyne" prescribed for a "slight indisposition." Such differences of phrase give to the better-known preface the ring of language written for the impersonal public and suggest, therefore, that it may have been composed specifically for the edition of 1816. One very notable difference between the two accounts has received less attention than it deserves. The "profound sleep" with its dream and the subsequent recording of it purely from memory are not to be found in the Crewe autograph. If Coleridge had actually dreamed his vision in sleep and then remembered it verbatim, it is unlikely that he would ever have toned down the marvel of this and have said only that he had composed the poem "in a sort of Reverie." Coleridge's stories never grew smaller, though they might grow more circumstantial, the farther away they got from the event. One is even led to wonder how real may have been the "man from Porlock" with his somewhat improbable "business," who has become almost a proverbial symbol for Philistine interruptions of genius and who makes his appearance only in Coleridge's published account. As a whole, the preface of 1816 sounds a good deal like the self-justifying memory of Coleridge on other occasions. He was here printing two poems written many years before and still unfinished. The number of uncompleted projects long left floating in his wake was already a grievous embarrassment to him, and now he was deliberately laying before the public two more of them. For the fragmentary state of this poem, however, a marvelous origin and the man from Porlock could bear the blame and serve as a natural shield against criticism, while Lord Byron's admiration and the description of the fragment as a "psychological curiosity" might justify its publication.

It may be asked—and has been—whether Coleridge's two statements are quite as irreconcilable as on the surface they seem; whether in the printed preface, even though he had said he "fell asleep," he may have meant the reader to understand by "a profound sleep, at least of the external senses" nothing more than his other note claimed, "a sort of reverie." If that were his meaning, some readers have thought, Coleridge need not be accused of inconsistent statements; the mistake would be merely that of the miracle-loving public that has misread his preface for a century and more. The suggestion is tempting, but I think it will not hold. Coleridge used the terms *dream* and *reverie* with precise and carefully defined meanings that preclude their being interchanged under these circumstances. The terms will engage us later on, but the subject of opium must be dealt with first.

Accounts of nineteenth- and twentieth-century literature have been sprinkled here and there with a good many highly colored and often delusory statements about the influence of opium upon creative imagination and the life of genius. The influences are seen as twofold, the "benign," as Mr. Kenneth Burke calls them, and the "malign." Opium, it has been thought, can inspire through dreams or trancelike reveries a special kind of poetry or poetic prose that could not be otherwise composed. Opium, on the other hand, is also held responsible for the gradual degradation and final ruin of the lives and hopes of those who take it. The drug lights a bright, beautiful, and eerie light at first; then, as years go on, it dims and extinguishes the light and punishes its victim cruelly. This is quite a Gothic conception, and some of the writing about opium has been almost as imaginative as the effects attributed to it.

Literary critics, however, have usually been imperfectly familiar with modern medical accounts of the effects of opium, and earlier medical writing on the subject is exceedingly unreliable. Even the "scientific" writers of the past seem to have sought their information in something of that spirit of independence of mere fact that sent Rousseau to seek out the habits of primitive man by sitting in suburban woods and thinking. The lag is not solely a lag among literary critics, for the older views are still current even among physicians who have not made a particular study of opiates.

De Quincey has a great deal to answer for to the medical profession. It would have delighted his vanity to know that almost alone he dominated the scientific as well as the literary explanations of the effects of opium for nearly a hundred years. And he is still, whether they know it or not, the chief authority behind the knowledge even of many physicians. Until as late as the 1920's, many of the most competent medical accounts of addiction to opium were drawn directly from the writings of De Quincey and Coleridge or from other writers who in turn had drawn from them. Having derived their principles from these sources, moralizing physicians of the Victorian era rounded the circle of their argument by applying them back again. Coleridge and De Quincey were held up in solemn warning as examples of how the drug leads to wretchedness and destruction. This extensive body of highly unscientific writing on the subject has not ceased to flourish. If familiarity with the drug were a criterion, it would be difficult to find better-informed witnesses than De Quincey and Coleridge. As it is not and as a complete study of their accounts would take us beyond the limits of this work without proving much, the problem will be approached from another avenue.

The old standard view, medical as well as literary, of the effects of opium runs something like this: (1) The drug injures and usually ruins the physical health and generally shortens the life of the person addicted to its use. Coleridge and De Quincey have to be taken as exceptions in the matter of longevity, since they lived to be roughly sixty-two and seventy-four, a record of survival not bad for their day. The generalization has been perpetuated, nevertheless. (2) Opium causes a gradual deterioration of intellect, psychological deterioration of the personality, and moral depravity. It is supposed thus to bring about changes in the actual character of the addict, making him a kind of person he was not and would not have become otherwise than through addiction and dooming him to unspeakable wretchedness in the end. He is supposed, further, to be easily identifiable by his pasty face, his queer look and manner, his shifty eye, and his emaciated form. (3) In the early stages the drug produces exquisite pleasure, but later the experience becomes one of horror, somewhat resembling the delirium tremens of alcoholism. (4) The drug is capable of producing dreams and visions of a most exquisite kind, utterly different in character from normal dreams. At first, they are beautiful, enchanting, their intensified sense impressions pleasurable in the highest degree. Afterwards the heightened acuteness of the senses merely accentuates their effect of horror, evil, loathing, and guilt.

Though modern medical and psychological knowledge of the effects of opium on human beings is still very incomplete, a few facts that bear upon Coleridge and De Quincey are well enough established to be summarized. As far as they go, their cumulative effect is to destroy or (on one or two points) to cast the gravest doubts upon the soundness of every one of these current beliefs. Before embarking upon discussion of them, however, I must mention, in order to rule out, certain aspects of the subject of addiction that will otherwise crop up inconveniently.

Some things are true of narcotic addiction today that were not true in eighteenth- and nineteenth-century England. Today, as every newspaper reader knows, addiction is a legal and social problem quite as much as an individual psychological or physical one. This is particularly so in the United States, where the use of narcotics except for strictly medical purposes is forbidden by law and where therefore most persons who have become addicted are unable to satisfy their need for the drug without becoming actual criminals themselves or falling into the power of criminals. The big-business-gangster market has become perhaps the major narcotic problem today because that has made it necessary or profitable (or both) to lure increasing numbers of victims into the trap of addiction. These persons, caught not only by the drug but also by the accompanying gangsterism, are almost surely doomed to deteriorate both physically and psychologically, and "morally" as well. The extremely high cost of illegal narcotics drains almost any common man's purse today and certainly any public school adolescent's; it thus often compels the habitué to choose between food and morphine. And as morphine satisfies a craving and at the same time diminishes the pangs of hunger, the choice is scarcely a choice for an addict. His health suffers. The need for money, together with the need for secrecy in securing and spending it, drives all but the most fortunate victims to lying, stealing, selling "dope" themselves, or otherwise falling into "moral" delinquency. All this is a matter of common knowledge, and I mention it only to get it out of the way and avoid confusion. For all its importance, it is not our business here. Some things that I shall say would be inapplicable to present-day America, but I shall not litter the pages further with reminders of the difference.[7]

2. PSYCHOLOGICAL EFFECTS OF OPIUM
MODERN INVESTIGATIONS

Opium more than any other cause has been held responsible for the failure of Coleridge both to fulfil all the promise of his genius and to win his everyday living by steady labors. During much of his life he depended upon gifts and loans from friends; his path was strewn with abortive plans and fragments. He himself attributed his "sloth" to opium, and that cause has not been much questioned.

A ruined life, however, we now know is not an inevitable consequence of addiction to opiates. Medical writers have shown that many addicted persons live entirely normal lives for a normal life-span. No one knows how many such persons there are, but they are not rare. These people do not deteriorate psychologically, intellectually, or physically; they continue their work in the world like others, provided only a regular supply of the drug is available for their needs; and they experience no marked effects from its use. Evidence for the truth of this is plentiful, despite the necessary secrecy of modern addicts. There is no indication, either, that life is shortened by use of the drug except on occasions of a grossly careless overdose.[8] Many addicts remain unrecognized as such, though addicted for many years. One medical writer, discussing work in the New York City Narcotic Clinic, cited as illustration the case of a signalman, obviously holding a responsible position, who had been addicted for twenty-five years without missing a day from work. He had never been reported for any sort of neglect and had never been recognized as an addict by his superior.[9]

Cases like this have been familiar for a century and more. The poet Crabbe, for example, used opium. His son, in a memoir published in 1834, described his father's middle years: "My father, now about his forty-sixth year,

[31]

was much more stout and healthy than when I first remember him." In early manhood he had had certain
frightening attacks which were finally diagnosed as digestive. "You must take opiates," said his physician. The
biographer continued:

From that time his health began to amend rapidly, and his constitu-
tion was renovated; a rare effect of opium, for that drug almost always
inflicts some partial injury, even when it is necessary: but to him it was
only salutary—and to a constant but slightly increasing dose of it may
be attributed his long and generally healthy life. His personal appearance also was improved with his health and his years. This is by no
means an uncommon case: many an ordinary youth has widened and
rounded into a well-looking, dignified, middle-aged man. . . . health of
itself gives a new charm to any features; and his figure, which in his
early years had been rather thin and weakly, was now muscular and almost athletic.

In the 1830's the pasty face and emaciated frame had not
yet taken possession of opium eaters. Coleridge's contemporary Wilberforce provides another instance, not
quite so perfect. His sons in their biography inform us that
he took opium for an illness in 1788, found it helpful, and,
having become addicted, continued to use it for the remaining forty-five years of his life. He was always "sparing," they said, in his use of the drug and never felt any
effect from it of any kind, good or bad, though he believed
that it kept him in better health ever after. For the last
twenty years, until his death at the age of seventy-four, he
kept his allowance of the drug stable, though he had increased it from time to time in earlier years. Though the
sons wrote more complacently than the facts warranted
(Wilberforce was not always sparing in his opium-taking),
the truth remains that he lived, on the whole and within
the limitations of his temperament, a normal and successful life. At the time the biography of him was written
(1838) little or no disgrace attended the habitual use of the
drug.[10] Though De Quincey's *Confessions* had been published and Coleridge's troubles were well known and

though medical authorities were growing slightly more aware than before of the dangers of opium, it was not until toward the mid-century that the name of "opium eater" came to be thought of as a stigma.

De Quincey mentioned as opium eaters, besides himself and Wilberforce, Lord Erskine, the former Prime Minister Addington, and Isaac Milner, Dean of Carlisle; Sir James Mackintosh was said always to have taken opium to calm his nervousness when he was to speak in parliament.[11] These are but a few stray instances of men whose health and careers seem to have been either wholly or relatively unimpaired by the use of opium. Such unspectacular figures, however, came to be quite overshadowed, not only in the view of the lay public but even among medical writers, by the histories of Coleridge and De Quincey.

Some modern studies have been undertaken to test the effect of addiction on health, physical fitness, and general efficiency. In general, the conclusions bear out the belief of Wilberforce and Crabbe that addiction *of itself* has little or no deteriorating effect. Addicts do usually deteriorate, but the cause is thought to lie in other factors than the drug itself. A few minor physiological effects are known to be brought about, but they are not permanent; they last only as long as the individual is actually under the opiate. Even under prolonged addiction, opium does not destroy the protoplasm of the tissues, as alcohol is said to do.[12]

Probably the most carefully controlled experiment having to do with physical fitness is one conducted some years ago at a Philadelphia hospital, in which observations were made of more than five hundred addicted persons who entered voluntarily for treatment. Besides the usual medical checking for general health, the patients' ability to withstand physical exercise was tested against that of two control groups of nonaddicted persons, one made up of ordinary hospital employees accustomed to a more or less sedentary life and a second of college athletes. As tested by heart action, pulse, respiration, and so on, recorded before and after exercise, the addicts were found to equal the control group of hospital workers and withstood strenuous exercise only slightly less well than did the college athletes. From these observations (which I have oversimplified in the telling), as well as from numerous others, the authors reported that they had detected no marked physical deterioration or lack of physical fitness in addicts who were receiving their required amounts of morphine.[13]

Approaching the problem not of health alone but of general efficiency and working by a different method, Dr. Lawrence Kolb, one of the most widely experienced investigators, studied the histories of a large group of persons who had become addicted accidentally through medical use of the drug. Some had evidently been abnormal psychologically before their addiction, and of these we shall speak later. Of the whole group, however, abnormal as well as normal, Dr. Kolb reported that three-fourths had had good employment records and that none who seemed to have been originally normal persons had had their efficiency reduced by opium. He described one alert old woman of eighty-one who had taken three grains of morphine daily for sixty-five years, yet had very successfully managed a household and reared her six children in the meantime.[14] Addiction to opiates, it is clear, does not of itself produce an abnormal life.

Discussion of the psychological aspects of addiction raises some minor difficulties of terminology. It is necessary to enter into the views on opium of authorities who often agree in their conclusions but differ in their use of terms or in their fundamental conceptions of human personality and the human mind. To translate these writers into the language of whatever psychological assumptions I myself choose to make would be unfair and would besides, I am afraid, embroil me in a discussion of the relative soundness of Mendelian, behaviorist, psycho-analytical, or other theories of personality, a discussion that would be both presumptuous and irrelevant. I shall let authorities speak, therefore, whether by direct quotation or otherwise, pretty much in their own terms even at the expense of consistency, only attempting to extricate their facts and observations with as few strands as possible clinging to them from the philosophical and psychological assumptions in which they are imbedded. When speaking for myself, I shall use such terms as *stable* or *normal* merely as the broadest and possibly least controversial terms.[15]

It is now well known, though it appears not to have been fully known in Coleridge's day, that all persons are subject to addiction. Everyone who takes opiates regularly for a time becomes addicted and suffers materially when the drug is withdrawn. The length of time required for habituation varies with the amount and frequency of the dose and with the individual, but it is said that three weeks of regular use will generally fix the habit.[16] On the other hand, it is widely agreed now that persons of unstable psychological makeup are much more likely to become addicted to opiates than are normal ones; that they are much less likely to control or stabilize their lives if they remain addicted; and, finally, that they are much less likely to be cured or to remain cured. Though this view is not shared by every modern writer quite without exception and cannot be regarded as proved in the sense in which a simple chemical reaction may be proved, it is the conclusion reached by those experts who appear to have had the greatest opportunities for investigating large numbers of cases in detail and over a considerable period of time.

Dr. Kolb, whom I have already cited, made a series of studies involving more than a thousand patients in the large United States hospital at Lexington, Kentucky, an institution wholly given over to treatment of drug addiction. His evidence is perhaps the most significant of all, but his summary will have to do duty here:

Drug addicts in the United States are recruited almost exclusively from among persons who are neurotic or who have some form of twisted personality. Such persons are highly susceptible to addiction because narcotics supply them with a form of adjustment of their difficulties. A very large proportion of addicts are fundamentally inebriates and the inebriate addict is impelled to take narcotics by a motive similar to that which prompts the periodic drinker to take alcohol. . . . Some drunkards are improved socially by abandoning alcohol for an opiate, but the change is a mere substitution of a lesser for a greater evil.[17]

Dr. Kolb supplemented this study with others covering a wide variety of cases, which reinforced his conclusion that purely physical dependence upon opium is likely to be temporary. In the great majority of cases of prolonged addiction, he found evidence of "nervous" abnormalities that antedated the addiction. The psychic causes that make a man particularly susceptible to opiates are also the causes most likely to take him back to the drug after a cure. Relapse, therefore, does not come about, as was once supposed, from something ineradicable that the drug has done to him physically; it follows from his already existing psychological inadequacies.[18]

In the course of addiction, a tolerance to the drug is established, the precise physiological or chemical causes of which are not yet fully understood though the phenomenon itself is one of the earliest and most widely known facts connected with opium. The tolerance may be increased enormously, as we know from the lethal amounts taken with impunity by many habitués, but there is always a considerable gap between the limit of tolerance and the "maintenance need." The amount of opium required, that is, to keep the addict comfortably free from the miseries and cravings of abstinence is materially smaller than the amount he can take without damage. His handling of this gap is crucial for the stabilizing of his life, but it depends upon other factors than the drug. In this phenomenon is anchored one of the main bridges between the physiological and the psychological effects of opium. The deterioration of character that is so commonly associated with opium users, particularly that which shows them growing more and more irresponsible, spending hours, days, or weeks in bed, abandoning for long periods the effort expected of normal persons to work or earn a living—this is believed now to have its roots not in the drug but in the original personality of the user, where the addiction itself has most often originated. Dr. Kolb reported from his investigations that those who deteriorated under addiction had been abnormal, usually extremely so, before their recourse to opiates. They had been drunkards, for example, or had had such acute symptoms of instability as nervous delirium or hallucinations in earlier life. They used the drug to facilitate a regression toward infancy that some part of themselves desired. Of itself, however, it not only does not ruin a man's character; apparently it does not alter it in any other way either.[19] The most careful and full studies of the subject tend to show that in lives which we might have supposed were ruined by opium the actual primary cause of ruin has been the original psychological makeup of the individual. The fundamentals of personality have not changed, however much aid the drug may have lent to the destructive element already at work.

The difference between psychological and medical (or accidental) addiction affects the history of individual cases broadly in two ways. The man whose need of the drug is primarily physical, having established the habit, continues to take it merely in order to avoid the discomfort or illness produced by its withdrawal. He may decide or be forced to go through the discomfort of a cure. If he does, he may remain cured permanently.[20] But if he does not, he can continue indefinitely to take only his maintenance dose. Since tolerance increases with custom, this maintenance requirement may creep up gradually, though apparently it does not always do so. There are no reasons, however, inherent in the drug itself for the taking of extra or enormous doses such as will send the addict into a half-stupor or narcotic sleep; what might be called the "normal" craving created by opium is satisfied by the maintenance dose and does not require more. When addiction is maintained thus, it need not interfere with a perfectly normal life as long as the individual has means to purchase what he requires without becoming embroiled in crime or debt. I am not even sure that it requires an exceptionally strong will to remain addicted at this level, in control of one's addiction. This kind of addiction, at any rate, is what we have in the Crabbes and their like.

The picture of Coleridge and De Quincey and of the vast majority of other addicts is very different. With a psychological basis for addiction, the temptation is always present to increase the drug beyond the maintenance level and up to the very limit of tolerance. The studies made at the Philadelphia hospital, for example, showed that when any disturbance occurred in the narcotic ward the patients always expressed a need for a larger amount of opium than usual. During the initial period of their experiment, while the patients were supplied freely with the drug, "the slightest degree of fear on their part always resulted in a temporary increase in dosage."[21]

These accounts bear a striking resemblance to some passages written a hundred and fifty years ago in Charles Lloyd's novel *Edmund Oliver* (1798). Some traits of the hero were patterned after Coleridge, and, though Lloyd was writing in anger or malice and is a far from trustworthy witness, his description of his hero's use of laudanum is of interest. Its details suggest that it was founded upon firsthand information, since obviously the modern knowledge I have been summarizing was not available to him. Lloyd's hero records in his diary: "I have some laudanum in my pocket. I will quell these mortal upbraidings," and "My brain phrensied with its own workings—I will again have recourse to my laudanum and lie down." Still later the young man of the novel, depressed, without money to pay his landlady, records of himself: "I have at all times a strange dreaminess about me which makes me indifferent to the future, if I can by any means fill the present with sensations—with that dreaminess I have gone on here from day to day; if at any time thought troubled, I have swallowed some spirits, or had recourse to my laudanum. . . ."[22] Almost all victims of opium at some time undergo a "cure." But the unstable, even though all physical discomfort and craving for the drug have disappeared, return again to their morphine weeks or months, occasionally even a year or more, later.[23] The words of Charles Lloyd, presumably about Coleridge, tell us why quite as accurately as the reports filtered through modern medical language, and somewhat more vividly. This evidence of the unstable or neurotic character of most persons who become addicted to opium I have set forth, however, not so much for the sake of painting a portrait of Coleridge as for its bearing upon the opium tradition. The original abnormalities of habitués came to be thought of as consequences of the drug.

The gift of extreme and mysterious pleasure is one of those powers conferred by tradition upon opiates; yet it too may be dependent partly or wholly upon the temperament of the user. Opium is known to have a pleasurable effect upon some people but not upon all; the actual proportion of each is not known. One experiment showed that from a single dose of morphine given to persons who did not know what it was, only one out of nine was pleasurably affected.[24] On the other hand, it is generally said that this euphoria is more likely to occur after addiction begins than upon an initial dose. No studies of opiate euphoria, so far as I know, deal with a sufficient number of cases to be significant, except those of Kolb. His observation has been that, apart from natural pleasure brought about by a swift relief from acute pain, persons who are psychological-ly stable do not experience "mental pleasure" from opiates. In most unstable persons, on the other hand, he found that the drug does produce pleasure during the early stages of addiction. The intensity of the pleasure appeared to be in direct proportion to the degree of instability. He cites typical accounts by patients describing their euphoria:

It makes my troubles roll off my mind.
It is exhilarating and soothing.
You do not care for anything and you feel happy.
It makes you drowsy and feel normal.
It causes exhilaration and a feeling of comfort.
A deadening, pleasurable effect.
. . . forgot everything and did not worry and had a pleasurable, dreamy sensation as of floating away.

One patient, typical of some others, said "it caused a buoyancy of spirits, increased imagination, temporarily enlarged the brain power, and made him think of things he otherwise would not have thought of."[25]

The last of these is the nearest we come to finding evidence of creative powers in opium. The explanation lies, however, in the euphoria that it produces, what to De Quincey was "its deep tranquillizing powers to the mitigation of evils" and to Coleridge a green and fountainous oasis in a waste of desert. The relaxation of tension and conflict, accompanied by a sense of pleasant ease, occasionally helps to release for a time the neurotic person's natural powers of thought or imagination or (rarely) of action, though it does not give him powers that he did not have or change the character of his normal powers. Coleridge recognized this effect upon himself when he said, in a passage to be discussed later, that opium by its narcotic effect made his body a fitter instrument for his soul. With some unstable temperaments the euphoria may be intense. Its effect is usually to increase the person's satisfaction with his inner state of well-being, to turn his attention inward upon himself while diminishing his attention to external stimuli. Thus it sometimes encourages the mood in which daydreaming occurs.[26]

The narcosis of opium has been popularly described as having the effect of heightening and intensifying the acuteness of the senses. This it quite definitely does not do. If anything, the effect is the reverse. Professor Meyer Abrams, citing De Quincey and Arthur Symons, once wrote of the "gift of opium" to these men as "access to a new world" such as ordinary mortals can never conceive, "a world of twisted, exquisite experience, sensuous and intellectual," in which "one can hear the walk of an insect on the ground, the bruising of a flower." He notes that De Quincey mentioned no intensification of the perception of light, but thinks that this was either an accidental omission or else the result of "an innate lack of sensitivity to light."[27]

A few experiments have been conducted for the purpose of testing precisely these things. They are not numerous enough, in my opinion, to constitute absolute proof if considered alone, but when they are weighed along with other evidence, I think we must accept them and must therefore relinquish the notion of those possible delights. Not even opium will bring us echoes of the centipede's rhythmic parade; he who would hear this must take cobra venom. The senses, it appears, are actually either unaffected or dulled—more often the latter—by opiates.

One experiment tested the acuteness of hearing in a considerable number of persons before and after the use of morphine. The injection was followed, the investigators reported, by "a marked dulling" of hearing, a decrease in acuity ranging from five to twenty decibels for various tones, the losses being greater in the upper tone registers. There vanish the shriek of the bat and the insect's footfall.

In a parallel study of vision, it was observed that acuity was usually unaffected but that the field of vision was "greatly" decreased for all colors but most markedly for red and green. Opium has long been known to contract the pupils temporarily, a circumstance that would naturally account for reduction of visual range. Some earlier observers had reported that there is sometimes a reduction in acuity also. Studies in the sense of smell are few and slight; as far as they go, they suggest that keenness in the perception of odors is diminished by opiates. For the sense of touch more studies are available. All seven of the recent experiments summarized in Krueger's *Pharmacology of the Opium Alkaloids* report a very material decrease in tactile sensitiveness under opiates.[28]

Though experimental work on some of these points has not been extensive enough to stamp the results as altogether final, they can hardly in practice be doubted because the observations are so fully consistent with each other and with other well-established facts. It is commonly known (and medically beyond doubt), for example, that addiction to opium always reduces and sometimes destroys sexual desire. Most obviously of all, the prime property of the drug is its narcosis of the sense of pain. Since the experimental work, as far as it goes, follows the same pattern as these known facts—narcosis, that is, of sensation of various kinds—and since no experiments are found to reverse this (no scientifically reputable study that I know of reports an increase in acuity of any sense), I think we are bound to give up any notion that the drug reverses itself, acting as a sort of antinarcotic on one or two senses while it narcotizes the others.

What a man actually sees or hears, however, is no necessary measure of what he imagines. The poets know what the feeling of solitude may do with a small noise:

> when a mouse inside the papered walls,
> Comes like a tiger crunching through the stones.

And everyone must have found a bright day look the brighter because of a mood. The euphoria of opium may affect a man in such ways as this, but we have no warrant at all to believe that the outside world enters his consciousness along nerve passages more exquisitely sensitized than our own. In that respect at least, his world is ours, except that it is probably a little dimmer.

The question of sense-perception leads to the final group of phenomena that tradition has associated with opium: kaleidoscopic imagery, the vision, and the dream. Of these it may be said in general and at once that no evidence warrants the belief that opium of itself produces any of them or that when the addict experiences them they are marked by the drug with a special character that they could not have had without it. It is surprising that even kaleidoscopic imagery should have edged its way into the opium tradition; this at least one might have supposed common enough to have escaped. Whether or not in a state between waking and sleeping everyone has seen imagery pass before his closed eyes I do not know; but certainly a great many quite normal persons do, and more would be aware of doing so if they began paying attention to it. In that half-waking state, the rational mind automatically suppresses awareness of fleeting imagery unless one deliberately notices it or unless it is for some reason especially insistent, as it is apt to be, for example, after fatiguing hours of unaccustomed motion. After walking or driving a car all day through unfamiliar scenes or working long at an unaccustomed physical task, a quite normal person may notice that his sleep is preceded by kaleidoscopic images of the day—leaf patterns or rocks, the pitching of hay, or whatever may have been going on. Such images are often vivid enough to be called "visions," however unpoetic their contents may be. One poet (who chooses to remain anonymous), whose waking life is more than usually preoccupied with visual experience, reports frequent, extremely vivid, and highly imaginative imagery of this sort. A familiar poem of Robert Frost describes a commonplace experience of the kind; his *After Apple Picking* tells over the moments before sleep in which sensations of the day are relived, the pressure of feet on a ladder, apple after apple in numberless succession. If the day's experiences have not been unusual or exhausting, the imagery is apt to be more imaginative and less exclusively tyrannized over by immediate memory.[29]

Very likely opium addicts who indulge in heavy doses and are reduced for hours at a time to a state just this side of sleep have quantitatively more of this experience than most people; they choose (a perhaps unconscious choice) to live more of their lives in this passive state than others do. No doubt the imagery is made pleasant if the drug has produced euphoria and the stupefaction is slight. But— once more—there is no reason to suppose that their mental cinema is different in kind from that of other people as a consequence of the drug. Nor does the drug itself actively produce the cinema. Imagery of this sort is essentially the same kind of experience that we refer to as daydream or reverie, though the degree of conscious thought and control will vary greatly from time to time and much ordinary reverie is occupied with the future rather than the past, or with "wish-fulfilment." As far as opium is concerned, the truth is the same in all these forms of waking dream. Doses above the maintenance level no doubt conduce to these passive states and prolong them; but as far as is known they do no more.

Some recent writers have accepted the statement of Coleridge in the Crewe manuscript that he had composed *Kubla Khan* in a reverie; most, however, appear still to regard the poem as a sleeping dream, recorded afterwards. In either case they have supposed that the "strangeness" of the poem is in itself sound internal proof that it must have been composed in an opium vision or dream. We are almost told that opium, not Coleridge, was the poet. Lowes's statement is probably the most famous of those insisting upon the dream:

> Nobody in his waking senses could have fabricated those amazing eighteen [final] lines. For if anything ever bore the infallible marks of authenticity it is that dissolving panorama in which fugitive hints of Aloadine's Paradise succeed each other with the vivid incoherence, and the illusion of natural and expected sequence, and the sense of an identity that yet is not identity, which are the distinctive attributes of dreams. Coleridge's statement of his experience has more than once been called in question. These lines alone, in their relation to the passage which suggested them, should banish doubt.

Lowes described the "dream-wrought fabric" in which we see "the unconscious playing *its* game alone," when the "sleeping images flock up . . . from the deeps" and "the will as a consciously constructive agency—was in abeyance," with "no intervention of a waking intelligence intent upon a plan." Hence, "the linked and interweaving images irresponsibly and gloriously stream, like the pulsing, fluctuating banners of the North [the Aurora Borealis]. And their pageant is as aimless as it is magnificent."[30]

Professor Meyer Abrams, whom I have already quoted in part, emphasized particularly the opium character of the dream. The drug admitted Coleridge and De Quincey, he wrote, to that world of "twisted, exquisite" sensation and experience so utterly different from our own that we can never comprehend it, though a glimpse is given in *Kubla Khan*, where the verse "caught up the evanescent images of an opium dream, and struck them into immobility for all time." The dream quality of the poem, he thought, is beyond the reach of analysis.[31] Mr. Hanson criticized this notion that opium had literally dictated the poem; he maintained that the drug only provided the opportunity for the composition, though he too was convinced that it must have been dreamed; it is "the great and inimitable dream poem," in fact, "the supreme example in English literature of the workings of the creative subconscious, unhelped—or unhindered—by conscious composition."[32] Still, in most readers of the poem the belief is firmly rooted not only that opium produces dreams but that these are so characteristic, so clearly unique, as to be identifiable as opium dreams upon internal evidence alone. Not long ago I came upon an article undertaking to show that Petrarch must have been an eater of opium because his poetry corresponds to what De Quincey described as the effect of the drug.[33]

With sleeping as with waking dreams, modern medical and psychological studies do not warrant the supposition that opium of itself either causes nondreamers to dream or transforms ordinary dreams into extraordinary ones. For this latter, the chief testimony has always been that of De Quincey, whose own statements are somewhat inconsistent. He sometimes described opium as producing dreams; yet he opened his *Confessions* with the remark that "if a man 'whose talk is of oxen,' should become an opium-eater, the probability is, that (if he is not too dull to dream at all)—he will dream about oxen."[34] The medical literature of the 1880's and 1890's does indeed record some horrible "opium" dreams by other opium eaters than De Quincey. Two of these are quoted by Professor Bald in a valuable study of Coleridge.[35] They can be accounted for otherwise, however.

Recent medical writers for the most part are concerned not with disproving old theories but with establishing positive truth. Hence much of the evidence on opium dreams is merely negative—the omission of accounts of them in otherwise full and detailed studies of symptoms, such as those already quoted from Kolb. An occasional statement, however, appears on the subject. Dr. Horatio C. Wood, more specific than most, follows a brief account of the euphoric effect of opium with a comment on the widespread idea that it produces "interesting dreams"—"an erroneous belief apparently founded largely on the writings of that famous English opium eater Thomas De Quincey." He suggests that De Quincey's dreams may have been "pure fiction" and concludes, "Certain it is that if they ever occurred they are a very unusual phenomenon." The few other informed modern writers who mention the matter at all agree.[36] The extent to which opium dreams have disappeared from medical and psychological literature is roughly indicated by the fact that neither Terry and Pellens' compilation on opium nor the more recent U.S. Supplement No. 165 indexes any entry under "Dream," though the former indexes "Delirium" and "Hallucination" (phenomena to be mentioned hereafter). The same thing is true, practically, of the annual *Psychological Abstracts* for the last twenty years: several hundred studies of opium are listed and almost countless entries under "Dream," but, with a single unimportant exception, none of the articles on either relates to the other. It is also perhaps significant that dreams, good or bad, are not mentioned by addicts when they are asked why they desire a cure or why they have relapsed afterwards.[37] Such reasons may have been given, but I have not met them in modern studies of the subject.

An occasional reputable modern authority, particularly of the older generation, still may be found to support the notion that opium produces dreams or hallucinations. Dr. Alexander Lambert at least as late as 1914 was of the opinion that acute addiction produces "nocturnal hallucinations which render [addicts'] nights times of terror."[38] This view, however, is not generally accepted by persons in touch with more recent studies. There are other more likely explanations of such hallucinations as may occur. In the studies of Dr. Kolb, one case of addiction is described in which the individual was subject to dreams, but Kolb does not suggest that these were produced by the opium. The case was one of an extremely abnormal person: a man who, although a highly trained physician, had never practiced or worked; who had regressed to an infantile dependence upon his mother; who at the age of fifty-three flew into childish tantrums that made even his mother consider having him committed as insane. He had become subject to "nightmares, during which he is noisy and swears a great deal. Because of this he has been compelled to move away from several hotels and boarding-houses. At the present time his body is covered with sores due to hypodermic injections." If the sores were usual with him as they are with many addicts who become careless with their needle, his nocturnal profanity is scarcely surprising. It has been suggested, too, that the constipation very commonly attending addiction may sometimes cause dreams which are then attributed to the opiate.[39]

Pain and illness of themselves tend to make us dream, and the comfort or sleep conferred by opiates during illness may well be haunted by passing imagery—pleasant or horrible according as the relief is complete or partial, or as euphoria is felt or not. Two persons have reported to me their own experience with what they believed to be opium visions. But those of one, it turned out in response to questions, had occurred in the midst of an almost fatal illness, during which the patient had been constantly delirious. The other person was also ill, had been suffering extreme pain, and at the time of the visions still had a very high fever accompanied by intense headache. The first person reported his visions as actual hallucinations; the second reported merely vivid kaleidoscopic images. Conceivably, these phenomena might have been caused by the narcotic; but the physical condition of the patients is more than enough to account for them on the basis of well-known medical fact as well as of common experience. The dreamers' readiness to assume opium as the cause, even under these conditions, illustrates the strength in the popular mind of the De Quincey tradition, which has in fact been so embellished with romantic and oriental curlicues that my first informant, though a person well informed in many respects, explained that he was able to sort out the opium vision from the delirium by the fact, as he remembered it after recovery, that it had contained an oriental figure. De Quincey himself might have elaborated that fantasy of the poppy soaking up from oriental soil images of Eastern faces to be scattered among the dreamers of the West. It should set geneticists back on their heels. But man is a highly suggestible animal, and, the De Quincey tradition being what it is, many of us will doubtless dream an oriental dream if we but look at a grain of opium.

No tradition such as this exists in the Orient itself, I am told. The word *opium* is not, as with us, axiomatically coupled with *dream;* some Chinese visitors to this country have said, in response to a question, that though they knew opium users, they recalled no association of the drug with dreams or visions. In the West, however, since the last century, we have all been exposed to the self-hypnosis of expectation. The person who expects dreams often has them; and the mere paying attention to them either helps to produce or causes us to remember them—as with a dreamless young man of my acquaintance, who, finding himself an anomaly among friends recounting their dreams, went home and had one.

It is well known that persons under emotional stress, whether temporary or constitutional, are, roughly speaking, inclined to dream more often and more vividly than most others. Very likely, therefore, opium users as a whole may be frequent dreamers because of their original instability. Particularly the less normal ones, those least able to control their addiction, who, taking large doses for their flights into forgetfulness, neglect more and more their normal responsibilities—these people enter a vicious circle.

They suffer increasingly from guilt and other emotional conflicts and in consequence may be likely to dream more and more. But the dreams would be neurotic dreams, not opium ones, the opium being causative, if at all, only in quite another sense than the traditional one.

The pleasant sensation of floating, endless extensions of time and space, distorted forms, horrible feelings of fear and guilt, and other special kinds of dreams traditionally associated with opium are actually all quite common among nonopium dreamers, especially if they are neurotic or troubled. The original instability of drug addicts has been illustrated by the case history of a woman who, before becoming addicted to morphine, had occasionally fallen into a state, sometimes brought about by music, during which she "forgot everything and did not worry and had a pleasurable, dreamy sensation as of floating away." Later she found that morphine helped produce the same effect.[40] The illusion of floating or flying occurs often in dreams not influenced by drugs. Long before Coleridge's day, David Hartley had noted as a commonplace of dreams the illusion of being transported from place to place "by a kind of sailing or flying motion."[41] The only actual dream recorded in Keats's letters (more exactly, the only dream indexed there), though not as far as we know an opium dream, exhibits several of the features that in addicts are commonly attributed to the drug:

> The fifth canto of Dante pleases me more and more—it is that one in which he meets with Paulo and Francesca. I had passed many days in rather a low state of mind, and in the midst of them I dreamt of being in that region of Hell. The dream was *one of the most delightful enjoyments I ever had in my life. I floated about the whirling atmosphere* as it is described with a beautiful figure to whose lips mine were joined, at [*as*] *it seemed for an age*—and in the midst of all this cold and darkness I was warm—even flowery tree tops sprung up and *we rested on them sometimes with the lightness of a cloud, till the wind blew us away again.* . . . O that I could dream it every night—.

Keats made of this a sonnet, the close of which might have
been thought inspired by the opium eater's confessions
except that De Quincey had not yet celebrated his pleasures and pains in print. "As Hermes once took to his
feathers light," the sonnet reads, so the poet fled

> to that second circle of sad hell,
> Where in the gust, the whirlwind and the flaw
> Of Rain and hailstones lovers need not tell
> Their sorrows. Pale were the sweet lips I saw
> Pale were the lips I kiss'd and fair the form
> I floated with about that melancholy storm.[42]

Keats's dream of floating and magnified time is but one
selected at random. Dreams of fear and guilt are even
more common, or else they are more often remembered
because more disturbing. De Quincey had been subject to
such dreams even as a child; apparently Coleridge had
known them very early too. But all these experiences are
commonplaces in psychological studies as well as in everyday life.

For some years a notion has been current that dreams
containing color imagery are extremely rare or even non-
existent. Whether it originated with Havelock Ellis or not
I am not certain; at any rate, since his day it has turned
up now and then, I believe, even in elementary textbooks
of psychology. Though I have made no attempt to in-
vestigate the question in any orderly way, I think it safe
to say that there can be no basis whatever for attributing
color in dreams to opiates. A little casual inquiry discloses
that, although more often than not dreams are remembered without color, nevertheless colored ones, sometimes
very vivid, are not uncommon. Most people who dream
pictorially at all report their recollection of a fair number
in color. From limited inquiries it would seem that differences here reflect varied temperaments: persons to whom
the life of the senses, particularly visual pleasure, is important dream in color not infrequently. Yet color dreams,

like so much else that is highly colored, have been incorporated into the legend of opium.

One other important factor has entered into the misconceptions about opium dreams, visions, and hallucinations; it is the confusion long current between the effects of *taking* the drug and the effects of *leaving off*. Before going into that, however, it will be necessary to see briefly a little of what was known or not known about addiction as a whole in Coleridge's own day.

3. SOME EIGHTEENTH-CENTURY ACCOUNTS OF OPIUM DREAMS AND ADDICTION

Dreams do not appear prominently in references to opium before the days of De Quincey or Coleridge. The pre-Romantic allusions cited by Professor Abrams mention no dreams and are precisely in keeping with modern medical findings: Homer's "drug to heal all pain and anger, and bring forgetfulness of every sorrow"; Virgil's "poppies soaked with Lethean sleep"; Chaucer's merely sleep-producing narcotic; Shakespeare's "drowsy syrups of the world." The same thing is true of the other historical sketches that I have seen.[43] Occasional passages in earlier writers, however, mention visions or dreams. Samuel Crumpe in 1793 wrote of the Eastern use of the drug: "The Persians say it entertains their fancies with pleasant visions, and a kind of rapture; they very soon grow merry, then burst into a laugh, which continues till they die away in a swoon."[44] Crumpe took his information from Chardin's *Travels through Persia*, a work, incidentally, that Coleridge probably read and that Robert Southey used as one of his sources for *Thalaba*. Chardin's report may have confused opium with hashish, which is known to be hallucinatory and to produce uncontrollable laughter.[45]

Hartley made an ambiguous reference to opium in his account of the theory of dreams. He had been explaining that in dreams the "State of the Body suggests" from among recent impressions such "ideas" as are suitable to the pleasant or painful state of stomach, brain, or some other part. "Thus," he remarked, "a Person who has taken Opium, sees either gay Scenes, or ghastly ones, according as the Opium excites pleasant or painful Vibrations in the Stomach"—according, that is, as it produces euphoria or, as often in unaddicted persons, nausea.[46] That he mentioned opium at all in this connection suggests that he may have thought there was a connection between dreams and the drug, though what he actually states is no more than that dreams reflect the pleasant or unpleasant, comfortable or uncomfortable, state of the body. Erasmus Darwin in *The Loves of the Plants* accompanied the "Sleep and Silence" of "Papaver" with dreams:

> Faint o'er her couch in scintillating streams
> Pass the thin forms of Fancy and of Dreams.[47]

His prose note describing the effects of opium says nothing of dreams, however. It is difficult to judge, from such remarks as these of Darwin and Hartley, whether anything more is implied than the mere obvious connection of dreams with any soporific agent, opium being practically the only such agent then known.

Robert Southey, however, once noted what he called "laudanum visions." In his *Common-Place Book* he made out a list of "Subjects for Poemlings," undated but probably belonging to the winter or spring of 1799. Among such projects as "Meditations on an empty purse" and a "Pharmaceutic ode," he entered: "Laudanum visions. I saw last night one figure whose eyes were in his spectacles; another, whose brains were in his wig. A third devil whose nose was a trumpet." Whether because he had been reading of them in Chardin or for some other reason (in July, 1799, he began the actual writing of *Thalaba*), Southey evidently thought his "visions" were induced by the drug. Perhaps they were; but perhaps, instead, they were induced primarily by the cold in his head. For in this same list of future "Poemlings" he set down another subject: "The cold in my head. French blacksmith. Ode." Southey's "laudanum visions" are all distortions of those members so sensitive during a cold—eyes, nose, and head. In later years he was chronically subject to some acute allergic condition, "summer cold" or "hay fever," from which he was at times almost desperate. Whether in 1799 his ailment was this or an ordinary cold, such images as he saw might well have haunted his restless half-sleep, with or without the laudanum.[48] Of such strands as this is the legend of the poppy embroidered. Had Southey's taste for comic verse not led him to project that ode to his cold, we should have thought we had in these visions of nose-trumpet, spectacle-eyes, brain-hair, what would appear a perfect, if not a poetical, example of the weird and distorted other world of opium.

These are a few early references connecting opium with dreams that have chanced to come my way. Presumably others exist, if from no other origin than the mere sleep- and stupor-producing power of opiates. But apart from this and from the natural connection of dreams with neurotic temperaments and physical suffering, the uncomprehended power of the drug was enough to hatch legends. The greatest reliever of pain known for three thousand years or more, an anodyne powerful beyond all others during ages when medicine could rarely hope to do more than ease pain, must have acquired the glamour of many false powers, not alone that of conferring dreams.

What Coleridge himself knew or thought of the effects of opium is a matter too complicated and uncertain to be worth tracing fully here. Of one thing, however, we may be sure among his contradictory accounts. When he professed to have been ignorant of what he was getting into, we must believe him.

There seems to have been only the dimmest knowledge in Coleridge's day, even among medical writers, of the dangers of addiction. Opium was believed to be a medicine; it was not merely an anodyne but a cure for—so it seems now to a cursory reader—perhaps three-fourths of the diseases to which man is subject. It was known to be habit-forming in some instances, but this knowledge seems to have remained on the fringes of the medical mind of the time and never to have been squarely examined. Perhaps physicians dared not admit fully even to themselves the dangers of the drug without which, it was said in the seventeenth century, "medicine would be a one-arm man." Samuel Crumpe, who wrote a book on opium in 1793, described its use for various ailments, including several that figure prominently in Coleridge's letters—gout, rheumatism, and dysentery. Crumpe apparently did not know that regular use of the drug invariably produces addiction. What he seems to have known is only that custom *may* render the use of opium necessary "to some constitutions." In these cases, he says, if any accident prevents the person from obtaining a supply, "the bad consequences resulting from such deficiency can only be obviated by the frequent and liberal use of other powerful stimulants." This and other brief remarks on the abuse of opium he appears to derive entirely at second hand from the accounts of the Eastern travelers Acosta, the Baron de Tott, and Chardin; and he thus travels through the entire territory of opium as if on the tacit assumption that for Englishmen it is a wholly beneficent medicine, though for orientals it may be an indulgence rather like drunkenness. There is no word of warning that an Englishman also might find the drug a curse, or even that an English addict had ever actually been known.[49]

We do not know whether or not Coleridge ever heard of Dr. Crumpe, who was an Irishman and whose book may not have been widely read. He did, however, know the work of Erasmus Darwin very well, and in the *Zoonomia* we may see something of what was believed about opium in England in the 1790's. We know that this work influenced Coleridge's thought on other subjects, and it may well have done so on opium. In Part III of the *Zoonomia*, which contains the "Articles of the Materia Medica," Darwin outlined a seven-part classification of medicines, one group of which is "Incitantia," or those things that "increase the exertions of all the irritative motions." The two chief medicines in this class—the only two, in fact, that Darwin considered well enough understood to be practical for internal use—are alcohol and opium. "To these," he wrote, for he was always alert to psychological aspects of medicine, "should be added the exhilarating passions of the mind, as joy, love," and for external use heat, electricity, ether.[50]

Eighteenth-century medical opinion was divided on the question of whether opium was a stimulant or a sedative. Darwin, like Crumpe, considered it a stimulant only. What we should now think the very obvious sedative effect was explained merely as exhaustion consequent upon stimulation.[51] In conformity with this belief, Darwin's class of "Torpentia" includes cold water and cold air, venesection, silence, darkness, turnips, potatoes, gooseberries, melons, cucumbers, broccoli, and numerous other substances—but not opium. Such a list as this brings home to us startlingly the paucity of actual drugs in use, or even in misuse, in Darwin's day and makes us realize what a genuine boon opium must have been. The conflicting theories about it seem to have made little difference in its prescription. Like other physicians, Darwin considered it good for almost everything.

He clearly recognized the phenomenon of tolerance in the use of opium, and he has one short passage on addiction that does not differ greatly from that of Crumpe. All medicines, he says, if repeated too frequently, "lose their effect, as opium and wine." Here he grows philosophical, explaining that man's system by nature accommodates itself to many sorts of things, from tobacco, which is disagreeable at first, to grief and pain, which also "gradually diminish, and at length cease altogether, and hence life itself becomes tolerable." In this setting, the special phenomenon of tolerance to opium could not have stood out very vividly. In another passage under the heading "Diseases of Sensation," he describes several kinds of delirium. After the kind induced by fever, he discusses a second that occurs "when the sum of general pleasurable sensation becomes too great" and the ideas aroused "are mistaken for the irritations of external objects." This delirium is produced by alcohol or opium. Some light is thrown upon what he meant when he added immediately: ". . . a permanent delirium of this kind is sometimes induced by the pleasures of inordinate vanity, or by the enthusiastic hopes of heaven." So this also does not go far toward warning the unwary about opiates: alcohol, opium, vanity, and the hope of heaven are merely lumped as possible sources of false euphoria or "delirium."[52]

After an essay on the uses of the "incitantia" alcohol and opium, Darwin has a paragraph of warning against the pernicious effects of continued heavy drinking, which may in the end, he says, produce dropsy, gout, leprosy, epilepsy, and insanity. Almost as a postscript to this warning he adds: "Opium, when taken as a luxury, not as a medicine, is as pernicious as alcohol, as Baron de Tott relates in his account of the opium-eaters in Turkey." In the medicines of this class, he continues, frequent repetition habituates the body so that the dose "may gradually be increased to an astonishing quantity, such as otherwise would instantly destroy life." When this occurs, it would seem that "these unfortunate people become diseased as soon as they omit their usual potations; and that the consequent gout, dropsy, palsy, or pimpled face, occur from the debility occasioned from the want of accustomed stimulus, or to some change in the contractile fibres, which requires the continuance or increase of it." But by this time the author has obviously forgotten opium and is thinking again only of alcohol. He utters a warning in this connection, but it refers to alcohol only: for patients suffering such debility from chronic alcoholism he suggests gradual reduction of liquor as long as digestion does not rebel, *and the addition of a little opium* and other medicines.[53] He gives no other warning against opium itself.

The impression one gets from Darwin and Crumpe—and they are in this respect apparently typical of medical opinion at the close of the eighteenth century—is that alcoholism was a familiar problem known at first hand but that—though they constantly prescribed opium to a large proportion of their patients—nevertheless, addiction to it was something they knew only by hearsay from somewhere else. In Turkey or Egypt there were oddities in the use of opium, if travelers' tales were to be believed—such is the impression the reader receives—but this did not imply any serious dangers to Englishmen in the use of the drug. There is no indication that among their own patients either Darwin or Crumpe had ever recognized an actual case of addiction as we know it.[54] Yet, with the drug so freely used, addicted patients must often have passed under their care. In these circumstances, Coleridge could have been no wiser than his physicians; he could not possibly have guessed what was in store for him when he began using opium habitually.

4. DEPRIVATION OF OPIUM, COLERIDGE'S "CURE" OF 1803, AND "THE PAINS OF SLEEP"

A prime source of confusion about opium was the long delay in accurate recognition of what are called "withdrawal symptoms." Ignorance of these contributed to many false notions about the effects of the drug, including the notions about dreams. The cause of these symptoms is not fully understood even today, but at least they have been clearly described. Some recognition of them appears in the earlier accounts of travelers in the East. Crumpe mentioned briefly from these sources the need for a liberal supply of wine if the accustomed opium were not available for "some constitutions" that had become dependent upon it,[55] and Darwin seems to have recognized the phenomenon dimly, though it was overshadowed in his mind by alcoholism.

Probably the fullest, certainly the most widely quoted, early account of withdrawal symptoms was that of Levinstein, which was not published until 1877.[56] For its day it was relatively accurate, and it remained for many years the classical treatment of the subject. A mistake by Levinstein upon one important point, however, created confusion that prevailed until 1918, when W. M. Kraus published a more accurate description.[57] The later account did not fully counteract even in medical circles the influence of Levinstein, whose misconceptions still have some currency. What he failed to understand was that withdrawal symptoms may and in fact often do occur in the midst of addiction. He therefore classified under the effects of opium itself some symptoms that are actually the effects of deprivation of opium. Levinstein's mistake was not his own but merely perpetuated for forty years more a misunderstanding already imbedded in the literature of opium. It was not realized that many, perhaps most, cases of addiction consisted not of a constant state of narcosis but rather of alternations between narcosis and incipient withdrawal illness.

Aside from relief of pain, the primary physiological effect of opiates on the human body is the functional inhibiting of some cellular and glandular activity. As tolerance develops, cells and glands become accommodated to the opium, and their functioning returns to what is approximately normal activity. After tolerance has been established for some time, if the opiate is quickly withdrawn, tissues and organs released from the influence become overactive until readjustment takes place. This is believed to be the primary, if not the whole, physiological origin of withdrawal symptoms; but there are psychological factors as well, which according to some authorities may be more important than physical sources of discomfort. As symptoms of withdrawal begin to appear about eight hours after a dose has been taken, addicts must use the drug at regular intervals three times within twenty-four hours—which they do not always do—in order to avoid daily intervals of discomfort. They suffer from deprivation too if they materially reduce the amount of their accustomed dose. If the opiate is broken off suddenly and not resumed, withdrawal symptoms run a course that rises to a peak of acuteness within two or three days and gradually subsides, the acute symptoms usually disappearing in a matter of two weeks or thereabouts.

According to the evidence of some modern studies, the acuteness of withdrawal illness may vary according to the instability of temperament among patients.[58] In symptoms as well as in cause, physical and emotional elements are inextricably mingled. Among the milder effects of abstinence are yawning, sneezing, chills, tearfulness, semblances of a cold, copious perspiration, tremulousness, intolerable restlessness, irritability, insomnia. Other more severe effects may follow promptly: asthma-like attacks, nausea, vomiting, acute diarrhea, abdominal pains, violent pains and cramp in the limbs, sometimes a collapse of heart action. There may be other emotional effects. Besides nightmarish dreams (as one would expect), there may be hysteria, hallucination, or even delirium. These may be tied up with other psychological problems that antedate the addiction. Dr. Kolb, for example, describes the case of one man who before he became addicted to morphine had had auditory hallucinations and who during his cure again heard "voices" several times.[59]

Many of these effects of abstinence used to be regarded as effects of the drug itself. Both constipation and diarrhea, for example—these may be particularly cited because Coleridge's frequent references to them have inspired a certain amount of amateur medical speculation—were formerly thought to be brought on by opium. Now it is known that only the first is produced by the drug; the contrary effect, however, often follows so promptly upon abstention that addicts may regulate their habits sufficiently to maintain health merely by postponing for a few hours their morning dose of morphine. A similar confusion prevailed with respect to psychological symptoms. The queer look, the pasty face, the shifty eye, and the nervous habits by which the addict has been thought to be marked out from normal human beings—these may actually appear at times when he is in need of a dose and is suffering withdrawal symptoms. So too with dreams and visions, at least of the horrible kinds. Jean Cocteau, undergoing a cure, described his own experience in psychological terms: the "tortures" of withdrawal, he said, "are caused by a return to life against the grain."[60] Dreams inspired by this "torture" have undoubtedly sometimes been translated into "opium dreams."

In the eighteenth and earlier nineteenth centuries many persons must have experienced accidental addiction and accidental cures, without ever knowing what was wrong. The discomfort of withdrawal would have been attributed to other causes, and if opium did not happen to be again prescribed and if the individual had not noticed any euphoric effect from the drug and so had not been tempted to use it in occasional large quantities as a means of relieving his troubles, he would have got over his addiction and been none the worse. There must also have been many who did not escape so easily, who, when a medical prescription of opium was discontinued, exhibited acute symptoms that would have been diagnosed as almost anything from gout and hysteria to dysentery or epilepsy. These symptoms would have been relieved or even "cured" by another prescription of the opiate, but the shadowy disease would again reappear whenever the drug was omitted, the physician himself remaining unaware of the cause. I have sometimes wondered what the old disease of "atonic gout" was. It seems not to exist today. In Coleridge's case, at any rate, the "atonic gout" from which he suffered in 1803 must have been primarily, if not wholly, an opium withdrawal illness.[61]

We do not know when Coleridge first took opium, when he first fell into addiction, when he first knew that he was addicted, or when he first attempted to abstain from the drug. This is rather a large order of ignorance, but we can do no better. We do not even know but that he may have gone through one or more periods of addiction and withdrawal illness without recognizing either. The habit, at any rate, was permanently fixed by 1801, and perhaps much earlier. He had used the drug more than once as early as 1791; by 1803 (probably by the preceding year) he knew only too well that it was an evil, at least for himself.[62]

Coleridge's letters furnished a very complete account of the symptoms of opium withdrawal many years before any of the well-known medical descriptions appeared. Neither he nor his physicians could have known the full meaning of what he endured; nor has that period of his life, I think, been properly understood since then. His poem *The Pains of Sleep*, published along with *Christabel* and *Kubla Khan* in 1816, had been composed in 1803, probably early in September. Its subject is the horrors of the poet's dreams. Almost ever since its publication it has been associated with "The Pains of Opium" in De Quincey's *Confessions*, and both together have become a textbook example of the horrifying dreams that opium produces after the pleasant dreams of early addiction have worn off. A different cause, however, was at work with Coleridge.

From about the middle of August, 1803, to the middle of October or somewhat later, Coleridge was attempting to do without opium at the same time that he was fighting an attack that he described as "atonic gout" (or gout of the stomach), complicated, it was suspected presently, by "mesenteric Scrofula." Nearly all his letters during these months describe his miseries at length and repetitively; and nearly all these miseries are classical symptoms of opium withdrawal as they are known today.

> But yester-night I pray'd aloud
> In anguish and in agony,
> Awaking from the fiendish crowd
> Of shapes and thoughts that tortur'd me!
> Desire with loathing strangely mixt,
> On wild or hateful objects fixt.[63]

The dream mentioned in these last two lines, though not referred to in his published letters, was probably not a poetic invention. The sexual desire that addiction inhibits is reawakened under withdrawal with increased intensity, often during sleep. The poem proceeds to other miseries:

> Sense of revenge, the powerless will,
> Still baffled and consuming still;
> Sense of intolerable wrong,
> And men whom I despis'd made strong!
>
> .   .   .   .
>
> Rage, sensual passion, mad'ning Brawl,
> And shame and terror over all!
> Deeds to be hid that were not hid,
> Which all confus'd I might not know,
> Whether I suffer'd or I did:
> For all was Horror, Guilt, and Woe,
> My own or others still the same,
> Life-stifling Fear, soul-stifling Shame!

[63]

These are typical neurotic dreams of fear, guilt, shame, powerlessness, and persecution, all heightened as they would naturally be by the emotional disturbances attending Coleridge's attempted cure. As his letters show, the lines were, if anything, an understatement of the actual experience. Explaining the circumstances of the poem to Southey, he wrote of the horrors and of his dread of falling asleep: "It is no shadow with me, but substantial misery foot-thick, that makes me sit by my bedside of a morning and cry.—I have abandoned all opiates, except ether be one . . . [editor's marks of omission]. And when you see me drink a glass of spirit-and-water, except by prescription of a physician, you shall despise me,—but still I cannot get quiet rest." A few days later he confirmed his abstinence in a letter to Tom Wedgwood; he was taking "nothing, in any form, spirituous or narcotic, stronger than Table Beer."[64]

Coleridge was on a tour in Scotland during much of this time, first with Wordsworth and his sister, afterwards alone. He was trying by exercise to move the "gout" from stomach to extremities. Despite his wretchedness, during the latter part of the tour he walked 263 miles, by his own calculation, in eight days. He wrote to Mrs. Coleridge on September 1: "While I can walk twenty-four miles a day, with the excitement of new objects, I can *support* myself; but still my sleep and dreams are distressful, and I am hopeless. I take no opiates . . . [editor's marks of omission] nor have I any temptation; for since my disorder has taken this asthmatic turn opiates produce none but positively unpl[easant effects]." Two days later he wrote again to his wife: " 'Twas an affair altogether of the body, not of the mind. That I had, it was true, a torturing pain in all my limbs, but that this had nothing to do with my tears which were hysterical and proceeded from the stomach."[65] From this confusion of mental and physical ills, one might imagine that Coleridge's hysteria had not been wholly dissipated when he wrote. These last words, however, accord well enough with at least one medical work that Coleridge had read, Darwin's *Zoonomia* again, in which hysteria is described as a disease sometimes attended by *vomendi conamen inane* ("an ineffectual effort to vomit") and other physiological symptoms. The first remedy that Darwin prescribed for it was opium.[66] Coleridge proceeded further with the account of his seizure, but some of the details apparently were too much for the delicacy of a later transcriber, for they have been obliterated. It was not his first attack. "I have been so particular in my account of that hysterical attack, because this is now the third seizure and the first from mere physical causes. The two former were the effect of agitated feelings. I am sure that neither Mr. Edmundson [his medical adviser] nor you have any adequate notion how seriously ill I am. If the complaint does not settle, and very soon, in my extremities, I do not see how it will be possible for me to avoid a paralytic or apoplectic stroke."[67] The episode was retold in a lighter spirit to the Beaumonts: "At Fort William, on entering the public-house I fell down in an hysterical fit, with long and loud weeping, to my own great metaphysical amusement, and the unutterable consternation and *beboozlement* of the landlord, his wife, children, and servants. . . ."[68]

Though the nightly horrors, from which he awoke screaming until his "night-yells" had made him a nuisance in his own house, were described as though they were the greatest source of his wretchedness, Coleridge had other miseries as well—pains in the head and limbs, asthma, restlessness, perspiration, abnormal sensitiveness to cold, "discomforts" almost worse than ill-health, dread of a paralytic stroke on his left side (whatever that may have meant), vomiting, abdominal cramp, diarrhea[69]—all common symptoms of abstinence from opiates. Coleridge may, of course, have been suffering from other ailments besides withdrawal of opium. His teeth were always a potential source of trouble, and one symptom that he reported at the end of this period of abstinence, swollen hands, I have not seen recorded as characteristic of the withdrawal syndrome. It is the only possible exception among his numerous complaints. Not only during the attempted cure of 1803 but for many years Coleridge was troubled with intestinal ailments. As far as we can tell from his descriptions, these might all have originated in irregular habits associated with opium. Coleridge's was one of those cases of addiction that consist not of smoothly consistent mild narcosis or even of this interrupted by spells of excessive indulgence but was rather an irregular succession of states ranging from acute narcosis to partial abstinence. Such a life would account adequately for all, or almost all, the symptoms Coleridge complained of from time to time, though obviously they might have been complicated by other causes too, for all we can tell now.[70]

In this illness of 1803, however, the most revealing sign of all was his remarkable physical strength, which he mentioned several times. He was so ill that he thought he might not live—yet he walked his twenty or thirty miles a day through rough Scottish country without ill effect. Even allowing for the walker's own count of his mileage, the feat required real strength. Coleridge kept referring to this almost with surprise. To Tom Wedgwood he wrote: "I am grown hysterical. Meantime my looks and strength have improved"; he had walked the 263 miles "with no unpleasant fatigue."[71]

This contradictory phenomenon has not been much dwelt upon in medical literature; but the carefully conducted study of Drs. Light and Torrance makes a point of it. Having found that their group of addicts while continuing to take a maintenance dose were the equal of the average sedentary persons in general physical fitness and ability to withstand exercise, they repeated the athletic phase of the experiment while the same addicts were

undergoing withdrawal. The patients were suffering acutely, many of them; some felt so ill they believed they could
not move. Yet even these, if they could once be persuaded
to go through the exercise test as they had agreed to do
before the experiment began—ill as they were, like Coleridge they completed the tests of exercise quite as well as
before, or even somewhat better. They were a trifle more
out of breath afterward (a result which the authors believed might have an emotional rather than physical basis); but in such tests as those of heart action and blood
pressure no more strain was evident than in the nonaddicted control group or than in their own earlier test when
they had been kept feeling "normal" through their usual
dosage. Dr. Light and his co-authors were led to the conclusion, cautiously stated, that most, if not all, of the
phenomena of withdrawal may be psychological in origin,
that they may derive from—to use M. Cocteau's words
again—the "tortures" of a "return to life against the
grain."[72]

It is clear, at any rate, that in 1803 Coleridge was undergoing a self-supervised "cure" but, not knowing its effects,
thought he was suffering from "atonic gout."[73] From
others' accounts of Coleridge's behavior at this time and
from the lengthened period of his ailments, we may doubt
that his abstinence was complete or systematic. There can
be no doubt, however, that he had reduced his consumption greatly or was doing without the drug altogether for
much of the time. The testimony of the letters is borne out
by entries in unpublished notebooks. The struggle was
given up, however. On November 23 he took a large quantity of laudanum; on the twenty-sixth he was ordering a
new supply through his friend John Thelwall. During part
of December he was again trying to abstain, but not for
long.[74]

An entry in Coleridge's notebook for early December
has been cited as an example of opium visions experienced

while the dreamer is in a state of waking reverie. Evidently at this time Coleridge recaptured the euphoria from opium that most often occurs, with those who experience it at all, during the early stages of addiction or upon return to the drug after abstinence.[75] He had apparently taken to sleeping alone in his study, an undoubted comfort in the unhappy state of his relations with Mrs. Coleridge. As his return to the drug had ended the siege of frightful dreams at least for the time being, sleep had become a delight instead of a terror. In this pleasant mood he experienced what were perhaps not so much opium visions as merely the natural imagery or recollections preceding sleep, such as anyone may have as he drifts off in a state of relief and temporary happiness after weeks of misery, but with that perfectly normal euphoria, in Coleridge's case, heightened by the return to opium.

When in a state of pleasurable & balmy Quietness I feel my Cheek and Temple on the nicely made up Pillow in Coelibe Toro meo, the fire-gleam on my dear Books, that fill up one whole side from ceiling to floor of my Tall Study—& winds perhaps are driving the rain or whistling in frost, at my blessed Window, whence I see Borrodale, the Lake, New-lands—wood, water, mountains, omniform Beauty—O then as I first sink on the pillow, as if Sleep had indeed a material *realm*, as if when I sank on my pillow, I was entering that region & realized Faery Land of Sleep—O then what visions have I had, what dreams—the Bark, the Sea, till the shapes & sounds & adventures made up of the Stuff of Sleep & Dreams, & yet my Reason at the Rudder/ O what visions, . . . & I sink down the waters, thro' Seas & Seas—yet warm, yet a Spirit/. . . .[76]

I do not find in this passage anything abnormal. Other things besides opium may put one into this half-somnolent state of physical and emotional contentment: the mere sudden cessation of an attack of acute pain will sometimes do it. Images of the sea—though dreams of bodies of water are sometimes taken to be indicative of particular neuroses—are not abnormal for anyone, still less for a man who overlooks a lake and has been a great reader of old accounts of voyages. The visions are not hallucinations, obviously, but imaginings encouraged by the will, with, as Coleridge himself says, Reason at the Rudder.

Several months earlier, in October, Coleridge had written specifically of the effect of opium. He was transcribing into a current notebook some notes originally made in November, 1799, and was here and there adding comments. The notes recorded his first visit to the Lake Country in 1799 and his first acquaintance with Sara Hutchinson. He paused in the transcription to exclaim "how imperishable Thoughts seem to be!" and added a condensed psychological comment:

> For what is Forgetfulness? Renew the state of affection or bodily Feeling, same or similar—sometimes dimly similar, and instantly the trains of forgotten Thought rise up from their living Catacombs!—Old men, & Infancy / and Opium, probably by it's narcotic effect on the whole seminal organization, in a large Dose, or after long use, produces the same effect on the *visual, & passive* memory.[77]

This passage has been cited as Coleridge's own statement of the creative powers in opium that could produce such a poem as *Kubla Khan*. In the light of recent medical knowledge, however, and in the light, too, of another statement of Coleridge, it suggests something rather different. The same idea, with the opium omitted, he had expressed more clearly and fully in a letter to Southey two months earlier. There, as in the notebook, he had been recalling the past and then, as he so often did, doubled back in thought to comment on the mental process he had just carried out. This led him to a generalization about memory and the nature of the whole associative process and to the propounding of a theory of association in disagreement with that of Hartley. Memory is awakened, he wrote, not by one *idea's* suggesting another idea, but by the occurrence of a whole mood or state of feeling, physical or emotional, that repeats or resembles a former one, in consequence of which memories belonging to that former state revive.

While I wrote that last sentence [he told Southey], I had a vivid recollection, indeed an ocular spectrum, of our room in College Street, a curious instance of association. You remember how incessantly in that room I used to be compounding these half-verbal, half-visual metaphors. It argues, I am persuaded, a particular state of general feeling, and I hold that association depends in a much greater degree on the recurrence of resembling states of feeling than on trains of ideas, that the recollection of early childhood in latest old age depends on and is explicable by this, and if this be true, Hartley's system totters. If I were asked how it is that very old people remember *visually* only the events of early childhood, and remember the intervening spaces either not at all or only verbally, I should think it a perfectly philosophical answer that old age remembers childhood by becoming "a second childhood!" . . . Hartley's solution of the phenomena—how flat, how wretched!. . . I almost think that ideas *never* recall ideas, as far as they are ideas, any more than leaves in a forest create each other's motion. The breeze it is that runs through them—it is the soul, the state of feeling.[78]

Coleridge's entry in the October notebook condensed what he had recently written to Southey, only with a different set of memories in mind. For as he wrote in the notebook he was thinking of the events recorded in the earlier notes of 1799 that he was engaged in copying out— his first meeting with Mary and Sara Hutchinson, the holding of hands, the first kiss. He was now more than ever in love with Sara. This is the context of the first part of his observation that the "state of affection or bodily Feeling" and not an "idea" conjures up the active and "living" past. Then, after the condensed reference to old men recalling childhood because they have grown physically and mentally weak and childish, he added that opium, in a large dose or after long use, probably by narcotizing the deeper, more living self, has the same effect but only on the "visual and passive" memory—without, he may have meant, the disturbing personal emotions that once accompanied those past events. He may have meant too, though I do not feel sure about this, that, like the repetition of childhood in age, a large dose of opium takes one back in memory to similar occasions of opium indulgence.

Coleridge obviously did not mean that opium in any literal sense inspired the memories or produced them, for he specifically refers to the *narcotic* effect upon the "whole seminal organization"; still more clearly, he was not referring to anything like *Kubla Khan*, for he was not describing creative activity at all but merely memory—and he underlined *passive*.

The nearest approach Coleridge himself made to an assertion that opium had a creative or formative effect upon his imaginings, if we except the inferences generally drawn from the preface to *Kubla Khan*, occurs in a later entry in a notebook of 1808:

Need we wonder at Plato's opinions concerning the Body, at least, need that man wonder whom a *pernicious Drug* shall make capable of conceiving & bringing forth Thoughts, hidden in him before, which shall call forth the deepest feelings of his best, greatest, & sanest Contemporaries? and this proved to him by actual experience?—But can subtle strings set in greater tension do this?—or is it not, that the dire poison for a delusive time has made the body, i.e., the *organization*, not the articulation (or instruments of motion) the unknown somewhat, a fitter Instrument for the all-powerful Soul.[79]

Here Coleridge did express the belief that opium had formerly made him capable of thoughts he would not have had otherwise, but even in this he is far from granting De Quincey's magic powers to the drug. He explicitly recorded his guess that it had not actually produced his fine thoughts but had merely put his body into a condition that made those thoughts possible. Even this notion he may have held only in retrospect: by 1808 he sadly needed excuses for his opium habit. He expressed the idea more succinctly in another note recently published: "Who can long remain body-crazed, and not at times use unworthy means of making his Body the fit instrument of his mind?"[80] With all his need for self-justification, Coleridge claimed no more than this for the drug. He seems never to have suggested that opium stamped a peculiar or unique character of its own upon his creative imagination; his

own statements, if read without the exaggeration encouraged by the subsequent tradition, are not as far as
has been supposed from conformity to scientific modern
knowledge. Once at least he expressed considerable skepticism. A certain John Webster in the seventeenth century
had published an account of a witch who, by means of an
ointment, put herself into "a deep sleep in which she
apparently dreamed of journeys and adventures which she
reported, when she woke up, as having really taken place."
This, Coleridge wrote in a marginal comment, "is not the
only well-attested instance of the use, and of the Cataleptic
properties of, narcotic Ointments and Potions in the
Pharmacy of the poor Self-bewitched." Like other "superstitions," he thought this no more than the decaying
corpse of "a defunct Natural Philosophy."[81]

5. YOUNG DE QUINCEY AND THE ROMANTIC CULT
OF THE DREAM

The fearful nightmares accompanying Coleridge's attempts at abstinence in 1803 bear some resemblance to
what De Quincey, perhaps remembering *The Pains of
Sleep*, christened "The Pains of Opium." De Quincey may
have been drawing upon a similar experience of deprivation of opium or of partial abstinence. In his literary version of his miseries, dreams or hallucinations predominate
over everything else; but then he had always dreamed.
His life is particularly useful to our study because it
provides a well-documented before-and-after-opium record
such as we do not have of Coleridge. On the whole, the
evidence suggests that opium eating did no more than lead
De Quincey further upon the road he had long been
following. Neither his character nor the direction of his
life can have been greatly altered by drugs. No doubt the
elaborate accounts of his early life that he himself wrote in
later years need to be read with allowance for a fictionizing
memory. Many family letters survive, however, early ones

of his own and of his mother especially, that give us a clear picture of him before he began taking opium.

As a boy, De Quincey was obviously unstable, though gifted. On more than one occasion in childhood, he tells us, he had fallen into a trance of some sort and had had visual and auditory hallucinations.[82] Short of a survey of his whole early life, which is out of the question here, the most revealing document is a diary that survives from the year 1803, when, not yet eighteen years old, having run away from school and quarreled with his mother and guardians, he was permitted to live alone in lodgings on a small allowance. He spent the time brooding over fears of not making a good impression upon others, calling upon a few older people, hoping to become an author, and devouring all the Radcliffean novels he could find in the circulating libraries. He was not taking opium and, as far as is known, had never taken it. Yet the literary projects he toyed with have a familiar ring to the reader of the Opium Eater's later confessions. One entry reads: "My Arabian Drama will be an example of *Pathos* and *Poetry* united;—pathos 'not loud but deep'—like God's own head."[83] Coleridge's *The Ancient Mariner* was evidently running in his head; and pathos, particularly of outcasts, always haunted him, for reasons not difficult for the student of his early life to guess. During the next two days he was taking home, reading, or returning to circulating libraries, besides Arabian travels, several romances whose mere titles tell us enough—*The Accusing Spirit, Castles of Athlin and Dunbayne, Sir R. de Clarendon*.[84]

The day after this Gothic debauch, De Quincey recorded what seems to have been half a reverie and half a plan for a bit of Gothic writing on his own account. He wrote:

Last night I imaged to myself the heroine of the novel dying on an island of a lake, her chamber-windows (opening on a lawn) set wide open—and the sweet blooming roses breathing y: odours on her dying senses. [One of his associations for this scene, he said, was derived from "The Farm," his home in earliest childhood. The entry continues:] Last night too I image [*sic*] myself looking through a glass. "What do you see?" I see a man in the dim and shadowy perspective and (as it were) in a dream. He passes along in silence, and the hues of sorrow appear on his countenance. Who is he? "A man darkly wonderful—above the beings of this world; but whether that shadow of him, which you saw, be y.ᵉ shadow of a man long since passed away or of one yet hid in futurity, I may not tell you."

There was something "gloomily great" about the man, De Quincey continued.

He wraps himself up in the dark recesses of his own soul; he looks over all mankind of all tongues—languages—and nations "with an angel's ken"; but his fate is misery such as y.ᵉ world knoweth not; and upon his latter days (and truly on his whole life) sit deep clouds of mystery and darkness and silence. . . .

The Bard of Gray figures in this phantasmagoria, and Schiller's *Geisterseher:*

I imaged too a banquet or carousal of feodal magnificence—such (for instance) as in Schiller's Ghost-Seer, in y.ᵉ middle of which a mysterious stranger should enter, on whose approach hangs fate and the dark roll of many woes, etc. I see Chatterton in the exceeding pain of death! in y.ᵉ exhausted slumber of agony I see his arm weak as a child's—languid and faint in the extreme . . . stretched out and raised at midnight— calling and pulling (faintly indeed, but yet convulsively) some human breast to console him whom he had seen in the dreams of his fever'd soul.

The half-reverie ends here, and its immediate sequel shows how deliberately it had been fostered. There are two kinds of pathos, De Quincey noted, the "near, tor- turing rend.ᵍ" and the "distant melting—soften.ᵍ pathos," the latter suitable for "y.ᵉ Poetical Tragical drama." "The last is what I aim at," the young author concluded.[85]

The remainder of the diary, though it contains no other succession of "imaged" scenes like this, bears out the spirit in which this was written. De Quincey was living in a world half-neurotic and half-literary, a world undoubtedly of experience twisted and distorted, quite without benefit, however, of opium. He was already expanding and contracting time and space like rubber bands; his thoughts were haunted by death and persecution; he was attracted by pathetic scenes of loneliness and isolation on island or sea; he was admiring Southey's *Ode to Horror*. Odd casual strangers encountered in real life became more odd as he contemplated them: "Read 99 pages of 'Accus^g Spirit';—walked into the lanes;—met a fellow who counterfeited drunkenness or lunacy or idiocy;—I say *counterfeited*, because I am well convinced he was some vile outcast of society—a pest and disgrace to humanity. I was just on point of hitt^g him a dab on his disgust^g face [De Quincey was miniature even when fully grown] when a gentleman (coming up) alarmed him and saved me trouble." This adventure was sandwiched between *The Accusing Spirit* and Mrs. Radcliffe's tale.

De Quincey lay abed until noon, though he had been invited out to breakfast at eleven; or he was called at seven and rose between nine and ten. He was excessively tardy in answering letters and wrote pompous apologies for his fault. He meditated writing a treatise "to prove that all animals are animated by demons." The idea, he noted, was not original, but "it would take." He pondered what should be his own future character. Should it be "wild—impetuous—*splendidly* sublime? dignified—melancholy—*gloomily* sublime? or shrouded in mystery—supernatural—like the 'ancient Mariner'—*awfully* sublime?" His mind ran upon heroes whose friends had died, upon "Spenser's ghosts whose 'stony eyes do glitter.'" He saw a press gang at work and noted the "most exquisite sorrow" contending with manliness in its victim's countenance. He listed subjects for "poetic and pathetic" dramas, tales, poems—of lost children perishing in frosty nights, of a black man, of a man dying "on a rock in the sea . . . within sight of his native cottage and his paternal hills," of two angels or spirits who "meet in the middle of the Atlantic."

He walked home from a visit "in a state of exquisite misery" for no apparent reason; he may have felt unwelcome, or had not found much to say. The next day he tried to impress the ladies of the evening before by wishing to visit hell to save himself from a state of "apathy" and talked of "the clouds which hang thick and heavy" on his "brain." His desire to impress others with his social and intellectual gifts was intense, and his suffering when he failed was acute: he went home "very miserable" after betraying a "want of skill in French," remained in bed the next day till almost noon, then walked past the "French prison" and read the article on "French" in the encyclopedia. And again he read romance after romance—*Alonzo the Brave and Fair Imogine* by Monk Lewis; *The Hosier's Ghost; Letters of a Solitary Wanderer* by Charlotte Smith, in five volumes; and much else of the same class, including various translations of German and French tales and plays. Horror and pathos were the keys of almost all that attracted him. He read poetry too, however, and regarded Wordsworth, Coleridge, and Southey almost with worship. He read, prophetically, an *Ode to the Poppy* in Charlotte Smith's metrical works.[86]

The eighteen years' interlude between this diary of 1803 and the *Confessions of an English Opium Eater* aged De Quincey, increased the range of his reading, and matured his tastes somewhat, though it did not perceptibly mature him as a human being. The difference between the *Diary* and the *Confessions* is obviously not the difference made by opium, for all the "opium" elements are already present in rudimentary form or in declared intention in the early notes. Little was needed, and that little no magic drug, to transform these youthful jottings into the highly colored *Confessions*. There was of course increased skill and experience. His great discovery in the *Confessions*, however, was the happy thought of making from his own life the thread upon which to string his preoccupations with death, loneliness, neurotic pathos, and grandeur. Evidently De Quincey had always longed to write about himself, perhaps without knowing it. The lost desolate children and little girls dying; the man dying on a rock at sea within sight of his "paternal hills" and home; the outcasts; the kaleidoscopic outpourings of his Gothic reading, with their mysterious, infinitely wretched and infinitely injured souls —all, clearly enough, were anagrams of himself. The chief source of his distinction as a writer may, in the long run, I suspect, prove to have been this discovery of his proper subject; without it he might have become little more than an ingenious hack writer and purveyor of only better-than-average tales of pathos and horror under the aegis of Mrs. Radcliffe and Ossian.

We cannot say to what extent De Quincey's famous dreams were fact and to what extent literary fiction. Whether the Malay who, according to the *Confessions*, came to his door and later haunted his dreams was much more than a vestige of his early plan for "a pathetic tale, of which a black man is the hero," we do not know. And how much "Ann of Oxford Street" may have been a fictionizing of his dreams and reveries of the dead sister, who, though a little girl when she died, was nevertheless more fully his mother than that strong-minded but unsympathetic parent Mrs. De Quincey, we do not know either. We must doubt, however, that the opium legend would ever have reached its present magnitude without the influence of the Gothic novel and German Romanticism, along with books of oriental travel, to people the dreams—and without the filter of De Quincey's temperament, through which so much of it has reached us.

The native tendency of both De Quincey and Coleridge toward neurotic dreaming undoubtedly converged with a literary vogue. Dreams, both the rational or psychological analysis of them and their special character as dreams— kaleidoscopic movement, preternatural brilliance, an air of being freighted with unknown meaning, the haunting through them of a mood melancholy, fearful, persecutory, or occasionally blissful—these things were already becoming a notable feature of romantic literature in England and Germany. The conclusion seems inescapable that the "dream" writing of Coleridge and De Quincey derives far more from the coalescing of individual temperament with literary tradition than from consumption of opiates.

Southey's poem *To Horror*, which De Quincey read in 1803, had been written twelve years earlier, before its author had met Coleridge.[87] The poem is not a dream, and its shifting scenes are mechanically contrived; but essentially it belongs to the dream tradition. On almost the opening page of Lewis's *The Monk* a dream is described at length. It begins with solitude and melancholy, as a reverie in which "a thousand changing visions floated" before the dreamer's fancy—visions sad, "but not unpleasing." These pass into sleep, where the scene becomes a church with "multitudes of silver lamps," "splendour," vaulted roof, distant music; a beautiful bride; an "unknown" of gigantic form with a complexion "swarthy, eyes fierce and terrible," mouth breathing "volumes of fire," and brow inscribed "Pride! Lust! Inhumanity!"[88] This scene perhaps contributed a strand to De Quincey's *Dream Fugue*, which draws more than once upon the dreamer's early plans and reading.

The current German literature, of which Coleridge and De Quincey read more than most of their English contemporaries, was full of dreams and discussions of dreaming. The preoccupation appears in Novalis, Tieck—almost everywhere, in fact.[89] Mr. Sackville-West has remarked the strong literary influence exerted by Jean Paul Richter upon De Quincey's visionary writing. Jean Paul made no bones about the artificial character of his dreams. "Permit me to embody in a dream," he wrote, "the few thoughts I have to offer on the education of princesses." These are the

opening words of a chapter in Jean Paul's *Levana*, the title
of which De Quincey later appropriated. Another chapter
of the same work contains what the author says is a
dreamed letter, complete even to a footnote reference, on
the subject of education. Jean Paul made no pretense of
the dream's being anything more than a literary convention. At the close of the chapter he uttered a comic protest
against being thought to have "dreamed in sport, and for
the sake of publishing." His introductory comment is a
fair statement of what occurs when most real dreams are
described afterwards: "Few men have experienced so rational a kind of dreaming as I have done. . . . I was
obliged, when awake, to help out this dream, even with
some changes in its order, so that it might—by the system
of opposite ends and aims, as well as of memory and oblivion—really appear what it is."[90]

Although the interest of romantic writers in dreams had
many aspects and derived from different motives with
different people, one superficial element no doubt was the
lure of the spectacular, which could not be so easily incorporated with themes of waking everyday life; another
more important one followed from the awakened interest
in psychology. Writers deliberately tried to reproduce the
shifting phantasmagoria of dreams as well as to fathom
their significance. In "The Pains of Opium"—that "eclectic
inferno," as Mr. Sackville-West happily calls it—are
mirrored undoubtedly some of De Quincey's real dreams,
with the hauntings of guilt and anxiety, always natural to
him, increased by the responsibility of his growing family
and failing fortune, and with the early fears, the persecu-
tions, and the lost world of lost children still vivid. The
Confessions exists in two versions, the later one containing
much that is not in the earlier. It is hardly to be doubted
that the first version too contains a good deal that did not
belong to the actual events. The *Confessions*, after all, was
written by a relatively young man seeking to make his

impression as an author, who had thought of authorship in terms of sensational fiction and drama. As an authoritative medical disquisition, the work should always have been suspect: it has too much in common with such pieces in the verse of Shelley as *Marianne's Dream* and the *Fragment: A Wanderer* or with the visions imbedded in *Alastor* and elsewhere. And if we were not so well accustomed to reading Keats's *La Belle Dame sans Merci* as poetry, we might as easily read that, too, as an opium vision.[91]

This literary tradition as much as real experience probably underlay the preface to *Kubla Khan*. By his own account, Coleridge had shared this romantic view of dreams as material for literary effects. During an illness in 1801 he told Thomas Poole that he hoped to look back upon it later "as a Storehouse of wild Dreams for Poems, or intellectual Facts for metaphysical speculation."[92]

Coleridge scattered abroad the terms *reverie, dream,* and *vision* rather more freely even than many of his dream-conscious English contemporaries, though perhaps not more freely than the Germans had been doing. *The Ancient Mariner* appeared in the second edition of the *Lyrical Ballads* in 1800, much to Lamb's disgust, with the subtitle "A Poet's Reverie." The preface to *Christabel* asserted that in the very first conception the author had had the poem present to his mind "with the wholeness, no less than the liveliness of a vision"; and either he or a friend whose shoulder he may have been overlooking wrote of "the visionary and dreamlike manner" pervading that poem.[93] Dream-images are particularly frequent in the poems Coleridge wrote during the years 1799–1800, the years of his first real familiarity with the current German literature that was so full of them—perhaps also the period that produced the "dream" of *Kubla Khan* and that saw the *Mariner* transformed into a "Reverie." But they haunt his earlier poetry too.

6. DREAMS OF VERSE—COLERIDGE AND "PERDITA" ROBINSON

Quite apart from medical, psychological, and literary probabilities, two or three circumstances of Coleridge's own life discourage belief that *Kubla Khan* was a literal opium dream or any other extremely remarkable kind of automatic composition, such as a complete semi-waking vision in which words and images created themselves for several hundred lines and were afterwards merely transcribed from memory. The chief circumstance is simply this, that Coleridge would never have kept the miracle dark for more than fifteen years. As no shame or disgrace was attached to the use of opium when the poem was written, he could have had no hesitation on that score in speaking of it. In view of his intense interest in mental processes and in dreams especially, it is not very likely that such an event as he described in the preface of 1816 could have occurred without his talking and writing to his friends about it. Coleridge habitually told the same story in letters to various people and did not confine himself to events that had occurred merely the day before he happened to be writing. The chance of his not having once, or more likely several times, recorded the dream of *Kubla Khan*, had it actually occurred, is small; and such letters would have been less likely to be destroyed or overlooked than most.[94]

He did, in fact, experience one dream of verse—small verse—which may have contributed to his note about *Kubla Khan*. Though he dreamed but four quite unpoetic lines, he recorded them with considerable interest in a letter to Thomas Wedgwood in September, 1803. Evidently he thought this phenomenon remarkable enough to be reported, though jocularly, in a quasi-formal-deposition style with time and place all complete. The doggerel dream may indeed have been dictated by lack of opium, for it occurred during the weeks when he was attempting to break the habit and was recorded in the same letter that informed Wedgwood of his taking nothing, "spirituous or narcotic, stronger than Table Beer." The verses I suppose suited the beer, and the reader may if he choose imagine that a more poetic draught would have produced better ones.

To diversify this dusky letter I will write as a Post-script an Epitaph, which I composed in my sleep for myself, while dreaming that I was dying. To the best of my recollection I have not altered a word.

The verses and a final comment follow beneath Coleridge's signature:

Here sleeps at length poor Col. and without Screaming,
Who died, as he had always liv'd, a dreaming:
Shot dead, while sleeping, by the Gout within,
Alone, and all unknown, at E'nbro' in an Inn.

It was on Tuesday Night last at the Black Bull, Edinburgh.[95]

It would be surprising that Coleridge should have reported this dream without referring at all to the infinitely more remarkable one of *Kubla Khan* several years earlier, if that had actually occurred.

Coleridge very often recorded dreams in his notebooks. On several occasions he woke recalling a sentence, which he then wrote down. Yet no notebook entry has been found of the dream of *Kubla Khan*.[96] In conversation also, as far as we know, Coleridge's friends heard nothing of it at the time. Years later, when Lamb told Wordsworth that *Kubla Khan* was about to be published, his turn of phrase does not suggest that he had any earlier knowledge of a marvelous origin. Coleridge was publishing *Christabel*, Lamb wrote, "with what he calls a vision, 'Kubla Khan.'"[97] As the poem itself was not new to Lamb, his phrase seems to imply novelty in the "vision" aspect of it.

An omission quite as damaging as this to belief in the poem as a dream occurs in an account by Clement Carlyon, who had traveled with Coleridge in Germany in 1799 and later entertained him and Humphry Davy at dinner when Coleridge visited London in the spring of 1803. The conversation on this occasion turned upon dreams and poetry. Coleridge talked about dreams and recited at least one of his poems, *The Devil's Thoughts* (written jointly with Southey); Davy recited verses of his own. For some forty pages Carlyon recounts not that discussion alone but also numerous descriptions of remarkable visions, dreams, and dream literature culled from many sources, including the writings of both Davy and Coleridge. If the composition of *Kubla Khan* had actually been attended by any astonishing psychological circumstances of dream, vision, or reverie, Carlyon's failure to mention it in these forty pages is most unaccountable, whether we suppose the omission originated with himself or with Coleridge.[98]

At least once later, probably in 1811 or 1812, before another audience, Coleridge did recite *Kubla Khan*. The occasion was recorded in the diary of John Payne Collier:

We talked of dreams, the subject having been introduced by a recitation by Coleridge of some lines he had written many years ago upon the building of a Dream-palace by Kubla-Khan: he had founded it on a passage he had met with in an old book of travels. Lamb maintained that the most impressive dream he had ever read was Clarence's, in "Richard III".... There was another famous dream in Shakespere, that of Antigonus in "The Winter's Tale," and all illustrated the line in Spenser's "Fairy Queen," Book iv. c. 5:

"The things which day most minds at night do most appear;"
the truth of which every body's experience proved, and therefore every body at once acknowledged.[99]

Collier refers to the dream palace, of which we shall have more to say later, but does not write as if the poem itself had been a dream or vision. The context, in fact, places the poem among purely literary dreams. Lowes dismissed the passage on the ground that it "obviously" represented "merely a confused recollection." As it is taken from a diary, however, and as Collier was not the man to forget or minimize a striking piece of information from his much-admired poet-acquaintance, it is unlikely that he heard any extremely remarkable tale about the origin of the poem.

This is a considerable list of omissions. The remarkable psychological curiosity of a highly wrought poem of from fifty to several hundred lines, created in a dream and remembered word for word, might conceivably have dropped out of the record of any one of the occasions we have glanced at but is hardly likely to have been lost from them all. This negative evidence alone should probably make an end of our belief in the tale told in the preface of 1816.

Among the numerous references to dreams in Coleridge's notebooks, one belonging to the winter or spring of 1800 is startling enough. "I have a continued Dream," he wrote, "representing visually & audibly all Milton's Paradise Lost."[100] What Coleridge actually meant by this is anybody's guess. By "continued" presumably he meant carried on from one dream to another. How he would *know* afterwards that he had dreamed the whole poem is hard to say. The feeling of continuity that dreams have—as Erasmus Darwin and Coleridge both said, there is ordinarily no surprise in them—disguises from the dreamer their discontinuity until they are checked afterwards by the waking mind. But if all the remembered parts relate consistently to the same known subject, their completeness could scarcely be checked at all by the waking mind. So it is with reverie too. A man may fancy he has composed a whole movement of a sonata or quartet in the brief interval before he falls asleep. But he could not produce the music afterwards, nor did he actually compose it; his failure is not alone the failure to remember it later. The illusion of smoothness and continuity that he afterward retains derives from the "streamy" nature, as Coleridge called it, of the reverie or dream state itself, not from continuity in the actual images, words, or tone combinations of the dream, which are in fact usually, I think, if not always, fragmentary and discontinuous, only here and there materializing or rising out of amorphous indistinctness into something definite enough to be communicable, even supposing it could all be remembered. The "streaminess" of that amorphous undercurrent of mood or self-awareness, or whatever one may call it, that constitutes the continuum of the dream or reverie carries over afterwards to create the illusion of completeness and continuity in the imagery that actually has only floated in scattered fragments upon the continuum. Thus a reverie characterized by a sense of musical progression, dotted with occasional bits of actual musical construction (theme, melody, harmony), becomes in memory a complete movement of a sonata, of which one cannot, however, quite reproduce most of the details. The same thing may presumably occur with a poet. Whether this was the way Coleridge dreamed *Paradise Lost* I do not know; it may have been. The reader, as Izaak Walton says, hath a liberty to believe as he chooses. He may feel that if Macaulay could recite all *Paradise Lost* waking, Coleridge could surely do so in his sleep. Be that as it may, Coleridge's note that his dream represented all Milton's poem "visually & audibly," is identical in substance and almost in language with what he wrote later of *Kubla Khan*, that "all the images rose up before him as *things*, with a parallel production of the correspondent expressions." The memory of his dream of *Paradise Lost* may have found its way into the preface to *Kubla Khan*.

One more coincidence appears from a new quarter. "Perdita" Robinson, actress, authoress, and abandoned mistress of the Prince of Wales, is apparently the earliest recorded admirer of *Kubla Khan*. Coleridge seems to have known something of her work earlier, but during the winter of 1799–1800, following his return from Germany, a mutually admiring friendship sprang up. He recommended her poetry to Southey for publication in the *An-*

nual Anthology; she wrote verses in tribute to his *Kubla Khan.* Apparently the two saw a good deal of each other in London that winter. A few months later she died. In the memoir published afterwards by her daughter, an account is given of the composition of a poem ten years earlier, under circumstances very like those Coleridge later described as attending *Kubla Khan,* except that the biographer's narrative was much less spectacular than his. Mrs. Robinson had composed a poem, *The Maniac,* in 1791 while at Bath in search of health. The anecdote was presented in the memoir "as an example of the facility and rapidity with which she composed":

Returning one evening from the bath, she beheld, a few paces before her chair, an elderly man, hurried along by a crowd of people, by whom he was pelted with mud and stones. His meek and unresisting deportment exciting her attention, she inquired what were his offences, and learned with pity and surprise, that he was an unfortunate maniac, known only by the appellation of *"mad Jemmy."* The situation of this miserable Being seized her imagination, and became the subject of her attention: she would wait whole hours for the appearance of the poor maniac, and, whatever were her occupations, the voice of *mad Jemmy* was sure to allure her to the window. . . .

One night after bathing, having suffered from her disorder more than usual pain, she swallowed, by order of her physician, near eighty drops of laudanum. Having slept for some hours, she awoke, and, calling her daughter, desired her to take a pen and write what she should dictate. Miss Robinson, supposing that a request so unusual might proceed from the delirium excited by the opium, endeavoured in vain to dissuade her mother from her purpose. The spirit of inspiration was not to be subdued, and she repeated, throughout, the admirable poem of The Maniac, much faster than it could be committed to paper.

She lay, while dictating, with her eyes closed, apparently in the stupor which opium frequently produces, repeating like a person talking in her sleep. This affecting performance, produced in circumstances so singular, does no less credit to the genius than to the heart of the author.

On the ensuing morning, Mrs. Robinson had only a confused idea of what had past, nor could be convinced of the fact till the manuscript was produced. She declared, that she had been dreaming of mad Jemmy throughout the night, but was perfectly unconscious of having been awake while she composed the poem, or of the circumstances narrated by her daughter.[101]

The origin of Mrs. Robinson's poem Coleridge may have heard from herself, or he may have read of it in the *Memoirs*.[102] The story is not quite so startling as the account he later published of *Kubla Khan*, but the resemblance is obvious. Miss Robinson offered it only as an instance of extremely facile composition; the piece was dictated while the poetess was apparently half-awake, though sufficiently under the influence of the drug to bedim her memory the next morning. This story was ten years old before it was told in print and may have grown a good deal in the interval; as it stands, it is not without some fog of half-contradiction. It still antedates Coleridge's preface to his poem by some fifteen years. In credibility it would seem to lie perhaps somewhere between Coleridge's tale and the common instance today of a man who has drunk too much and cannot remember how he got home, though he may have driven his own car with accustomed or at least tolerable skill and possibly unusual speed. The claim is not made that Mrs. Robinson had dreamed her poem and then remembered it verbatim afterwards. The account does not suggest that opium lent a special quality to *The Maniac*, nor did it: the poem is indistinguishable from the author's other verse. Its subject sounds, no doubt, like a traditional "opium" theme; but romantic literature was too full of maniacs for any special significance to be attached to this one, and there is nothing especially wild, maniacal, or dreamlike about the poem itself.

The coincidence of the circumstances in which *The Maniac* and *Kubla Khan* were said to have been composed is remarkable, if it is coincidence—which I doubt. It seems rather as if the account that Coleridge published in 1816 may have had a composite origin in which the story of

Mrs. Robinson's poem, his own dream of *Paradise Lost* (whatever it may have consisted in), and the doggerel epitaph he dreamed in 1803 had a major share. I wonder, too, whether Plato may possibly have had a finger in the preface, as he probably had, through the *Phaedo* and perhaps the *Ion*, in the poem itself. For in the *Phaedo* Socrates reports that he has been told in *dreams* that he should make *music;* so at last he does compose a few *verses* "in obedience to the dream."

The foregoing exposition, particularly the barrage of medical authorities on opium, has taken us far from *Kubla Khan*, and a perhaps overponderous engine has been raised up for the destruction of shadows. But a tradition so firmly established requires a good deal of investigation if it is to be questioned. I would not myself say that modern medical or other evidence has proved that opium could not possibly ever be responsible for any dream. Few things in medicine and far fewer in psychology are ever proved in that sense. The difficulty, if not the utter impossibility, of securing conclusive proof founded on controlled experiments that could rule out suggestibility and other irrelevancies, when dealing with such subjective phenomena as dreams and such dangerous material as habit-forming drugs, will be obvious to anyone familiar with experimental techniques. But we should not be led therefore to ignore the findings of medical and psychological observers. The weight of these is against the notion of *Kubla Khan* as any kind of special "opium dream." Neither Coleridge's preface nor De Quincey's *Confessions* can hold water as countermedical evidence in favor of such dreams. In Coleridge's own life the inconsistency of his two accounts, the coincidences such as that involving "Perdita," and particularly the great gap of silence for sixteen years or more between the dream and the more sensational of his two accounts of it, despite known occasions suitable for breaking the silence—these circumstances, apart from either poetic or medical probabilities, almost alone reduce the dream to dust. The important point, however, is not whether we can catch Coleridge, as Lamb said, "quizzing the world with lies." It is merely that if we wish to know what the unconscious mind of genius is like, we shall have to search elsewhere than in *Kubla Khan*. That poem is no doubt "inspired," but the breath that entered it is of neither sleep nor opium. So we need not read as glorious nonsense lines that make quite rational sense, nor need we in this or other "opium" writings find some unique, but at the same time mechanical, essence of poppy instead of universal man, whether normal or neurotic, behind highly colored imagery, oceans, flight, tinkerings with time and space, or fabulous serpents.

Serpents seem to have drifted into the opium tradition, possibly by way of De Quincey's crocodiles; so we may expect one day an opium-dream interpretation, as well as a Jungian and a Freudian one, of Genesis, Eve and Satan, or Milton's Hell. Yet what child who has been to a zoo or read fairy tales has not found his fears take form in dreams as wild beasts or serpents? And all one needs is the descriptive talent of a De Quincey and a temperament that has remained imaginatively close enough to the fears of childhood to turn the remembrance into the phantasmagoria of "opium visions." There was a taste for these things in the last century, an interest in exploring dream worlds; and so people wrote of them, particularly people of certain temperaments. Shelley's *Marianne's Dream* is much more labored than *Kubla Khan*, less expert, and much less poetic; yet—though it was not inspired by opium—by comparison with it *Kubla Khan* reads like an exercise in logic. Had Blake been an opium eater, his poetry and art, unaltered from what they now are, would be taken for the quintessence of the exquisitely distorted world of drugs. The *Mad Song* and, in a different medium, the fearful picture of Nebuchadnezzar are straight out of that tortured dream world—or so we should think if we did not know otherwise. But as Blake was not known to be a drug addict, we discuss his imaginings in terms of Swedenborg and symbolism instead. It is this kind of misleading psychological thought behind the opium tradition that may perhaps warrant, if anything can, the marshaling of so many cannon merely against Coleridge's preface to *Kubla Khan*.

The note in the Crewe manuscript very likely had some slight basis in fact, though not enough to mark the phenomenon as really exceptional. Coleridge may have been in a sort of "reverie" as the note says, perhaps a somewhat deeper reverie than that of a reader or spectator enthralled by novel or play, as he described the state of "dramatic illusion." No doubt he had been taking opium; perhaps, too, the euphoric effect of opium rendered his process of composition more nearly effortless than usual. But he was wide enough awake,[103] we may suppose, to write down his poem more or less as he composed it, and there is no reason to think that it was printed without revision and polishing. There is reason to suspect that the whole was not composed at one sitting. Finally, we cannot suppose that opium created the particular character of the poem. Had there been anything really strange in the facts, I think we should have heard of them earlier—from Carlyon's long discourse on Coleridge and dreams, from Collier's or Lamb's remarks on the poem, or from Coleridge himself.

I am inclined to the belief that Coleridge's original inclination toward daydreaming, encouraged by the use of half-stupefying doses of opium, had combined with his introspective habit of observing his own mental processes and with his interest in Hartleyan psychology to make him consciously capture and use in both his poetry and his prose the content and perhaps one might say the "tech-

nique" of the daydream. And yet even of this I am not sure. For as I see how general was the interest at that time in such phenomena as dreams and how much Coleridge's own theory about them derives from his predecessor Erasmus Darwin, his preoccupation seems to melt into the general pattern of thought current among English and German poets, critics, and philosophers, and I find hardly anything, on this subject, that sets him apart from the others except as each individual personality and temper stands out from any other.

7. ERASMUS DARWIN AND COLERIDGE; THEORY OF DREAMS, REVERIE, AND DRAMATIC ILLUSION

In the midst of the welter of eighteenth- and nineteenth-century writing on dreams and psychology, a number of parallels between the thought of Coleridge and that of his elder contemporary, Erasmus Darwin, seem to have escaped notice, though they throw light here and there upon Coleridge's writings. Some of his ideas have been assumed to be more transcendental or more obscure than they are, and others have been thought more original because we no longer read Darwin except sometimes to sample his bad poetry. When Coleridge described an attack of hysteria as "proceeding from the stomach"; when he wrote that his friend Charles Lloyd's illness might "with equal propriety be named either Somnambulism, or frightful Reverie, or Epilepsy from accumulated feelings";[104] when he insisted that nightmare is not properly a dream but rather a species of reverie allied to somnambulism; or when he wrote that *Kubla Khan* had been produced in a deep sleep "at least of the external senses," he was not either using language carelessly or uttering new psychological views founded on opium and introspection, but was simply writing within the psychological framework elaborated by Darwin in the *Zoonomia*. And though a treatise on medicine is not at first glance the most likely source for a famous literary theory, the *Zoonomia* appears also to have had a good deal to do with Coleridge's theory of dramatic illusion.

In their day the works of Darwin made a great impression—with good reason, for he was a remarkable and original man. His poetry, to be sure, was soon found out, and his scientific speculations were soon superseded. His reputation therefore faded quickly. He still holds a place, however, in the history of evolutionary thought, for he formulated a number of the ideas later developed by Lamarck and Charles Darwin. In an era when it was fashionable to see nature as all-beneficent, he was as keenly aware of the bleak underside as of the fair surface. He described the murderous struggle for existence: even the gentle nightingale, the lamb, and the dove he shows devouring life voraciously, in the verses of *The Temple of Nature*. He observed and theorized about heredity, mutation, the adaptation of species to environment, and survival of the fittest. He did not stop there but elaborated a modern theory of artesian wells and himself had one of the few in England; he expressed modern views on sanitation and fresh air, planned an ingenious flying machine to be propelled by gunpowder or compressed air, urged "microscopic researches" that he thought might lead to "the discovery of a new world."[105] His speculations seem to have been endless, and time has not rendered most of them absurd.

Of the greatest interest for Coleridge, however, must have been the range and originality of Darwin's psychological theories. Though founded on the English materialist philosophy, Darwin's thought is marked by a strong tendency to approach both mental and physical phenomena from a subjective analytical point of view, and often by awareness, derived from introspection, of what human experience feels like from within. His natural bent was away from purely mechanical modes of thought. The whole of nature, he premised, "is one family of one parent"; this to him meant life, the "spirit of animation," an organic more than a mechanistic conception. His writing, despite its unreligious tone, may be one of the less illustrious sources of Coleridge's belief in the "one Life within us and abroad."[106]

The *Zoonomia* was published in separate parts between 1794 and 1796, though much of it had been written long before. Its purpose was to systematize the facts of animal life and by this means to "unravel the theory of diseases." In his Preface Darwin deplored the school of thought that regarded the human body as "an hydraulic machine, and the fluids as passing through a series of chemical changes, forgetting that animation was its essential characteristic." The work as a whole is a composite of philosophical physiology, psychology, and medicine. It anticipates in many curious ways the psychosomatic medicine of modern times, for it is built upon a firm belief in the interaction of mind and body.[107] Few books look as absurd today as medical treatises that antedate Pasteur, and the *Zoonomia* is not altogether an exception. But some even of its absurdities have a more modern ring than most works of its day because of Darwin's inveterate devotion to psychological observation. His prescriptions are startling no less for their recognition of emotional forces than for their revelation to us of the paucity of useful drugs in the eighteenth century. For one form of "diabetes" as he knew it, for example, he prescribed: "Opium. Joy. Consolations of friendship." In a chapter on instinct that should delight psychoanalysts, he traced man's standards of the beautiful in landscape, painting, sculpture, even the forms of some antique vases, to the infant's association of pleasure with the form of the mother's breast. Human delight in soft textures and in the curving lines of hills he accounted for in terms very like Freud's. The configuration of the face in smiling he traced, similarly, to the shape of the infant's lips as its muscles relax after nursing. He found the origin of fear in what would now be called the "trauma of birth," describing the psychological and physiological effects of the shock to the infant upon entering the world.[108] Whatever one may think of such ideas as these, they are at any rate modern. Even when the assumptions underlying his conclusions are most outmoded, Darwin still shows considerable insight. His account of the effect that over-anxiety may have in bringing about the very results we fear is not invalidated by the fact that modern genetics destroys the illustration he offers.

Coleridge had known the work of Darwin since his youth and in 1796 met the doctor in Derby. He was contemptuous of the poetry in *The Botanic Garden* and disapproved of Darwin's lack of religion; but at least for a time he had the greatest respect for him otherwise. Darwin was "the everything, except the Christian!" he wrote in 1796; he "possesses, perhaps, a greater range of knowledge than any other man in Europe, and is the most inventive of philosophical men." Moreover, Darwin "thinks in a *new* train on all subjects except religion." A year later Coleridge still thought him "the first *literary* character in Europe, and the most original-minded man," and in his enthusiasm once planned to address a "Hymn" to the great doctor "in the manner of the Orphics." However much Coleridge disapproved of those writers who would derive man from the orangutan, he could not have failed to be impressed by the *Zoonomia*, the purely medical portions of which would have been no obstacle to him but rather an attraction added to the philosophico-psychological discussions. But his admiration soon gave way to animosity, and his later references to Darwin, for what reasons I do not fully know, are hostile or contemptuous. He seems not to have acknowledged any intellectual debt to him and by 1804 was accusing him of plagiarism.[109] I suspect that a comparative study of Darwin and Coleridge might reveal other connections, but my concern now is only with their views of dreams and the psychological and literary ramifications of that theme.

The theory of dramatic illusion, which Coleridge elaborated chiefly for its own sake but incidentally also for the purpose of demolishing what little remained of the old unities of time and place, was expounded in two notable passages in his lectures, as well as more briefly elsewhere. In his notes for the lecture of 1818 on *The Tempest* he attacked as absurd "the whole edifice of French criticism respecting the so-called unities of time and place." This led to a discussion of the two extreme views of imitation in dramatic art: the one, that drama produces actual delusion in the spectator; the other, voiced by Dr. Johnson and others, that the spectator is throughout "in the full and positive reflective knowledge" that what he is witnessing is not true. Coleridge held that there is "an intermediate state," which he called "illusion," or in the more famous phrase that he applied to poetry in the *Biographia literaria,* the "willing suspension of disbelief for the moment." He could best explain this, he said,

by referring you to the highest degree of it; namely dreaming. It is laxly said that during sleep we take our dreams for realities, but this is irreconcilable with the nature of sleep, which consists in a suspension of the voluntary and, therefore, of the comparative power. The fact is that we pass no judgement either way: we simply do not judge them to be unreal, in consequence of which the images act on our minds, as far as they act at all, by their own force as images. Our state while we are dreaming differs from that in which we are in the perusal of a deeply interesting novel in the degree rather than in the kind, and from three causes: First, from the exclusion of all outward impressions on our senses the images in sleep become proportionally more vivid than they can be when the organs of sense are in their active state. Secondly, in sleep the sensations, and with these the emotions and passions which they counterfeit, are the causes of our dream-images, while in our waking hours our emotions are the effects of the images presented to us. . . . Lastly, in sleep we pass at once by a sudden collapse into this suspension of will and the comparative power: whereas in an interesting play, read or represented, we are brought up to this point, as far as it is requisite or desirable, gradually, by the art of the poet and the actors; and with the consent and positive aidance of our own will. We *choose* to be deceived.

From this fact Coleridge argued that improbability is a flaw in drama only when it obtrudes itself upon the spectator's mind as an improbability, and this in turn "depends on the degree of excitement in which the mind is supposed to be."[110]

Schlegel is generally thought to have been Coleridge's source for one essential portion of this statement, though the questions of precedence and indebtedness have not been answered beyond the possibility of doubt. Schlegel had said: "The theatrical as well as every other poetical illusion, is a waking dream, to which we voluntarily surrender ourselves. To produce it, the poet and actors must powerfully agitate the mind, and the probabilities of calculation do not in the least contribute towards it."[111] Most of what Coleridge was to say, however, Darwin had already said. Part I of the *Zoonomia* contains a chapter on sleep, followed by one on reverie. These, supplemented by passages scattered elsewhere in the same work and by prose interludes in *The Botanic Garden*, appear to have become a part of Coleridge's intellectual furniture and surely lurked behind his accounts of dramatic illusion. There are obvious differences, to be sure. Coleridge was writing criticism, though from a psychological point of view, whereas Darwin was writing a philosophico-medical treatise, with many side glances in all directions, literature being the least of them. Yet he too wrote of the unities and Shakespeare, particularly *The Tempest* and the opening of *Hamlet*.

Sleep, Coleridge said, is characterized by "a suspension of the voluntary and, therefore, of the comparative power" and by "the exclusion of all outward impressions on our senses." That was the definition of Darwin precisely. He had distinguished sleep from waking by three conditions: (1) the "volition . . . is entirely suspended during sleep"; (2) there is an "absence of the stimuli of external bodies"; (3) "during the suspension of volition we cannot compare" our "ideas" with known fact or with each other, as we do when awake.[112] Such "comparison" is an "act of reasoning of which we are unconscious except from its effects in preserving the congruity of our ideas." To this activity, which is exerted "every minute of our waking hours" though it had not hitherto received a name, Darwin affixed the term "intuitive analogy." Somewhat oddly, in the *Biographia literaria* Coleridge remarked that he was reviving the terms "intuition" and "intuitive" from the elder sixteenth- and seventeenth-century writers, though in the very same paragraph he described the revival of old terms for new purposes as "the plan adopted by Darwin in his *Zoonomia.*"[113]

Coleridge's further observations on the superior vividness of dreams and on their inner causes had also been made by Darwin. The absence of stimulus from without, the latter had said, renders our dreams more vivid than the images of reverie: we recall "the figure and the features of a long lost friend whom we loved, in our dreams with much more accuracy and vivacity than in our waking thoughts." He had also expressed a belief that man's inner emotional life, and not mere association of ideas, produces dreams. "In sleep," he wrote, "when you dream under the influence of fear, all the robbers, fires, and precipices, that you formerly have seen or heard of, arise before you with terrible vivacity."[114] This is a conception more modern and probably truer than the idea of dreams that underlies *The Road to Xanadu*, which seems in practice, though not altogether in theory, to hark back to purely associationist notions.

In one short passage in the chapter on sleep Darwin developed almost the whole of Coleridge's theory of dramatic illusion, in brief form, through an almost identical train of thought. Sleep led him from dreams, through reverie, to the "reverie" of the reader or audience of plays and fiction, thence to a comment on Shakespeare, and finally to the dramatic unities. Here, as the doctor himself would have expressed it, the "catenation of ideas" as well as some of the constituent parts corresponds point-by-point with Coleridge's.[115] After speaking of the rapidity of dreams (we may dream "a whole history of thieves or fire in the very instant of awaking"), he had proceeded:

So when we are enveloped in deep contemplation of any kind, or in reverie, as in reading a very interesting play or romance, we measure time very inaccurately; and hence, if a play greatly affects our passions, the absurdities of passing over many days or years, and of perpetual changes of place, are not perceived by the audience; as is experienced by every one, who reads or sees some plays of the immortal Shakespear; but it is necessary for inferior authors to observe those rules of the $\pi\iota\theta\alpha\nu\acute{o}\nu$ and $\pi\rho\acute{e}\pi o\nu$ inculcated by Aristotle, because their works do not interest the passions sufficiently to produce complete reverie.

Coleridge diverged from Darwin's view on two points. Darwin had said that in sleep we believe our dreams to be true, that while they are in progress they deceive us because the will and consequent comparing power are suspended. This Coleridge specifically rejected, but used the same reason for opposing as Darwin had given in propounding the idea. Coleridge said we neither believe nor disbelieve but simply pass no judgment either way. His observation was ingenious but possibly not wholly sound; for, though it is true that we pass no specific judgment on the reality of the images and events of dreams, nevertheless our experience in dreams usually "feels" as "real" as our waking life. In either state, the mind proceeds upon the unformulated assumption that the external objects it perceives are actually there. A distinct judgment occurs, whether in waking or in dreams, only when doubt arises. The sleeper makes a judgment of sorts in those occasional dreams during which he knows he is dreaming. On this question Coleridge's analysis was no improvement upon Darwin's.

Coleridge's other point of difference lay in the idea, which is generally traced to Schlegel, of the distinction drawn between delusion and illusion through the notion of the voluntary suspension of disbelief. Darwin had anticipated this theory too, but only incidentally; he had not proposed it as a critical doctrine, nor did he maintain it consistently when he wrote of literature. It followed from his definition of reverie as a state in which the *voluntary* and comparing powers are active but in which stimuli from outside are not attended to unless the subject of our reverie ceases to interest us or unless the outside stimulus interrupts by violence. If the subject presented to us, "whether a romance or a sermon," interests our attention with enough "pleasurable or painful sensation" to excite our "voluntary exertion," reverie is the result.

In the Interludes of Darwin's *The Loves of the Plants*, dialogues between the Poet and the Bookseller explore more fully the literary application of this theory of sleep, dreams, and reverie. "You will allow," the Poet addresses the Bookseller, "that we are perfectly deceived in our dreams: and that even in our waking reveries, we are often so much absorbed in the contemplation of what passes in our imaginations, that for a while we do not attend to the lapse of time or to our own locality; and thus suffer a similar kind of deception, as in our dreams. That is, we believe things present before our eyes, which are not so." (Compare Coleridge's statement that dreaming and engrossment in a novel differ "in the degree rather than in the kind"—from which he proceeds to his Darwinian definition of sleep.) The art of a painter or poet may present to our imaginations a "train of ideas" so interesting that we cease to attend to other external objects. When this occurs, if we cease also to exert "voluntary efforts to compare these interesting trains of ideas with our previous knowledge of things, a complete reverie is produced: during which time, however short, if it be but for a moment, the objects themselves appear to exist before us. This, I think, has been called by an ingenious critic [Lord Kames], 'the ideal presence' of such objects." In the next Interlude Darwin passes beyond Kames and approaches more nearly the later statements of Schlegel and Coleridge. The audience of a tragedy, he says, experiences a perpetual swift alternation, shifting "almost every moment," between belief and disbelief.[116] For Kames's "ideal presence" he substitutes in one passage the term *theatric reverie*. In producing this, he remarks more than once, "the great Shakespear particularly excells."

As in Coleridge's account, the question of "belief" in dramatic fiction leads to that of "probability." Must the events of drama be probable? Coleridge said No: improbability is a flaw only when the excitement created by the poet is insufficient to make us forget the improbability. Darwin's Bookseller had raised the same question, and his Poet had replied: "Not if they so much interest the reader or spectator as to induce the reverie above described." Shakespeare departs from probability and nature, Darwin observed, in producing the sublime, the beautiful, and the novel (i.e., invented beings such as Ariel and Caliban); yet he "so far captivates the spectator, as to make him unmindful of every kind of violation of Time, Place, or Existence. As at the first appearance of the Ghost of Hamlet, 'his ear must be dull as the fat weed which roots itself on Lethe's brink,' who can attend to the improbability of the exhibition." Similarly, in many scenes of *The Tempest*, we are so carried away that we "relapse with somewhat of distaste into common life at the intervals of the representation." Fiction and drama require only so much verisimilitude or probability as will prevent our reverie from being dissipated "by the violence of improbability or incongruity."[117]

In his treatment of this whole subject Coleridge is much closer to Darwin than to any other predecessor that I know of. Darwin's ideas were, of course, not wholly original. He himself cited Lord Kames for one of them and in other passages acknowledged debts to Burke, Hartley, and others. But a glance at Darwin's most notable predecessors serves only the more to emphasize his departure from them and the extent of his apparent influence upon Coleridge.[118] The whole train of ideas is strikingly similar in Coleridge: the same observations on dreams, despite his dissent from the notion that we believe in them while they last; the same definition of sleep; the "complete reverie" in which the objects "appear to exist before us"; the prominence of the notions of volition and of the power of comparison in accounts of dream and reverie, the "theatric reverie," "illusion," or "poetic faith"; the application of all these to readers or audience of novels and plays, to Shakespeare (Darwin illustrated some points by occasional reference to the ancients—Homer, Lucretius, Ovid—but referred to practically no modern writers except Shakespeare), in particular to *The Tempest* and the first scene of *Hamlet,* and to the unities of time and place. We find, further, both writers introducing nightmare into their discussion. Darwin's Bookseller had asked if the "reverie of the reader" might not be "dissipated or disturbed by disagreeable images being presented to his imagination," and the Poet had answered: "Certainly; he will endeavor to rouse himself from a disagreeable reverie, as from the nightmare."[119] There is no more about nightmare here, but a few pages later, in the poem itself and in the illustrative notes, nightmare reappears through "the evening fog," bringing dreams of the "Murderer with his knife behind" and other horrors, along with a reference once more to Shakespeare and the definition of sleep versified—"The WILL presides not in the bower of SLEEP." A long note elaborates this definition and adds a full exposition of nightmare. "When there arises in sleep a painful desire to exert the voluntary motions, it is called the Nightmare or Incubus," the account begins and is developed to the length of a paragraph. The effect of all this is reinforced by the full-page engraving of Fuseli's "Nightmare," in which a distressed lady hangs halfway out of bed, with the blind-eyed mare pushing through the curtains behind and a grotesque, leering half-demon squatting upon the sufferer's breast,[120] or as the poet writes, "on her fair bosom sits the Demon-Ape."

Coleridge introduced the subject of nightmare at some length into one of his three discussions of dramatic illusion.[121] He probably had Darwin's lines and the illustration from Fuseli specifically in mind, for he referred to the "assassin . . . stabbing at the side" (Darwin's "Murderer with his knife behind") and to impressions of bed, curtains, and "a goblin sitting on the breast" (he had been impressed by Fuseli's illustration some twenty years or more earlier).[122]

In sum, Coleridge's celebrated accounts of dramatic illusion might fairly be described as consisting of the ideas of Erasmus Darwin refined at one point by means of Schlegel—unless it should prove eventually that Coleridge was right in his claim, at present unsubstantiated, to have developed his theory before Schlegel had done so, or at least independently of Schlegel. This claim becomes possibly more rather than less believable when Darwin enters the scene, for little was needed after Lord Kames to reach the theory offered by Coleridge and Schlegel, beyond Darwin's account of the matter, united with Darwin's own definition of reverie, which he himself did not fully bring to bear on his literary remarks. Darwin the critic was obviously more naïve than Darwin the psychologist and scientist: he did not even make the fullest possible use of what Kames had thought out; and, writing in the early 1790's or before, his emancipation from the doctrine of the three unities was but partial and timid. Nevertheless, and after all possible allowances have been made, he seems to have provided the main ground from which Coleridge's accounts of illusion sprouted. His observation, made more than once, of the activity of the voluntary powers during reverie and his suggestion that theatric reverie consists in a rapid alternation (as if it were a kind of vibration) between belief and unbelief seem to me to fall little short of Coleridge's account of it as "intermediate" between the two states or, in the more celebrated phrase, as "the willing suspension of disbelief." Coleridge polished the theory, however, and made it accessible by extricating it from the mass of Darwin's somewhat unreadable prose.

On this note I must return from a subject that is largely digression, even though it may overshadow in literary importance the remainder of what I have to say about Coleridge and Darwin. Coleridge wrote a good deal about dreams, reveries, optical illusions, apparitions, and the supernatural; and he planned to write more than he did. His writing on these themes often seems cryptic today, and a few of his comments may strike one, according to one's bias, as inspired or eccentric or perhaps merely irresponsible. In the light of Darwin's psychology, however, some of them prove to be neither wayward nor inspired but, when properly understood, part of a systematic order of thought, though not one originated by himself. His account, in the preface to *Kubla Khan*, of his "profound sleep, at least of the external senses" and of the words and images that "rose up" before him without any conscious "effort" was not merely an elaborate way of describing a special kind of reverie, as has been suggested in order to reconcile the statements of the preface and the Crewe manuscript. It was phrased strictly in accordance with Darwin's definition of true sleep and sleeping dreams. Coleridge had the definition clearly in mind at the time, too, for he employed it in a letter discussing dramatic illusion, written within two or three weeks of the publication of *Kubla Khan*.[123]

The preface and the letter belong to the spring of 1816. One of the other passages on dramatic illusion was apparently written in 1818. But as early as 1796 Coleridge had already become embroiled in Darwinian terminology. In November of that year he had described his friend Charles Lloyd's psychological illness in a letter. It may, he wrote, "with equal propriety be named either Somnambulism, or frightful Reverie, or *Epilepsy from accumulated feelings*."[124] This diagnosis owes nothing to poetic imagination but is strictly in keeping with Darwin's account of reverie in its abnormal manifestations as one of the "diseases of Volition," allied specifically to epilepsy. Somnambulism also Darwin classified as a form of reverie rather than sleep, on the ground that the somnambulist's volition and sometimes his comparing power are active: the somnambulist moves about under his own control and may even speak coherently.[125] So Coleridge, in using the terms as synonymous, was merely applying what he had recently learned from the *Zoonomia*. Perhaps it was he too who, after nursing Charles Lloyd to partial recovery, sent him off to consult Dr. Darwin about his health.[126]

Coleridge was greatly interested in the phenomenon of nightmare, no doubt from bitter experience. We have seen how he lugged in the topic somewhat irrelevantly when he wrote of dramatic illusion. But his psychological analysis of the phenomenon owes more perhaps to Darwin than to personal experience of "the pains of opium."[127]

Other observations on sleep and dreams are perhaps also traceable to Darwin, though some of them are common to earlier writers as well. In the draft of a lecture on "Dreams and Apparitions" Coleridge used as one of his arguments the fact that "the strangest and most sudden transformations [in dreams] do not produce any sensation of surprise." Darwin too (like Hobbes and others before him) had commented on the inconsistency of our dreams and "the total absence of surprise" in them. "Thus," he said, "we seem to be present at more extraordinary metamorphoses of animals or trees, than are to be met with in the fables of antiquity; and appear to be transported from places, which seas divide, as quickly as the changes of scenery are performed in a playhouse; and yet are not sensible of their inconsistency, nor in the least degree affected with surprise." Coleridge's accounts of delirium, too, were composed partly within the framework of the *Zoonomia*, though he was more preoccupied with associationism as well as more overtly critical of it than was Darwin, who often departed from it without troubling to argue his point. The remark in *Anima poetae*—"And what is the height and ideal of mere association? Delirium."— is implicit but not explicit in Darwin; and Coleridge's belief that dreaming is the nearest approach to delirium probably reflects Darwin's statement that "dreams constitute the most complete kind of delirium," which is marked by "endless trains" or "perpetual flow of ideas." Coleridge had the finer phrase, however, "the streamy nature of association."[128]

8. "WHAT IS THINE, WHAT IS MINE"

Viewed against the background of Darwin's thought, Coleridge's scattered statements on a number of subjects both lose and gain. They lose a good deal of the originality we have attributed to them but gain in coherence and consistency. Statements and phrases which by themselves have seemed erratic or arbitrary prove to be not so at all. On the other hand, remarks of Coleridge that had seemed to spring full-fledged from his own brilliant and original insights prove to be in fact Darwin's insights, sometimes more subtly expounded or developed by Coleridge, sometimes not. It was not, probably, a question of plagiarism— though Coleridge was ungenerous, under the circumstances, in his contemptuous references to Darwin and in calling *him* a plagiarist. The works of Darwin were easily accessible; however out of fashion *The Botanic Garden* and the *Zoonomia* had fallen by the time Coleridge used ideas from them in his lectures in London, they were probably not wholly forgotten. In employing terms in Darwin's sense and accounting for psychological phenomena by means of Darwin's explanations, Coleridge was using not indeed the current ideas of the day but at least matter that might have seemed more or less in the public domain. M. Jean Cocteau, saying that we live today in a period of such individualism that "we no longer speak of disciples; we speak of thieves," marks a danger to beware of.[129] Coleridge, however, does not seem ever to have acknowledged the smallest debt to Darwin. It is just possible, though quite unlikely, that by the time he expressed the ideas in public lectures he had forgotten what they owed to his predecessor.[130]

Having trod a number of times not gently upon Coleridge's veracity and having the prospect of doing so again, I should like to add a word here. The definitive study of Coleridge's character and temperament has yet to be made (assuming, as we should not, that a study of temperament could or should be definitive). The two chief modern biographical volumes, those of Mr. Hanson and Sir Edmund Chambers, have other aims, and Mr. Fausset's analysis does not always win agreement. This is not the place for such an attempt, nor I the author. But meanwhile, as everyone else must do who writes about Coleridge, I find myself faced at many turns with some inaccuracy in his statements. One is tempted to creep about dodging them as far as may be, or to try desperately to read them in some way that will fit the facts. But neither of these seems quite the spirit in which to treat a poet-critic-philosopher after a hundred and fifty years. One can say instead that Coleridge was forgetful, absent-minded, vague; that he was interested in truth, not mere fact; that he was above pettifogging details; but these also will not do, not really. Coleridge was not vague; he was very precise, circumstantial, and factual, whether the facts were so or not. And most people now know that forgetfulness and absentmindedness are not primary elements but have their causes. One can always fall back on moral disapproval, but that is a glass house and, what is more, explains nothing.

One of the most attractive features of Coleridge was his power and willingness, only very occasional, to see past his own façade. He did this once in a letter to Southey that has not been much noticed, though it is a revealing statement. Characteristically, the passage, itself perceptive and unassumingly modest, is sandwiched between a self-defensive protestation at one end and a boast at the other. Coleridge had been accused of vanity, but his fault was not that, he wrote. It was *"an instinct to have my power proved to me by transient evidences*, arising from an inward feeling of weakness, both the one and the other working in me unconsciously." He went on to an equally honest and penetrating statement about his personal relations with others, and then concluded: "A sense of weakness, a haunting sense that I was an herbaceous plant, as large as a large tree, with a trunk of the same girth, and branches as large and shadowing, but with pith within the trunk, not heart of wood—*that I had power not strength, an involuntary impostor, that I had no real Genius, no real depth.* This on my honor is as fair a statement of my habitual haunting, as I could give before the tribunal of Heaven."[131]

This abysmal self-doubt coexisted, as he would have said, with an egotism equally extreme, an egotism which could assert for his projected essay on poetry that it would supersede all past works on metaphysics and morals.[132] His egotism demanded of him that his achievement be unique and supreme, transcending all that his precedessors had done; yet he felt himself as weak as an overgrown herbaceous plant, "an involuntary impostor." And, to go no deeper into the matter than recognition of that conflict, it is no wonder that he sought opium for its "deep tranquillising powers to the mitigation of evils."[133] Few of us, I suppose, can claim never to have taken liberties with truth or fact from an "instinct to have our power proved to us by transient evidences" or to avoid making an unfavorable impression. With Coleridge the extremes of his need to impress, however transiently, and of his unbelief almost in his own essence drew him into that sizable class of persons whose need to say whatever will make themselves momentarily most comfortable tends to obliterate either fact or truth. They may know faintly somewhere in their minds what the truth is, and they may even know faintly that others will find it out tomorrow; yet to say what is not true meets the momentary but imperative need of today, and so it is said. Coleridge's misdating of his poems—his habit of assigning them a date too early, attributing them sometimes to his youth or boyhood—arises not from sublime indifference to mundane dates but from the self-mistrust that finds them not the supreme poetic achievement that he requires them to be; the misdatings are, in fact, gestures of deprecation.[134] But in Coleridge the need of the moment to melt away the conflict of self-doubt and self-claim was often self-defeating. His "lies" were not usually of the well-ordered kind, calculated to succeed and establish him credit in the world. They were momentary even when they were repeated from time to time, and were almost always doomed to sink him into a deeper morass than before.

The teasing problem of Coleridge's unacknowledged borrowings might be examined in this same light, though it is complicated by other factors that are beyond our consideration here. His failure to finish so many of his works perhaps has in part a similar origin. The "Sloth" that he deplored was the symptom, not the disease; and opium, in turn, was the instrument more than the cause of that Sloth. Unfinished work cannot be judged, it escapes the final test; and Coleridge did not feel sure enough of his genius to meet the test. This, I think, though I have set it forth only briefly and inadequately, is something of the state of mind in which *Kubla Khan* was published, and this spirit of mingled deprecation and assertion of uniqueness I think also underlies the preface that he wrote for it.

~ III ~

The Echoes

1. LOWES AND THE TRAVELERS

In *The Road to Xanadu* Lowes was concerned to show through analysis of the sources of *Kubla Khan* the links by which man's unconscious mind, without the slightest intervention of consciousness or will, associates elements the most disparate and, if the mind be that of genius, transforms and fuses them into a poetical entity. It will be impossible here to summarize adequately the elaborate pattern of "hooks and eyes of memory" that Lowes traced, but it is necessary to have some sort of working summary before us, however little justice it may do the original.

The materials that entered into Coleridge's dream, according to Lowes, were nearly all drawn from books of travel. These were not all associated with a single region or epoch but were drawn from almost every continent and age. Roughly speaking, he found three main groups of material: old accounts relating to Asia, especially Tartary, Cathay, and Hindustan; old and modern accounts of the sources of the Nile in Africa; and a book of travels in North America. The primary works were Purchas's *Pilgrimes* and *Pilgrimage*, Bruce's *Travels To Discover the Source of the Nile*, Maurice's *History of Hindostan*, and Bartram's *Travels through North and South Carolina*. Besides these, Lowes found important sources in the classical writers, chiefly historians and geographers—Herodotus, Pausanius, Strabo, Seneca, Virgil—and in Burnet's *Telluris theoria sacra* and its English version. There were other incidental sources—Bernier's *Voyage to Surat*, the works of Athanasius Kircher and Major Rennell, and some others. Still more incidentally and almost as if it were an afterthought, he noted slight connections with the English poets Milton and Collins, which had been pointed out earlier by others.

The opening lines Coleridge himself had traced to this passage in *Purchas His Pilgrimage:*

> In *Xamdu* did *Cublai Can* build a stately Pallace, encompassing sixteene miles of plaine ground with a wall, wherein are fertile Meddowes, pleasant Springs, delightfull Streames, and all sorts of beasts of chase and game, and in the middest thereof a sumptuous house of pleasure, which may be removed from place to place.[1]

Pleasure-house, garden, trees, and fruit Lowes also found in Purchas's *Pilgrimes*, along with a spelling closer to Coleridge's in the name *Xandu*. Gardens, trees, fragrant blossoms, winding streams, "five miles," and springs Lowes related also to Bartram, Bruce, and Bernier. Bartram provided an "inchanting and amazing chrystal fountain, which incessantly threw up, from dark, rocky caverns below, tons of water every minute" and a creek that "meanders six miles through green meadows." In Bernier, whom Lowes felt certain, chiefly from internal evidence, that Coleridge must have read, the word *domes* is used once in connection with two "cabinets" built in a canal in the pleasure-garden of Chah-limar; in a different passage of the same work is described an "eremitage" with a garden, which was said to float upon the water. Coleridge's River Alph has no connection with Xanadu, but Lowes noted ancient accounts in Virgil, Pausanius, and Strabo of the legend of the Alpheus, which was said to flow under land and sea from Greece, to reappear as the fountain of Arethusa in Sicily. In some of these passages the Nile is also referred to incidentally. Imagery connected with the Nile as a "sacred" river, other fountains, the Nile again flowing *per praecipitia hominibus inaccessa* (Coleridge's "caverns measureless to man"), and another sub-

terranean river Lowes found scattered through a variety
of works ranging from Bruce and Bartram back to Herodotus. These various sources take care, roughly, of the materials in the first paragraph of *Kubla Khan*. The imagery
of the second paragraph in part repeats and overlaps that
of the first, and so do the sources presented by Lowes. But
some of the scenery is different. There is the "deep
romantic chasm," a "savage place," "holy" and "enchanted," and there is the fountain whose play is not continuous but "half-intermitted" and which throws up huge
rock "fragments." There are also the "mazy motion" of
the river, the "ancestral voices prophesying war," and the
"caves of ice."

Some of these images Lowes found in Major Rennell's
Memoir of a Map of Hindostan, where Cashmere is described in words suggesting those of Coleridge: "romantic," "fertility," a "capital river" which had opened a
channel among the mountains, "encircles," "holy land"
where "miraculous fountains abound," "garden in perpetual spring." Lowes quoted from Bruce, with reference
to the Abyssinian landscape, extracts containing the
words "romantic," "grove of magnificent cedars," "cover," "savage," "inchanted," "prodigious cave," etc. These
are not taken, however, from a single continuous passage
in Bruce but are scattered through more than seventy
pages of the narrative. Bernier and Bartram yield similar
details, and the latter provides two specially notable
instances of springs or fountains that gush irregularly and
cast up rocks, sand, or shells. As sources for Coleridge's
"ancestral voices prophesying war" Lowes presented
passages in Purchas, Bruce, and Beckford's *Vathek*.
Purchas had mentioned that "no warres are begunne or
made" without the word of the Tartar priests. In Bruce
the traveler is told that "the Begemder people have a
prophecy, that one of their governors is to fight a king at
Serbraxos, to defeat him, and slay him there," and that

afterwards Abyssinia will be "free from war." These do not suggest very vividly the prophetic ancestral voices in *Kubla Khan*, but even more strained is the parallel drawn from *Vathek*. Beckford says nothing of war but merely describes how at the edge of the abyss Vathek for a moment mistook the sound of waters for voices.[2]

Coleridge's "caves of ice" had been traced originally by E. H. Coleridge to a passage in Maurice's account of Hindustan that tells of "an Image of Ice" in a cave in the mountains of Cashmere, which grew and diminished in size as the phases of the moon altered. Coleridge had copied this passage into a notebook, probably as material for his projected series of hymns to the sun, moon, and other elements. Lowes also drew attention to "a grotto of odd congelation" mentioned by Bernier.[3]

As the major source for the closing paragraph of *Kubla Khan*, Lowes presented the account in Purchas's *Pilgrimes* (not the *Pilgrimage*, from which the opening lines were drawn) of the false Paradise of Aloadin, where the imagery of trees, fruits, palaces, and houses of pleasure is repeated. The palaces were equipped with pipes for serving wine, milk, honey, and clear water. There were Tartar "Damosels skilfull in Songs and Instruments of Musicke and Dancing." Into this Paradise Aloadin brought youths who had been drugged into unconsciousness; they awoke, enjoyed the pleasures, and believed themselves actually in Paradise; afterwards they were put to sleep and awoke again to find themselves outside. Through their desire to return, Aloadin secured such power over the youths that they became fearless of death and would even commit murders at his desire. Coleridge's "damsel with a dulcimer" and his dreamer, the "I" of the poem, Lowes identified with Aloadin's youths and damsels in their sensual Paradise. Oddly, ignoring Coleridge's shift to the first person in this passage, Lowes regarded the dreamer rather vaguely as a mere type figure among the Tartar youths.

He found a few other connections with Bruce here—the reference to Abyssinia and "Mount Abora," which he traced to the place names "Abola" and "Astaboras," though he gave some weight also to the association with Milton's Mount Amara, "where Abassin kings their issue guard," a source that had been pointed out earlier by Professor Lane Cooper. Finally, the "flashing eyes" and "floating hair" in *Kubla Khan* were traced to a different episode in Bruce, in which the narrator was riding in company with the king of Abyssinia, who was "dressed in the habit of peace, his long hair floating all around his face, wrapt up in his mantle, or thin cotton cloak, so that nothing but his eyes could be seen.[4]

This completes the essential, but certainly not satisfactory, summary of Lowes's study of the sources of *Kubla Khan*. Only by repeating the book itself would it be possible to do justice to the elaborate web of connections that are there presented; so this sketch must suffice. Lowes found one or more sources, some of them compelling belief more readily than others, for most of the images in the poem. For the woman wailing beneath a waning moon for her demon-lover he seems not to have found any special origin; either the poet's dream became more inventive at this point or the expounder missed an additional key somewhere. There are no "ancestral voices" either; no triple magic circles are drawn, nobody plays upon a dulcimer, and nobody shouts "Beware!" For some of the other images, too, the parallels given seem a trifle far-fetched. Lowes himself, according to reports, was not entirely satisfied with his explanation of the "damsel"; a question particularly remained of why the "Abyssinian maid" should sing of "Mount Abora."[5]

As Lowes reconstructed the origin of *Kubla Khan*, the process ran something like this. Sitting in his chair, overcome by the opiate, as described in the preface, Coleridge fell into a deep sleep just as he had been reading the

sentences quoted from Purchas's *Pilgrimage*. The laws of
Hartleyan association then took over. The *Pilgrimage*
recalled the *Pilgrimes*, each of these recalled another
passage in another work by the association of an image of
fountain, river, pleasure-house, garden, or place name;
and the next one recalled still another by reminders sometimes close, sometimes tenuous. The sleeping memory was
led from the Nile to the Alpheus or from Bruce on Africa
to Pausanius on Greece through Herodotus, who mentions
both together. All the while, through the mysterious working of genius, these fleeting memories from books coalesced
spontaneously into visual images and were transformed
into corresponding words automatically and organized unconsciously into finished poetic form. Coleridge himself
might not have agreed with all this, for Lowes's exposition
was more purely Hartleyan than, except perhaps in quite
early years, he would have approved. In the last chapter I
quoted one note that furnished an oblique, anticipatory
criticism of Lowes's view of the workings of the mind.
Coleridge had questioned whether ideas (the term *idea*
included images) ever are suggested by other ideas. Association operates not by idea-links, he thought, but by
feeling-links; it is the state of feeling, physical or emotional, rather than a mechanical link between one image
and another,[6] that revives in the memory images from the
past. To this question we shall return later.

The complexity of the evidence being what it is, some
carts in these chapters necessarily precede some horses. I
shall therefore take up the echoes that seem to be audible
in *Kubla Khan* from the works of Coleridge's contemporaries, before considering whether such echoes are even
possible chronologically or whether originals can be distinguished from echoes at all. There is no question of
thrusting aside Purchas and Bruce in order to insert
Landor and Southey, Milton, or Wieland as the chief

sources of imagery in *Kubla Khan*. There can be little
doubt that at one time or another Coleridge read many,
possibly most, of the works that Lowes discussed; and
there is no doubt, either, that at least some of those works
found their way by avenues direct or indirect into the
poem. Nevertheless, the suspicion arises that whatever
spirit dictated *Kubla Khan* may have descended from the
literary tradition more than from the travelers. Coleridge's
use of Milton must await later chapters because of its
connections with the date and the ultimate poetic effect of
his poem. Among contemporary works, however, *Kubla
Khan* exhibits likenesses to Walter Savage Landor's *Gebir*
and Wieland's *Oberon* and many far closer links with
Southey's *Thalaba*. The synthesis of miscellaneous travelers and geographers of Asia, Africa, Europe, and the New
World did not take place first in the sleeping brain of Coleridge at his lonely farmhouse near Porlock. Behind Landor
were Bruce and Milton, and behind Milton was Purchas;
behind Southey's *Thalaba* were all these, besides Wieland's
Oberon and almost countless others. The rage for oriental
material in the eighteenth century had already annihilated
distinctions of time and place. Egypt, China, Tartary,
Persia, Abyssinia, and sometimes, for good measure, Peru
were all boiled up in the same pot and sauced now and
then with Greece, Italy, or France. Among Europeans
writing of the East, minor themes drifted invisibly from
one to another poet and romancer. There was the theme,
for example, of the living man who is permitted to visit
Paradise and who returns with a token as proof. Coleridge,
in a typically Coleridgean note published in *Anima poetae*,
preserved the delicate essence of this theme: "If a man
could pass through Paradise in a dream, and have a flower
presented to him as a pledge that his soul had really been
there, and if he found that flower in his hand when he
awoke—Ay! and what then?"[7] A variant of this had appeared earlier in Wieland's *Oberon*, when Huon, having

fallen in love with a goddess or angel seen only in a dream, wishes he might have brought from his dream a token, "were it but the flower that in her bosom bloom'd!"[8] Southey introduced the theme into *Thalaba* in a version taken from Sale's Introduction to the Koran. The story there was attached to the invisible Paradise-palace-city of Irem that figured prominently in both *Thalaba* and *Gebir*. And in his *Common-Place Book* Southey recorded still another variant, which he quoted at length from Medjireddin's *Fundgruben des Orients*. According to this, a man descended into a pit in the mosque at Jerusalem and returned with a leaf behind his ear, which he said he had gathered in Paradise. As Mohammed had foretold that one man should enter Paradise alive and walking upright and as the leaf did not wither, the man's claim was acknowledged.[9] Even the concluding lines of *Kubla Khan* may be playing with echoes and overtones of this theme: the poet, like these other travelers or dreamers, would be looked upon with the awe due to one who had entered the sacred garden and "drunk the milk of Paradise," if he had only been able to bring back his token—not a flower, but "music loud and long," the poem of the Paradise itself. Perhaps not; perhaps, that is, I have spun the thread too thin, for Coleridge's conclusion has other stronger affinities. My point at the moment is not in any case *Kubla Khan* but something more general; it is the way in which even small rivulets of thought or imagery eddied on from person to person, forming intricate patterns in the carpet of the day, a rich complex of associations shared by writers and readers.

2. "GEBIR"

Landor's poem *Gebir* was first published anonymously in the summer of 1798, almost simultaneously with the first edition of the *Lyrical Ballads*. Apparently it attracted no attention at first, and we hear nothing of it from members of Coleridge's circle until a year later, when Southey reviewed it for the *Critical Review*.[10] Coleridge read it during that next summer of 1799, after his return from Germany in July. Partly because of the enthusiasm of Southey, *Gebir* came to exert an occasional influence upon Landor's own and the following generation of poets, leaving some trace upon the writing of Keats, Shelley, even Tennyson, perhaps Wordsworth, but most of all upon Southey himself. Coleridge too, I think, came under its influence. And, *Kubla Khan* aside, the mark of a serpent in *Gebir* may have been printed upon *Christabel*.

Coleridge had more than a poetic reason for reading *Gebir* with an attentive if not a sympathetic eye. Southey, with whom he was newly reconciled after a long quarrel, was praising the poem in unbounded terms to all his friends. He found in it "some of the most exquisite poetry in the language" and said as much in print only a few months after he had set down, also in print, Coleridge's own *Ancient Mariner* as a mere "Dutch attempt at German sublimity." Landor's Preface too was characteristically provocative and must have offered to Coleridge a challenge at almost every point. The unknown author mentioned the main source of his tale—the mere "shadow" of his subject, he said—as the story of Gebirus and Charoba, "a wild and incoherent, but fanciful, Arabian Romance," which he had found in Clara Reeve's *Progress of Romance*, a volume he had met with "on the shelf of a circulating library." His tone, for a new and unknown poet, was arrogant, even a little bumptious. Unlike Coleridge, who at that time took his profession as a poet most seriously, Landor described *Gebir* as "the fruit of Idleness and Ignorance"—for, he said, had the author been "a botanist or mineralogist [the poem] never had been written" (Coleridge had said he should "not think of devoting less than 20 years to an Epic Poem" if he should undertake one).[11] "A poem like mine," Landor's Preface avowed further, "should never be founded totally on fiction" (Coleridge's *Ancient Mariner* had been fiction; so was the yet unfinished *Christabel*). "I have written in blank verse," Landor continued, uttering now a real challenge, "because there never was a poem in rhyme that grew not tedious in a thousand lines." *The Ancient Mariner* had stopped short of a thousand lines, but *Christabel* was intended to be much longer; so was *The Three Graves*, which Coleridge was attempting to complete shortly after he had read *Gebir*. All were in rhyme. Landor's Preface added, on the virtues of blank verse as opposed to rhyme: "My choice is undoubtedly the most difficult of the two: for, how many have succeeded in rhyme, in the structure at least; how few comparatively in blank verse. There is Akenside, there is, above all, the poet of our republic."[12] This is all that the Preface had to say of Milton, but the reader of *Gebir* cannot miss the prevailing influence of *Paradise Lost*.

Gebir and *Kubla Khan* bear marks of resemblance that seem as if they should be more than fortuitous. The likeness is not one of plot, for Coleridge's fragment, as far as it goes, has none; nor is it, nominally at least, of locale, for the events of *Gebir* take place in ancient Egypt with a minor excursion to Italy, whereas Kubla's summer palace was far to the east in Xandu (or Xamdu, Xaindu, or Shang-tu), not very far from Peking. The poems do show some likeness in theme. Both contrast Paradise gardens with the world of caverns below. Both are concerned with the process of building: magnificent gardens and "pleasure-dome" on the one hand; on the other, a magnificent city and palace, described in so outdoor a spirit as to seem in retrospect more garden than city or palace. In both poems the effect of movement is secured partly through the fact that these scenes are shown first as decreed and in progress rather than already built. Movement comes too from the rivers that haunt the lines of both poems, in Coleridge's the "Alph" with (according to Lowes) the Nile lurking somewhere about, in Landor's the Nile, attended toward the end by the rivers of all Europe.

In the actual execution of *Gebir* a good many more reminders of *Kubla Khan* crop up. There are "sunless" caverns and subterranean rivers so important that they occupy a whole book of the poem. From the cavern's opening issues a "mingled sound" of the river and the voices of ancestors (a parallel to *Kubla Khan* before which the dim resemblance of Vathek described by Lowes pales considerably). This is the world of the dead, and here amid the "confused roar" of Acheron in its subterranean channel, "ancestral" voices warn the hero against war. All this is remarkably like the "mingled measure" that also comes "from the [river-]fountain and the caves," amid the "tumult" of which "Kubla heard from far Ancestral voices prophesying war." Landor even used the phrase "heard afar" and describes Acheron as flowing not steadily but with "lapses," like Kubla's "half-intermitted" river-fount. Landor's river hurls no rocks, but later on Mount Aetna hurls them in similar language and amid the names of many rivers. There is, besides, hair that floats; music of dulcimer; a waning moon beheld by an enchantress in league with the evil powers; a "high gilded dome"; a royal bath like a pleasure-house, with "crystal roof" in an "aerial sunny arch" inclosed in Arabian gold that suggests the images of "sunny dome" and "dome in air." And the image of a palace is used for the sun setting with its orb reflected "midway in the wave."

It is difficult to exhibit fairly and fully a series of parallels when they must be extracted from their setting. Almost a sixth sense is wanted to discriminate between accidental and essential resemblances, and there always lurks the danger of translating a generic likeness into an influence. The literature of England for some years before and after 1800 was honeycombed with caverns and bursting at the seams with fountains, springs, cataracts, rills, and "meanderings," not to mention also chasms and fragrant groves. Lowes made insufficient allowance for the ubiquity of these properties and sometimes paid them more heed than they deserved. It would be absurd to find *Kubla Khan*'s progenitors in every literary cavern or mazy river. And on the other hand, when the current literature was so full of these, one can scarcely suppose that Coleridge passed them all by unheeded, only to borrow the same image from a single sentence tucked away in an old travel book or in a Greek work remembered from his school or Cambridge days. Such epithets as *wild* and *mazy* turn up everywhere in the latter half of the eighteenth century; damsels and music are scarcely less frequent. Mrs. Radcliffe's romances and verses, which Coleridge certainly knew, were full of these things, and the lesser and greater writers echoed them. In the year of *Gebir* and the *Lyrical Ballads*, the *Monthly Magazine* announced a new novel entitled *The Subterranean Cavern*, in four volumes.[13]

Gebir employs most of these common romantic properties, and so does *Kubla Khan*. So too, quite often, do the sources discussed by Lowes, for a number of the less ancient travelers, geographers, and translators were readers of one another and of Milton and Spenser. On the other hand, though the chief poetic effects of *Kubla Khan* grow out of what Coleridge did with his imagery rather than out of the imagery itself, he also used some images that are at least slightly off the beaten track. The dome, for example, does not haunt most other romantic literature or the earlier poetic tradition as it haunts *Kubla Khan*, where it occurs five times and dominates the whole as if present in every line. Domes are not even so pronounced a feature as this in most travelers' accounts of the East. The subterranean river, the intermittent river-fountain, the demon-lover, and the heat-cold contrast in the "miracle" of the "sunny dome" and "caves of ice"—these are not quite the standard properties of romantic poetry that caverns, mazy streams, chasms, and fragrant groves are. Coleridge also employed a few mildly unusual epithets. In pointing out parallels, one cannot take the romantic commonplaces too seriously; they are significant only when from a special combination of elements or from a special association, phrase, atmosphere, or trick of style they seem to offer more than a generic resemblance. The warning is easily spoken but not easily minded, as I fear the reader may now and then silently remark hereafter.

The likenesses between *Gebir* and *Kubla Khan* are more striking as I have summarized them than they are likely to appear when they are not lifted from their context. In order not to warp the argument by overjudicious selection, it will be best to return the phrases and images to their places, exhibiting them as nearly as possible in their original surroundings, though at the expense of some repetition.

Gebir is the story of a young king reared at Gibraltar, "among those mountain-caverns, which retain His labours yet, vast halls, and flowing wells." He had been "incens'd by meditating on primeval wrongs," his father before death having bound him by a promise to make war upon Egypt for the purpose of reclaiming the land once ruled by his ancestors. So Gebir sailed for Egypt with ten thousand gigantic followers. Landing near the Nile, they advanced upon the city armed not with conventional weapons but each bearing a huge stone upon his "tow'ring" head (I, 12–28).

Charoba, the young queen of Egypt, is alarmed, but on the advice of her old nurse, who thinks to destroy the invader more conveniently by guile than by force, greets Gebir hospitably and persuades him to undertake, instead of war upon her city, the rebuilding of the ancient lost city on the coast. It was the city once founded by Sidad, Gebir's ancestor; it is also the city, palace, and garden of

Irem, with which Southey's *Thalaba* opens. Gebir's followers set to work busily. "Fragments" are "weigh'd up"
from the ancient streets; "again the sun shines into what
were porches"; the men seize "the flowers and figures
starting fresh to view"; they polish "the growing green of
many trackless years." "Far off, at intervals, the ax resounds"; "here, arches are discover'd . . . there . . . a marble . . . some high pillar." But after seven days of building,
the whole is destroyed mysteriously overnight; and each
night thereafter the day's work is overthrown (II, 1–36,
64–65).

Gebir's adventures are interwoven with a contrasting
story of love between his brother Tamar and a sea nymph,
an affair that ends happily later on, with nuptials, a magical flight-voyage to Italy, and a prophecy of the ultimate
triumph of their descendant Napoleon "from the Garonne
to the Rhine." When these secondary lovers first meet,
they wrestle, Tamar wagering upon his victory a sheep
against her seashells. Then follows the famous passage [*Parallel images*
that Landor later believed had inspired the more famous *and phrases from*
seashell lines in Wordsworth's *Excursion:*[15] Kubla Khan][14]

> I have sinuous shells [the nymph tells him], of pearly hue *Sinuous rills*
> Within, and they that lustre have imbibed *Sunny dome*
> In the sun's palace porch; where, when unyoked, *Shadow of the*
> His chariot wheel stands midway in the wave. *dome of pleasure*
> Shake one, and it awakens; then apply *floated midway*
> Its polished lips to your attentive ear, *on the waves*
> And it remembers its august abodes,
> And murmurs as the ocean murmurs there [I, 170–77].[16]

When Gebir finds his buildings leveled, he consults his
brother's nymph, who explains to him that Egypt is a land

> Of incantation; demons rule these waves;
> These are against thee; these thy works destroy [II, 206–7].

He must offer sacrifices before his partly built palace, she
says. Completing the prescribed ritual, he finds himself on
the edge of "a black abyss." And now he begins to hear

voices in "a mingled sound" that soon prove to be "ancestral" voices.

The word *ancestor* (or *ancestral*) is not one of those that haunt romantic literature; it seems, in fact, to be rather uncommon, except for the "ancestral hall" or "ancestral mansion" that appears now and again. In *Gebir*, however, both the word and the idea recur so frequently and sometimes in such unexpected situations as to become a noticeable mannerism. We meet it in unnatural as well as in natural phrases, and once it is used close to *prophetic* as in *Kubla Khan* (VI, 199–200). At first Gebir did not identify the voices:

And from this chasm Ancestral voices

> He thought he sometimes heard a distant voice
> Breathe through the cavern's mouth, and further on
> Faint murmurs now, now hollow groans reply.
>
> .   .   .   .
>
> He entered; and a mingled sound arose
> Like that— . . .
> Of birds that wintering watch in Memnon's tomb [II, 241–49].

Where was heard the mingled measure

The narrative is interrupted at the opening of Book III by a passage in epic style beginning with praise of Shakespeare and continuing with reflections on the inadequacy of any poet's power to re-create the past through imagination. Rivers are used here as symbols. The poet in youth "drank of Avon"; but he may never, while alive, cross that greatest of subterranean rivers, "the stream of jealous Acheron" or descend the "unsearchable abodes" of Night, to bring back into daylight dead heroes. Once night has fallen, once the present is past, can anyone, he asks, "bring back the far-off intercepted hills, Grasp the round rock-built turret, or arrest the glittering spires?" Can anyone by means of language "the parting Sun's gigantic strides recall?" After this Landorian substitute for an invocation to the Muses, the tale itself is resumed. But the poet of *Kubla Khan* dealt with the same question: he *could* re-create the past vision, the "dome in air" (Landor's

Alph the sacred river ran through caverns measureless to man

With walls and towers were girdled round Sunny dome

Could I revive within me . . . I would build that dome in air, that sunny dome

"round rock-built turret"?), if he could but regain his vision.

The scene of *Gebir* for the remainder of Book III is the cavern world of the dead, in the description of which Landor combines classical, Miltonic, Dantesque, and oriental imagery. Though Landor the poet cannot visit the subterranean world, in the person of his hero he can. The actual visit is confined to the abode of the wretched, but Gebir is told also of that other region of the dead, the beautiful garden and groves of the blest.

Upon entering the cavern, he heard his name called twice but thought it only "the strong vibration of the brain That struck upon his ear." The form of a man, however, approached, and

> as he came
> His unshorn hair, grown soft in these abodes,
> Waved back, and scatter'd thin and hoary light.
> Living, men called him Aröar: but no more
> In celebration, or recording verse,
> His name is heard, no more by Arnon's side
> The well-wall'd city, which he rear'd, remains [III, 19–28].

His floating hair

Aröar, spirit of an ancient warrior, undertakes to guide and inform Gebir. Here, he explains, lie Gebir's fathers, the race of Sidad, great men once, "but their pleasure was in war." So they had received punishment from the gods,

> by whose decree
> Depriv'd of life, and more, of death depriv'd,[17]
> I [Aröar] still hear shrieking, through the moonless night,
> Their discontented and deserted shades [III, 35–43].

As Gebir advanced with his guide through this cavern world, the subterranean river became audible in the distance:

> a roar confused
> Rose from a river, rolling in its bed,
> Not rapid— . . .
> Nor calmly— . . .
> But with dull weary lapses it still heaved
> Billows of bale, heard low, but heard afar [III, 74–79].

With ceaseless turmoil seething . . . amid whose swift half-intermitted burst . . .

And mid this tumult Kubla heard from far ancestral voices

The billows are of the river, but the bale is the bale of the ancestors. The sound is "heard afar" even by living men above ground, when hell opens to let Night loose in the world and men lie in bed hearing their own hearts beat. Thus Landor heightens the significance of the sound of river and voices. In this dim world below there is no life— no nightingale and no lark, nor flower nor herb nor grasshopper. Only "twilight broods here . . . glowing with one sullen sunless heat" (III, 80–89).

Where Alph the sacred river ran through caverns measureless to man down to a sunless sea Sank in tumult to a lifeless ocean

Before Gebir encounters his ancestral spirits, however, Aröar makes some observations upon cosmology and further describes the regions of the dead. He speaks of the sun's fire—"glowing oceans of the sun"; of ice—"crystal cliffs of hail"; of ocean—the "cold and blue abyss." Turning to the world of death, he describes the "happy fields" that lie beyond the other subterranean river, fiery Phlegethon, which separates the wretched from the blest. In that Paradise garden gentle breezes

Like rebounding hail

Paradise Fertile ground Gardens where blossomed many an incense bearing tree Enfolding sunny spots of greenery

> scatter freshness thro' the groves
> And meadows of the fortunate, and fill
> With liquid light the marble bowl of Earth.

There flourish "thick myrtle bowers" and "odors rising half dissolved," olive groves, "tufted banks," and "enough of sunshine to enjoy the shade" (III, 97–129, 269–311).

Gebir, however, in search of advice, not cosmology, has asked "what region held his ancestors," and at length their forms are revealed in situations that arouse horror and pity. They do not recognize him.

> "O my sires,
> Ye know me not!—They answer not, nor hear.
> . . . .
> . . . what wretch
> Is that with eyebrows white, and slanting brow?
> . . . .
> He too amongst my ancestors? . . .
> . . . .
> He was a warrior, then, nor fear'd the Gods?"
> "Gebir, he fear'd the Demons, not the Gods" [Aröar
> replies] [III, 180–94].

At length Gebir finds himself embraced by the ghost of his father, who now utters bitter repentance of the vow he had once exacted from Gebir, the vow to make war upon Egypt. He vanishes, but Aröar enforces the moral: the father's words must turn the son's feet from the evil intention of war—have indeed already done so in part, since Gebir has had the courage to penetrate these depths. But now again the cavern's mouth is near. Beyond it are his own people, and Gebir returns to the mortal world much as Milton's Adam departed from Paradise:

Ancestral voices prophesying war

> he arose,
> And bent towards them his bewilder'd way.

The nurse still secretly plots destruction, though by now Gebir and Charoba are unadmittedly in love. The Egyptians have now become afraid of the invader king, who is known to have visited the cavern world of the dead; even Charoba confesses that the thought "thrills" her with "affright," though she thinks he must be "belov'd of heaven" or he could not have reascended into daylight. There are "prophecies," "tumult," alarm as winter closes and spring comes, "urged slanting onward" by the breezes (IV, 52–58). Men murmur against the strangers who are building a fairer city than their own. "O profanation! O our ancestors!" they cry (IV, 88–95). But the Nile has risen, and a festival is ordered. There is an expedition upon the great river, with sacrifices, tame crocodiles, sweet airs of music, gilded barges with oars of palm that rise "glittering and aslant" or seem "to tremble wearied o'er the wave." A throng "shone out in sunny whiteness" with "the bright-eyed waters dancing round." In a procession upon "stately" camels, attended by Ethiop slaves, ambassadors of false peace bear gifts to Gebir. At sunset they approach Gebir's pavilion raised on the plain. His men, resting from their labor of building, are surveying the spacious site where walls are still being erected. Some sing of brooks in "smiling meads"; some, remembering home,

The sacred river

Sunny dome would prefer bare rafters to the "high gilded dome" (IV, 156–206).

Book V is the book of demon-enchantresses. The nurse Dalica journeys to her old home, the deserted city of Masar, once "throng'd by palaces," but now a wilderness *A savage place as* of plain and mountain, haunted by the hyena, where only *holy and enchant-* a few descendants of an ancient race remain to practice *ed as e'er beneath* their magic, with such incantations as had once made the *a waning moon* moon itself shudder. Dalica's sister is one of these en- *was haunted by* chanters. Arriving by night and challenged by her sister *woman . . .* in the dark, Dalica raises her sickle to inclose within its curve the "fading moon" and speaks the secret "hallow'd words." Her sister at first thinks her a fiend:

> "Woman of outer darkness, fiend of death,
> From what inhuman cave, what dire abyss,
> Hast thou invisible that spell o'erheard?" [V, 1–54, 61].

The sisters are united. She of the wilderness knows the deepest secrets of evil enchantment. Her eyes "watch the waning moon, . . . where the founts Of wisdom rise, where sound the wings of Power" (V, 81–84). Her aid is wanted, for Gebir must be killed by treachery. The enchantress weaves a fine garment, dipped in the poison of the cerastes *Weave a circle* and other magic poisons. "Thrice she dipt" it, "thrice *round him thrice* waved it thro' the air," and it is ready for its deadly use.

The other pair of lovers, however, Gebir's brother Tamar and the sea nymph, are united, and the "sacred gate" of dawn opens over the waves for their wedding day. The ceremony is attended with "sweet-flowing music," the ocean peopled with nymphs. When night has come and "the moon appear'd To hang midway betwixt the earth and skies," the nymph leans over her lover asleep "in Ocean's grot where Ocean was unheard." Awaking, the mortal youth for a moment thinks he has awakened "from dreams of pleasure to eternal sleep." The nymph has a sad prophecy to utter about Gebir but first urges Tamar not to succumb to grief, which can create nothing but more of

〔 128 〕

itself. The habit of grief, she says, is mild at first and "casts no shadow as he comes along":

> "But, after his embrace, the marble chills
> The pausing foot, the closing door sounds loud,"

and none but the fiend in the end triumphs from the encouragement of grief (VI, 34–86). Her prophecy is of Gebir's death. But as that fate cannot be averted, she takes Tamar off upon a watery tour of rivers, to "sport at leisure" where Rhine rolls—"What River from the mountains ever came More stately!" At her touch his grief gives way to "pleasure." Then, to his delight, the "sacred" isle of Venus is before them, whence they hear the "symphony of lutes" murmuring of love. Far off appear the "thousand towers of Crete." The youth hears "the voice of rivers" as they journey—Peneus (which, like its neighbor in Greece, the Alpheus, disappears beneath the earth), Amphrÿsos, Spercheios, Enipeus,

Alph the sacred river

A stately pleasure-dome

Her symphony and song

> where the winds
> Scatter'd above the weeds his hoary hair.

His floating hair

They see Ithaca, "like a blue bubble, floating in the bay." Then, following the long list of rivers, the greatest sight of all looms, Aetna, hurling rocks skyward:

> Behold the vast Eridanus . . .
>
> . . . .
>
> Of noble rivers none with mightier force
> Rolls his unwearied torrent to the main.
> And now Sicanian Etna rose to view.
>
> . . . .
>
> He heard it roll above him, heard it roll
> Beneath, and felt it too, as he beheld,
> Hurl, from Earth's base, rocks, mountains, to the skies
> [VI, 122–80].[18]

And from this chasm with ceaseless turmoil seething as if this earth in fast thick pants were breathing a mighty fountain momently was forced amid whose swift half-intermitted burst huge fragments vaulted And mid these dancing rocks . . . it flung up momently the sacred river

In a later edition Landor defended his image of Aetna on the ground that "Virgil has said the like of a river," though his images of volcano and river coalesce without the assistance of Virgil. Coleridge also later united the same images, possibly with *Kubla Khan* in his memory—for he repeated the words "mighty fountain" in a letter describing a mountain storm, "as if it was some mighty fountain just on the summit of Kirkstone, that shot forth its volcano of air, and precipitated huge streams of invisible lava down the road to Patterdale."[19]

Tamar, learning of his future descendant Napoleon from the nymph's "prophetic" lips, suddenly thinks of "his ancestors and home" as they pass Gibraltar. But he must not weep for his home with its "caves abhorr'd, dungeons and portals that exclude the day," for those "mansions" had bred the plan for war. So they pass on to another beautiful river with elms that cast a "mingled shade" over the water, craggy rocks, lofty precipice, valley, grove, flowers, and "festoons of pensile vines" in "arches." Its stream "recoils struggling" and hurries to the "vast abyss" (VI, 186–282).

The seventh book closes the poem with a return to the affairs of Gebir and Charoba. The atmosphere is one of festivities haunted invisibly by danger, treachery, war. In spite of difficulties—evil eyes penetrating "thro' palaces and porches," "suspicions, murmurs, treacheries," and the horn that summons first to the chase but "second to the war"—a marriage has been arranged. "Link'd together by the seven-arm'd Nile," Egypt and Iberia are to be united.

A sunny pleasure dome
That dome in air
A damsel with a dulcimer
Mid this tumult Kubla heard from far . . . war

Landor describes the preparations for the wedding. The queen's bath resembles a pleasure-house, with doors of cedar and marble walls; "Arabian gold inclosed the crystal roof" in an "aërial sunny arch." As Charoba bathes, "o'er the palace breathes the dulcimer." Amid the festivities are heard curses and quarrels, "threats and defiance and suburban war," but these are only for the sake of securing a better view of the procession to come. The stream

Meandering with a mazy motion

Meander himself is introduced. Flowery turf is rolled to form a seat (Wordsworth and Coleridge were apparently not the only poets interested in building a "seat of sod").

Egypt, however, is doomed to be bathed in blood. As Gebir in state awaits his bride, the nurse approaches ceremoniously and throws the poisoned cloak over the king. The effect is immediate; Gebir totters to the shore of the Nile; the waters murmur drearily in his ear and rise "wild, in strange colours, to his parching eyes." As he falls dying upon the shore, Charoba, ignorant of the nurse's treachery, nevertheless knows the "demons" have "dyed that robe with death." She appeals to the dead, her parents, for aid. Gebir revives sufficiently to make his farewell epic speech about death, grandeur, and glory, and then dies.

Set thus in the midst of their original surroundings, the parallels between *Gebir* and *Kubla Khan* are not nearly so striking as when they are viewed separately. One could not, on grounds of resemblance alone, say that the author of *Kubla Khan* must unquestionably have read *Gebir*. Nevertheless, reading Landor's poem as a whole, I find besides the specific parallels a certain kind of richness that suggests *Kubla Khan* as it does not suggest any other poem of Coleridge's and that goes a little beyond, I think, the Miltonic texture traceable in both. The movement of *Kubla Khan* is liquid, that of *Gebir* only partly so—more nearly, if the image can be excused, a half-flowing, half-marble movement. Yet *Kubla Khan* seems rather like a light distillation from the longer work, with story and persons sunk out of sight and only atmosphere and the distilled spirit of scenery retained. A fair number of the images that Lowes traced to many scattered sources are found together here in Landor's single work. And some verbal echoes that on the surface appear trivial or accidental may actually be more significant than they seem.

Midway in the wave, for example, is not a conspicuous phrase. But it occurs in the most famous descriptive passage in *Gebir*. Standing at the end of an iambic line, its metrical effect is a little out of the ordinary and is identical with the effect in *Kubla Khan* of *floated midway on the waves* (*wave* in the manuscript version). In *Kubla Khan* the visual image as well as the phrase is like Landor's; for Landor was describing the sun as a palace with its circular reflection (palace suddenly transformed into chariot wheel) "midway in the wave." In *Kubla Khan*, it is the half-circular shadow of the sunny dome that is reflected. The use of the word *midway* in Coleridge's passage I suspect may derive more from the sound haunting the poet's ear than from the sense; his palace would in natural course be reflected "on the waves" but not so particularly "midway" on them. It will be necessary to return to this phrase later on, for it has other connections with the dating of Coleridge's poem. In *Gebir* the image is preceded only two lines earlier by the "sinuous shells," associated with images of brightness. *Sinuous* is a striking and felicitous epithet there; and though it is not one of the common romantic epithets for *rills*, Coleridge uses it for his garden, "bright with sinuous rills." In the sound of the phrases and in the weight of their cadence within the lines of verse there is a certain likeness: "And there were gardens bright with sinuous rills" and "But I have sinuous shells, of pearly hue" (followed by *lustre*). In *Gebir* these phrases and images all lie within four of the eight lines that, rightly or wrongly, were suspected to have inspired Wordsworth's shell passage.

Another echo in which both sound and sense play a part is distinctly of the sort apt to travel from one poet's inner ear to another's. After bursting as an intermittent fountain, Coleridge's sacred Alph flowed through subterranean caverns to a "lifeless ocean" which is also a "sunless sea." Through Landor's caverns the Acheron—also, of course, a sacred river, though the word itself is not used here— heaves, intermittently also, in a region where life has been removed by descriptive detail. This passage ends with the phrase "one sullen sunless heat." The epithet *sunless*, not itself entirely inconspicuous, is rendered more prominent through the assonances of the two preceding words, which double or treble every sound in the key word, *s, u, n, l*—*one sullen sunless*—and all these in turn make more prominent the following contrasted vowel sound in *heat*, the same contrast as in Coleridge's *sea*. Landor's phrase is overwrought and is composed with less grace than Coleridge's *sunless sea* but for that very reason would strike a sensitive ear the more forcibly. This parallel is a tenuous and subjective thread with which to weave an argument of influences; but, as with the other verbal echoes between *Gebir* and *Kubla Khan*, the phrases appear not in isolation but combined with similar patterns of thematic material.

These are some of the bits and pieces of links that appeared when I attempted to see what lay behind my first uncritical and subjective impression that *Gebir* was floating somewhere in the mind that composed *Kubla Khan*. Obviously, tenuous connections such as these are a quicksand only too likely to sink the critic. Yet the line between good and inferior poetry is often even finer and more subtle. The poet's ear is attuned to distinctions scarcely louder than the shriek of the bat, and we are as likely to miss our way by avoiding as by seeking the oversubtle. In any case, as there must be a limit to even a tolerant reader's patience with these fine-spun links, I shall pass on to *Thalaba*.

3. "THALABA"

If Coleridge knew either *Thalaba* or *Gebir* before he composed *Kubla Khan*, he must have known them both. Southey was at the height of his admiration for Landor's poem when he composed his own oriental tale, and Coleridge was making the acquaintance of both works at the same time. In writing of *Gebir*, I have been betrayed by Landor's charms into a superfluity of narrative. *Thalaba*, though a much longer poem, does not so tempt the reader.

As the parallels are sprinkled much more thickly, however, quite as much must be said. Mistaking incoherence of structure and multiplicity of matter for richness, Southey wrote a poem that is almost beyond the range of intelligible summary. Fortunately this does not matter.

At first Southey called his poem "The Destruction of the Dom Danyel" (pronounced Dōm, as he showed by occasionally marking it so). He described its theme in a letter to William Taylor of Norwich in September, 1798: "I have also another plan for an Arabian poem of the wildest nature; the title—'The Destruction of the Dōm Danyel,' which, if you have read the continuation of the Arabian Nights Entertainments, you will recollect to be a seminary for evil magicians under the roots of the sea. It will have all the pomp of Mohammedan fable, relieved by scenes of Arabian life, and these contrasted again by the voluptuousness of Persian scenery and manners." To another friend he expressed the hope that in his "Dom-Daniel" he might "wield the wand of enchantment at least as ably as Wieland," and even, a few months later, hoped to emulate the *Orlando Furioso*.[20]

The "continuation," an altogether different work from the real *Arabian Nights*, was *Arabian Tales: or, a Continuation of the Arabian Nights Entertainments. . . .*[21] Coleridge very likely saw it, if he did not already know it, when he and Southey were writing "at the same table" in the late summer of 1799. Its fourth volume recounts the life and death of Maugraby the magician, chief servant to Zatani (Satan). There are stories here within a complex story framework, all the action being played out against a background of Hell and Paradise imagery. The Paradise, however, is a false one used by Maugraby much as Aloadin used his false Paradise of pleasures. What concerns us in this medley of tales is the imagery and a few situations, which I shall attempt to extract without disturbing the peaceful decay of the remainder.

Maugraby takes a young prince of Syria through a mountain cavern that opens upon a wide fertile plain watered by rivulets. Suddenly a palace appears in the midst of this plain. There is a pavilion with beautiful fountains at the corners and a central fountain whose sunlit water glides over bright stone and sinks into openings below. The garden is filled with birds, flowers, "odoriferous shrubs," a thick wood, cedars. Its fertility is emphasized by its being unnatural, for palace and plain are surrounded by the summits of Mount Atlas and would by nature be barren except for Maugraby's magic powers. Another "terrible fountain," at which Maugraby tortures his victims, appears from time to time.[22] Dedication to the service of Zatani takes place in the temple that "lies under the sea, near Tunis" and is reached by descending through nine gates of the Dom-Daniel, "the chief roots of which lie concealed under the waters of the ocean." The prince, however, has a mysterious dream sent by Mohammed, which enables him to rescue victims of the magician and to destroy the golden image within the Dom, though not the Dom itself.

Cavern
Twice five miles
of fertile ground
. . . were girdled
round
Gardens bright
with sinuous rills

Incense-bearing
trees
A cedarn cover

Through caverns
measureless to
man down to a
sunless sea

There is a mingling of geographical elements: reference is made to the great wall dividing China from Tartary; mortals are transported by evil magic to suffer naked at one moment upon the icy pinnacles of Caucasus and in the next upon the burning sands of Arabia. Beautiful young women play and sing. Everybody traces magic circles for every sort of purpose: this seems to be one of the more rudimentary tricks and one of the first that Maugraby teaches his pupils.

Weave a circle
round him thrice

The chief subsidiary story, which becomes in actual substance the central one, is literally a demon-lover tale. Through Maugraby's magic, an Egyptian princess falls in love with a youth whom she has seen only in a dream. Spurning a worthy human lover, she cares only for the "phantastic" lover of her enchanted dreams, the demon—

A vision in a
dream

A woman wailing
for her demon-
lover

though she does not know this—Maugraby himself, who lures her to his home, "the caverns under the sea, adjacent to the Dom-Daniel of Tunis." Here she is made to suffer in unspeakable ways into which we need not enter, though the author does. She sees the spirit Asmodius, the demon-lover of the Book of Tobit (to which Coleridge's demon-lover lines have sometimes been traced) with an "assembly of magicians, such as they usually hold at the wane of the moon." In the end, the princess helps her rescuers to break the enchantments and destroy Maugraby. To escape from the enchanted land it is necessary again to penetrate a subterranean cavern that opens into a beautiful but dangerous garden region filled with tempting, deadly fruits and waters. The princes reach at last the place of "magical beauties," "where stands the lofty dome," beneath which rests the fatal urn that they seek. They strike it with the magic ring and the whole is destroyed, including Maugraby and his "vast caverns." But the Dom-Daniel remains, awaiting a future destroyer.[23]

Through caverns . . . to a sunless sea

As holy and enchanted as e'er beneath a waning moon was haunted by woman wailing for her demon-lover

Southey undertook to carry on from there. He seems to have had demon-lovers on his mind during the autumn of 1799, for in an unpublished letter of December he wrote of the story in Pausanius of "Euthymus fighting a Demon and delivering a damsel" as a fit subject for "a wild poem."[24]

Like the tale of Maugraby, *Thalaba* is full of domes and the word *dome* (or *Dom*); it has subterranean and sub-oceanic caverns, Paradise gardens, and of course damsels, mostly Arabian. In the copious illustrative notes following each book, Southey quotes at length from his numerous sources. These include most of the works Lowes described as the primary sources of *Kubla Khan*—Burnet, Purchas, Bruce, and the rest—but at times *Kubla Khan* is much closer to *Thalaba* than to those earlier works. Southey's material appears here and there also to have some connection with entries in Coleridge's notebook, the famous

Gutch Memorandum Book, which in its turn has been associated with *Kubla Khan*. The links are complicated.

Thalaba contains two elaborately described and spectacular Paradise gardens, both false ones. The first, which opens the poem, is another version of the city and garden of Irem that Landor had introduced as the ruined "ancestral" city which Gebir undertook to rebuild. As Southey's poem opens, the boy Thalaba wanders with his mother alone in the desert, where (before the first dozen stanzas are finished) the sky rests "like a dome upon the circling waste." Suddenly before them

> high in air a stately palace rose.
> Amid a grove embower'd
> Stood the prodigious pile;
> Trees of such ancient majesty
> Tower'd not on Yemen's happy hills,
> Nor crown'd the lofty brow of Lebanon.[25]

A stately pleasure-dome
That dome in air

Forests ancient as the hills

These "ancient" forest trees were more than common romantic scenery, for they represented a remarkable horticultural feat. Shedad, who had ordered the building of Irem, "bade the full-grown forest rise, his own creation"; he would not "wait for slow Nature's work." So "hither, uprooted with their native soil," by "the labour and the pain of multitudes" the mature trees were brought to spread "wide their shadowy arms" (Southey probably read of this accomplishment in the Russian *Memoirs* of Peter Henry Bruce).[26] There were "golden towers" and walls of silver, "bowers," "aromatic paths," and all the other appurtenances suitable for a Paradise garden. In the verse itself the palace is not called a dome, but the illustrative notes emphasize that image. Even the unremarkable use of *dome* for the sky Southey accentuated by quoting from Le Suire's *Le nouveau monde:* "La mer n'est plus qu'un cercle aux yeux des Matelots, Où le Ciel forme *un dôme* appuyé sur les *flots*" (I transcribe Southey's version). Both the sound and meaning of *flots*, here combined with *dôme*, suggest Coleridge's words; and for the palace and its

Sunny dome
Walls and towers
Incense-bearing trees

Dome . . . floated midway on the waves

golden towers he cited accounts in Tavernier and Hakluyt of "domes" and palaces gilded or covered with gold leaf. In another long note Southey transcribed an account of the legend of "this garden or paradise" of Irem from George Sale's translation of the Koran. Shedad, according to Sale's version, had built the city and palace, "adorned with delicious gardens," hoping to inspire veneration of himself as a god. The city is "still standing in the deserts of Aden," but is invisible except very rarely when God permits it to be seen by some chosen mortal.[27] Sale's Irem is thus quite as visionary a paradise as that of Kubla with its "dome in air" that Coleridge would have re-created in music, had he not lost his vision.

Southey tells the tale of Irem at considerable length in his verse, through the mouth of the one living man whom Thalaba finds there. The survivor tells how the palace had *Caverns* been built, how "the central caverns gave their gems" for *Cedarn cover* its adornment and the woodman's ax "open'd the cedar forest to the sun." Its garden contained "copious springs," fragrant flowers, and the marvelous "full-grown forest" of "ancient" trees already noticed. Shedad, Thalaba hears, had aimed to create such a garden as once "was lost in *Paradise* Paradise" with trees like those "in Eden's groves." The palm "tower'd," "tall as the cedar of the mountain." By way of comparison the Egyptian pyramids are drawn in— those "aweful piles," their spacious vaults "fill'd with *A miracle of rare* miracles and wealth miraculous" (I, 29). But the pyramids *device* themselves are as nothing to Shedad's miraculous palace, which has a sapphire floor and a dome "in air" that is not only sunny but that glows like sunrise even at night:

That dome in air   Here self-suspended hangs in air,
              As its pure substance loathed material touch,
                   The living carbuncle;
That sunny dome   Sun of the lofty dome,
              Darkness hath no dominion o'er its beams;
                Intense it glows, an ever-flowing tide
              Of glory, like the day-flood in its source [I, 30].[28]

[138]

When the "stately pile" with its "high tower top" was
complete, multitudes came to behold the "palace sparkling
like the Angel domes of Paradise" and its "Garden like the
bowers of early Eden." In this passage Southey introduced
comparisons to the sea, voices "like the ocean roar," and
"one deep confusion of tumultuous sounds" (I, 33–34).

A stately pleasure dome

Gardens
Paradise

Tumult . . .
ocean . . . mid
this tumult . . .
voices

But even before the building was completed, there had
been warnings—not, as in *Gebir*, from ancestral voices, but
prophecies nevertheless of "woe" in the midst of the
Paradise: "Often the Prophet's voice Denounced impending woe" (I, 24). And after the work was finished the
prophet's

Voices prophesying war

All who heard should cry Beware

> large eye roll'd in horror, and so deep
> His tone, it seem'd some Spirit from within
> Breathed through his moveless lips the unearthly voice.

his flashing eyes . . .

For the Sarsar, the "Icey Wind of Death," destroyed all.
Ever since, the one survivor had lived alone beside "the
fountain's everlasting flow" (I, 41–48). Outliving his companions and even himself, surviving to tell his tale to
Thalaba, he perhaps owes something to the Ancient
Mariner. He is at last summoned by the Death Angel, and
now suddenly "the Palace and the groves were seen no
more," by Thalaba or the reader; the Paradise in a vision
vanished into nothing as it had come. Only wilderness
remained.

A vision
Paradise

Southey's second Paradise appears in the sixth and
seventh books and is avowedly patterned upon that false
one of Aloadin to which Lowes traced some of Coleridge's
garden imagery and his lines about the damsel and what
he called the "Tartar youth."[29] In the illustrative notes,
Southey again quotes from his sources at length—from
Burnet's *Telluris theoria sacra;* from Purchas, both the
Pilgrimes and the *Pilgrimage;* from Odoric's travels in
Hakluyt; and from "that undaunted liar, Sir John Maundeville."[30] This last account interested him especially. He
had apparently not at first copied it out fully, for in a letter

of October, 1799, he asked his friend Bedford to transcribe it for him. It is an account, he said, of "a sort of Apollo-Gardens or Oriental Dog and Duck" to which Aloadin conveyed young men "after an opium dose." Referring again later to Mandeville's account, he says he should like to trace its historical origins; Purchas relates it from Marco Polo, he notes.[31] The "opium" was Southey's addition to Mandeville, but it returns us once more to Coleridge's preface of 1816, for in the notes to *Thalaba* Odoric is quoted with reference to this same Aloadin, "Senex de Monte," who would give a man "a certeine potion, being of force to cast him into such a slumber as should make him quite void of all sense, and so being in a profounde sleepe, to convey him out of his paradise" and thus by promise of a return would win the youth's allegiance. According to Purchas as cited in *Thalaba*, Aloadin administered "a sleepy drink" that cast the youths "into a trance" before as well as after their admission to the Paradise. There is much milk and honey, too, in Southey's notes. The passage from Mandeville, for one, quotes: "*Dabo vobis terram fluentem lacte et melle.*"

On the conventional assumptions about *Kubla Khan*, as to both its dream origin and its date, these parallels with *Thalaba* imply a good many coincidences which, added to the others marked in this and the next chapter, stretch probability to a thin thread. But we have not finished with *Thalaba*'s paradises. In his verse the details about Aloadin from Purchas, Mandeville, and Odoric are given with much additional embroidery. The surroundings outside the garden are described first. There are two "rills," one "boiling," the other with "wave intensely cold." The Arabian youth hears these blending with other tones, in "deep low murmurings,

> Which from the fountain caves
> In mingled melody"

came to him "like faery music" (VI, 9). It is "a scene of wonders." Here, as in *Kubla Khan*, the geography is

[Preface]: An an-odyne

The Author con-tinued . . . in a profound sleep

For he on honey-dew hath fed and drunk the milk of Paradise

Where was heard the mingled meas-ure from the foun-tain and the caves

marked by a main river with subsidiary rills: "a thousand streamlets" stray "in mazy windings o'er the vale," their "labyrinthine channels islanding A thousand rocks," just as the "ethereal ocean" of the sky "circles" the clouds. These rocks of variegated colors sparkle in the sun; among them "gush'd the fountains up," and beyond them rolls the broad river that "received and bore away the confluent rills." The scene is as strange and beautiful as that where "the hundred sources of Hoangho burst" (VI, 10–12).

Sinuous rills

A mazy motion

A mighty foun-tain . . . 'mid these dancing rocks

The sacred river

What Lowes regarded as one of the most indubitably dreamlike characteristics of Coleridge's poem, the min-gling of imagery from the Middle East, Africa, and Tartary, is exhibited in Southey's paradises in broad-awake, if soporific, lines. The Hoangho was the Yellow River of China (farther south than the region of Cublai's palace), "sacred" like all the great Eastern rivers. Southey's phras-ing must also have suggested to a reader at the turn of the century the Nile with its much-talked-of but still mysteri-ous sources. In the notes Southey marks a closer associa-tive link than Lowes found between Aloadin's Paradise in the Middle East (the location varies, as Southey noted, with the teller of the tale; it may be Arabia or Persia, or elsewhere) and Cublai; he quotes Odoric's statement that it was the Tartar conquerors—the very race, therefore, of Genghis and Cublai—who at last overthrew Aloadin's Paradise. There needed no ghost of Coleridge's dream to combine these things.

Thalaba's entrance to the false Paradise was through a narrow ascending valley, a "silent, solitary glen" evidently patterned in part after a scene much nearer at hand than the Nile or the Hoangho—the Valley of Stones near Lyn-mouth in Devonshire, which Southey had visited in August, 1799, just before he joined Coleridge at Stowey. The scene had made such a strong impression that he described it at length in several letters, remarking upon the "serpentining perpendicularity," the "huge stones and

That deep roman-tic chasm

Huge fragments vaulted

fragments of stones," the two rivers each flowing down a combe, "rolling down over huge stones like a long water-fall" and joining together as they enter the sea, so that "the rivers and the sea make but one sound of uproar." There were also, as we know from Hazlitt, ocean caverns there. The whole, Southey thought, resembled "a palace of the Preadamite kings." He thought it should have been the scene of another of the ancient demon-lover legends, this time multiplied into the fifty daughters of Diocletian who cohabited with devils—a tale of which Coleridge also had made a note in the Gutch Memorandum Book.[32]

Mingled measure from the foun- tain and the caves

When Thalaba finally entered the Paradise, he thought he must be dreaming an "unsubstantial dream." He "closed his eyes, and open'd them again," but the scene was still there; it was no dream. So we have another surfeit of ter-raced palaces, "pavilions" bright with "sunny" gold, "mingled joy," winding streams, "sounds of harmony" from "far music" and distant song, a "wilderness" of roses and perfumed orange groves and waterfalls. All the "rills" of the garden run together into a single wide stream spanned by the arches of a "straight and stately bridge" that is in some respects very similar to Kubla's pleasure-dome with its shadow reflected "midway" on the water, for the bridge is a pleasure-house too, with an upper and a lower story. Like Kubla's pleasure-dome it is shadowed in the water:

A vision in a dream
Close your eyes with holy dread for he . . . hath . . . drunk . . . of Paradise
Rills
River
Stately pleasure- dome

> Strong in the evening and distinct its shade
> Lay on the watery mirror, and his eye
> Saw it united with its parent pile,
> One huge fantastic fabric. Drawing near,
> Loud from the chambers of the bridge below,
> Sounds of carousal came and song,
> And unveil'd women bade the advancing youth
> Come merry-make with them! [VI, 28].

The shadow of the dome of pleasure floated midway on the wave

Damsel . . . sing- ing of Mount Abora [earthly Paradise]

Southey's notes embroidering this stanza quote travelers' accounts of Eastern bridges that served the double purpose of pleasure-house and span. In one such building the central arch was hollowed and fitted with chambers and had large covered balconies above, where people in summer took the air "with great delight." In another, large enough "to find entertainment for a whole caravanne," each arch contained a room and stairs to descend. If Coleridge's "midway on the wave" was not a meaningless phrase, the idea of *midway* may have derived from these bridges that would actually have been reflected in *mid*stream.

After wandering about, Thalaba entered a "banquet room" with a fountain, and instantly "through all his frame Delightful coolness spread." The very light itself came "cool'd." The guests drank cool wine and ate fruits that had been dried in summer's heat, apricots "cased in ice," the "sunny" orange on a "plate of snow" (VI, 20–25). Southey does not describe his banquet-room as "caves of ice" like Kubla's, but he labors to convey the contrast of the cool, dim-lighted inclosure and iced foods with the tropical climate outside. A note reinforces the contrast and connects the scene with the pleasure-bridges: "When Tavernier made his first visit to the Kan at Erivan, he found him with several of his officers regaling in the *Chambers of the Bridge* [Southey's italics]. They had wine which they cooled with ice, and all kinds of fruit and melons in large plates, under each of which was a plate of ice." This "stately" bridge-arch-pleasure building, reflected in the river, with cool, dim lower chambers and iced foods—associated as it is with all the other appurtenances of a Paradise garden, damsels, music, and an Arabian maid—appears, certainly on the surface, much more nearly related to Coleridge's pleasure-dome with "caves of ice" than the brief phrase in Maurice noted by E. H. Coleridge and Lowes. There is also, however, an actual palace of ice still to come.

In the midst of these scenes, whenever the ladies of pleasure attempted to lure Thalaba, he called to mind the image of "his own Arabian Maid,"[33] from whom he had

A miracle of rare device a sunny pleasure-dome with caves of ice

A damsel . . . in a vision once I saw
It was an Abyssinian maid

long been parted. Once, as he closed his eyes and "call'd the voluntary vision up," he opened them to see the Arabian maid herself, in fact this time and not in vision, fleeing from a pursuer. This Arabian "damsel" Thalaba had met early in his travels. She had lived a simple life "beneath no lamp-illumined dome." Thalaba had played upon his reed for her and composed poetry of love and woe, but visions and dreams had drawn him away to fulfill his mission (III, 22–24).

Southey's Paradise has one further feature somewhat suggestive of Kubla's "deep romantic chasm," "measureless" caverns, and "lifeless" ocean. When Thalaba and his Arabian maid tried to escape from the evil Paradise by following the river, they heard its "deepening sound louder and louder in the distance,"

But O that deep romantic chasm . . . with ceaseless turmoil seething as if this earth . . . were breathing a mighty fountain momently was forced

Caverns measureless to man Sank in tumult to a lifeless ocean

Voices prophesying war

> As if it forced its stream
> Struggling through crags along a narrow pass.
> And lo! where raving o'er a hollow course
>   The ever-flowing flood
> Foams in a thousand whirlpools! There adown
>   The perforated rock
> Plunge the whole waters; so precipitous,
>   So fathomless a fall,
> That their earth-shaking roar came deaden'd up
>   Like subterranean thunders [VII, 6].

And for a final parallel with Kubla's Paradise, Southey's too is under threat of war. But Thalaba, not war, destroys Aloadin and his magic Paradise and departs with the Arabian maid. Like Landor, Southey was unable to resist the closing lines of *Paradise Lost:*

> Awe-struck and silent down the stony glen
> They wound their thoughtful way [VII, 23].

In contrast to the two false paradises of the poem stands the book of the "Dom-Daniel caverns, under the Roots of the Ocean." These words, which had evidently mesmerized their author, recur like a refrain. Perhaps Southey looked upon the phrase as the equivalent of a Homeric epithet. It derives from Burnet, who was apparently equally pleased with it. At any rate, the sonorous "Dom-Daniel" with its cosmic adjuncts dominates *Thalaba* somewhat as Coleridge's dome with its reduplicated epithets dominates *Kubla Khan*. Though, strictly speaking, only two books are devoted to this satanic region, Southey evidently intended that the Dom-Daniel should haunt the whole portentously; destruction of it is the mission assigned to Thalaba. The first of the cavern scenes occupies Book II, following immediately upon the Paradise of Irem. The scene, laid for an assembly of the master-magicians, is sprinkled by the poet with ghoulish debris scarcely more awe inspiring than Tam O'Shanter's supernatural properties, though there is no hint of amusement behind Southey's pen. The first exhibit is an infant's head upon a platter, the dead eyes gleaming with "demon light." There is an important magic ring whose crystal has been formed by subterranean fiery fountain and frozen dew of Caucasus. Within an inner den burns the Eternal Fire, which "stream'd up" from a "chasm," like "waters gushing from some channell'd rock"; no eye beholds the source of this *Caverns measure-* fountain that springs from the primeval "Abyss" (II, *less to man* 25–26).

We have seen no intermittent fountains thus far. Toward the end of the poem, however, Thalaba, in search of the Dom-Daniel, journeys to a wellhead, an extraordinary spring, clear and dangerously deep, whose

> loosen'd bed below,
> Heaved strangely up and down,
> And to and fro, from side to side,
> It heaved, and waved, and toss'd
> And yet the depths were clear [XI, 30].

This well, unlike Kubla's, was unruffled on the surface though tumultuous beneath. In a note Southey explained that his description was taken from an actual spring known as the "Boiling-Well" near Bristol. Coleridge would have known the place, which reminds us of his own note, printed in *Anima poetae* on a spring "with the little tiny cone of loose sand ever rising and sinking at the bottom," though he was evidently writing of a different spring.[34]

Upon that "Boiling-Well" in *Thalaba* a boat awaited the youth, with a "Damsel," supernatural or visionary, at its helm. This is the beginning of a journey by water that leads ever downward, ever faster, from well to rill to river to ocean to cavern to abyss and the Dom-Daniel. Without using Coleridge's phrase "through caverns measureless to man," Southey labors to produce and exaggerate just that effect. At first the boat "falls" down the "winding" stream through "green and fertile meadows." Increased by many "rills," the stream broadens into a great river down which the boat still "falls," the sinking and swelling roar of waters increasing until at nightfall the "great ocean" opens before the boat. Under a cliff that once more recalls the cliffs and caves of Devonshire near the Valley of Rocks, the Damsel finds the "cavern arch." As the boat enters the ocean cavern, the dim light grows fainter, sounds are "deaden'd," and farther on the air itself becomes motionless, "lifeless." But the Dom-Daniel caverns are "beneath the roots" of the ocean. So Thalaba alights and proceeds alone ever downward through the "dead" air until he reaches a precipice overhanging a "dreadful gulph," above which the faint light "floated" but "mingled not" with the darkness. At the bottom of this he at length enters the Dom-Daniel, slays the evil magicians, and in the inmost cave speaks the proper words addressed to Mohammed and stabs the "Living Image." The whole, all the "thundering vaults," falls in destruction, for the Image had "sustain'd the ocean-weight," whose "waters arch'd the sanctuary" (Book XII, *passim*). Thalaba is at once translated to Paradise, the real one at last, where his Arabian maid awaits him.

We have already encountered a damsel or two, but there

The sacred river ran then reached the caverns measureless to man and sank in tumult to a lifeless ocean

A sunless sea

are others scattered through the poem, one of particular interest who begins as one of the bad ones but, repenting, becomes one of the good. Thalaba met her first in a cave as a woman with gray hair but a "damsel's" face, spinning and singing. She talked to him always in song, sweet but mysterious, for Thalaba "knew not the words." She bound his hands with gold-spun magic thread which he could not break, and delivered him to her brother-demons. Later, repentant, she unwound the thread, singing to him again in a voice

so musical,
That sure it was not strange,
If in those unintelligible tones
Was more than human potency,
That with such deep and undefined delight
Fill'd the surrender'd soul.
The work is done, the song hath ceased;
He wakes as from a dream of Paradise [IX, 42].

Southey overdid everything: he has not one Paradise garden but two, and other minor ones; not one damsel but four or five; sorcerers, a whole tribe; and caverns upon almost every page, more or less loosely connected usually with the central suboceanic caverns. The reader of *Thalaba* naturally telescopes all these repetitions in memory, for in the poem they are often not distinctly enough drawn or not essential enough to the fabric of the whole to be kept in their places. A second boiling spring appears in a scene that has obvious connections with both Landor and Coleridge. A "bitumen-lake" is fed by springs that roar, "boil," and "gush tumultuous out" with "torrent force" from the depths of a cavern which "no eye of mortal man, if unenabled by enchanted spell," had ever penetrated. The cavern contains serpents whose necks swell, like those in *Gebir* and *Christabel*, and the way is lighted by a sorcerer carrying a dead hand for a candlestick.[35] Guided by this light, Thalaba advances to another fountain within the cave, one that gushes not steadily but intermittently, like

A damsel . . . in a vision once I saw . . . singing of Mount Abora Could I revive within me her symphony and song to such a deep delight 'twould win me . . .

. . . drunk the milk of Paradise A vision in a dream

Caverns measureless to man
From this chasm with ceaseless turmoil seething a mighty fountain momently was forced amid whose swift half-intermitted burst huge fragments vaulted

〖 147 〗

Coleridge's. Under the "spacious vault," with "everlasting roar," "black river-fountains burst their way" with "whirlwind's force." The flood gushes upward, then

> the deaden'd roar
> Echoed beneath, collapsing as it sunk
> Within a dark abyss,
> Adown whose fathomless gulphs the eye was lost [V, 22–23].

Caverns measure-
less to man . . .

Finally, reinforcing the hint of pleasure-dome with ice-caves that we saw in the pleasure-bridges, an actual palace of ice and an ice-cave almost found their way into the poem but became somewhat transformed during the process of composition. In the tenth book, Thalaba journeyed through the bitter region of ice and snow near Mount Caucasus, in the midst of which he came upon a house in a fragrant tropical garden, kept warm by a magic fountain of fire with rivulets that wound among the groves and flowers. The garden had been built for his damsel-daughter by a sorcerer, who daily created out of snow, to wait upon her, human forms of men and women that breathed and moved but remained chill to the touch and melted away each night. In the published form of the poem, the damsel's house is small and lowly and of unspecified material. The original plan, however, was different. As the tale was outlined in Southey's *Common-Place*

A miracle of rare
device a sunny
pleasure-dome
with caves of ice

Book, Thalaba was to find "a young woman, a damsel, in an ice palace," which may have been, but probably was not, the same as an "ice-cave" mentioned on the next page of the outline.[36] From the phrasing of Southey's sketch it appears that the passage may have been not only planned but actually written first in these terms but altered before publication.

An actual ice-palace or cavern-ice-palace, however, must have provided the chief suggestion for both Southey and Coleridge. In the *Biographia literaria*, quoting, he said, from an essay written during his Cambridge days, Coleridge referred to "the Russian palace of ice, glittering, cold and transitory."[37] This was no figment of imagination; it was the actual pleasure-palace of the Russian empress, which had struck a poetic imagination before Coleridge's. In the fifth book of *The Task* Cowper had used it for an extended comparison with his winter scene in nature. The "glitt'ring turrets" and "grotto within grotto" of ice-hung trees in winter reminded him, for the space of some fifty lines, of that "most magnificent and mighty freak," the artificial Russian palace of ice, whose "marble" was not stone but "the glassy wave." "Silently as a dream" its fabric had risen (like Kubla's dream-palace) without sound of hammer or saw. It was indeed a miracle of rare device—a "brittle prodigy," Cowper called it—its interior adorned with "long wavy wreaths of flowers" made of ice, and tables, seats, and throne surrounded by the ice-mirror walls. With all this in sight and with an ice-cave of Southey's interwoven in so many other connections with Coleridge, Lowes's parallels between *Kubla Khan* and Maurice and Bernier seem rather marginal than central.

The reader must have had a surfeit of *Thalaba* by this time; and so, though there are other passages in the poem itself, in the preliminary sketch and notes for revision and in the illustrative prose notes, which may have some bearing upon *Kubla Khan* (the aerial gardens of Babylon, for example, with sounds of "dulcimer and lute"; Thalaba's hair that "floats straight in the stream of the wind"),[38] we shall nevertheless pass on to the third of the contemporary poems that seem most closely woven into the web.

4. "OBERON"

Wieland's version of the tale of Huon of Bordeaux, *Oberon*, was published in the English translation of William Sotheby in 1798. Southey apparently read it late that year or early in 1799 but did not think very highly of it. "It only diverts," he said, "it does not kindle the imagina-

tion."[39] Coleridge had evidently at least looked at the
original as early as December, 1797. He had begun to
study German sometime earlier, and told Cottle then that
he was "translating" the poem. His imagination, however,
was probably converting wish into fact. It is doubtful if
he could have gone far in *Oberon* with the knowledge he
then had, and apparently his burst of study was somewhat
abortive, for when he went to Germany a year and a half
later he still knew very little of the language.[40] Whatever
may have been true of Wieland in German, Coleridge
probably read Sotheby's translation either shortly before
he left for Germany or during his stay there.[41]

There is little, however, in *Oberon* that Coleridge would
not see elsewhere—in *Thalaba, Gebir, Rasselas, Paradise
Lost*—and its influence was probably rather to reinforce
these than to contribute much else. Wieland's poem contains possibly even more caverns than *Thalaba.* We meet
one almost upon the first page of Sotheby's translation,
and with the eighteenth stanza we are right in the midst of
the familiar properties and the familiar epithets: rocks,
caverns, "mazes," "enchanted"; followed shortly by
"giant cedar," "wild," "savage" (used to mean merely
wild or primitive), "grot," "trance," hair that "floats,"
"delightful dream"; and soon again by the combination of
cave with fountain and honey. So opens the first canto.
And the second begins with a journey down a "romantick
height" with "groves of ancient cedars," "mazy vales," a
"fertile" glade and mead, the "maze of many a silver rill,
That danc'd in sparkling currents down the hill," and a
wood haunted by a demon. This is certainly reminiscent of
Kubla's "ancient" forests and "deep romantic chasm"
that "slanted Down the green hill athwart a cedarn cover!
. . . enchanted . . . haunted by woman wailing for her
demon-lover," his "sinuous rills," "mazy motion," and
"fertile ground."[42] Though these details, individually considered, are but stock properties in the cult of the "pic-

turesque" and undoubtedly owe as much to the new
fashions in landscape gardening as to poets, still the concentration of so many of them in these scenes of *Oberon* and
Kubla Khan suggests perhaps something more than chance
independent echoes. They are worth recording, at any
rate, because Lowes sometimes carried us much further
afield to trace slighter links.[43]

In the story of *Oberon* dreams play a leading role. As in
the Arabian Tale of Maugraby, the princess-heroine, a
sultan's daughter engaged to marry an Eastern prince, fell
in love with a knight seen only in her dreams. She knew by
his long golden hair that he was a Western youth. The
image of the "floating hair" is more memorable in *Oberon*
than elsewhere, for it is a part of the plot. Introduced early
in the poem, it later becomes the means by which, when
Huon removes his oriental turban and his golden curls
"float," the princess recognizes in real life the lover of her
dreams. Huon also sees her first in a dream. Lulled asleep
supernaturally by a song, he dreams of her as a goddess-
woman in a setting, once more, of rills and shady groves.
He is reluctant to awaken: "Leave me, at least, the visionary maid!" he cries; and many stanzas of the next canto
are filled with his account of her. The language plays every
variation on the themes of dream, vision, and Paradise. If
only he might have brought a token with him from
his dream, "were it but the flower that in her bosom
bloom'd!"[44]

Oberon, like *Thalaba*, contains an earthly "Paradise," a
fruitful garden inclosed by almost impassable mountains
and inhabited by a hermit. It is described with the familiar
furniture of maze, fragrance, crystal stream, winding rills,
the inevitable grotto or cave, and the magic song of an
enchantress. The place is a fairy Paradise made fertile in
the midst of its mountains by the magic, this time, of
Titania.

I have not dwelt upon *Oberon* at length here because

nearly everything in it that suggests Coleridge appears, with a great deal more besides, in *Thalaba*. But *if* Coleridge knew *Thalaba* before he wrote *Kubla Khan*, then he also certainly knew *Oberon* and *Gebir*, and both must have been fairly fresh in his mind. These two poems also had left visible marks upon *Thalaba*.

This group of three interrelated poems, together with Milton's *Paradise Lost*, which hovered over them all, contains almost every image and many verbal reminders of *Kubla Khan*. Coleridge was reading and discussing them all within the space, approximately, of a year or two. The question is whether the matrix within which Coleridge's poem developed is not this closely knit literary one, enriched by the wider literary tradition of which all the poems form a part—a tradition within which the geographical materials that have been regarded as the special raw material of Coleridge's dream-poem had already been poeticized quite out of their raw state. The sources to which Lowes called attention with so much ingenuity and eloquence were indeed, many of them, material upon which this whole poetic tradition drew, and Coleridge himself certainly read some of them. But it may well be that his imagination when he wrote *Kubla Khan* was working for the most part directly upon the tradition itself. If that is so, his synthesis is something else than we have supposed.

The question remains, however, whether he could have known the two latest of those works, *Thalaba* and *Gebir*, before he composed *Kubla Khan*. If he wrote it, as has been thought, in 1797 or 1798, he could not.

~~ IV ~~

The Date

Chaucer has been a great convenience to incompetent or harassed authors: if the reader like not what he finds, let him "turne over the leef and chese another tale." The defense was a nice one for Chaucer, who did not need it. For the rest of us it is a confession of incapacity when our subject has got beyond us. Still, I know no better. The power to transform a complex mass of fact, probability, and speculation into a neat single-dimensional chain that will retain for a reader the detective suspense enjoyed by the author in assembling it is something that mere wishing will scarcely achieve. Most of us, I suppose, have wished upon occasion to break the cramping limitation, inherent in language, upon the organization of thought—have needed to say two or three things at once, as one can do in music or painting, or even as one might by a diagram on a wall. With the chain of words there is only a before and an after, though what one sometimes requires is an all-over patterned fabric of links. Any substitute for this author's dream of a perfect expository medium must be marred by omissions, repetitions, and broken threads, and often by inordinate dulness. I have found no means of condensing to readable proportions the mass of individually small details bearing upon the date of *Kubla Khan*. If the reader wishes to spare himself and will take the author's word for the conclusion or inconclusion, let him pass over to the next chapter.

Concerning the date of the composition of *Kubla Khan*, only two things can be said with anything like certainty.

One of these is merely negative: that no evidence now available enables us to date the poem with assurance. The other, as far as it goes, is positive: we know that the poem was in existence by October, 1800. In the past its composition has been assigned tentatively to various times between May, 1797, and midsummer, 1798. There appear to be grounds, however, for extending the range further. The poem may have been composed as late as the autumn of 1799 or even in May or June, 1800. Reasons can be marshaled both for and against these later dates as well as the earlier. It is a pity we cannot reach a definite conclusion, for though a year or two would ordinarily matter little, in this instance it makes some real difference. The later date, throwing the poem into the midst of a very different set of circumstances and influences, alters materially the effect one may suppose the poem to aim at. So it would seem worth while to examine the available evidence, some of which has not been noticed in the past, despite all that has been written on the subject.

1. COLERIDGE'S STATEMENTS; THE EVIDENCE FOR 1797 AND 1798; THE QUARREL WITH CHARLES LLOYD

The evidence bearing upon the date of the poem falls roughly into four general divisions. The first consists of three, or possibly four, statements by Coleridge himself; the second, of certain circumstances of his life and his reading. The third comprises the references to the poem by others—and the lack of them. Finally, there is internal evidence from the language, versification, and style of the poem itself, the most interesting and most slippery of all the evidence.

The earliest date to which the poem has been assigned, 1797, rests entirely upon Coleridge's two statements: one in the Crewe manuscript, placing the event at Culbone, near Porlock, in the fall; the other in the preface of 1816, which gives the date as "summer" of that year. Had the poet been generally a trustworthy witness for the dates of his writing, there would have been little else to say: lacking other decisive evidence, his word would have been taken as final. Coleridge, however, was one of the very last persons to be relied upon for an accurate date or indeed for faithfulness to chilly fact of certain other sorts as well. The difficulty goes beyond that of a mere faulty memory. In 1803, for example, he sent *The Pains of Sleep* to a friend as verse he had just written about his current miseries; less than a fortnight later he described it to another correspondent as a poem he had written nine years earlier (the air of precision in the "nine" is characteristic); writing to a third old friend, after another interval of less than two weeks, he reverted to his original account of it as a new piece.[1] From time to time his greatest friends and admirers have had to take account of this weakness of Coleridge on factual matters. As early as 1800, Lamb referred to it kindly as his "daily & hourly habit of quizzing the world by lyes, most unaccountable & most disinterested fictions." Dorothy Wordsworth later on wrote with pain and disillusion that "his whole time and thoughts (except when he is reading and he reads a great deal) are employed in deceiving himself, and seeking to deceive others. He will tell me that he has been writing, that he *has* written, half a Friend; when I *know* that he has not written a single line." Finally, Coleridge's grandson, E. H. Coleridge, expressed the point gracefully in his notes for a projected biography: "Coleridge's anecdotes about himself must be judged by the same standard which Charles Lamb applied to the morality of the characters in Wycherley's and Congreve's plays —the scene is laid in Arcadia."[2]

Instances of misdating are not confined to one or two occasions. *The Monody on Chatterton* (the first version) is believed to have been written when Coleridge was eighteen

instead of sixteen, as he maintained. Though our knowledge of the history of *Christabel* is by no means complete,
it is certain that "the first book and half of the second"
were not finished in 1797, as in 1815 he told Byron they
had been. His misdatings, moreover, were usually not
vague but very precise. The brief poem *What Is Life?* was
actually written on August 16, 1805, when the poet was
just short of thirty-three; yet in 1819 he said quite definitely that the lines had been written "between the age of 15
and 16." The statement has an almost hallucinatory exactness: it was not merely "about" that age but precisely
"between." *Time, Real and Imaginary* he described as a
"school boy" poem, though it too appears in fact to have
been written a good many years later. In the *Biographia
literaria* he recalled the date of publication of his first
volume of poems as 1794 instead of 1796. The more than
four hundred lines of *Religious Musings* were described in
the subtitle as "A Desultory Poem, written on the Christmas Eve of 1794." Coleridge was undoubtedly capable of
fluent extempore composition: nonetheless, *Religious
Musings* was a work seriously in progress for nearly two
years; Coleridge built all his poetic pretensions on the
poem, he told John Thelwall in 1796. Of all the errors of
this kind, I remember seeing only one in which he assigned
a date later than the correct one; that was obviously a slip
due to confusion between the dates of composition and
publication.[3] The others, in the main, were probably no
mere accidents but derived from some such psychological
reasons as were suggested in an earlier chapter. His general
habit was to assign a date too early, sometimes by many
years. The actual known percentage of his errors is high,
especially in view of the large number of poems that were
automatically dated by newspaper publication, which
naturally placed some clog upon imaginative chronology.
Because of this frequent inaccuracy, Coleridge's own
retrospective dates have not usually been regarded as

final when they have conflicted with other likely-looking evidence.

It is not possible to say how long after the event Coleridge wrote either of those two notes ascribing the composition of *Kubla Khan* to the year 1797. The preface printed in 1816 reads as if it had been written for publication and most likely belongs to that or the preceding year, though one cannot be sure. The Crewe manuscript is probably earlier. The watermark, the closer resemblance of the text to Purchas and Milton, and the character of the explanatory note all point to an earlier date. The note does not, however, appear to have been written immediately after the poem was composed.[4] Both notes appear to be retrospective and are therefore weak reeds to lean upon. Their date of 1797 has been either questioned or abandoned by most writers on Coleridge in the present century, chiefly because it appears to conflict with another statement by Coleridge himself.

The second date, 1798, was first adopted by Dykes Campbell and E. H. Coleridge. Finding a manuscript note of 1810, in which Coleridge connected his retirement between Linton and Porlock and his recourse to opium with the mental distress resulting from a quarrel with Charles Lloyd, they believed Coleridge should have written "the summer of 1798" in his preface, since the quarrel, E. H. Coleridge said, was at its height in May of that year.[5] Both editors felt that the later date was more probable on stylistic as well as biographical grounds: they found it difficult to believe the verse of *Kubla Khan* could have wholly preceded the composition of both *The Ancient Mariner* and *Christabel*. Other recent writers have agreed with this judgment. To Mr. Hanson the poetic quality and particularly the metrical excellence of *Kubla Khan* suggest that it was the last rather than the first of the three.[6]

Coleridge may have made one other statement about the date of the poem, but this I have been unable to trace

with any certainty. Mr. Robert Graves accepted May,
1798, as the true date, "in spite," he said, "*of Coleridge
himself having nine years later postdated it to the summer of
1799*, and in 1816 having predated it to 1797." Mr. Graves
does not say where he saw Coleridge's reference to "the
summer of 1799," and, though it is of the greatest interest
for the purpose of this chapter, I have failed to find a hint
of its trail before it reached Mr. Graves.[7]

There has been no disposition to question the place
association with the Porlock region, nor does there appear
to be any reason for questioning it. On that point all three
of Coleridge's statements agree; furthermore, that kind of
association is not likely to have been subject to the particular pressures that falsified Coleridge's memory or
utterances about dates. The connection with Porlock
would naturally belong to the time when Coleridge was
living at Nether Stowey; that is, during 1797, or 1798
before his departure for Germany at the end of the summer, or after his return in July, 1799. Or it might have
occurred while he was in Bristol, Stowey, and Porlock
again in the late spring and early summer of 1800. Various
attempts have been made to trace Coleridge's movements
while he lived at Stowey, in the hope of finding out when
he went or might have gone to Porlock under circumstances that might have produced the poem. The most
exhaustive study was made by Sir Edmund Chambers in
an article on "Some Dates in Coleridge's *Annus mirabilis*."
Tracing the poet's doings and whereabouts step by step,
he settled upon a day or two about May 9, 1798, as the
most likely occasion for that sojourn at Porlock. In his
recent biography, however, Sir Edmund has become
dubious of Coleridge's absence from the Stowey neighborhood at this time. He has found reasons for rejecting that
and other dates in 1798 and has concluded that Coleridge
was probably right, after all, in assigning *Kubla Khan* to
the fall of the preceding year. Observing that in a letter to

Thelwall written presumably on October 14, 1797, Coleridge mentioned that he had just been "absent a day or two" from Stowey, Sir Edmund has suggested that he went to Porlock and wrote *Kubla Khan* during that absence.[8]

This date, however, is open to two objections. It conflicts with the implications of Coleridge's note of 1810, an objection that Sir Edmund recognizes but does not think insuperable. There is a further obstacle: Coleridge probably spent the "day or two" before the fourteenth not in Porlock but in Bristol, for the records of the Bristol Library show that on October 13 he returned two books which he had borrowed in August.[9] Though he might have sent the volumes to Bristol by someone else, the dates of the library register and the "day or two" of absence from home coincide so perfectly as to make that supposition unlikely. It is not easy, at any rate, to send him to Porlock without any positive evidence, in the face of strong, if not conclusive, indications that he was in Bristol.

Most other recent writers on Coleridge have preferred to place *Kubla Khan* in 1798. Since the prime reason for rejecting the preceding year—Coleridge's statement connecting Porlock and opium with his quarrel with Lloyd—holds equally for any date before late April, 1798, Mr. Hanson suggested three occasions during May on which Coleridge might have stayed briefly at Porlock. One of these is the same date, about May 9, that Sir Edmund Chambers had originally fixed upon but later found reason for doubting. The whereabouts of Coleridge is not recorded from the afternoon of Tuesday the eighth, when the Wordsworths had tea with him at home in Stowey, to the night of Saturday the twelfth, when he must have slept at home, since he "walked in to Taunton" from Stowey the next morning to conduct chapel services. Dorothy Wordsworth's journal records that she wrote to Coleridge on Wednesday the ninth, the day after she had seen him at

tea; and this fact originally led Sir Edmund to the speculation that Coleridge might have been absent from home,
since Alfoxden, where the Wordsworths were staying, was
but a short walk from Stowey. However, though an absence is not impossible, it is not necessarily implied by the
letter from Dorothy. It is no more unlikely that she would
write to Coleridge at home than that she would send a
letter after him to Porlock on the very day of his departure
for such a brief absence (if he went at all) as from Wednesday to Saturday, when she had seen him late on Tuesday. Whether he was at home or elsewhere, she would have
written, I imagine, only if some unusual circumstance had
arisen. Sir Edmund, in any case, now thinks the letter
Dorothy mentioned was to Cottle and that Knight misread "Cot." as "Col." in the manuscript (now lost) of her
journal.[10] If that is true, no absence from home is even
remotely implied.

A walk to Linton mentioned in an undated letter of
Coleridge to Cottle has been suggested as another possible
occasion for the opium dream at Porlock, which lay on his
route; but as he specifically said he "walked in one day
and returned in one," that occasion will hardly do. One
other possible date has been offered, a day or two after
May 20. On the sixteenth Coleridge had left home with the
Wordsworths to see the Cheddar rocks. They slept that
night at Bridgewater, and the next at Cross. Coleridge
must have returned home on the eighteenth, while Wordsworth proceeded on from Cross to Bristol. Mr. Malcolm
Elwin argues that Coleridge very likely went to Porlock
for a few days after the twentieth. His friend and neighbor
Poole was suffering from grief over a brother's death,
Wordsworth was in Bristol, and Dorothy, Mr. Elwin
thinks, could not with propriety have seen Coleridge in
her brother's absence. At a loose end for congenial company and depressed by his quarrel with Charles Lloyd, he
probably sought solitude and opium at Porlock. There is

no evidence that he did so, however; and again the records of the Bristol Library stand in the way, though not as firmly as for the earlier date. On May 22 Coleridge is recorded as having returned two books, and on May 25 he withdrew two others, though, as Wordsworth was probably still in Bristol, it might have been he who took out and returned the volumes in Coleridge's name.[11] There are more formidable objections, however, to the supposition of any absence from Stowey immediately after May 20, for two other visitors have to be accounted for. Cottle came, apparently after Dorothy's journal ends on May 17; and Hazlitt came. Cottle's visit I cannot date; Hazlitt stayed three weeks; and though he mentions no dates, the beginning and end may be marked with some probability: he seems to have arrived on or about May 20 and to have left on June 10. During his visit there were excursions about the vicinity of Stowey and a walk to Linton, but there seems to have been no opportunity for Coleridge to "retire" to Porlock, nor does Hazlitt mention any such production as *Kubla Khan*.[12]

Altogether, there is a good deal of difficulty in accepting any of the specific dates in 1797 or 1798 that have been suggested for that elusive and special retirement at Porlock. Of them all, that of May 9, 1798, raises the fewest obstacles, but even that has been given up by Sir Edmund Chambers and almost wholly by Mr. Elwin; against the others there are very material objections. The most that can be said for any of them is only that we have no incontrovertible proof anchoring Coleridge at home during a space of three or four days. There is no positive evidence of any kind, no reference to a stay at Porlock that could have been *the* stay, no reference even to an absence from home that is not pretty certainly explained otherwise. Unless we are certain that the possibilities are limited to these two years, it may be well to speculate farther afield, for when Coleridge gave a date that was wrong, he was as apt to err by several years as by one.

The note of 1810, upon which the date 1798 has mainly rested, requires inspection. When Campbell and E. H. Coleridge discovered it, no other date than that published by Coleridge had been thought of, and they naturally interpreted the note in a way that would conflict as little as might be with the original preface. If the passage is read carefully, however, in the light of the known facts of Coleridge's life, the retirement near Porlock referred to in it (without a date) will be seen to fit the events following his return from Germany in 1799 more easily than those of 1798.

The entry was written under the date of November 3, 1810, and bore the heading "Ego-ana." After some bitter reflections on his past relations with Wordsworth and his love for Sara Hutchinson, Coleridge went on to his quarrel with Charles Lloyd. The origin of that quarrel may be summed up briefly. About the end of 1797, Southey and Lloyd took offense at three sonnets published by Coleridge, under the name of Nehemiah Higginbottom, in the November issue of the *Monthly Magazine*. The verses were parodies of Lloyd's and Lamb's poetry and—so they thought—of Southey's, though Coleridge maintained that his own work and not Southey's had been the butt of his third sonnet. In the following April, Lloyd's novel *Edmund Oliver* appeared. It was dedicated to Lamb, published by Coleridge's friend Cottle, and composed unmistakably with Southey's knowledge. Its hero was obviously patterned in part after Coleridge: his appearance was described, as well as the military aberration of his Cambridge years, the disappointment of his early love for Mary Evans, and his use of laudanum and spirits to help drown trouble and responsibility. To Coleridge this naturally seemed a betrayal of confidence by one who had lived in his house and whom he had nursed in illness. Though

Lloyd was the author, Coleridge considered him but the instrument of "another man's [Southey's] darker passions," for the unfriendliness between himself and his brother-in-law was of much longer standing than the Higginbottom affair.[13] In the summer of 1799, immediately after Coleridge returned from Germany, the breach with Southey was ended. The primary blame for the quarrel was now thrown upon Lloyd, who continued to be an active source of trouble for the next several years.

This is the situation of which Coleridge wrote in the notebook of 1810. The passage follows immediately after a statement of his belief that he had never really possessed Wordsworth's friendship or Sara Hutchinson's love. Another heading, "Elucidation," introduces the remainder of the entry:

If ever there was a time and circumstance in my life in which I behaved *perfectly* well, it was in that of C. Lloyd's mad quarrel & frantic ingratitude to me—He even wrote a letter to D. W. [Dorothy Wordsworth], in which he not only called me a villain, but appealed to a conversation which passed between him & *her*, as the grounds of it—and as proving that this was her opinion no less than his—. [Spring, 1798] She brought over the *letter* to me from Alfoxden with tears—I laughed at it—After this there succeeded, on his side a series of wicked calumnies & irritations—infamous Lies to Southey & to poor dear Lamb—in short, a conduct which was not that of a fiend, only because it was that of a madman—on my side, patience, gentleness, and good for evil—yet this supernatural effort injured me—what I did not suffer to act on my mind, preyed on my body—it prevented my finishing the Christabel—& at the retirement between Linton & Porlock was the first occasion of my having recourse to Opium—And all this was as well known to W[Wordsworth] & D W. as to myself—Well! he settled in the North—[December, 1799] & I determined to leave all my friends & follow him—[Summer, 1800] Soon after came—Lloyd & settled at Ambleside [September, 1800]—a thick acquaintance commenced between him and the W—so that the fear of *his* coming in & receiving an unpleasant agitation occasioned such Looks & Hurry & Flurry & anxiety that I should be gone from Grasmere, as gave me many a heart ache—It was at this time that speaking of C Ll.'s conduct to me & others I called him a rascal—*D W* fired up, & said, *He was no rascal*—in short, acted with at least as great warmth on his behalf, as she ever

could have done on mine—even when she had known me to have acted
the most nobly—At length, a sort of reconciliation took place between
me & C. Ll—and about six or 8 months after, some person told *D. W.*
that C. Ll. in a public Company had given it as his opinion, that
Coleridge was a greater poet, & possessed of more genius by nature,
than *W. W.* Instantly, D. W. pronounced him a VILLAIN. And thence-
forward not a good word in his favor!!——[14]

Though it cannot be verified in every detail, the note is
on the whole consistent with events as we know them,
except for the reference to opium, which must be considered hereafter. Several points can be roughly fixed. If
Dorothy Wordsworth brought over from Alfoxden a letter
of Lloyd's attacking Coleridge, she must have done so
between early December, 1797, when the Higginbottom
sonnets appeared, and June 25 or 26, 1798, when the
Wordsworths left Alfoxden. It was probably sometime in
May, however, for not until about that time did the
mutual resentments become acute. On May 20 Coleridge
was unable to keep his own troubles out of even a short
note of sympathy to Poole on his brother's death: "So
many unpleasant and shocking circumstances have happened to me in my immediate knowledge within the last
fortnight, that I am in a nervous state, and the most
trifling thing makes me weep." Lloyd's novel would have
been one of those "shocking circumstances"; Lloyd's
letter to Dorothy Wordsworth may have been another.[15]

About that time Lloyd, we know, communicated to
Dorothy, apparently by letter, something detrimental to
Coleridge that she passed on to him. "Lloyd has informed
me through Miss Wordsworth," Coleridge then wrote to
Lamb, "that you intend no longer to correspond with
me."[16] The letter from Lloyd to Dorothy Wordsworth that
Coleridge remembered in 1810, perhaps the very one im-
plied in this statement to Lamb, almost certainly belonged
to the spring of 1798 and probably to the first half of May.
Thus far, at least, Coleridge's narrative fits the known

facts. It does not mention *Kubla Khan* at all but does refer to "the" retirement between Porlock and Linton as if there had been only one or perhaps only one that was memorable for indulgence in opium. Because of this definitive phrasing and the fact that the first outbreak of the quarrel with Lloyd occurred in the late spring of 1798, E. H. Coleridge drew the conclusion that his grandfather had misdated *Kubla Khan* by a year.[17] The calumnies, the lies to Southey and Lamb, the injury to Coleridge's health, and the failure to finish *Christabel* are by this reading all concentrated within that spring and summer—either that, or they were jumbled and misdated in the note of 1810.

It is evident, however, that in 1810 Coleridge was surveying not a single season but the whole history of his relations with Charles Lloyd from the beginning of Lloyd's "ingratitude" and the open break in 1798 to the time, as late as 1802 or even later, when Lloyd ceased to be in a position to interfere with his friendships. E. H. Coleridge appears to have telescoped into a month or two events that had actually been spread over several years. Both the ill health and the inability to finish *Christabel* are more easily placeable, as will be seen shortly, in late 1799 and 1800 than in 1798. So also is the reference to the "first" indulgence in opium, though it is of course entirely wrong for either date. And the "series" of "calumnies" did actually continue to irk Coleridge from May, 1798, at least through the whole of 1800. In fact, the period of his greatest bitterness toward Lloyd came after, not before, the months in Germany. All this had better be shown somewhat more fully.

Lamb and Coleridge we know were offended with each other in the spring of 1798, largely because of Charles Lloyd. Most of the events, however, that showed how far Coleridge was being undermined by Lloyd occurred after May. The breach with Lamb lasted until the end of 1799.[18] While Coleridge was abroad, from September, 1798, to the

following July, Southey, Lloyd, and Lamb drew together
in a friendship that excluded him. He was reconciled with
Southey in August, 1799; and only after that, instead of
regarding Lloyd as a mere tool of Southey's malice, did
Coleridge look upon Lloyd as the primary troublemaker.
All through the latter part of 1799 and early 1800 Coleridge's letters betray his continued sense of Lloyd's in-
juries, even while they show, a trifle ostentatiously, the
"patience, gentleness, and good for evil" that in 1810 he
remembered having displayed. Writing to Southey on
October 15, 1799, Coleridge reported that Lloyd and
Edmund Oliver had recently been damaging his reputation
with Christopher Wordsworth at Cambridge. He commented on this as mildly as he could:

> My dear Southey! the having a bad heart and not having a good one
> are different things. That Charles Lloyd has a bad heart, I do not even
> think; but I venture to say, and that openly, that he has not a good one.
> He is unfit to be any man's friend, and to all but a very guarded man
> he is a perilous *acquaintance*. . . . Of confidence he is not worthy. . . .
> I have great affection for Lamb, but I have likewise a perfect Lloyd-
> and-Lambophobia![19]

A few weeks later Coleridge laid aside his forbearing
tone in the privacy of a notebook where he was jotting
down matter for a satire. Among the "characters" for this
he listed "Lloyd & his Gang." The word *Gang* reveals
something of the depth of bitterness that lay beneath his
milder public words. That was in November, 1799; in
January he again returned to the subject in a letter to
Southey:

> Poor Lloyd! Every hour new-creates him; he is his own posterity in a
> perpetually flowing series, and his body unfortunately retaining an ex-
> ternal identity, *their* mutual contradictions and disagreeings are united
> under one name, and of course are called lies, treachery, and rascality!
> I would not give him up, but that the same circumstances which have
> wrenched his morals prevent in him any salutary exercise of genius. And
> therefore he is not worth to the world that I should embroil and em-
> brangle myself in his interests.[20]

As a rule, Coleridge was a most unmalicious man, and his letters about Lloyd are written in an exceptional spirit, for him; the tone of condescension softens the words but not the barbs.

As his note of 1810 said, the trouble did not end even that winter in London but pursued him northward later in the year. After their return from Germany the Wordsworths had gone to stay temporarily with the Hutchinsons at Sockburn in Durham. At the end of December, 1799, they settled in their cottage at Grasmere. In the spring of 1800 Coleridge decided to live near them and in June took his family north to stay. Three months later Dorothy Wordsworth mentioned with regret that Charles Lloyd was coming to live at Ambleside. She thought him "a dangerous acquaintance." But soon after his arrival his dangerousness was forgotten; he became a frequent and welcome visitor at the Wordsworths'. Coleridge's memory in 1810 of the "thick acquaintance" and of the embarrassment caused by the Wordsworths' fear that he and Lloyd might meet, the "Looks & Hurry & Flurry & anxiety that I should be gone from Grasmere" when Lloyd was expected, is confirmed by implication in Dorothy's journal, though nothing is specifically said.[21]

The phrasing of the note of 1810 associates the retirement near Porlock not with the opening of the quarrel but with the "series" of events that followed; and in the sequence of Coleridge's narrative Porlock did not precede but followed the failure to finish *Christabel*. He may not have meant strictly that the abandonment of *Christabel*, which did not take place at a single moment, entirely preceded the Porlock episode; he seems rather to have been placing them together in the note. But he did not put the retirement first.

Christabel is supposed to have been begun in 1798, or possibly 1797. Coleridge himself, however, does not mention it, so far as we know, until October 15, 1799, when he assured Southey, who wanted it for the *Annual Anthology:* "I will set about 'Christabel' with all speed." Between October and early December he was trying or intending or promising to complete it, but by the end of that time he had lost his "poetic enthusiasm" and thought he would not be able to do so. He made another abortive effort upon it in the summer of 1800 after he went north; and that autumn he was again at work, presumably completing the second part. Thus there are contemporary records of two and probably three (perhaps overlapping) attempts and failures to finish the poem—all of them in late 1799 or 1800, all of them occurring while Coleridge was seriously concerned over the damage he believed Charles Lloyd was doing to his friendships, all of them during or immediately following periods of notable ill health, and two of them of sufficient importance to have been described repeatedly in his correspondence.[22] Coleridge's note of 1810 might have referred to any one of these unsuccessful efforts or to a telescoped memory of them all. We may assume earlier efforts to finish the work if we choose, but we know of none, the earlier letters being barren of any recognizable references even to the beginning of the poem, in contrast to late 1799 and 1800, when Coleridge's local air was thick with avowed efforts and failures to finish it. His subsequent association of these failures with the Porlock episode would seem to point therefore to some date toward the close of 1799 or to 1800.

On one circumstance the note of 1810 is undoubtedly inaccurate. Whatever dates may be assigned to the other events, it is certain that Coleridge had used opium or laudanum long before the quarrel with Lloyd could have arisen. He had used it in 1791; and for a time in 1796 he was taking it "almost every night," not as medicine for toothache or rheumatic pains but, as he explained, because his wife's illness and the blunders of his printer had left him "tottering on the edge of madness." Some writers have been disposed to think that in 1810 he intended to refer not to his first medical use of the drug but to the first use of it for psychological reasons, though that notion cannot stand in the face of either his own letter of 1796 or Lloyd's descriptions in *Edmund Oliver*, which, however malicious, can scarcely be read merely as Mephistophelian prophecy. About opium Coleridge's later statements are known to be extremely unreliable, as even he confessed.[23] Nevertheless, he seems to have had some more or less abiding memory in later years of a connection between the period after his return from Germany and his addiction to opium. There may be something real in that memory despite inconsistencies. The dates he gave or implied range from 1799 to 1800 (possibly, but not probably, 1801); the causes vary from unnamed illness to swollen knees and rheumatism or rheumatic fever. The reference in the note of 1810 to a period of ill health caused by Lloyd's attacks can scarcely have referred to the spring or summer of 1798 unless it was a pure figment of imagination, for during that time Coleridge seems to have been quite well.

On the other hand, two memorable attacks of rheumatic illness after July, 1799, can be dated without dependence upon his later memory. Both were accompanied by distress caused by Lloyd, and both fit very well with some of his later accounts of the origin of his addiction. Apparently the more acute but briefer attack began late in September, 1799. On the thirtieth, Coleridge described it in a letter to Southey as the worst since his rheumatic fever at school. On October 15 he was still harassed by pain and digestive illness. The letter recording this is the same one that told of his Lloyd-and-Lambophobia, recounted new damage Lloyd had done him, and referred back to *Edmund Oliver*.[24] A second illness the following year at Keswick evidently lasted longer in an intermittent way and left him weaker, though it may possibly have been less acute. Coleridge appears to have exaggerated this one somewhat in his letters because he was having to borrow money from Poole, whom he had neglected, and from the Wedgwoods, and was behind in other commitments. It was still, however, one of the memorable illnesses of his life, and it occurred precisely at the time when Lloyd was obviously winning favor with the Wordsworths.[25] In later memories Coleridge seems to have telescoped these two attacks of 1799 and 1800–1801. Both were notable at the time not only for pain but also for periods of euphoria during intervals of relief or in convalescence, and the descriptions of these in his letters point to the effect of opium.

One of his later memories of the origin of his slavery to the drug specifically dates it from this second illness. Another connects it with the acute rheumatism after his return from Germany but does not make clear which illness he meant. In one letter, probably written in April, 1832, he wrote that he had been taking large amounts of laudanum for thirty-two years. Figured with literal exactness, the date would fall about halfway between the two actual illnesses; it would also correspond very closely to a visit to Porlock that we know occurred in May or early June, 1800. In another letter, dated April 22, 1832, when he was making one last effort to free himself from the habit, he wrote, with a final burst of optimism, of the miracle of his "sudden emancipation from a thirty-three years' fearful slavery." That would seem to refer to 1799. Writing to Byron in April, 1816, Coleridge rejoiced in "the happy knowledge" that opium may be abandoned "even after 15 years habit." Though this has been interpreted as a reference to 1801, I do not think Coleridge was counting fifteen years back from the date of the letter, for he was writing then not as one still under slavery to the drug but as one who had been free from it for two years. The escape (actually only partial, of course) had taken place in May and June, 1814. So again the "15 years habit" ending in 1814 points back to 1799. Finally, many years later,

Carlyon testified to having heard from John Chester, the Stowey friend who had been his companion in Germany, that Coleridge's addiction had originated in a rheumatic attack after his return from Germany.[26] Chester would have had direct knowledge of Coleridge's illness and use of opium in 1799, but not of the later one of 1800–1801.

All these accounts, though they are inconclusive and not in all points consistent, suggest that one or the other or both of those illnesses of 1799 and 1800–1801 were permanently associated in the mind of Coleridge with the beginning of his addiction. He was quite likely wrong. They may well, however, have brought his first *recognition* that he was addicted to the drug. They may have marked the beginning of his consumption of it in "enormous quantities" instead of in the moderate doses sanctioned by medical authority, though he had almost certainly become addicted earlier through (and to) smaller doses. The universal ignorance about addiction and withdrawal symptoms would probably leave a man unaware that anything had happened to him as long as he stayed within the limits of medically allowable doses. When he found himself taking with relative impunity what he knew were lethal quantities, and irresistibly going back for more, then he might begin to know that something was wrong. It might well be an event, or a period of time, that would later rise up in his memory as the first hint that what Chardin and Baron de Tott had reported of Eastern opium eaters might come to be true of himself, an Englishman. The first of the two illnesses, that of September-October, 1799 (but not the second, which took place after his removal to Keswick), would be fully consistent with the reference in 1810 to the retirement between Linton and Porlock and the recourse to opium there.

On the whole, then, the retrospective statement that Coleridge committed to his notebook in 1810 summarizing his quarrel with Charles Lloyd—which has been the foundation of the most widely accepted date for *Kubla Khan*—seems to be, for Coleridge, relatively accurate. It is corroborated in a general way by his own earlier letters and by a good deal that we know from other sources; its contents are part of the known fabric of his life as the published preface to *Kubla Khan* and the note in the Crewe manuscript are not. Campbell and E. H. Coleridge seem to have been justified in allowing it to outweigh the others. Most likely the poem was composed, or perhaps only begun, during the "retirement" mentioned there. The circumstances of the note, however, suggest a time after, rather than before, the ten months spent in Germany. The "series" of calumnies had scarcely had time to be built up, nor had Coleridge had time to hear of most of them before that. And it was not in 1798 but only after July, 1799, that his resentment became fixed primarily upon Lloyd instead of Southey. Obviously, the "retirement" must have occurred before his final departure for the north in June, 1800: after that he could not have gone to Porlock. Circumstances thus point to the months between late September, 1799, and—to be very specific— June 12, 1800. During that period two occasions are likely. One of them we know actually occurred. It was not a mere passing-through on a walk to Linton; it was probably a stay of at least several days' duration; Coleridge was probably alone; his solitude might well have been broken by "a person from Porlock." But the discussion of this will have to wait.

2. CONTEMPORARY REFERENCES—NEGATIVE

The earliest unequivocal reference that I know of to the existence of *Kubla Khan* occurs in a poem by "Perdita" Robinson, written in October, 1800. There is a possible earlier one, however, in the journal of Dorothy Wordsworth. These must be discussed later on. The absence of other references to the poem on occasions when one might expect to hear of it, however, raises the temperature of doubt about the dates 1797 and 1798. George Bellas Greenough and Clement Carlyon both left accounts of their meetings and travels with Coleridge in Germany. They made copies of some poems and heard him recite others. Between them they mention some eight or ten that range in date back to early 1797, but *Kubla Khan* is not among them. Although the tour of the Harz region might have been expected to recall the scenery of the poem to mind, Coleridge apparently was not inspired, like Boswell and Johnson on Macbeth's witches' heath, to recite the appropriate lines when the party saw caves, an underground river, or other suggestive properties.[27] These omissions are not very material, since neither Carlyon nor Greenough set out to copy or name all Coleridge's verse and *Kubla Khan* was at that time only a fragment and not yet a famous poem. But it does read aloud exceptionally well and might have been "chaunted" or mentioned on one of these occasions if it were in existence; or its phrases might have found their way into one of the three descriptions of the tour.

More significant, however, is Southey's failure to mention it later, during the autumn of 1799, when Coleridge was pulling out old pieces and writing and half-promising new ones for the *Annual Anthology* and the *Morning Post*. The lines might have been a trifle fantastic for newspaper publication, but they would have been conspicuous in the *Anthology* only by their superiority. Prodding Coleridge for contributions, Southey mentioned a number of poems and fragments, but never *Kubla Khan*.[28] There is, however, one unnamed fragment mentioned by Coleridge as a possible contribution to the *Anthology*. Though we have no means of identifying it, the poem was evidently not a figment of his imagination, for Humphry Davy had seen and admired it; moreover, it was evidently new. When Coleridge told Southey in December, 1799, that he feared

he had "scarce poetic enthusiasm enough to finish 'Christabel,' " he added that the poem "with which Davy is so
much delighted" he "probably may finish time enough."
He mentioned it again later in the same letter: ". . . were I
sure that I could finish the poem I spoke of." It might
conceivably have been *Kubla Khan;* the loss of "poetic
enthusiasm" mentioned in the letter does at any rate recall the theme of its concluding lines. Speculation on this
point, however, is a quicksand.[29]

3. SCENERY OF 1799, FIRST- AND SECOND-HAND
THE REUNION WITH SOUTHEY

The dominant features of Kubla's landscape in Coleridge's poem are the dome, the measureless caverns, the
underground river and sunless sea, the garden, ancient
trees encircling sunny spots of greenery, the deep chasm
slanting down a hill among cedars, the intermittent fountain throwing up rocks, the mazy river, the rills, the
miraculous combination of sunny summery dome and icy
caves, and the two images brought in for comparison—
demon-lover and prophetic ancestral voices. To these are
added in the concluding lines the maid with dulcimer
whose music might bring back the poet's inspiration, the
picture of the inspired poet, the magic circle, the milk and
honeydew of Paradise. Apart from the proper names, the
materials of the poem are not really oriental. This is surprising in view of the resemblance of the imagery to that
of *Thalaba,* but it is obvious nevertheless. Even the "incense-bearing trees" are no more than a Miltonic orientalism. In so far as the materials underlying *Kubla Khan*
were real and not literary, they seem rather like a combined distillation of the German Harz region and Somerset,
with perhaps a feature or two of south Devon added.

The year 1799 is the year more than any other in which
all these images appeared, some of them repeatedly, both
before Coleridge's eyes as scenery and before his mind as

reading. In May he toured the Harz country; in September he rambled in south Devon among scenes that were probably not new to him but that he was seeing afresh through their novelty to Southey and with fresh recollections of Germany and the Quantocks; in late October and November he saw the Lake District for the first time on a walk with Wordsworth. Of the first and last of these three jaunts he made detailed notes.

Those of the Harz tour included full descriptions of two huge, many-chambered, stalactite-hung caverns, one of them, Bauman's Hole, once the most famous of all European caverns. He wrote also of an actual cave not quite "of ice" but floored with snow, in exciting contrast to summery verdure overhead, that created the memorable illusion of two climates united at one spot. He wrote of a plain with walls and towers; of an underground well or pool and wild chasms, of a stream that ran underground; of a rotunda of greenery surrounded by trees; and, finally, toward the end of the tour, of a famous Dome Church, actually known by that epithet. All this Coleridge recorded doubly, in notebook and letters, obviously with an eye to future literary use. At one point he remarked that the scene, if sufficiently heightened, would do for a novel or poem.

Coleridge's descriptions are too long to quote fully, but some of the details should be seen as he wrote of them:

... an enormous cavern, which we descended. It went underground 800 feet, consisted of various apartments, dripping, stalactitious, and with mock chimneys; ... a most majestic natural arch of rock ... this antechamber is open at the top ... and on the edges the beeches grow and stretch their arms over the cavern, but not wholly form a ceiling. Their verdure contrasted most strikingly with the huge heap of snow which lay piled in the antechamber of the cavern into a white hill, imperfectly covered with withered leaves ... a slope of greenery almost perfectly round ... ascended a smooth green hill, on the top of which stood the ruined castle.... Here again I could see my beautiful rotunda of greenery.[30] ... Sometimes I thought myself in the coombs about Stowey, sometimes between Porlock and Linton—only the stream was somewhat larger. Sometimes the scenery resembled parts in the river Wye. . . . The whole was a melancholy and romantic scene that was quite new to me.

There were "dancing waterfalls" and "rock fragments" and other rocks "unusually wild in their shape."[31] After crossing a river, the party entered a second cavern.

It was a huge place, 800 feet in length, and more in depth—of many different apartments. . . . One thing was really striking—a huge cone of stalactite hung from the roof of the largest apartment, which, on being struck, gave perfectly the sound of a death-bell . . . the effect was very much of the fairy kind. . . . After this, a little clear well and a black stream pleased me the most; and multiplied by fifty, and coloured *ad libitum*, might be well enough to read of in a novel or poem.

Coleridge summed up this portion of his journey with the comment: "Interesting in the highest degree is it to have seen in the course of two or three days so many different climates, with all their different phenomena!"[32] He took up the same theme in the next day's instalment, with the scene from the Castle Hill of Blankenburg, which he attempted to draw as well as describe: "a plain of young Corn—then Rocks—walls and towers—And pinnacles of Rock, a proud domain." A small lake was crossed at one end by a bridge, beside which the water "plunged itself down, . . . into a chasm of 30 feet in depth and somewhat more in length (a chasm of black or mossy Rocks) and then ran under ground." He described a "stream" of beech trees "flowing adown the Hill" and other hills that "ran aslant." Reaching "the silent City of Goslar," he went to see "the Dome Church . . . a real Curiosity—it is one of the oldest, if not the oldest, in Germany." He proceeded to a long description of this Dome Church—its pictures and altar, its superstitions, including one episode of a woman and a devil—not quite demon-lovers, however. Finally again he turned to the description of a "green meadow" that was "completely encircled, by the grandest swell of woods" he had ever beheld, "a complete Bower," from which he emerged beside a "deep dell" with "Orchards in blossom."[33]

These are the salient passages in the accounts of the cavern and river scenery that impressed Coleridge in Germany. Though they constitute perhaps the most elaborate and sustained of all the natural descriptions he ever wrote, he was dissatisfied with them. To his wife he remarked that they might possibly recall to himself "real forms" if he should read them again, though they must be meaningless to her. "In addition to the difficulty of the thing itself," he said, "I neither am, nor ever was, a good hand at description. I see what I write, but alas! I cannot write what I see." The same and more was written to Poole:

These lines, my dear Poole, I have written rather for my own pleasure than your's—for it is impossible that this misery of words can give to you, that which it may yet perhaps be able to recall to me. What can be the cause that I am so miserable a Describer? Is it that I understand neither the practice nor the principles of Painting? or is it not true, that others have really succeeded? I could half suspect that what are deemed fine descriptions, produce their effects almost purely by a charm of words, with which and with whose combinations, we associate *feelings* indeed, but no distinct *Images*.

Coleridge was at this time collecting materials for a life of Lessing, whose ideas lurk beneath this sentence, a point to which I shall have to return hereafter.[34]

It seems unlikely that the reminders of *Kubla Khan* in these letters came about through Coleridge's having the already written poem in mind. The very elements that we find in the poem seem here in Germany to have surprised him by their novelty. He had seen caves before, and he was most likely familiar with Wookey Hole Cavern, out of which the River Axe issues in full current.[35] But the contrast of seasons—the view of summer from the snowy cave and other swift alternations between snow and blossoming trees—seems to have been a novelty to him as it would scarcely, I think, have been had he already written of that "miracle of rare device," the "sunny pleasure-dome" in its summer gardens with the "caves of ice." He seems not once to have been struck by any resemblance of the present scenes to imaginary ones that he himself had already created. The relative absence of verbal echoes bears out this impression. Except perhaps for "slant," which was a favorite word with him for several years, nearly every word or phrase that might verbally suggest the poem (there are actually almost none except "walls and towers" and the rock "fragments") is dictated by the necessity of his subject. The letters and notes are all written with an eye strictly upon what was before him and give no impression of a literary origin. Coleridge often echoed his own former language when the situation was appropriate; yet here there are no phrase echoes that sound retrospective.

For some months after his return from Germany, Coleridge was surrounded with materials bearing upon *Kubla Khan*, as he had been in no single earlier period of his life. Scenery, conversation, and reading all play a part. He returned in July, 1799. On the twenty-ninth, hoping to make peace, he wrote a friendly letter to Southey, who had been staying with his wife at Minehead. Southey responded and on August 12 joined the Coleridges at Stowey. First, however, he walked on to Porlock, where he stayed overnight, and then proceeded along the coast of north Devon to see Lynmouth and the Valley of Rocks.[36]

Southey had completed the plan for his poem on "The Destruction of the Dom-Daniel" some months earlier and had already been reading avidly, taking notes, and copying out numerous passages from travelers' accounts and other works on the East. During July he had been reading the Koran, and on the day Coleridge first wrote to him he was writing to a friend about Mohammed.[37]

It was with head and luggage full of these materials that

Southey arrived at Coleridge's house for a reunion that was to last almost continuously for the next five weeks. Though the brothers-in-law remained "wholly immersed in conversation,"[38] Southey nevertheless reported a book and a half of the "Dom-Daniel" completed before the end of August, while he was still at Stowey. By September 6 the second book was almost finished. During these weeks various joint literary plans were afoot. The two poets were to collaborate upon a poem in hexameters on the subject of Mohammed. Little of this was ever produced, but it remained a live project for some months. Southey's reading for *Thalaba* was already stuffing him with Eastern material for "Mahomet," and Coleridge no doubt joined in that reading. He was to help Southey, too, with contributions to the *Annual Anthology*. An immediate tangible result of their labors together was the satirical poem *The Devil's Thoughts*, which appeared in the *Morning Post* on September 6 and attracted a good deal of public attention.[39]

At this time Coleridge quite likely saw a sentence in a letter of William Taylor that actually related to *Thalaba* but that reminds one of the close of *Kubla Khan*. "I am glad," Taylor had written to Southey some months earlier, "you are intending to *build* with the talisman of *song* a *magic palace* on the site of the *Dom*daniel of Cazotte."[40] To "build" a "palace" with "song," associated with magic ("weave a circle round him thrice") and the word "dome," is just what Coleridge's lines say: "with music" (after the Abyssinian maid's "song") the poet would "build that dome in air." If Coleridge did not see this letter before he wrote his poem, the coincidence is striking, for it is practically impossible that Taylor should have seen *Kubla Khan* if it existed when he wrote his letter. Coleridge must, in fact, have seen either this letter or an issue of the *Monthly Magazine* that had appeared during his absence from England, for some verses of Taylor's in the letter, afterwards printed in the magazine, furnished the basis for Coleridge and Southey's *The Devil's Thoughts*. These verses of Taylor provide also a verbal or place-name association that has bothered critics of *Kubla Khan*, who have often wondered why Coleridge's "maid" was "Abyssinian"; Taylor's lines contain an incident about a girl and an "Abyssinian bishop."[41]

On August 27 the Coleridges and the Southeys set off together from Stowey for south Devon, the former bound on a visit to his relations at Ottery and the latter temporarily without a home. For a short time they all stayed uncomfortably at Ottery; then the Southeys found lodgings at Exeter, eleven miles away, "a very walkable distance." Not many days later the Coleridges joined them there, and the two men soon went off for a five-day ramble in that country. Both continually compared the scenery unfavorably with the north coast of Devon and Somerset. Coleridge wrote that, with due exceptions, the scenery "is tame to Quantock, Porlock, Culbone, and Linton." Southey was fresh from his tour along the coast to Linton, and they had evidently been comparing notes. One of Coleridge's notebooks has brief entries about "Lesley Cleve" (Lustleigh Cleave), with its torrent, rocks, and foam. Southey made notes of the rivers and of Becky Falls with its "huge round stones." Since Coleridge made no elaborate notes of his excursion as he had made of the Harz tour, we do not know whether when they "walked around Torbay" they visited the celebrated Kent's Hole Cavern or not, but they may very well have done so. Southey had caverns in his mind several weeks later, when he wrote to Coleridge in rather surprising language about the paintings of the artist William Jackson of Exeter; he described them as "cavern drippings chiselled into ramifications." Coleridge's *Lines Composed in a Concert-Room*, which appeared in the *Morning Post* on September 24 and was probably written during the stay in south Devon, con-

tains a line about the "moan of ocean-gale in weedy caves,"
which E. H. Coleridge thought might have been suggested
by a recent visit to Kent's Hole.[42] At Torbay the travelers
very likely saw also the fluctuating intermittent fountain
or spring of Laywell, for Southey made two notes, without
dating them, from the *Philosophical Transactions:* "Lay
Well, ebbing and flowing, near Torbay," and "When the
ebbing and flowing well in Torbay disappoints spectators,
the common people account for it by the influence which
some one of them has upon the fountain."[43] The fountain
of *Kubla Khan* that rose and fell like the earth's breathing
resembles not only the parable of Plato and the springs of
Bartram but suggests also this fount of Laywell, which is
not much more than twenty miles from Coleridge's early
home at Ottery St. Mary and which he very likely visited
and certainly passed very close by, on this September
tour. On the twenty-fourth the Coleridges returned to
Stowey, after more than five weeks of almost continuous
companionship with Southey.

Late in October Coleridge went north to see the Wordsworths, who were then staying with the Hutchinson family
at Sockburn. The visit was crucial for Coleridge. For the
first time he met Wordsworth's future wife and her sister
Sara Hutchinson, for whom he conceived the most serious
and lasting love of his life.[44] He had no sooner arrived,
however, than he set off, not overwillingly, with Wordsworth and Cottle to see the Lake District. Among his
notes of this tour a few details stand out. These were a
magic "Druidical circle" and another green circle bounded
by trees, upon both of which Coleridge dwelt and the second of which he sketched as well. He described Lyulph's
Tower reflected in the water, gleaming "like a ghost dim
and shadowy in the water—and the bright shadow thereof,
how beautiful it is, cut across by that tongue of breezy
water! And now the shadow is suddenly gone, and the

Tower itself rises emerging from the mist. Two thirds are still hidden, but the pinnacles are clear—and in a moment all is snatched away—A mazy dance, a fleeting pageantry of realities and shadows!" In another scene a "conical shadow," this time of a mountain, lay upon water that, like a mirror, reflected both dark and "sunny" clouds. Streams and waterfalls and reflections in water recur. Winding rivers are common enough, but the Tees required a special phrase: "Well may one call this noble River the peninsulating Tees,"[45] its windings being so tortuous that one might sometimes see a sail apparently on land, half a mile from where one thought the river ran. He kept recurring to the subject in varying phrases: the "curve of the River how elegant," "curve of the River, not indeed the line of exquisite Beauty as at Herworth Croft, but . . . ," "the river in wild turns below."

There were "black" chasms and "frost shattered chasms of stone—stone cataracts." There was one where "two streams run athwart each other." Elsewhere a "ridgy mountain" runs down and "enfolds the scene." There was an "encircled" lake, a hill "running slant down into a Lake" with "a chasm, then a Hill steep as a nose running behind the embracing Giant's arms with a chasm interposed." Some hills "intermitted on each side." A wood sloped down to a "serpent river." At Scale Force he found the chasm "so wildly wooded that the mosses & wet weeds & perilous Tree increase the Horror of the rocks"; where the chasm deepens, he said, he "never saw Trees on rock Zigzag in their Lines more beautifully." There was "a Hill in a curve . . . green on the Top, but all else black & precipitous snow-patched & snow-streaked all over. . . . A House or Outhouse, of most savage aspect—. . . three slender but stately Trees behind."[46]

Some of these images suggest *Kubla Khan*—the deep and dark chasms, undoubtedly "romantic," the excessively winding streams, and so on; but the likenesses are generic

rather than particular, and much the same could have
been found in Mrs. Radcliffe without recourse to the Lake
District. Accurately visualized, the differences between
these scenes and those of *Kubla Khan* are even greater than
they seem, for Coleridge and Wordsworth were making
their tour between October 27 and November 18, hardly a
season in the north of England to suggest oriental luxuries.
Yet the echoes are there, and perhaps all the more note-
worthy from the fact that the scene itself could hardly
have suggested the poem. Certain words stand out—*enfolds* (and *encircled* and *embracing*), *savage, stately, slant,*
the "bright shadow" of a tower in the water, *mazy, athwart,
intermit*. The last two words Coleridge seems particularly
to have liked during this autumn and the following year.

Through the six months of 1799 in which Coleridge was
seeing so much scenery, both new and familiar, he was
perpetually making comparisons. In Germany he was reminded of the Wye and the coombs about Porlock and
Stowey; in south Devon he made comparisons with
"Quantock, Porlock, Culbone, and Linton"; finally, now
in the north, he was reminded of the "Somersetshire
Hills," the cleaves of south Devon, and again the Wye. It
is scarcely an exaggeration to say that he was haunted
during these months by the mingled succession of scenes,
particularly of cavern, waterfall, stream, steep slanting
chasm, and encircled places. He was equally haunted, I
think, by doubt of his own descriptive powers.

The unprecedented spate of descriptive letter-writing
and note-taking, unmatched elsewhere in Coleridge's life,
which opened with the letters from Germany in May,
closed fittingly with a letter, this time not his own but
from Wordsworth to him, begun on the following Christmas Eve just after the Wordsworths had moved into
Dove Cottage. This description, one of the most elaborate
to be found anywhere in Wordsworth's letters and obviously composed with care (praised by Knight as "one of

the best specimens of his prose writing that we possess"),[47] is an account of the journey with Dorothy, mostly on foot, from Sockburn to Grasmere. The prevailing theme is waterfalls, and after brief accounts of two others Wordsworth exerted himself fully upon the third, Hardraw Force. The season was December, and there was a kind of cave, hung with icicles and "fountains of ice"; there were "fragments" of rock encased in ice white as snow. But— here is the striking feature—before he had done with the cave, though the scene was midwinter, he had turned it into summer, had introduced Arabia, the "heat of a July noon," and "a long summer day to dream in," with special note of this summer-winter contrast. He had also used the expressions "momently," "interrupted," and "midway in its fall" to describe the "irregular fits of strength" with which the cataract fell. And the scene was "enchanted" beyond his powers to express. The whole passage is important enough to quote. He and Dorothy approached the cataract from below, walking up the brookside between "winding rocky banks" until it came into full view.

It appeared to throw itself in a narrow line from a lofty wall of rock; the water which shot manifestly to some distance from the rock seeming from the extreme height of the fall to be dispersed before it reached the bason. . . . After cautiously sounding our way over *stones of all colours and sizes encased in the clearest ice* formed by the spray of the waterfall, we found the rock which before had seemed a *perpendicular wall extending itself over us like the cieling* [sic] *of a huge cave;* from the summit of which the water shot directly over our heads into a bason and among *fragments of rock wrinkled over with masses of ice*, white as snow, or rather as D. says like congealed froth. The water fell at least ten yards from us and we stood directly behind it, the excavation not so deep in the rock as to impress any feeling of darkness, but lofty and magnificent . . . a scene so exquisitely beautiful. . . . On the summit of the cave were three festoons or rather wrinkles in the rock . . . hung with icicles of various length, and . . . the stream shot from between the rows of icicles *in irregular fits of strength and with a body of water that momently varied.* Sometimes it threw itself into the bason in one continued curve, sometimes it was *interrupted almost midway in its fall* and, being blown towards us, part of the water fell at no great distance from our feet like the heaviest thunder shower. . . . The rocks on each side, which, joining with the sides of the cave, formed the vista of the brook were chequered with three diminutive waterfalls or rather veins of water each of which was a miniature of *all that summer and winter can produce of a delicate beauty.* The rock in the centre of these falls where the water was most abundant, deep black . . . and hung with *streams and fountains of ice and icicles* that in some places seemed to conceal the verdure of the plants and the variegated colours of the rocks and in some places to render their hues more splendid. *I cannot express to you the enchanted effect produced by this Arabian scene* of colour as the wind blew aside the great waterfall behind which we stood and hid and revealed each of these faery cataracts *in irregular succession* or displayed them with various gradations of distinctness, as the intervening spray was thickened or dispersed.—In the luxury of our imaginations we could not help feeding on the *pleasure which in the heat of a July noon this cavern would spread through a frame exquisitely sensible.* That *huge rock* of ivy on the right, the bank winding round on the left with all its living foliage, and the breeze stealing up the valley and bedewing the cavern with the faintest imaginable spray. And then the murmur of the water, the quiet, the seclusions, and a *long summer day to dream in!*[48]

There can be little question that a connection of some sort exists between this letter of Wordsworth and *Kubla Khan.* It stands, however, in a more ambiguous relation to the poem than does Coleridge's description written in Germany, because in Wordsworth's account the contrast of ice-hung cave and summer heat was not present in the actual scene but was added gratuitously by the imagination of the writer. In the caverns of Coleridge's Harz tour the contrast had been a striking feature of the scene itself; in describing it as he did, Coleridge had merely stuck to the facts. In Wordsworth's letter the icy cave is almost the only feature of the real scene that bears more than a distant likeness to *Kubla Khan;* even the general features of winding streams, rocks, and chasms would scarcely strike the spectator as a likeness in midwinter. The other resemblances are rather verbal and imaginative than factual. It is quite as likely, therefore, that the poem had printed its language upon the descriptive prose of Wordsworth's letter as that the letter should have influenced the poem.

What does seem certain in the midst of these uncertainties is that between May, 1799, and the end of the following winter there was a concentration of interest among Wordsworth, Coleridge, and Southey upon many of the images, ideas, and words that we find in *Kubla Khan*. The summer-winter contrast of the "huge fragments" of rock that were like "hail" in Kubla's summer garden, as well as the "miracle" of the "sunny dome" and "caves of ice," have their parallel in Wordsworth's "fragments of rock wrinkled over" with white ice and his ice-adorned December cave that suddenly turned into Arabia, as well as in the wintry cave with summery verdure of Coleridge's German tour. This mingling of summer and winter was more than a passing thought with Wordsworth too, for it figures in his poem *The Brothers*, which in this same Christmas Eve letter he said he had begun, and which was founded upon an incident he and Coleridge had heard of during their tour in November. The contrasts in that poem involve "winter's work" on a "July evening"; a sailor "between the tropics" hearing in imagination his northern inland sounds of waterfall, caves, and trees; a "May-storm" that brings "January snow"—all in the early part of the poem.[49] On their excursion together the two poets must have been discussing their work, comparing German scenes with those before them, probably discussing the poetic use of these very summer-winter contrasts and probably also the theories and difficulties of descriptive writing—with the theories of Lessing, too, hovering in the air. It was a period that seems to have produced some of the most elaborate and conscious prose description that either poet ever wrote. Other reminders of *Kubla Khan* appear in poems Wordsworth was composing at that time. He interrupted his work on *The Brothers* to write *Hart-Leap Well*, in which he described the building of a "pleasure-house" (also called a "palace") beside a "fountain in a dell"; and sometime in 1800 he described a hillock of stones as "the rude embryo of a little Dome Or Pleasure-house, once destined to be built."[50] Emphasis upon the process of building, as well as upon pleasure-house and dome, is here.

Images of ice-caves and heat-cold or summer-winter contrasts were almost epidemic that year in Coleridge's circle. There was *Thalaba* with its two "rills" of contrasted "boiling" and "intensely cold" water, the summer heat opposed to the cool chambers "hollowed" beneath the pleasure-bridges with their fruits incased in ice, and the plan for an "ice cave" and a damsel's palace of ice set in a garden made balmy by magic fiery streams. In a comic ode written shortly before Christmas, Southey used the image of snow falling upon tropical sands.[51] The second *Annual Anthology*, which was in preparation during the autumn of 1799, contained Cottle's *Markoff: A Siberian Eclogue* with the line "I, who in caves of ice have oft reclined"; and the first *Anthology*, which had just appeared, included Southey's "monodrama" *Chimalpoca*, in which "the icy caverns of the North" are said to represent the tropical notion of hell. Of this image Coleridge shortly afterward wrote an inversion: "I am sitting by a fire in a rug great coat. Your room is doubtless to a greater degree air tight than mine, or your notions of Tartarus would veer round to the Greenlander's creed. It is most barbarously cold."[52]

Maurice's image of ice in a cave in the mountains of Cashmere, which Lowes believed suggested the "caves of ice" in *Kubla Khan*, lacks this characteristic feature of heat-cold contrast that particularly made Kubla's caves "a miracle of rare device." It, too, however, presumably came before Coleridge's eyes in 1799, for the Gutch Memorandum Book, in which Coleridge had recorded it, almost certainly was in use while Coleridge and Southey were working together in August and September and undoubtedly was used during the succeeding months (see Appendix II).

The region about Bristol, which Coleridge had known since before his marriage, had its caverns, its underground river, and its subterranean lake that ebbed and flowed. Shortly after his return from Germany he must have encountered these again, and even the fabulous River Alpheus itself, not at first hand but, possibly for literary purposes more memorably, in print. The issue of the *Monthly Magazine* current when Coleridge reached Stowey and the preceding issue—those published in June and July, 1799—contain interesting accounts of the "State of Manners &c at Bristol" and the "Environs of Bristol." Who the author, "A. B.," was I do not know, but he must have been someone belonging to the circle of Coleridge and Southey.[53] The first instalment, which surveys the eminent citizens, mentions very few persons outside that circle: among clergymen only the Rev. John Estlin, Coleridge's friend; of printers, only Cottle. Most flattering mention is made of Southey, Cottle, George Dyer, even the newcomer Humphry Davy, who was not yet much known, as well as Dr. Beddoes. Lovell too, the brother-in-law of Coleridge and Southey, though he was already dead and had never been eminent, is mentioned kindly. The particular persons selected for notice would hardly have been the choice of any writer outside the group of Southey's friends. The Bristol Library is described, and George Catcott, its sublibrarian, whom Coleridge knew, is characterized as "remarkable in his younger days for riding over five inch bridges, clambering steeples, and exploring subterranean caverns." Explaining the diminishing commerce of Bristol, the author refers to the African slave trade: "Like some fabulous river that I forget, it disappears in one place, only to rise in another." That river, no doubt, is the Alpheus of legend. It is also Coleridge's Alph, as well as the Alpheus of *Lycidas*. The Sicilian-fountain end of the tale was introduced later in the year, along with the snow-tropic contrast and a serpent with powers that recall *Christabel*, into Southey's ode to the cold in his head.

In the subsequent article on the environs of Bristol, the writer turns from eminent persons to scenery. He gives an account of "the unfortunate cavern called Pen-park hole," where a ghost had once been seen: "At the bottom is a lake of water, which is supposed to ebb and flow; but according to what stated times is not known." There are dangerous holes above this "Avernian receptacle." Two miles away in distance, but immediately following it in the article, is "a conspicuous place, called Blaze-Castle," situated "on an eminence in the midst of a wood, above which it towers to a great height." It is "a fanciful appendage to the pleasure-grounds" of a gentleman and is of "very con-siderable" size. The article goes on to describe Brockley Coomb, "a deep, rocky vale, running transversely into the side of an immense hill, and forming the coolest, and most sequestered summer's retreat imaginable. The trees here are of the largest growth." Along the sides of this vale are "masses of rock, jutting out above the stateliest trees," with other equally tall trees above. The place had been familiar to Coleridge as early as 1795 and had impressed him then sufficiently to inspire a poem.[54] But it was the writer in the *Monthly* and not Coleridge's younger poetic self who particularly noted the line of the coomb running "transversely" into the hill, with its immense trees—all the details of Kubla's "deep romantic chasm" that "slanted" down the hill "athwart" the wood of cedars.

The article in the *Monthly* proceeds to a description of the rocks at Cheddar and the "winding vale," narrow and exceedingly deep, with sides "in many places, an hundred and thirty yards in perpendicular height." Here a subter-ranean passage is said to connect with "the famous sub-terranean cavern, called Wookey-Hole, about six miles off"—source of the River Axe (the existence of this passage was said to have been traced by a lady's lapdog that fell in at one end and emerged at the other). There is an account, too, of a spectacular hurling through the air of huge rock fragments along the Avon. The scene is near Clifton, where a Roman ruin and cliffs tower above the river. From these, "great portions of rock are frequently dislodged, and scattered in all directions. Masses of stone, on these occasions, larger than any among our druidical remains, are sometimes seen whirled from an eminence of seventy or eighty yards."[55] There can be little doubt that Coleridge read all this soon after his return to England, for he kept up with the *Monthly* regularly. It is all very English, to be sure, and not in the least oriental. But Mr. Wylie Sypher some years ago showed that some of the scenery of *Kubla Khan* might be traceable to that of Cheddar, Wookey Hole, and Culbone rather than to Eastern travelers' accounts.[56] These descriptions in the *Monthly Magazine* would have recalled to Coleridge sights that he had seen but would also have added to them. The "great portions of rock" that were occasionally "whirled" eighty yards through the air he was not likely to have witnessed; yet they remind one of the "huge fragments" hurled by Kubla's fountain. The writer in the magazine compressed into a single vivid article what for an actual observer would have meant scattered impressions gained from numerous excursions.

4. COLERIDGE'S READING, 1799: PURCHAS, "THALABA," "GEBIR," AND OTHERS—MILTON ESPECIALLY

The printed word interested Coleridge no less than the outdoor world, and the weeks following his return to England were not filled solely with scenery viewed at first or even at second hand. There was poetry and the intention, at least, of producing more. There was the plan for "Mahomet" in hexameters. On the part of Southey, the

"Dom-Daniel," now transformed into "Thalaba," was still progressing, and Coleridge was reading it. Sandwiched into the middle of Southey's accounts of progress is his excited discovery of *Gebir*, which he had been reviewing for the *Critical*. He "would go an hundred miles to see the anonymous author." Coleridge read that poem too. Writing to Southey shortly after his return from Exeter, he compared the genius of Bampfylde to that of Charles Lamb and "the Gebir-man." His interest was more than momentary; during the following winter in London he was still trying to learn the identity of the author. The work seems to have gone the rounds of Coleridge's circle. By the end of October Lamb had evidently seen it, and Southey continued to reread and praise it.[57] Landor's poem must have been firmly printed on Coleridge's mind through conversation as well as reading during the five weeks with his brother-in-law's enthusiasm.

Most of the sources to which Lowes traced the imagery of *Kubla Khan* came before Coleridge's attention—either by actual reading or by reminders—during the late summer and autumn of 1799. At this time nearly all Southey's reading was of the East, and Coleridge evidently shared at least some of it. Southey was "gutting the libraries" at Exeter, he told Cottle while Coleridge was still with him, and "laying in a good stock of notes and materials." He had found books of travels into Egypt, the Levant, Persia, the East Indies.[58] Other books he had with him, and many notes from his reading had already been prepared for the ornamentation of *Thalaba*. These refer to almost every one of the sources mentioned by Lowes. Some we know Coleridge had read in earlier years; of others there is no record apart from Lowes's hypothesis. But it is certain that most of them would have come to his attention now through Southey and other channels.

James Bruce's *Travels To Discover the Source of the Nile* is one of the works that Lowes believed had a very great influence on *Kubla Khan*. The sacred River Alph, the fountains, and the human figures at the end, all, he thought, were deeply indebted to Bruce and in a lesser degree to earlier accounts of the sources of the Nile, particularly that of Herodotus. Some of the parallels drawn between Bruce and *Kubla Khan* are exceedingly thin—such mere words or phrases, for example, as "romantic," "fountains of the Nile," "island of green turf." Still, Bruce and the Nile probably enter somewhere into the ancestry of the poem. In 1799 reminders of Bruce were thick and in at least one instance were coupled with the very chapters in Herodotus that Lowes thought significant. Southey refers to Bruce's *Travels* in *Thalaba* and quotes from it in his notes. Also, shortly after Coleridge returned from Göttingen he must have read some discussion relating to Bruce and the sources and course of the Nile printed in the *Monthly Magazine*, together with a translation of Herodotus' chapters on the subject. The author, by what appears to be an odd coincidence in view of Coleridge's recent residence there, was "Professor Heeren of Göttingen." How this German Professor Heeren, who knew little if any English, got into the *Monthly* at just this time with a translation *from Greek into English* of the very chapters of Herodotus to which Lowes traced something of *Kubla Khan*, is a mystery beyond the range of the present chapter (see Appendix I). But Coleridge was reading the *Monthly Magazine* regularly, if not also writing for it, and must therefore have seen the professor's contribution after its publication, if not before.

Bartram's *Travels* is almost the only book regarded as an important source for *Kubla Khan* that Southey did not quote in his notes for *Thalaba* and that is not mentioned in his and Coleridge's correspondence of 1799. But that book too Coleridge may have been rereading or looking into; for it may have been while preparing his contributions for the *Annual Anthology* of 1800 that he added to the poem *This*

Lime-Tree Bower the footnote taken explicitly from Bartram.[59]

Besides the contagion of Southey's reading, writing, and conversation, Coleridge had two special reasons for indulging in a spree of travel literature. One was the poem on Mohammed, already noticed. The other was a project for bread and butter that seems to have escaped comment from Coleridge's biographers. It appears to have been a geographical book of some sort, probably an early version of the project he offered a year later to Godwin as

... a system of Geography, taught by a re-writing of the most celebrated Travels into the different climates of the world, choosing for each climate one Traveller, but interspersing among his adventures all that was interesting in incident or observation from all former or after travellers or voyagers: annexing to each travel a short essay, pointing out what facts in it illustrate what laws of mind, &c. If a bookseller of spirit would undertake this work, I have no doubt of its being a standard school-book. . . . I mentioned it to you because I thought this sort of reading would be serviceable to your mind: but if you reject the offer, mention it to no one, for in that case I will myself undertake it.

Coleridge first mentioned his plan indefinitely in a letter to Southey on September 25, 1799: "I shall go on with the Mohammed—(tho' some thing I must do for pecuniary emoluments). I think of writing a schoolbook—." On the thirtieth he mentioned it again, as "a lucrative speculation (and it will be an entertaining job)." He wished Southey— and this is what seems to mark it as some sort of historico-geographical work more or less like that described later to Godwin—to borrow for the purpose from William Taylor "Herder's Ideas for the History of the Human Race [and] Zimmerman's Geographie der Menschen." The idea may have sprouted in part from the travel books with which Southey and he had occupied themselves in Exeter. It would indeed be "an entertaining job" for Coleridge to tinker with, if not to execute. Two weeks later he referred to it again. "Mohammed I will not forsake," he wrote, "but my money-book I must write first." He was probably carrying on at least the painless part of that task, the reading; in October he went to Bristol in search of material for it. The project may have been alive during the winter in London as one of the "compilations for booksellers" that engaged him. At any rate, the plan described to Godwin the following autumn was not an isolated notion, for he had evidently been immersed in travel books. In one letter he spiced a solemn reflection on Baptism and Eternal Life with not very elegant Eastern images from his reading—"the Llama's dung-pellet, or the cow-tail which the dying Brahmin clutches convulsively." He urged Godwin to read more travels and voyages. He had another plan for Godwin's pen—to write a play on "the death of Myrza as related in the Holstein Ambassador's Travels into Persia"—and he proceeded to give the page reference for this in "Harris's Collections."[60]

Thus, for some fifteen months after Coleridge returned from Germany, the travelers and geographers were engaging his attention, at least sporadically. One book of travels, *Purchas His Pilgrimage*, we know unequivocally that Coleridge had been reading when he composed *Kubla Khan*. Not only does his preface tell us he fell asleep over it, but his opening lines clearly paraphrase a passage from it. Lowes found numerous links between this book and Purchas's *Pilgrimes*, which indicated to him that the second as well as the first influenced *Kubla Khan*, in consequence, he supposed, of the unconscious associative memory that called up a formerly read passage of one work from a present reading of the other. But it seems quite certain from other sources that Coleridge must have been reading the *Pilgrimes*, if not also the *Pilgrimage*, at some time during these fifteen months, for Lowes pointed out that a passage from the same volume of it that described "Xandu" crept into *The Ancient Mariner* between the first edition (published in September, 1798, apparently just after Coleridge left England) and the second edition of 1800.[61]

[194]

Though there is no clear proof that Coleridge was reading the *Pilgrimage* then also, circumstances make it highly probable. Southey used both works for *Thalaba*. He quoted from the *Pilgrimage* in the notes to stanzas that were completed while he was with Coleridge in August, 1799, as well as in the Aloadin section later on. The *Pilgrimage* would have been of the greatest interest for Coleridge's schoolbook because of its combined historical and geographical character: it sets forth, as the title-page says, "Relations of the World and the Religions observed in all Ages and Places discovered, from the Creation unto this Present." As Book III also contains an account of the life, religion, and successors of Mohammed, Coleridge would have had every reason to take up the work during the summer or autumn of 1799 as material for both his poetical "Mohammed" and his schoolbook.

Some earlier readings would have been revived in the memory of Coleridge in 1799 through their reflection in the Gutch Memorandum Book, which appears to have been in use again after his return from Germany.[62] There would have been reminders of Bartram, of the cave of Plato's *Phaedo*, of the Book of Tobit with its demon-lover. A demon-lover theme of quite another sort, with the couples multiplied fifty fold, recorded in the notebook from Milton's *History of Britain*, was being discussed by Southey, Humphry Davy, and Coleridge between August and October, 1799. "Dioclesian King of Syria / fifty Daughters in a ship unmann'd / same as Danaides—land in England—commit / with Devils": this was Coleridge's cryptic version of it. Davy had plans for a poem on the subject.

Two apparent echoes of the notebook occurred in *The Devil's Thoughts;* and at least three others appear in *Thalaba:* one a project mentioned twice in the notebook, of turning Burnet's chapter on mountains into English blank verse; a second, the brief solitary note "Cavern-candle," which suggests that most gruesome of all cavern candles with the dead hand for candlestick in *Thalaba;* and the third the odd entry, "A dunghill at a distance some-times smells like musk, and a dead dog like elder flowers." I do not know whether Coleridge had read this or whether his nose told him; at any rate, one of Southey's choicer demons in the same candle-lighted cavern exclaims: "Thou should'st . . . die civet-like at last In the dung-perfume of thy sanctity." (The civet, it will be understood, was a common source of musk.) In the same cavern of *Thalaba,* lighted by the same "enchanted" candle, are the two snakes with "swelling necks" that take us back to *Gebir* and forward to *Christabel.* And between Southey's cavern candle and his odoriferous musk-dunghill, the cavern itself is described in terms reminiscent at once of the sunless ancestral abode of the dead in *Gebir* and Kubla's measure-less cavern with its underground river and intermittent, rising and falling fountain:

> *a spacious vault,*
> Where the black *river-fountains burst* their way.
> Now as a whirlwind's *force*
> Had center'd on the spring,
> The *gushing* flood *roll'd* up;
> And now the deaden'd roar
> Echoed beneath, *collapsing as it sunk*
> Within a *dark abyss,*
> Adown whose *fathomless gulphs* the eye was lost
> [V, 32; italics mine].

Dim flames "flung" through the cavern their uncertain light into the "black darkness of the vault." Besides the images themselves of dark measureless ("fathomless") cavern, river, rocks, and geyser-like fountain, there is a fairly thick concentration of words that suggest *Kubla Khan: sunk, fountain, forced, burst, vault,* and not far off *enchanted, Holy,* and *unholy.* In these nine stanzas Southey spun a complex web. How many of his threads were bor-rowed from Coleridge and how many lent it is not possible to say. At any rate, the Gutch Memorandum Book as well as *Kubla Khan* is involved, and the dates range from August or September to October or perhaps early November, 1799.

Kubla's River Alph obviously inherits its name from the Greek river Alpheus. Lowes cites Pausanius as a source for this, and Pausanius is cited by Southey at the very beginning of *Thalaba*. Besides the "fabulous" underground river of the *Monthly Magazine* in 1799, the Gutch notebook, and the stream and waterfall that he saw sink into the earth in Germany, Coleridge would have met the Alpheus in a literary setting during that same autumn, for he was then reading the *Aeneid*, another source cited by Lowes. Phrases in *Kubla Khan* have been traced to Collins's ode on *The Passions*, and early in December, again writing to Southey, Coleridge mentioned Collins's odes.[63] Poetically, however, the presiding influence over *Kubla Khan* was not Purchas or any of the travelers or *Thalaba*, but Milton.

Echoes from the fourth book of *Paradise Lost* were noticed long ago in Coleridge's fragment. The purely poetical aspects of this influence will be considered later on, but the subject has something to do also with dates, for Coleridge was more than usually haunted by Milton during the months that followed his return from Germany. His admiration for Milton had begun early and continued as long as he lived, though the central place in his pantheon was eventually given over to Shakespeare. In 1795 he had obviously been reading both Spenser and Milton intensively and acquisitively. After that there was a lull, during which Milton was reflected in his poetry and correspondence only now and then, as in *The Nightingale* of 1798, which recalled the earlier *To the Nightingale* of 1795. *Gebir* and conversation with Southey toward the end of the summer of 1799 would have brought Milton into focus again for Coleridge, if nothing else did, for the Miltonism of *Gebir* was noted by reviewers and could not be missed, and

Southey avowedly had *Paradise Lost* in mind, particularly the fourth book, when he composed *Thalaba*.[64] One of Coleridge's stanzas in *The Devil's Thoughts* refers to lines in the midst of the Paradise scene of Book IV, when the Devil, speaking as a ventriloquist's dummy for Coleridge, claims intellectual kinship with a bookseller:

> He [the Devil] went into a rich bookseller's shop,
>   Quoth he! we are both of one college!
> For I sate myself, like a cormorant, once
>   Upon the tree of knowledge.

When it appeared in the *Morning Post* of September 6, 1799, the stanza was annotated: "This anecdote is related by that most interesting of the Devil's Biographers, Mr. John Milton, in his *Paradise Lost*, and we have here the Devil's own testimony to the truth and accuracy of it."[65] So the one scene of *Paradise Lost* that was unmistakably imprinted upon *Kubla Khan* was specifically in Coleridge's mind in September, 1799. It must have remained there too, or else returned, for it was during that winter that Coleridge recorded his remarkable "continued Dream, representing visually & audibly all Milton's Paradise Lost." The topography of Milton's Paradise is the topography of Kubla's; and even Coleridge's "incense-bearing" trees I think stem from an elaborate simile in Milton's scene, one that Southey also transplanted bodily into *Thalaba*.[66]

Southey and Davy apparently were reading Milton's *History of Britain* (the source of Coleridge's note about Diocletian's daughters and the fifty demon-lovers) during the autumn; in late September Coleridge was ordering (and probably had already been reading in Exeter) Milton's prose works and two weeks later was referring to them again. Milton's poetry left conspicuous, and evidently conscious, traces upon at least one poem written in December, the *Ode to Georgiana, Duchess of Devonshire;* and a notebook entry warrants the guess that he may have had *L'Allegro* and *Il Penseroso* specifically in mind in November.[67]

Milton's *Lycidas* has numerous connections with *Kubla Khan*. For one thing, it provides the most familiar English reference to the River Alpheus and the Fountain Arethusa. But another point of contact bears upon the date. Coleridge, it will be recalled, wished to build his dome with music "loud and long." Now "loud" music is not very romantic, unless it is martial, or perhaps sung by a bird. As described by poets, even unromantic poets, music is apt to be soft, low, lofty, melodious, even majestic; rarely is it just plain "loud." Not even Gray, striving for a good deal of noise in *The Progress of Poesy* and *The Bard*, makes it so. Coleridge, it is true, used the epithet occasionally, for the notes of birds, the music of the spheres and of angels, the hymn of piety, and the music of rejoicing (the Hermit and the "loud bassoon" of *The Ancient Mariner*). *Loud*, however, is not what one would expect in the context of *Kubla Khan*, with its maid and dulcimer and its Paradise garden. One poetic passage this epithet almost inevitably awakens in the memory of a reader—Milton's "Begin, and somwhat loudly sweep the string," in *Lycidas*. In 1799 and 1800 Coleridge was haunted by "loud" music *of poetry*, I suspect because he was haunted by *Lycidas*, as well as other work of Milton. I do not think he ever used the image in his earlier verse, unless *Kubla Khan* is earlier, or in his later. But in *A Christmas Carol*, published first on Christmas Day, 1799, and written shortly before, he wrote of "sweet Music's loudest note, the Poet's story."[68] In Part II of *Christabel*, which was in progress probably then and certainly in the later months of 1800, Bard Bracy's music is "loud" five times in three different places. The noise is obviously not accidental; it is insistent. "Go thou, with music sweet and loud," says Leoline to the Bard, and shortly afterwards, "Your music so sweet, More loud than your horses' echoing feet! And loud and loud to Lord

Roland call." Bracy himself uses the word in another connection: "I had vowed with music loud To clear yon wood from thing unblest."[69] In all these passages, including the one in *Kubla Khan*, Coleridge apparently had in mind loudness as a special characteristic of poetic inspiration described under the convention of music. It is the same conception in each instance; it is a definite and an unusual one; and it does not appear elsewhere in Coleridge's verse. It reflects, possibly, not only Milton but his preoccupation with the question of his own "immortal bardship," a preoccupation that crept at that time even into a jocular letter to his penmaker.

With all these things in view—the continuing interest of Coleridge himself and Southey in *Paradise Lost*, especially the Paradise garden of Book IV; the passing around of the Diocletian story, his purchase of Milton's prose and current references to it; and his use of Milton's rhymes and metrical effects, which I shall discuss presently—I know of no other such Miltonic months in Coleridge's life as those running, roughly, from August, 1799, to the spring of 1800. How strong the tie is between these circumstances and *Kubla Khan* can only appear through consideration of Coleridge's stylistic and metrical habits at that time and earlier, and then, finally, through a view of some poetic effects of *Kubla Khan* itself, which I shall try to present later on.

I have surveyed—too fully perhaps, and yet with numerous omissions—some of the sources that are generally believed to underlie the imagery in *Kubla Khan*. As with Milton, so with the others, inspection of available evidence suggests a concentration of those works before Coleridge's eyes or ears shortly after his return from Germany, such as we have no evidence for at any other period. As far as sources go, therefore, the likelihood is great that these materials would have drifted together into a poem at that time rather than have floated to the surface of the poet's mind from possible or actual reading scattered over many earlier years. All the important sources and many of the minor ones that Lowes's elaborate analysis set forth are known to have been before Coleridge's attention in the latter months of 1799 and the early part of 1800. The weight of the evidence from his reading thus favors a late date for the poem, and it is considerably reinforced by the parallels with *Thalaba*, for if *Thalaba* followed *Kubla Khan* by a year or two, as has generally been assumed, we are forced to imagine two accidental, yet elaborate, "catenations" of identical, yet essentially unrelated, reading, one in Coleridge's unconscious mind in 1797 or 1798, and another, conscious and carefully documented, in Southey's preparations for *Thalaba* in 1799. It is not easy to imagine Southey, broad awake, methodically retracing Coleridge's dreaming footsteps.

5. SELF-ECHOES: IMAGERY, LANGUAGE, VERSIFICATION

Any attempt to establish the chronology of a poet's work on evidences of style is a slippery business, as we all know from the studies of Shakespeare; but style does nevertheless throw light on the matter sometimes. With respect to *Kubla Khan*, something can be learned from a few points in the language and something more from the meter and other matters. Coleridge was not averse to echoing his own past poetry. This being so, we cannot always draw reliable conclusions about the dates of his poems from resemblances of theme or image. His earlier poetry yields more than one "rude romantic glen" and magic fountain, more than one Muse or Castalian spring of inspiration, and many dreams. As early as 1796 there are Passions in a "roundelay" that "weave an holy spell," and, then or even earlier, an "arched dome"; as late as 1811–12 the poet's "magic circle" of "pleasure" appears in a lecture.[70] More often, however, he repeated himself or played variations upon the same theme either at the same time or when circumstances placed before him his own past words. Making due allowance for such revivals out of his distant past, we still, I think, find in *Kubla Khan* numerous and significant affinities with the poetry of 1799 and 1800 that would lead us to place it there, tentatively at least, if we had no other evidence to go on.[71]

The self-echoes linking *Kubla Khan* with this later date appear in the imagery, language, and metrical pattern. Of these, the imagery is the least important because it is least distinctive and can to some extent be matched in kind, if not in quality, by Coleridge's own poetry of other periods and by that of his contemporaries. Yet it tells something.

A number of translations or adaptations from the German poets belong to the period following Coleridge's return to England or possibly, some of them, to the latter part of his stay abroad. The alterations and expansions that Coleridge made in these give some hint of his current interests. A cove or inlet in the original of one poem, for example, is transformed into a "sea-cave," and a path that merely wound cursorily up the hill becomes one that "stole in mazes up."[72] His poem *On a Cataract*, from Stolberg's *Unsterblicher Jüngling*, opens on a sort of "measureless-to-man" note that does, to be sure, largely correspond to the original. The subject is a stream that issues from a rock, and Stolberg himself had said of it: "Kein Sterblicher sah Die Wiege des Starken," which Coleridge renders quite literally, "Never mortal saw The cradle of the strong one." But he exaggerated or largely invented the cataract and cavern elements, just as he had added a cave to the preceding poem. The "Felsenkluft" from which Stolberg's stream flowed becomes for Coleridge "the cell of thy hidden nativity" or, in his subtitle, a "cavern near the Summit of a Mountain Precipice"; the "fountain" is gratuitously made "slumberless" and "ceaseless" and is born in a "holy" twilight. Coleridge adds an "antistrophe" of his own:

> Above thee the cliff inaccessible;—
> Thou at once full-born
> Madd'nest in thy joyance,
> Whirlest, shatter'st, splitt'st. . . .

Coleridge increased the violence of Stolberg's imagery; inclosed the ravine into a cavern, with its interior never seen by man; and added the images of shattering, splitting rock that remind one slightly of the rock fragments hurled by Kubla's subterranean river, and of the *Monthly Magazine*'s rocks "whirled" from the precipice above the Avon.[73]

In another adaptation from Stolberg, the *Hymn to the Earth*, Coleridge writes of the poet's harp, his song, and his voice that "floats"; of "joy" that inspires his music, and a "stream flowing in *brightness*." These words and images bear a greater resemblance to his own "dream" of *Kubla Khan* than to the lines of Stolberg, who barely mentions a song in passing as "Feiergesange" and later "heiligen Liedern."[74] The epithet *measureless* is used here too—its sole appearance anywhere in Coleridge's poetry except for the two occasions in *Kubla Khan*—though there is nothing in the German original to suggest either the word or the image. Another lyric from Schiller, *The Visit of the Gods*, closes somewhat as does *Kubla Khan*, with the poet, his lyre, the underground River Styx, and the magnification of himself as godlike. In this Coleridge is merely following his original, except that he turns Schiller's "come" to "float" and invents a phrase in which he can use "bright" once more. Here it is the gods who are "bright"; generally at this period it was his streams—"this stream so brightly flowing."[75] E. H. Coleridge also placed among the poems of 1799, though he said there is no evidence by which it can be dated, a two-line translation from Schiller illustrating "The Ovidian Elegiac Metre," in which the sole image is of a rising and falling fountain:

> In the hexameter rises the fountain's silvery column;
> In the pentameter aye falling in melody back.[76]

Finally, a stage direction in the translation of *Wallenstein*, on which Coleridge was engaged during the winter of 1799–1800, presents the heroine playing a "symphony" and then singing a song. The passage introduces one upon which Coleridge bestowed exceptional pains, evidently considering the song a poetic highlight in the drama. Schiller had mentioned no playing of a "symphony": his word was *präludiert*. Once, in 1796, Coleridge had used the word *symphony* in the verse of *Joan of Arc*. There it was the poet's music played upon the harp taken from "Freedom's trophied dome." "Such symphony requires best instrument," he had said there. Only in *Kubla Khan* and *Wallenstein* did he use the word again (in connection, at any rate, with his poetry), and in these there are the like circumstances of a maid playing the symphony and singing a supernal song. "A guitar lies on the table," he wrote in *Wallenstein*, and the heroine Thekla "seizes it as by a sudden emotion, and after she has played a while an irregular and melancholy symphony, she falls gradually into the music and sings." The Abyssinian maid's instrument was a dulcimer, but she too played a "symphony" and sang a song. Again the association favors 1799 or 1800 for *Kubla Khan*, for Coleridge had then been hearing Landor's "symphony of lutes" as well as the dulcimer in *Gebir* and had perhaps also re-encountered his own early "symphony" when foraging through his old verse for Southey's *Annual Anthology*. As we shall see, Coleridge's verse of 1799–1800 carries numerous echoes of his early verse of 1793–96, and so does *Kubla Khan*.[77]

I have not been able to keep imagery and words entirely apart. The shorter translations of Coleridge show kinship to *Kubla Khan*, sometimes through his choice of the piece itself, sometimes through his alterations. Caves, with or without underground rivers bursting from them, are added to the originals. Opportunities that do not exist are invented for using the words *bright, ceaseless, measureless, inaccessible, holy, float, symphony*—all words or images prominent in *Kubla Khan*. The translations reinforce a number of other indications that at this period of his life— from the time in Germany when he questioned his own power of descriptive writing—Coleridge was exceptionally conscious of the question of his poethood. He expressed the thought once jocularly, referring to his poetical self as "my immortal Bardship," in a letter of October 8, 1799, that closes: "Given from Apollo's temple in the odoriferous Lime-Grove—alias Street—in what Olympiad our In-spiration knows not, but of the usurping Christian Æra 1799, Oct. 8. / S. T. Coleridge." This note is to his pen-maker about pens—"Hexameter and Pentameter Pens —."[78] The note is a joke, but the preoccupation with his poetic immortality at that time was very real. It was the theme of the lines he rendered from Schiller, in which the poet is lifted from earth to his proper dwelling with the gods on Olympus, and of his addition to Stolberg, in the *Hymn*, of poetic harp, song, joy-inspired music. It is also the theme of the closing lines of *Kubla Khan*.

Certain original poems written after Coleridge's return from Germany exhibit other parallels to *Kubla Khan*, chiefly verbal ones. I have already spoken of Coleridge's unusual use in 1799 and 1800, and not elsewhere in his poetry, of the word *loud* to describe the music of poetic inspiration. The *Lines Composed in a Concert-Room*, which may have been written while Coleridge was with Southey at Exeter, were first published on September 24, 1799, and Coleridge still had them in mind to revise for the *Annual Anthology* in December.[79] Here we have a poem of about the same length as *Kubla Khan* that opens in a quite differ-ent vein but soon shifts to the theme of music produced out of the poet's past recollection. A man breathes "sad airs, so wild and slow" into his flute, but more particularly the poet addresses a "dear Maid" whom he would seek again:

> *Such songs* in *such* a mood to hear thee *sing*,
> It were a *deep delight!*

This is very close indeed to the words of Kubla's poet: if he could but recall the vision of the maid (Abyssinian), her "song" would give him "such a deep delight"—and so on. As we saw in the last chapter, it is also very like the passage in *Thalaba* about the unintelligible song "that with *such deep* and undefined *delight* Fill'd the surrender'd soul," the song that was also like "a dream of Paradise."[80] This grammatical construction seems to have been running in Coleridge's mind, for in the first act of his translation of *Wallenstein* he used it again: ". . . placed such power In such a hand." Though the expression seems ordinary enough in prose, meter heightens it; moreover, I do not find precisely this in either earlier or later verse of Coleridge.[81] Other verbal echoes of *Kubla Khan* are thick in the lines given over to the maid of the Concert poem: "floating," "ocean" joined with "caves," "fling" (in *Kubla Khan*, "flung"), "brightness," "holier," "stately," "tower'd" and the rhymes *remeasures-pleasures* and *caves-waves* played off against each other very much as they are in *Kubla Khan*. These echoes are all concentrated within nineteen lines in the Concert poem—most of them, in fact, within a bare dozen. Finally, *Lines Composed in a Concert-Room* exhibits the same elaborate patterning of sounds that we find in *Kubla Khan*, a point to be discussed shortly.

Among the other poems of 1799, reminders, somewhat negligible, occur in the small fragment of *Mahomet*. In the *Ode to the Duchess of Devonshire* Coleridge used again conspicuously as a refrain the rhyme of *pleasure-measure;* he wrote there also of dreams, "circlets," and "enchanting music" and employed the epithets *ancestral* (the earliest, apart from *Kubla Khan*, and one of the few appearances of the word anywhere in Coleridge's poetry), *stately*, and *bright*. These are all concentrated within ten lines, yet the subject is entirely distinct from that of either the Concert poem or *Kubla Khan*. *Bright* is a common enough epithet in prose or verse, and Coleridge had used it sometimes earlier in perfunctory or obvious ways to describe eyes or sunlight, or even a vision. But the word is susceptible of highly poetic uses, and of these Coleridge seemed especially aware in 1799. Particularly then he noticed the charm of "bright" waters. The "stream so brightly flowing" of the *Water Ballad* (?1799) and the "bare stream flowing in brightness" of the *Hymn to the Earth* (1799) are but less refined versions of Kubla's "gardens bright with sinuous rills"; and the "bright shadow" on the water reflecting Lyulph's tower, in the account of his tour of the Lakes, belongs to the same order. Such uses of the word were not quite wholly confined to this period—two or three times in the verse of 1793–95 Coleridge wrote something like them, the closest being "river . . . winding bright and full" in 1795—but they are more prominent in 1799 than at any other time, possibly, again, because of Landor, who wrote of "bright-eyed waters" and a "sunbright bay" in *Gebir*, or because of the return to his own early verse.[82]

In *Love*, composed after or during his visit to the north in October and November, 1799, there are again dreams, the poet's song and harp, something resembling a demon-lover who starts up from a "savage den" or "darksome shade" or "green and sunny glade." There is also the expression "midway on the mount."[83] This phrase is one of two, already mentioned in other connections, that deserve attention. *Midway on the wave* (or *mount*, etc.—the noun varies) and *momently* both appear in *Kubla Khan* and nowhere else that I know of in Coleridge's poetry except in pieces composed between autumn, 1799, and spring, 1800. At first glance they seem like trivial expressions likely to appear anywhere by chance, but they are not quite that. *Momently*, in the sense of *recurring at short intervals*, appears not once but twice in *Kubla Khan:* the "fountain momently was forced" and "flung up momently the sacred river." Coleridge used it again that winter in the translation of the first act of *Wallenstein:* "The whole scene moves and bustles momently."[84] Wordsworth used the word in the same sense and in a context almost identical with that of *Kubla Khan* in his letter of Christmas Eve, 1799, from which I have already quoted: "The stream shot from between the rows of icicles in irregular fits of strength and with a body of water that momently varied."

Midway on the waves (*wave*, in the Crewe holograph) is used in *Kubla Khan* to describe the reflection of the dome upon the water. Landor, we saw, used *midway in the wave*, along with "palace," to describe the reflection of the sun's "wheel" in the water, in the "sinuous" shell passage that he later thought had influenced Wordsworth. In *Gebir* the phrase is underlined for the auditory memory by another that holds the same metrical position in the line, "wearied o'er the wave," and by a more notable one in which "the moon appear'd to hang midway betwixt the earth and skies." In Wordsworth's Christmas Eve letter to Coleridge, the very sentence following the "irregular fits" of the stream that "momently varied" described the cataract as sometimes throwing itself in a continued curve, sometimes "interrupted almost *midway in its fall*."[85] All this relating to a stream and waterfall, reinforced by other echoes near by, seems to me too like Coleridge's "sinuous" rills, his river and fountain "flung up momently" with "half-intermitted burst," and the dome's reflection "midway on the wave" to be purely accidental. In *Love*, which was printed just three days before Wordsworth's letter was begun, Coleridge used the metrically similar phrase "midway on the Mount," and about the same time, in *The Piccolomini*, "midway on the ocean." Like *momently*, the phrase, I think, is more significant than at first glance one might suppose. In his earlier poetic practice, Coleridge had used *midway* only prepositionally: "midway the Aonian mount" in 1796 and "midway the smooth and perilous slope reclined" in 1798.[86] He used *midway on* only (unless *Kubla Khan* is an exception) after he had read Landor's most spectacular passage in *Gebir* and within days or weeks of the time that he was seeing the expression in Wordsworth's letter.[87] The commoner syntax of Landor's phrase is at once more graceful and more emphatic; the extra metrical stress laid upon the following preposition gives to the whole phrase a more measured and spaced-out value than *midway the wave* would have. Obviously a poet may use either, according to metrical need; but the fact remains that Coleridge saw the phrase used conspicuously by Landor in August, 1799, and by Wordsworth in December and that, whether by chance or otherwise, he used a similar phrase only in *Kubla Khan, The Piccolomini,* and *Love.* The phrase is particularly conspicuous metrically in *Kubla Khan* because, preceded by "floated," it marks the beginning of a shift from iambic to trochaic movement that continues for several lines and helps to create for the ear a floating effect. The lines are shortened at this point, and the accent backs up on itself, very smoothly; the effect is to transform a forward rhythmical movement to a motionless rocking. Furthermore, as was observed earlier, Coleridge's image as well as his phrase resembles Landor's, for Landor was describing the *sun* as a *palace* with its *circular reflection* and Coleridge the *reflection* of his *sunny dome* (= pleasure-house or palace with semicircular outline). *Midway* was natural for the sun's image on the sea in Landor but is not the expected phrase for a pleasure-house that would be supposed to stand on the river's edge. And Landor's image occurs in the same sentence as his "sinuous shells" with its verbal half-reminder of Kubla's "sinuous rills," the only use Coleridge ever made of the epithet *sinuous* in his poetry. Finally, the word *intermit* occurs in his verse only in *The Piccolomini* and *Kubla Khan* ("half-intermitted" in the latter). Again the significance of the repetition is increased by other factors. The verb, unlike its adjective *intermittent,* is not very common. There is no excuse for it in Schiller's original (the German word is *aufhören,* which, as far as I can learn, never implies recur-

rence and is accurately translatable only as *stop, cease,* or
end). It is, in fact, slightly inappropriate to the context.
The word was evidently running through the mind of
Coleridge late in 1799, for he used it in a letter of October
15 and again in the notes of his tour with Wordsworth on
November 11, though I do not think he used it frequently
during other periods.[88]

Perhaps too much stress has been laid upon these small
phrases and words, but, if so, it is because they struck my
ear more forcibly than did chasms, rills, and some other
scenic furniture. It is common experience that small verbal
habits are picked up, used for a brief time, and then
dropped. This would appear to have happpened in Coleridge's writing with the "loud" music of poetic inspiration,
"ancestral," "momently," "intermit," "midway on the
————," "such a deep delight," of which none appears
earlier in his poetry and only one ("ancestral") afterwards.
Besides these, "slant," "bright" streams, and "symphony," and the *measure-pleasure* rhyme seem particularly, though not exclusively, associated with the same
months. Whether these count for little or much, they are at
any rate consistent with most of the other evidence. In
language and imagery, as well as in the complex network
of its sources, *Kubla Khan* falls into the pattern of Coleridge's writing and other interests of 1799–1800 more
naturally than into that of either of the two preceding
years.

Finally, in verse form also its affinities lie with the later
rather than the earlier dates. The *Ode to Georgiana,
Duchess of Devonshire*, written between December 20 and
23, 1799, has already been mentioned for its verbal echoes
of *Kubla Khan*. It was obviously, and I think quite consciously, written under the influence of Milton's shorter
poems. In one stanza Coleridge employed the most spectacular of all Milton's rhyme effects, that of the monotone
ō, which runs through the sonnet *On the Late Massacre in*

Piemont with no relief but the single *ay*-rhyme at the end. Milton's rhyme-words were *bones, cold, old, Stones, groanes, Fold, roll'd, moans, sow, grow, wo[e]*, and *they, sway, way*. The fourth stanza of Coleridge's *Ode to Georgiana*, though longer than a sonnet and mingling other rhymes, concentrates among twenty-two line-endings *those, owes, groans, tones, roll, soul, rose, woes*, and *day, away*, and reinforces these by other internal rhymes—*owe, growing, moment*. Milton's sonnet

roll'd
Mother with *Infant* down the Rocks.

Coleridge's stanza half echoes this too, with

O'er the growing sense to *roll*,
The *mother* of your *infant's* soul!

The meter of the *Ode to Georgiana* is somewhat Miltonic in other ways and may have been consciously reflecting *Il Penseroso* and *L'Allegro*.[89] Milton had opened each of these poems with ten lines of alternating three and five stresses, and then dropped into tetrameter couplets for the remainder. The effect of the irregular opening carries over so that the reader is hardly aware upon reaching the end that the variations were not continued. The couplets themselves are also varied metrically, for they shift smoothly back and forth between iambic and trochaic effects. Though the whole pattern is systematic and fixed, except for the iambic-trochaic shiftings, the impression that lingers in the reader's ear afterward is of a relatively unfixed form, made up of a prevailing but insubstantial four-stress line varied by lines of three and five stresses. This resembles the metrical effect of both *Kubla Khan* and the *Ode to Georgiana*. The first is written in a variety of five-, four-, and three-stress lines, the prevailing character being that of the four-stress rhythm with which the poem begins and ends, though there are actually about as many pentameter lines. The verse has a more willowy, vagrant air than Milton's but is technically much like it. And when

[211]

Coleridge reaches the lines about "the shadow of the dome of pleasure" and the "damsel with a dulcimer" he too shifts his pattern between iambic and trochaic rhythms in a movement that is important to the whole poetic effect.

The *Ode to Georgiana* follows a similarly irregular pattern. It too is founded on a four-stress base, with good-sized patches of five-stress lines and some of three; it shifts here and there to a trochaic rhythm. Its metrical likeness to *Kubla Khan* is partly disguised by the conspicuous two-line refrain and frequent couplet rhymes, but it exhibits some of the same over-all lightness and varied smoothness that characterize both that poem and the two of Milton. The rhyme pattern also of the *Ode to Georgiana* as a whole resembles that of *Kubla Khan*, with its mingling of alternate, inclosed, and couplet pairings; and these similarities are reinforced by the verbal echoes already mentioned. The *Ode*, we have seen, displays prominently in its refrain the rhyme of *pleasure* and *measure*, which occurs twice in *Kubla Khan*, once as a regular end-rhyme and once as a rather distant interior correspondence of sounds—"pleasure-dome" and "measureless" (ll. 2–4). Milton uses the same rhyme in *L'Allegro* (ll. 69–70), and again in the slightly altered form of *leasure-measure* in *Il Penseroso* (ll. 49–50).

Speculating freely and on technical grounds alone, one might imagine the verse of *Kubla Khan* written as a refinement upon the interesting but somewhat more obvious patterns of the *Ode to Georgiana*. We know from his own statements that Coleridge wrote the latter poem during a period when his mind was on Milton. *Kubla Khan*, however, shows further points of resemblance to Milton's pair of poems. Like them, it turns at the end to the theme of music, more or less closely associated with poetry. And Milton's two poems have meadows, brooks, towers, "tufted trees," "poet's dream" and "haunted stream," "winding," "mazes running" (of music), "heave," "holy," an "Ethiope Queen" (Abyssinian) and a "Tartar King" (Kubla was a Tartar), bowers, glades, "Muses in a ring," forests, enchantments, a "covert," honey, an awakening from a dream to the sound of music, and so on. The spirit of Milton's two poems is quite different from that of Coleridge's dream-fragment, but then so is Schiller's *Die Götter Griechenlands*, for which, either then or later, Coleridge meant to employ the same "style and metre."

The *Ode to Georgiana* is not the only poem of those known or believed to have been composed in 1799–1800 in which Coleridge used a free or irregular metrical pattern like that of *Kubla Khan*, with tetrameter lines predominating but combined smoothly with passages of five-stress and occasional three-stress lines. Other variations of it appear in two brief fragments of 1800, *Apologia pro vita sua* and *A Thought Suggested by a View* and in the longer pieces *The Mad Monk* and *A Stranger Minstrel*. There is nothing particularly notable about such a metrical form except, for our present purpose, this: that, *Kubla Khan* aside, Coleridge had not used it before 1799 and that it is particularly unlike anything he is known to have written in 1797 or 1798. At a much earlier time he had made two attempts at a somewhat similar free-sounding verse of irregular lines: certain stanzas of *Songs of the Pixies* (1793) and the verses *To the Rev. W. J. Hort* (1795) show some kinship with the meter of *Kubla Khan*.[90] In 1797 and 1798, on the other hand, Coleridge's ear seems to have been haunted mainly by the pentameter, especially in blank verse, with a few excursions into other meters. He tried out at that time the six-line stanza of Burns in some verses *To a Young Lady* (1798):[91] he freed the ballad stanza in *The Ancient Mariner*. *France: An Ode* (1798) looks irregular at first sight but is actually no free or neo-Pindaric ode, for meter and rhyme both are rigidly fixed, identical in every stanza; it is probably the most rigid piece of mechanical discipline to which Coleridge ever submitted himself in verse. Its prevailing rhythm is set by the pentameter lines that dominate the whole. *The Raven* was a departure, probably deliberate, from what had become an almost habitual pentameter music. As Coleridge implied in his note, the poem is modeled after the meter of the February Eclogue in *The Shepheardes Calender*. Its gallop exhibits certain kinds of irregularities, but they are nothing like those we have been discussing.[92] The most celebrated of his irregular meters, that of *Christabel*, bears no resemblance to that of *Kubla Khan* in its general plan or in the execution of the part usually assigned to 1797 or 1798, for the metrical lightness there derives chiefly from anapestic movement, of which *Kubla Khan* has none.[93] No verse, then, distinctly resembling that of the "dream"-fragment appears among the poems known to have been written in 1797 or 1798. In 1799 and 1800, the *Ode to Georgiana* and the several others of a like sort were a conscious departure from Coleridge's recent metrical forms, and *Kubla Khan* most closely resembles these.

A final point concerns the rhyme. *Kubla Khan* contains one unrhymed line. Before 1799 there are (if my observation has not failed) just five other blank lines in all Coleridge's rhymed verses. There may, in fact, be only three. Those three are in juvenile verses, and of them only one was ever allowed to see print during Coleridge's lifetime. They were due probably to imperfect craftsmanship rather than deliberate intention. The other two blank lines, not attributable to youth, appear in Part I of *Christabel*. These may have been written in 1797 or 1798. But as the birth of that poem is shrouded in mystery, individual lines cannot be certainly dated; these might just as well have been written when Coleridge was working on the poem, as we know he was, in late 1799 or 1800. So there are, at most, two unrhymed lines, and perhaps none at all, apart from *Kubla Khan*, in the rhymed verse composed between the end of 1790 and 1799. From the latter date onward, on the other hand, he frequently interspersed

his verses with unrhymed lines. The practice may have
been suggested to him by one or two of the German lyrics
which he translated, or by Milton's sprinkling of blank
lines in *Lycidas*, which in later years he commented upon
and which his own rhyming in *Kubla Khan* closely resembles. Whatever the reason for it, the change was
abrupt. I count thirty-four or thirty-five blank lines in the
rhymed verse of 1799 and 1800 alone, as well as a new use
of daring off-rhymes—*lids-sheds, plaint-wonderment, re-
leased-kissed*. Of these also, *Kubla Khan* exhibits one or
two not quite so venturesome instances.[94]

In sum, Coleridge's return from Germany was signalized
by notable changes in his poetic style and technique. How
deliberate they were and whether they began before or
after his arrival in England I cannot be sure, since the
precise date of some of the translations is not known. As
the few poems that we are sure were written while Coleridge was still in Germany show no traces of the new style
(except for one translation made in April that contained,
like its original, several unrhymed lines), I am inclined to
think it developed chiefly afterwards. If so, many things
combined to produce it: German lyrics, *Thalaba*, *Gebir*, the
reperusal of Milton and of his own early verse, his concern
about his own descriptive powers, and his theory about
"charm of words" derived from the *Laocoön* of Lessing—
all these had a share. The characteristic changes in the
language, meter, and rhyme of the poetry of this period are
all exhibited in *Kubla Khan*. If that poem actually was
written in 1797 or 1798, it is a surprising anticipation of his
later style.

6. "PERDITA" ROBINSON'S IMITATION; DOROTHY WORDSWORTH'S "KUBLA"

There is one fly in the beautiful smooth consistency of
the theory I have been presenting of a date later than 1798
for the "dream" of *Kubla Khan*. At the beginning I mentioned one clear terminal date, the only fact, so far as I

know, that is really certain. The poem was in existence by October, 1800, for "Perdita" Robinson had unmistakably seen it by that time.

Mrs. Robinson has stepped into the magic circle of *Kubla Khan* several times. We have seen how, by an odd coincidence if not some stronger link, her dreamlike dictation of *The Maniac* had anticipated the account printed by Coleridge of his "opium-dreamed" poem. During the winter of 1799–1800, Coleridge saw a good deal of her, admired some of her poems, and recommended them to Southey for the *Annual Anthology*, where they duly appeared. She had contributed occasionally to the *Monthly Magazine*, and during this winter both she and Coleridge were writing with some regularity for the *Morning Post*.[95] In verses written in October, 1800, *Mrs. Robinson to the Poet Coleridge*, she combined a general tribute to Coleridge's genius with an attempt to redescribe the scene of *Kubla Khan*. Without naming the poem, she made quite clear that she was quoting from it and writing of it.[96] Coleridge returned the compliment in *A Stranger Minstrel*, written in a verse form much like that of *Kubla Khan*. We do not know when Mrs. Robinson had first become acquainted with the latter poem, whether during the winter when she was seeing Coleridge a good deal or afterwards; but her poetical compliment establishes its terminal date.

The fly in the theory is not Mrs. Robinson's, however; it is a word, imbedded in the journal of Dorothy Wordsworth, that may imply the existence of the poem in 1798. The single word *Kubla* occurs in the account of the Wordsworths' journey from Hamburg to Goslar in the first week of October, 1798. On the third morning of that expedition, Dorothy ate a breakfast of bread and apples in the streets of Brunswick, then "carried *Kubla* to a fountain in the neighboring market-place, where [she] drank some excellent water" before entering the Goslar diligence.

If one knew that in writing this Dorothy Wordsworth

meant she had actually carried Coleridge's poem on that morning in Brunswick, there would be no more to say; we should have its terminal date clearly marked by that date —officially, October 6, 1798, and unofficially a month or so before that. It is difficult to imagine that the word *Kubla* issuing from Dorothy's pen could refer to anything else than the poem *Kubla Khan*. On the other hand, in this context a poem is almost the last thing one can imagine her speaking of. The word is therefore a puzzle however one takes it; one has only a choice of unlikely alternatives. As far as I can see, they are these: an improbable event on the morning of October 6 and an even more improbable recording of it if it occurred; or a slip of the pen of a kind that is not of itself improbable but that would not often coincide with the crux of a mystery and that seems to have been copied a second time; or, finally, an improbable nickname for some possession. Of these, only the first alternative would establish the existence of *Kubla Khan* in 1798, and it is perhaps the least likely of the three.

A suggestion has been put forth recently that, in the playful private language sometimes used by Coleridge and the Wordsworths, their drinking "can" might have been named in honor of Coleridge's Kubla.[97] For a breakfast on the street and a drink of water in the market place, a can would at any rate be a good deal more suitable than a poem; and the pronunciation (*Khan* was commonly spoken to rhyme with *ran*) and the common spelling *Can* would have encouraged the pun. This inspired guess, made in recent months independently by two persons, though it may solve the puzzle of Dorothy's meaning, still does not supply a date for Coleridge's poem. It does not tell us that the can was called "Kubla" that morning in Brunswick. The theory that the *Kubla* of the journal was either a nickname or a slip of the pen would imply only that the poem was in existence *when Dorothy wrote this part of her journal in its present form*. That date we do not know, but we do know that it was not immediately after the event. She may have written the phrase before she left Germany in the spring of 1799; on the other hand, she may not have written it until the winter of 1799–1800 at Grasmere or even later. The evidence for the date of this writing, as far as I have been able to make it out, will be found in Appendix III. It is a morass too deep even for this swampy chapter, though its importance should give it a place here. Largely because of Dorothy's *Kubla*, at any rate, the date of Coleridge's poem must remain unsettled; unless or until new evidence comes to light we can hold only the most tentative opinion.

7. WHAT COLERIDGE SAW OF "THALABA"

Two matters remain before we have done with the date of *Kubla Khan*. We have not yet considered how much of *Thalaba* Coleridge is likely to have seen before he must have composed his own poetic fragment; nor have we considered possible occasions between his return from Germany and his removal to Keswick when he might have retired to Porlock and written it.

As Southey's poem was not published until the summer of 1801 and *Kubla Khan* was certainly composed at least a year earlier, Coleridge's debt—supposing him to have owed one—could not have been to the complete printed work. In pointing out the parallels earlier, I did not pause to mark stages in the completion of *Thalaba* or to distinguish between the portions Coleridge might have seen completed and those he could have known only in fragments or from notes and conversation, but treated the whole as a unit, which I must now take apart.

For some months before he began the systematic writing of the poem, Southey had been elaborating the plan for it and had been making notes for the plot and scenes. He had also been reading, copying out passages that might be of use, and making numerous preparatory notes of other sorts. Some portions of the verse itself seem to have been written before their turn came round in the story, possibly even before the regular writing was begun. By the middle of July, 1799, he had completed the plan and had embarked upon the writing. Toward the end of August he reported a book and a half finished; by September 6 he had got almost to the end of the second book; on October 18 he was approaching the end of Book IV. Meantime, by August 12 he had joined Coleridge at Stowey. From then on until about September 23 or 24 the two poets remained together or within walking distance, first at Stowey, afterwards at Ottery and Exeter, and during their walking tour in South Devon. Progress on *Thalaba* was retarded, but its themes drifted into other joint activities when Milton's Paradise (Book IV of *Paradise Lost*) found its way into *The Devil's Thoughts*, the joint epic on Mohammed took shape, in air at least, and "the atmosphere of Mohammed's Paradise" entered Southey's correspondence. Coleridge read what had been written of *Thalaba* by approximately the third week of September; that was Books I and II and perhaps part of III. He must also have seen, heard, or heard about the plans and materials for the remainder. Being rarely unfertile in suggestions, he very likely contributed ideas, suggestions for reading and notes, not impossibly even bits of verse, to the work-in-progress. His own notebook (the Gutch Memorandum Book) contributed small bits. At the end of September he was advising Southey by letter to substitute "Allah" for "God" in the poem; "the so frequent repetition" of "God," he thought, gave a too "sermonic cast" to the poem and might offend Christians as well.

Beyond this, the connections between Coleridge and *Thalaba* grow more uncertain. The poem, however, progressed. Between October 22 and 25 the fourth book was completed and the fifth begun; by December 27 the sixth was partly finished and the notes for the whole done except for "the trouble of arranging and seasoning them." By January 8, 1800, Book VI was done; on the sixteenth Book VII was far advanced; and by February 3 Book VIII was complete. Meanwhile, Southey had been polishing and revising the earlier portions. Then, on April 24, having tried unsuccessfully to persuade Coleridge to go abroad with him, he sailed for Lisbon. Waiting at Falmouth for a favorable wind, he wrote "half a book of *Thalaba*," probably the beginning or end of Book IX. In letters from Lisbon he recorded progress on the rest—the tenth finished in June, the remainder by July 23. Further polishing followed.[98]

Coleridge could not have seen Books X–XII and almost certainly not Book IX before he wrote *Kubla Khan*, for these were not sent back from Lisbon until October. He knew what was to go into them and may have seen rough drafts and fragments composed earlier, but that would have been all.[99] The first eight books (possibly but not likely the ninth) were left in England. He probably saw all these, but we cannot be sure. No meeting with Southey is on record between the time of their parting in Exeter late in September, 1799, and the Southeys' departure for Portugal the following April, though half-intended meetings are referred to in the letters of those months and one or more may have taken place.[100]

Even if the two did not meet, Coleridge may have seen the intervening books of *Thalaba*, III–VIII. Shortly after December 15 Southey sent up from Bristol by Mrs. Coleridge, to Coleridge in London, some manuscript material that may have included, but probably did not, part of the poem. Copies were being made, however, during the winter, one of them specifically for Coleridge to use in treating with a London publisher for the work. As Southey later abandoned the plan to publish immediately, we do not know whether he actually sent the copy (or part of it) to Coleridge or not.[101] When he left England in April in a state of discouragement over his health, he deposited one copy of the completed books with C. W. W. Wynn in London. Coleridge was to take charge of its publication if Southey should die abroad.[102] Coleridge may have seen this copy. Or he may have seen some less perfect copy or fragments among the things Southey left with Charles Danvers, with whom he had been staying in Bristol. A notebook of Coleridge's shows that he conversed with Danvers in Bristol two weeks after Southey had sailed.[103]

To sum up briefly, then, Coleridge certainly saw Books I and II of *Thalaba* in August and September, 1799. He certainly also became familiar at that time with detailed plans and notes for the rest. He may have seen part of Book III and almost certainly other fragments written before their turn. Books III or IV–VIII he may have seen at some undetermined time, most likely between January and May, 1800. Or he may not.

If we reinspect the parallels between *Thalaba* and *Kubla Khan* with these facts in mind, this is what we find. First— except for one passage to be mentioned presently—there are no significant *verbal* resemblances in the last four books of *Thalaba*, those which we know Coleridge could not have seen before his own poem must have been composed. There are a few phrases, but only rather common ones like the "green and fertile meadows," which are not as close to the words of *Kubla Khan* as is the "fertil ground" of Milton's Eden. Thalaba's hair "floats" in the wind in Book XI, but neither the word nor the image is very unusual; and Huon's hair in *Oberon* "floats" much oftener and more insistently.[104] There are broad likenesses of material and scenery, the most notable being the damsel's garden in an icy region warmed by magic, with its inhabitants made of snow. The really significant resemblance of this scene to *Kubla Khan*, however, is found not in Southey's passage as finally written but in his original sketch for it, where the damsel had a miraculous "ice-palace" or "ice-cave" in a garden warmed by a fountain of fire. This sketch Coleridge certainly read or heard described—even perhaps contributed to—while he was with Southey in August and September, 1799.[105]

The one close verbal parallel in these later books occurs at the close of Book IX. Maimuna, the repentant demon, who had bound Thalaba with a cobweb while she sang an unintelligible song, now loosed his bonds and again sang, in a

> low sweet voice so musical,
> That sure it was not strange,
> If in those unintelligible tones
> Was more than human potency,
> That with *such deep* and undefined *delight*
> Fill'd the surrender'd soul.
> The work is done, the song hath ceased;
> He wakes as from a dream of Paradise
> [IX, 42; italics mine].

This I noted earlier as strikingly like Coleridge's "damsel with a dulcimer," whom the poet saw "in a vision" and whose song would win him "to such a deep delight" that he might create the "dome" in his own song, and people would then say that he had "drunk the milk of Paradise." It was almost the same phrase—"such songs in such a mood to hear thee sing, It were a deep delight"—that Coleridge had used in the Concert poem, which he sent to a newspaper apparently just before he left Southey in Exeter, *at the time when Book II of Thalaba was being completed.*[106] Yet Book IX, it is almost certain, Coleridge did not see before he wrote *Kubla Khan.* The natural supposition would be that, in this instance at least, Southey had Coleridge's phrases in mind when he wrote of Maimuna. That may be so. But if we turn again to the sketches for *Thalaba* in the *Common-Place Book* we find that the unintelligible song had no part in the plans for Book IX but *originally belonged to Book II instead,* where another demon was to "attempt by magic to destroy the boy [Thalaba], as by holding his hand and singing to him a song in words unintelligible."[107] Book IX gave Southey a great deal of trouble; it underwent major alterations both while in progress and afterwards between the first and second editions. The unintelligible song, inessential to the story in either book, was therefore evidently transferred from Book II when new matter was required for Book IX. So the song that produced "such deep . . . delight" as to seem like a "dream of Paradise" presumably stood where Coleridge would have seen it in September. He was probably present at the birth and may even have lent to the song more than an appreciative ear. I have spoken earlier of these and other links between the Concert-Room poem and *Kubla Khan;* here they are unmistakably interwoven with *Thalaba* as well, though whose phrases they were at first we cannot tell.[108]

Everything, then, that is significant in the last four books of *Thalaba* appears to have been known to Coleridge before the last week of September, 1799. Books VII and VIII have no strong verbal resemblances to Coleridge's poem; and those in Books V and VI, conspicuous as they are, might almost all have come from Coleridge's familiarity with the plan and notes. This is true even of the account of the false Paradise avowedly modeled after that of Aloadin. The topography of the Paradise of Book VI is like Coleridge's, with its small winding streams flowing into the larger river, its banquet hall, its bridge that is also a pleasure-house, its association of the Eastern Tartar conquerors with Aloadin's garden, and much else; but these are not verbal associations. One distinct cluster of echoes there is, however; it also takes in *Gebir* and Collins's *The Passions: An Ode for Music*. Though the chronology is uncertain, the links are evident. Coleridge wrote of "the *mingled measure* From the *fountain* and the *caves*," amid which "ancestral voices" prophesied war; Southey wrote of the "murmurings, Which from the *fountain caves* In *mingled melody* . . . came." Landor had written memorably of a *"mingled sound"*—voices of the dead—that issued from his *cave*, where the voices of "ancestors" warned Gebir against war; and Collins had written of the *"mingled measure"* that stole "through *glades* and *glooms*." Only in *Thalaba* and *Kubla Khan* does the "mingled" music take in both caves and fountains; only in *Kubla Khan* and *Gebir* does it add voices of ancestors and war. On December 27, 1799, Southey said he had written part of Book VI; his "mingled melody" occurs in the ninth stanza. Only a week before this Coleridge had mentioned Collins's odes to him in a letter. With Collins thus inserted into the confusion (more of Collins than this phrase lurks below the surface of *Kubla Khan*), anyone would be rash who presumed to know who owed whom what, as between Southey and Coleridge, in the passages of "mingled measures." The answer can only be guessed at within the limits of the known facts, which are (1) Landor's precedence of *Thalaba* and (2) his ignorance, if not also his precedence, of *Kubla Khan*, and (3) Collins's precedence of all the others.

In book V of *Thalaba* also, one passage suggests *Kubla Khan* strongly in language as well as imagery. It is the cavern scene that I discussed earlier: the "river-fountains" that "burst" their way, rising and falling; and the "fathomless gulphs." This scene, however, may have been written in some form before the rest of Book V: according to an early sketch, the episode was intended for Book IV. It is in any case closely linked with Coleridge, for in it are two of the echoes that appear to have been derived from Coleridge's notebook, the gruesome "cavern-candle" and the dunghill smelling like musk, as well as the serpents with "swelling necks," like the snake in Part II of *Christabel*. This scene, therefore, would seem to have been pretty well developed while Coleridge and Southey were still together, unless we are to suppose that Coleridge's notes were made from a later reading of *Thalaba*, a somewhat

improbable supposition. Quite apart from the date of
Kubla Khan, this cluster of links suggests that Southey's
scene may have taken shape at Stowey or while Coleridge
remained with him in Exeter. His sketches do not mention
a cavern as the scene for this episode in Book V, nor is a
cavern mentioned in the Koran or in Sale's notes to the
passage of the Koran that he used for it. So the scene may
have owed something to the caverns Coleridge had recently
visited in Germany and to Kent's Hole and the ebbing and
flowing well near Torbay. It may also originally have belonged to the Dom-Daniel scene of Book II and have been
transferred later to Book V when another cavern was
added there.

Apart from this and the "mingled measure" passage, the
significant verbal parallels between *Kubla Khan* and
Thalaba, those that are not fairly common in other poetry
at the end of the eighteenth century, occur in Book I and
the portion of Book IX that was originally intended for
Book II—the books that Coleridge is known to have seen
before the end of September, 1799. The resemblances elsewhere are owing to identity of material, sources, ideas for
scenery, and preliminary notes. The sonorous name of the
Dom-Daniel, for instance, which Southey wrote sometimes
with the marked vowel Dōm-, sometimes as Doam- or
merely Dom-, runs through all his early accounts of the
work; and its power over a sensitive ear like Coleridge's to
convert the "pleasure-houses" of the Eastern books they
were then ransacking into the "pleasure-dome" of Kubla
is not difficult to imagine. The word *dome*, repeated some
five times in fifty-four lines, rides Coleridge's fragment as
conspicuously as it does Southey's plan. The "ice-palace,"
too, and the "ice-cave" of Southey's written plan were
certainly, as we have seen, circulating among friends during the summer and autumn of 1799, with the very phrase
that Coleridge used, "caves of ice," appearing in Cottle's
contribution to the *Annual Anthology*. Again it is not

possible, or important, to establish precedence in use of the phrase; the currency is the point.

The general question of precedence between *Kubla Khan* and *Thalaba*, however, is a rather different question, if only because of the oddness of what must have occurred if we suppose Coleridge's poem actually to have preceded by a year or more the inception of *Thalaba*, as the usually accepted dates would imply. *Thalaba* could not possibly have been derived from Coleridge's fragment. So we should have to suppose that a synthesis (conscious or unconscious) from books Coleridge had read at various times in the past—some of them, according to Lowes, probably many years before—took place one summer at Porlock. Then, a year or two later, Southey systematically went through the same books—all or practically all of them, and some others—to make another poetic synthesis, deliberate this time and different, but founded on almost exactly the same materials. It is much easier to imagine Coleridge's small distilled piece and Southey's sprawling one as interlocking at a time when we know both men had most of that material at the surface of their minds. If this latter is what really happened, Southey's first two books, his detailed plan, much of his reading, and many of his notes must have preceded the composition of *Kubla Khan*;[109] Books III–VIII might equally well have preceded or followed it; and Books IX–XII as a whole followed or were written independently, in Portugal.

However all this may be, the literary rapport between Coleridge and Southey after their reconciliation is abundantly clear. Quite apart from their joint projects, the mingled measures they shared with Collins, and Southey's apparent use of the Gutch notebook—the special serpentine properties of the Lady Geraldine in *Christabel* are interwoven with the cavern serpents and the vampires of *Thalaba* and with that other mythical snake, the seps, which Southey made occasion to insert into the ode to his cold in December (not forgetting Landor's snake either). I do not know when Christabel's father was christened "Sir Leoline," but he too is bound up somehow with *Thalaba*. Southey planned to make use of an episode about a "Leoline and Lady," improbable as that name may be for an Eastern romance. On January 20, 1800, however, his *Common-Place Book* notes that "the Leoline and Lady story is clumsy" and must be "exterminated."

These and numerous other intimate connections between Southey and Coleridge at the turn of the century form a not wholly insignificant, though a neglected, chapter in the intellectual and poetic history of S. T. C.

8. PORLOCK

I have not yet conveyed Coleridge to Porlock; and if he cannot be got to Porlock, he cannot have written *Kubla Khan*. So at least we assume, for the association in his memory between place and poem is not so likely to have strayed as his dates often did. There are only two likely occasions for that sojourn, the first hypothetical, just before or possibly just after October 15, 1799, the second not only likely but actual, in May or June, 1800.

Coleridge paid a visit to the Wordsworths at Grasmere in April, 1800. He left them on May 4 and was in Bristol by the seventh. On May 21 he was writing from Poole's house at Stowey; by June 12 he had returned to Bristol. As early as February he had spoken to Poole of settling in Porlock if he could not find a house that would suit him at Stowey. His visit in May and June was for the purpose of looking for a house—ostensibly at least, for he was actually pretty well decided upon settling at Keswick. During part of that time he was in the Porlock neighborhood.[110] If there was only one real "retirement" near Porlock in Coleridge's life and if the note of 1810 in which he connected it with inability to finish *Christabel* is accurate, this spring of 1800 would fit very well in timing with a letter written to Wedgwood after he reached Keswick, in which he spoke in strong terms of the depression that had interfered with his finishing *Christabel*, though the cause he named to Wedgwood, the labor of translating *Wallenstein*, was understandably less personal than that recorded in the notebook. The perennial mystery of the "person on business from Porlock" who, according to the preface of 1816, had interrupted for more than an hour the automatic recording of his dream-poem but whose existence has often been doubted, is more easily explicable at this time than at any other. We know of no acquaintances that Coleridge had in the neighborhood; but if he were house-hunting, a man might very well have come to see him on that "business."

Charles Lloyd was still on his mind, too, though I think not as much as he had been during the previous autumn and winter and as he was to be again soon afterward when both families were settled near Wordsworth. We do not know of any ill health, such as Coleridge's two notes to *Kubla Khan* and his entry of 1810 mention; but as the details of his life just at that time are not fully traceable, some brief unrecorded indisposition is entirely possible. We know that Coleridge saw Charles Danvers at Bristol on May 7 and might there have been reading at least fragmentary or imperfect portions of Books III–VIII of *Thalaba* if he had not seen them earlier. One possible date for the poem, then, would be during these weeks at Bristol, Stowey, and Porlock, roughly during the month following May 8, 1800.

As far as we know, though a brief unrecorded visit sometime during the preceding winter or early spring is not impossible, Coleridge was not in the Bristol or Stowey neighborhood and thus not within easy reach of Porlock at any time between late October of the preceding year and this visit. A brief stay at Porlock shortly before or perhaps just after October 15, 1799, is a second possibility and is at worst no more fanciful than the hypothetical occasions that can be found for the year 1797 or 1798.

On September 24 the Coleridges had returned to Stowey from their stay at Exeter with the Southeys. Between the twenty-fifth and the thirtieth Coleridge had an attack of rheumatism more acute, he said, than any he had had since school days. On October 15 he was better but still suffering from intermittent pain and digestive sickness. "Since I received your former letter," he wrote that evening to Southey from Stowey, "I have spent a few days at Upcott; but was too unwell to be comfortable, so I returned yesterday."[111] The visit to Upcott, near Combe Florey, some seven miles from Stowey, would have been to the Wedgwoods. Coleridge might, finding that visit a strain but not eager to return home directly, have gone on alone for a day or two to Porlock. Or he might have gone to Porlock before his visit to the Wedgwoods. He had been in his wife's company almost constantly since July, an unusually long stretch, and some reaction was evident, for in this same letter to Southey he remarked, ostensibly with reference to someone else: "The wife of a man of genius who sympathises effectively with her husband in his habits and feelings is a *rara avis* with me."[112] Although in Germany he had expressed the greatest eagerness to rejoin his wife and child at home, this feeling had obviously not hastened his return. It apparently did not long survive that event either.

It is possible, too, that Coleridge went to Porlock after his letter of October 15 and before going on to Bristol a short while later. The attraction of the Porlock-Linton region had been strong. In Germany and more recently in south Devon, he had been comparing the scenes unfavorably with those of "Quantock, Porlock, Culbone, and Linton." In the following February and again in May, as we have seen, he even thought of settling there if a house were not available at Stowey. I doubt whether he would deliberately have left that region unvisited for a whole year after his return from Germany or whether he would willing-ly have gone to London for the winter without at least one jaunt to those favorite scenes. Southey had just come from a tour of that part of the coast when he joined Coleridge in August and, in fact, had just written a sonnet to Por-lock.[113] Coleridge would probably have revisited the place after his long absence abroad if he had had any oppor-tunity.

Both of Coleridge's explanatory notes to *Kubla Khan* and also the entry in his notebook of 1810 connected the retirement at Porlock with ill health. This would fit the early or mid-October date quite well. The disparity in his reported ailments is not very material—a "slight indis-position" and more general "ill health" in the published preface of 1816, "injured" health from worry about Lloyd in the note of 1810, "a dysentery" in the Crewe manu-script, and the remains of rheumatic pain with sleepless-ness and digestive illness actually reported on October 15. Whatever the state of Coleridge's addiction to opium may have been at the time, he would have been using the drug for rheumatic pains, and, unless his doses were very care-fully spaced, an occasional "dysentery" would have oc-curred in natural course.

It is tempting to "extract" still more (I find Mr. Emp-son's word useful, after all) from this letter of Coleridge to Southey on October 15, and I shall proceed to do so, with due warning that hypothesis has here entire rein.

> For in truth, my dear Southey! [he wrote] I am harassed with the rheumatism . . . but when the pain intermits [*intermits* here, and later in the letter with reference to *Gebir* and genius *ebullient*, a word Cole-ridge associated with fountains—these we could stretch into reflections of a recent "half-intermitted burst" of Kubla's fountain] it leaves my sensitive frame *so* sensitive! My enjoyments are so deep, of the fire, of the candle, of the thought I am thinking, of the old folio I am reading, and the silence of the silent house is so *most and very* delightful, that upon my soul! the rheumatism is no such bad thing as *people make for*.

And yet I have, and do suffer from it, in much pain and sleeplessness and often sick at stomach through indigestion of the food, which I eat from compulsion.[114]

Coleridge sounds as if he were thinking of a series of evenings—more than one, perhaps even more than two; and yet he had returned home only "yesterday." Perhaps his own house was silent now and then, and he could sometimes, he said, ignore its confusion. But one of his great complaints and the reason he later gave Poole for refusing to live there again was precisely its not being quiet and there being no study to which he could retire from the uproar of the household. So if Coleridge had been to Culbone and if he were not going to say so, this description of his quiet evenings could be read as partly a recollection of the lonely farmhouse where he had spent a recent evening or two. And—since I am rewriting the letter for him, I might as well go on—the "old folio" could be *Purchas His Pilgrimage*, continued from Porlock. I spin the folio into Purchas not quite wholly from thin air, for, as I suggested earlier, Coleridge very likely *was* reading the *Pilgrimage* as well as the *Pilgrimes* of Purchas not long after he returned from Germany.

Purchas at Porlock or Culbone at any date, early or late, is not something to be taken for granted without thought. It is conceivable on a prolonged visit, and the later one in 1800 may have been that; those that have been suggested for 1797 or 1798 were not. These places were a longish walk from Stowey. *Purchas His Pilgrimage* in the edition of 1614 is a heavy and unwieldy *folio* of nearly a thousand pages; other editions, I think, are no lighter. Even a library cormorant like Coleridge would be more likely to take along some smaller volume that could be stuffed into a pocket or that would not weigh down a knapsack excessively; and I doubt whether Purchas was commonly found on the shelves of Porlock farmhouses. I do not know whether Coleridge ever owned the *Pilgrimage* or not. But if he had gone to Porlock direct from a visit to the Wedgwoods, he might have taken with him from Upcott even a heavy book that he wished to borrow for more than a day or two's use at an inn. His plan for a geographical schoolbook, to be compiled from the writing of famous travelers, had been hatched only about two weeks before, and Purchas would be a prime work for that.[115] The language in which he described to Southey this "delightful" quiet reading suggests the euphoria produced by opium; it is like the language Coleridge used elsewhere in describing that effect.

The letter of October 15 upon which I am raising a largely fanciful edifice contributes several other useful if airy bricks. It shows Coleridge's bitterness toward Charles Lloyd and his concern that Lloyd was damaging his reputation with Christopher Wordsworth at Cambridge; there is a long circumstantial passage about this, and the letter closes with his "Lloyd-and-Lambophobia." It shows too that he had *Gebir* in mind (its unknown author's genius is a *"powerful* or *ebullient* faculty") and Milton. It may possibly also refer to an unnamed poem that Southey had not seen: "I will set about 'Christabel' with all speed; but I do not think it a fit opening poem [for the *Anthology*]. What I think would be a fit opener, and what I would humbly lay before you as the best plan of the next Anthologia, I will communicate shortly in another letter entirely on this subject." The likelihood that this "fit opener" had anything to do with *Kubla Khan*, however, is diminished if not altogether annihilated by the next letter, in which Coleridge suggests that the opening poem should be something "in couplets, didactic or satirical," which would please both the genuine lovers of poetry and "the ignoramuses and Pope-admirers." He says he had planned such a piece but had not written it.[116] I do not recognize *Kubla Khan* in this unwritten piece, and perhaps not either in the unnamed and unfinished fragment, not imaginary, that "delighted" Davy, presumably when they met in Bristol before the end of October. But one cannot be sure, for Coleridge's ideas might have changed from letter to letter. He seems, at any rate, to have written some unidentified and unfinished poem during this interval.

If *Kubla Khan* were composed in October, 1799, its connection with *Thalaba* would have been on the basis of the first two completed books and the notes, plans, and fragments for the remainder. The reminiscent words of Coleridge's notes describing the Lake District, written some two or three weeks later—*savage, stately, slant, athwart, mazy*—none of them unusual singly, but sprinkled rather thickly, would have been echoes of the recent poem. This date would mean, too, that Wordsworth's Christmas Eve letter, with its "momently" and "midway in its fall" and its gratuitous introduction of the Arabian summer into an icy northern December scene of chasm and cataract, drew upon a recent memory of the verses he might have read for the first time during Coleridge's visit a month or six weeks earlier. And only a short time afterward Coleridge's brief friendship began with "Perdita" Robinson, the one person who can be said positively, with no ifs or buts, to have seen the poem before the following October. If it were fresh and on the table for possible completion after Coleridge went to London at the end of November, it could easily have come before her appreciative eye then. The October date fits the chronology given in Coleridge's note of 1810. It also falls into the midst of the flurry of Diocletian's daughters and their demon-lovers, whom we saw in the Gutch Memorandum Book, in Southey's letters, and in Davy's plans for a poem, all current within recent weeks.[117]

9. AND SARA HUTCHINSON

And now, as I have set no limit at all to this ice-palace of speculation, I shall add a cupola that fits temptingly, though it may be only, like Erasmus Darwin's palace in Coleridge's phrase, "glittering and transitory." I think Sara Hutchinson may properly crown the edifice.

It seems almost certain that some gap in time, perhaps a small one of days or weeks only, separated the composition of the first part of *Kubla Khan* from the final eighteen lines. The lines imply as much themselves, for they are an explanation of the poet's inability to write the rest of the poem, and he would, one supposes, have given himself at least a little time for a renewed burst of inspiration before writing off the poem as unfinishable. Lowes never satisfactorily explained the Abyssinian maid. Many years after his book was written he expressed dissatisfaction with his own account but was still puzzled over her.[118] The association of women and music was by no means unusual in Coleridge's poetry. There are lines on the subject in his early writing, and the theme appears in the *Lines Composed in a Concert-Room*. It is explicit in later verses: "'Tis my faith, that there's a natural bond Between the female mind and measured sounds."[119] In all the other poems, however, the introduction of woman (or Muse) and song is both conventional and natural in a way that it is not in *Kubla Khan*, where the "vision" of the Abyssinian maid is abrupt, dreamlike if one must have it so, at any rate conspicuously nonlogical in sequence.

Not long after October 15, 1799, Coleridge went to Bristol and presently from there traveled north on his visit to the Wordsworths at Sockburn, where he first met Sara Hutchinson. After his tour of the Lake District with Wordsworth, he returned to Sockburn and spent almost a week with the Hutchinsons. It almost seems, from one of his notes, as if he went north half-expecting to fall in love with Sara or Mary. At any rate, his feeling for Sara sprang into love at first sight or very nearly that, and some lovemaking occurred before he left. His poem *Love*, written during or shortly after this visit, is thought to be an indirect commemoration of the event. Three years later (if the date attached to the lines by E. H. Coleridge is correct) he addressed his love—"Asra" by now—as a "living fount" that, like Kubla's fluctuating one, "doth heave and fall" and that springs up "like vernal waters . . . through snow."[120] The lines of verse quoted in his preface to *Kubla Khan* are from a poem she is thought to have inspired, and the poem *Separation*, which is specifically addressed to her, carries an echo of *Kubla Khan* in the lines

> Wealth's glittering fairy-dome of ice,
> Or echo of proud ancestry.

Another poem addresses her as "maiden mild," associates her name and voice with music, and tells how she stood before him "like a thought, A dream remembered in a dream," all of which half-suggests the damsel with dulcimer of the "vision in a dream" of *Kubla Khan*.[121] And Miss Coburn tells me that Coleridge once addressed Sara Hutchinson as his "Moorish maid." If we do not feel convinced that *Kubla Khan* was dictated by a dream, word for word at a single sitting, and if we consider the date of about mid-October, 1799, as a likely occasion for the composition of the major part of it, the events that occurred shortly afterward in the meeting with Sara Hutchinson would explain very well the hiatus in the poem, its abrupt shift from the apparently settled subject of Kubla and his summer palace and garden to an irrelevant Abyssinian maid, the earthly but unattainable Paradise of Mount Amara of which she sings, and the poet himself, who, after being entirely absent from the early part of the poem, is suddenly injected in the first person into the closing lines to tell us that he has had (and lost) a glimpse of Paradise.

The still later date that I have suggested as possible for *Kubla Khan*, that of Coleridge's known visit to the Porlock region in May or June, 1800, would likewise accommodate the presence of Sara Hutchinson in the poem, though it would not, like that of 1799, illuminate the sudden shift of themes that sets apart the closing lines.

As for the mysterious poem that had "so much delighted" Davy and that on December 19 Coleridge did not know whether he would be able to finish for the *Annual Anthology* or not, it might possibly be *Kubla Khan*, though on the whole I doubt it. He wished to give that unknown poem a fictitious title or none at all, he said; and I doubt whether, even if the maid were not at first Abyssinian, the original form of *Kubla Khan* would have been likely to need concealment. The reference might have been to the poem *Love*, which was originally printed under the red-herring title *Introduction to the Tale of the Dark Ladie*. There are objections to that identification too, however; for the poem that on the night of Thursday the nineteenth he was not sure of being able to finish within a month or two must have been actually finished and delivered to the newspaper by the very next day: the *Introduction to the Tale of the Dark Ladie* appeared, apparently complete, in the *Morning Post* on that Saturday (December 21). I know of no other poem than these two which could have been written at that time and which might have required the concealment of a fictitious title.[122]

This is as far as we can go (a cautious person would no doubt say much farther) toward establishing the date of *Kubla Khan* on the basis of evidence now known. The date of October, 1799, seems to me slightly more likely than that of the following May or June, but either would appear possible. Uncertainty must remain about any date after 1798 because of Dorothy Wordsworth's word *Kubla*. But to reject the possibility of the later dates requires, I think, a good appetite for coincidences. Improbability is involved, no matter what alternative one chooses, but I suspect that greater obstacles stand in the way of the old dates, 1797 or 1798, than of these new ones.

Perhaps I have labored the problem too long. It seemed to me, however, that the detail was essential if the question were to be raised at all. Coleridge's preface of 1816 placed the fragment of *Kubla Khan* on a solitary shelf where, as I think, it has misled us, not altogether intentionally, about the creative imagination of genius long enough. The poem should stand where it belongs, in the literary tradition, and the date of its composition is material, though not crucial, to this.

V

The Poem

1. LITERAL MEANING

The prime question that has been put off so long remains. What, one must ask, is the residue of all this sifting through a network of parallels, debts, dates, and medical reports? If the dream was not a dream, and the date was perhaps not the date, and the new unconscious synthesis of unnumbered travels and histories was not new and probably not unconscious, we are faced by certain other final questions, unless all the negatives in these chapters amount merely to a bid for the alias invented by Coleridge, "Idoloclastes," or Mr. Auden's "Will his negative inversion." The poem itself with its essential questions remains untouched; yet it should be worth looking at on its own account, bare of the mythology in which it has been clothed. Though one is defeated in advance, knowing that even the most assiduous stalking enables no one to impale the living essence upon the critical page, one feels, nevertheless, an obligation to approach as nearly as one can to the thing-in-itself, once having set forth on the expedition in the first place.

Still there are as many negatives as positives to be dealt out, partly, no doubt, because one postpones the most difficult task. *Kubla Khan* has been read with equal conviction as cosmic allegory and incantatory nonsense; and with reference to both meaning and form it has been described equally as a fragment and a perfectly rounded complete whole. It has been called the quintessential poem of romanticism, even while its magical virgin birth placed

it quite outside literary tradition or pedigree. To the
aesthetic purist these may still be peripheral questions;
they must be acknowledged, however, to lead at least in the
direction of the poetic essence itself. They will serve for a
beginning.

First as to meaning. One of the earliest symbolic interpretations and perhaps the most aberrant of them all has
already been mentioned, that of Mr. Robert Graves in
The Meaning of Dreams, which Lowes dissected not very
mercifully but not unjustly either, though from a point of
view that in its turn was vulnerable.[1] As Mr. Graves reads
the poem, Coleridge was "thinking of himself in terms of
the serene and powerful Kubla." The pleasure-dome is the
bower into which Coleridge retired by means of opium.
But this retreat is not perfectly secure, for there were the
prophecies of war. These Mr. Graves suggests may have
been, on one plane of symbolism, Charles Lamb and
Charles Lloyd prophesying an evil fate for the drugtaker;
on another they were "probably" the actual threat to
England from the war with France, under which "it was
hardly the duty of an Englishman, even a genius, to bury
himself far off in the West Country and weaken his spirit
with opium." The romantic chasm and the "woman wailing for her demon-lover" are referable to the "former
strong passion that Coleridge had felt for his wife," for the
loss of which his wife is now reproaching him. The caves
into which the river sinks are a sexual symbol (if I understand Mr. Graves correctly), complicated by the current
pregnancy of Mrs. Coleridge. The river is the life of man
from birth to death. The poem shows us that "Coleridge
has determined to shun the mazy complications of life by
retreating to a bower of poetry, solitude and opium." The
Abyssinian maid is an unidentified beloved who usually
lay beside him in his opium dreams. The caves of ice may
represent the purely intellectual character of the poet's
attachment to Dorothy Wordsworth. The close of the

poem is a justification of his opium habit "on the ground that the vivid and emotional visions which the drug gives him" will some day be converted into "poetry that will stagger the world," a claim to greatness that Coleridge is using "as a weapon against his ambitious and disillusioned wife." This is indeed a heavy enough weight of meaning to strain the supports of any dome, and certainly of Coleridge's frail and airy one.

Lowes, as we have already seen, went to the opposite extreme with his notion of the poem as an exquisite but meaningless phantasmagoria of drifting images and phrases from books floating upon the unconscious mind of the dreamer and dissolving into each other as dreams do. Lowes's view of dreams was not that of modern psychology. He disavowed any interest in the significance of a dream except for its shifting character and its poetic beauty. The point of view from which he wrote, in fact, is not very far from the old Hartleyan notions:

Suppose a subliminal reservoir thronged, as Coleridge's was thronged, with images which had flashed on the inner eye from the pages of innumerable books. Suppose these images to be fitted, as it were, with links which render possible indefinite combination. Suppose some powerful suggestion in the field of consciousness strikes down into this mass of images thus capable of all manner of conjunctions. And suppose that this time, when in response to the summons the sleeping images flock up, with their potential associations, from the deeps—*suppose that this time all conscious imaginative control is for some reason in abeyance*. What, if all this were so, would happen?[2]

Psychoanalytical thought has one answer to this question: with conscious control in abeyance, the images fall under control of the unconscious mind and become symbols of desires, fears, conflicts, expressing the will or wish of the dreamer no less purposively than if they were conscious, but at the deeper levels of unadmitted desire or conflict. Lowes's answer was not this, for the dreamer in *Kubla Khan*, he thought, is "merely the detached and unsolicitous spectator." And the only force determining the form and sequence of the imagery is the "subtle potency of the associative links." There is no plan, no "deliberate manipulation." It is in effect a poet's exercise of free association without any implication that *free* is more than *chance* association or than Hartley's juxtaposition of atoms; the "bewildering hooks and eyes" of the unconscious memory alone were the "irresponsible artificers of the dream." And so in the poem the "linked and interweaving images irresponsibly and gloriously stream, like the pulsing, fluctuating banners of the North. And their pageant is as aimless as it is magnificent."[3]

It is evident from Lowes's language that he was too dazzled to see quite what was before him, his appreciation having outrun perception. It has happened to many readers, not of this poem alone, perhaps most often to us in America. We are inclined, possibly, to read poetry rather more hastily and more impressionistically than the English do, and are determined, when we do read it closely, to do something to it or extract something from it rather than merely to see what it is and enjoy it. Coleridge's preface and the music of *Kubla Khan* have so particularly encouraged the impressionistic approach to that piece that we are apt to read it with but half-conscious attention as a kind of glorified nursery rhyme even while we call it the quintessence of poetry.

At any rate, to one who reads *Kubla Khan* attentively without ulterior motive and without fixed preconceptions, *Kubla Khan* has, throughout, a perfectly normal meaning, one that is as logical and, as far as one can tell, as conscious as that of most deliberately composed poems. This is evident, once we cease to be dazzled by the familiar prefatory note and Kubla's bewitching scenery. Indeed, one hesitates to explain the meaning because of its obviousness and because it must be a commonplace to many. The authority of Lowes, however, has attached many readers to the phantasmagoric view of the poem. To lay such a powerful ghost as this, it is necessary to labor the obvious. In doing so I shall keep strictly, for the moment, to the surface of the poem, to what is actually said, with no side glances for symbols and none for Coleridge's possible intentions.

The first part is merely the picture that everyone knows of the strange and beautiful Paradise or pleasure-grounds, enriched and poeticized ultimately from many sources. The topography of the scene is somewhat unprecise, so that the reader could scarcely draw a map of it. But the actual statement and the separate elements of the picture are perfectly clear. Almost, though not quite literally, like the stream in *Paradise Lost*, Coleridge's "sacred river" rises from the earth in a fountain, winds through the garden, and sinks again underground. The poet leaves off without finishing or putting to use these pleasure-grounds, either dissatisfied with his presentation of them or unable to continue, or both. In the last eighteen lines, which Lowes was sure "nobody in his waking senses could have fabricated" with their "dissolving panorama" and "vivid incoherence," the poet makes an explicit statement about what precedes. In a vision, he says, he once heard music sung and played by a damsel. Her song was of an earthly Paradise. If he could only revive within himself that music, the joy it would give him would enable him really to re-create the scene of Kubla's Paradise, in poetry that would be truly immortal. He would then be looked upon with awe as one of the inspired great ones, the poet-prophets of the world. Here are the lines:

> A damsel with a dulcimer
> In a vision once I saw:
> It was an Abyssinian maid,
> And on her dulcimer she played,
> Singing of Mount Abora.
> Could I revive within me
> Her symphony and song,

To such a deep delight 'twould win me,
That with music loud and long,
I would build that dome in air,
That sunny dome! Those caves of ice!
And all who heard should see them there,
And all should cry, Beware! Beware!
His flashing eyes, his floating hair!
Weave a circle round him thrice,
And close your eyes with holy dread,
For he on honey-dew hath fed,
And drunk the milk of Paradise.

This is the poet's explanation of his failure to complete the poem.[4] As Coleridge said often in his waking hours, so he says here: he *could* have accomplished something truly worthy of himself, *if only*——.

In part, the thought is related to the later ode *Dejection*. The mood of gloom is not mentioned explicitly, but Coleridge feels the same lack that he described in the ode, a lack of inner joy or delight—what Gerard Hopkins afterward called "the fine delight that fathers thought." This is needed to stir his creative imagination. In the familiar passage from *Dejection* he wrote:

> . . . thou need'st not ask of me
> What *this strong music in the soul* may be!
>
> . . . .
>
> This beautiful and *beauty-making* power.
>   *Joy*, virtuous Lady! Joy that ne'er was given,
> Save to the pure, . . .
>
> . . . .
>
> Joy, Lady! is the spirit and the power,
>
> . . . .
>
> *And thence flows all that charms or ear or sight,*
>   All melodies the echoes of that voice,
>
> . . . .
>
> But now afflictions bow me down to earth:
> Nor care I that they rob me of my mirth;
>   But oh! each visitation
> *Suspends what nature gave me at my birth,*
>   *My shaping spirit of Imagination.*[5]

This is precisely the negative equivalent of the poet's words in *Kubla Khan*:

> Could I revive *within me*
> Her *symphony and song*,
> To such a *deep delight* 'twould win me,
> That *with music loud and long*,
> I would build that dome in air. . . .

In both poems joy or delight is represented as an inner music that inspires the poet to create; the presence of a woman is imagined; and the epithets for the music, "loud and long" in the one, find echo of both sound and sense in the "strong" of the other. If, then—to return to the direct statement of *Kubla Khan*—the writer, "I," had this inspiration that is rooted in joy, "with music . . . I would build that dome . . . those caves of ice! And all who heard [my music] should see them [domes, caves] there, And all should cry, Beware! . . ."

The figure with "flashing eyes" and "floating hair" in the final lines Lowes traced to a confluence of Bruce's king of Abyssinia, whose hair on one occasion floated, and the "youths" who were followers of Aloadin—an impersonal mysterious figure beheld by Coleridge in his dream. Conceivably, the figure from Bruce may have entered into the imagery in some degree, but its essence is surely not what Lowes supposed: the poet is not dreaming about two impersonal figures, an Abyssinian maid and a "Tartar youth." This would indeed produce the "vivid incoherence" that Lowes admired. But the incoherence is created only by the reader's ignoring the grammatical structure, and hence the statement as a whole, for the sake of dwelling upon isolated phrases and images. If there is any dreaming going on in these final lines, it is the reader's, not the poet's. The lines beginning with the "damsel" exhibit a perfectly clear rhetorical and grammatical sequence. The pronouns have obvious antecedents, and the progress of thought from line to line is entirely natural and orderly. It seems impossible not to read the poem as sense, once the connections have been made.

Any interpretation of the poem as symbolic or impressionistic must at least be in consonance with this primary literal reading. Mr. Kenneth Burke puts "Beware! Beware!" into the poet's "pontificating" mouth;[6] but if the poet intended to lecture himself on his opium or the world on anything else, he concealed himself wholly behind the brows of the awed spectators. It is clearly they who speak the words *about* the poet. Coleridge is explicit in this. "Close your eyes," "weave a circle round him thrice." The circle is one of separation from the beholders; he who is possessed by god or daemon—inspiration—is mysteriously set apart.

The origin of the concluding lines Lowes must have missed only because it was too obvious: essentially, the picture is but the ancient conventional description of the poet with his "eye in a fine frenzy rolling." This conception was old even in Plato's day, and practically every detail used by Coleridge was a commonplace in it. The descriptions derived a good deal from the accounts of persons possessed by the god in Dionysus worship and the Orphic cults—flashing eyes and streaming hair, as well as honey, milk, magic, holiness, and dread. It was of course all perfectly familiar to Coleridge. Plato's *Ion* gives what is probably the most famous passage of this kind, and at the risk of further laboring the obvious I shall quote it here. Though it does not mention every detail that Coleridge uses, it gives the main ones, including specifically the comparison of poetic inspiration with the frenzy of the orgiastic cults:

In like manner the Muse first of all inspires men herself. . . . For all good poets, epic as well as lyric, compose their beautiful poems not by art, but because they are inspired and possessed. And as the Corybantian revellers when they dance are not in their right mind, so the lyric poets are not in their right mind when they are composing their beautiful strains: but when falling under the power of music and metre they are inspired and possessed; like Bacchic maidens who draw milk and honey from the rivers when they are under the influence of Dionysus but not when they are in their right mind. And the soul of the lyric poet does the same, as they themselves say; for they tell us that they bring songs from honeyed fountains, culling them out of the gardens and dells of the Muses; they, like the bees, winging their way from flower to flower. And this is true. For the poet is a light and winged and holy thing, and there is no invention in him until he has been inspired and is out of his senses, and the mind is no longer in him; when he has not attained to this state, he is powerless and is unable to utter his oracles.[7]

Coleridge's Inspiration, music, holiness inspiring awe, milk and honey, are all explicit here; and the flashing eyes and floating hair are implicit in the "Corybantian revellers" and "Bacchic maidens." So much for the straight literal reading of *Kubla Khan*.

2. PART OR WHOLE

The idea has been advanced more than once in recent years that the poem is not a fragment but a complete and perfect whole. This view has attracted so many readers and, if sound, would have such real bearing upon the poetic effect of the lines that the basis for it had better be examined. Coleridge himself called the poem a "fragment"; and, haunted as he was by the ghosts of his many unfinished works, I should think it unlikely that he would have added by a deliberate falsehood to the number of that congregation in limbo. He also treated it as a fragment, keeping it, as he did *Christabel*, unpublished for many years, though his usual custom was to publish finished works promptly except for a few obviously intimate ones the publication of which would embarrass himself or others—verses such as those unmistakably addressed to Sara Hutchinson, for example, and *The Pains of Sleep*.

It is difficult, on the other hand, to imagine the poem carried beyond its present close. Conceivably, following a momentary cross-current of thought in the passage that introduces the Abyssinian maid, Coleridge might have written the poem into a hole from which he could not extricate it. He might, that is, have destined the poem to progress in one direction but, having once interrupted this current to comment on the inadequacy of his inspiration, have found he had actually written what must put an end to the work, a continuation of the original being unthinkable afterwards. Coleridge would not be the first poet whose matter had got beyond its inventor's control and taken him where he had not meant to go. But that is not what one means by a finished poem. It is conceivable, too, that he had in mind a three-part musical form with a more beautiful and heightened return to the original garden theme— the Inspired Poet, having recovered his "vision," now demonstrating what he could really do. The poem might then have remained incomplete from Coleridge's inability to transcend what he had already done as the theme would require. On the whole, however, I think this not the most likely reconstruction of Coleridge's intention (though the idea of translating musical into poetic forms had occurred to poets in Germany and might have been familiar to Coleridge).[8] There is nothing like it to be found elsewhere in his work, and I doubt whether *Kubla Khan* represents a departure of that sort from his usual practice.

The most likely explanation of the actual form of the poem would seem to be also the most natural. As it stands, it clearly consists of two parts, the description of Kubla's Paradise gardens and an explanation of why the poet could not after all finish what he had begun, or, to speak within the framework of the dream, why he could not re-create the vision he had seen. The whole reads like a fragment with a postscript added at some later time when it has become obvious to the poet that he cannot finish the piece. The postscript is skilfully linked with the rest by the recurrence of the dome and caves of ice; but these and other devices do not conceal, and I imagine were not meant to conceal, the actually disparate parts. If a man begins a poem, gets stuck, and then adds the comment, "I cannot finish this," even though he versify his comment to match his fragment, he is not likely to produce a whole in the poetic or aesthetic sense, though he does bring his piece to an end beyond which it could not be continued.

To me, at any rate, the poem has never sounded complete in any other sense than this. Several things in it, furthermore, have charm and interest if one reads it as a fragment but are poetically unsatisfactory if one tries to regard it as an organic whole, even a dreamed whole. One of these is Kubla's hearing of the "ancestral voices prophesying war," which Coleridge makes impressive and then drops. It is true that if the poem is read as an actual incoherent and unaltered dream one cannot cavil at the flaw, since the dream produced it; but I do not find enough incoherence for that. So the "ancestral" threat of war is too prominent and at the same time too much out of key with the other images—too pointless, in fact, since no further use is made of it—to be satisfactory poetically if the fifty-four lines must be regarded as a finished piece; the image remains unassimilated. Only if one reads those words as a hint at something to come in the poem, do they charm the mind as they should with their portentousness.

I think Coleridge would have agreed. On just such a point in *Christabel* a comment survives which was probably Coleridge's in substance and perhaps in language as well.[9] It concerned the lines about the mastiff bitch and Christabel's mother:

> Sixteen short howls, not over loud;
> Some say, she sees my lady's shroud.

These details, so the comment runs, not only give "a prevailing colour or Harmony to the whole," but are "indicative also that my Lady's spirit is to make a principal interest in the after story." They prepare us also for the "visionary and dreamlike manner which pervades the Poem." Christabel's mother, the writer points out, is dropped into the story again, though no structural use is made of her in the fragment as it exists. He justifies and explains these unused references on the specific ground that they would have been an important structural part of the finished poem. Every event in the fragment "is completely in Harmony with the general wildness of the Poem, and is yet consistent and connected with and dependent upon the other." Coleridge would probably have justified the "ancestral voices" of Kubla, from the poetic standpoint, only by a similar unfulfilled intention of something to come later in the poem. The two lines on the woman wailing beneath a waning moon for her demon-lover also seem poetically in keeping in a fragment but would be out of proportion in a short whole. Shifting the scene from day to night as they do and introducing two figures, obviously not as part of a shifting dream-sequence of irrelevancies but in the language and syntax of a conventional literary comparison, the lines are nearly as much out of drawing as an elaborate Virgilian simile would be in a lyric.

The division of *Kubla Khan* into its two parts also seems fatal to the unity of the poem if it must be regarded as a complete whole. The first part is given over entirely to Kubla's pleasure-grounds, the demon-lover lines being not a new scene but only a comparison. In the last eighteen lines, time, place, and speaker all are changed. The first part is wholly impersonal; the last is written wholly in the first person. The poet enters in the thirty-eighth line unannounced, but, unlike the stars of *The Ancient Mariner*, his place is not prepared and appointed, nor does he enter as a lord that is certainly expected; he rather breaks in. Professor Wilson Knight has ingeniously compared the form of *Kubla Khan* to that of an enlarged Petrarchan sonnet.[10] Read thus, however, it can only be an imperfect "sonnet," for the requirement of that or any other two-part poetic form, that the sestet must throw some transforming light upon the octave, is not met in Coleridge's poem. The last eighteen lines terminate but do not fulfil the first part—or so it seems to me. I do not find that the main descriptive portion—the gardens, the fountains, the romantic glen—becomes any different in memory after I have read the concluding lines, for the break remains too complete despite the links in imagery. The conviction does not rush upon me at the end that the split is after all no split; for the end makes the beginning no brighter, no dimmer, deepens the meaning by no tragic implications or irony or illuminating reversal. A fulfilment is still absent at the end, partly because *action*, not pure description, has been left in the air. The place is *being built* before one's eyes. Kubla *decreed* the pleasure-dome; and so the ten miles of ground *were girdled round*. The progression thus started cries out to continue, like an unresolved cadence in music.

On the whole, not only do the first thirty-six lines of the poem refuse to sound as if they had been dreamed; they sound more than anything else like a fine opening for a romantic narrative poem of some magnitude. *Oberon*, *Gebir*, *Thalaba*, the unwritten "Mahomet," *Christabel*, even Cottle's *Alfred*, to name only such poems as were present to Coleridge's mind in 1799 (and there were others earlier) —into this tradition *Kubla Khan* might have fitted very well.[11] The historical Cubla was an attractive subject for such a poem. Though he shared the usual adventures of the successive Tartar conquerors with their wars and prophecies of wars, he was said to be distinguished above the others by a breadth of mind and a tolerance foreign to most oriental rulers. Marco Polo, in Purchas, reported that Cubla expected persons of all religions to pray to their own gods; toward Christians especially he was well disposed. Most significant of all for a poet was his good name among authors. D'Herbelot records that Cubla was praised by oriental historians for having loved and "gratifié" men of letters of all nations and sects: he accorded them many privileges and exempted them from every sort of tribute and subsidy.[12] As all this would have fallen in with the interests of Coleridge, he might have played briefly with the idea of weaving a poetic tale about this figure. The subject had the additional advantages that he mentioned in recommending "the death of Myrza" as a literary subject to Godwin—"crowd, character, passion, incident and pageantry"—and was besides "so little known that you may take what liberties you like without danger." Apparently, in Germany in 1799, he was actually interested in a modern theme of a like sort, for he made a note about a recent Tartar khan with roughly similar interests: "In the year 1783 The Tartar Chan, Schapin Gueray, who had been driven out of his dominions by his Subjects, & reinstated by the Russian Court, set on foot a Translation of the Great French Encyclopaedia into the Tartar Language."[13] The poem itself tells us something of the poet's intention if we are entitled to suppose that Coleridge meant what he said. The "music" of the lost inspiration, he says, would have been "loud and long." I have already referred to his fondness during 1799–1800 for "loud" music, out of *Lycidas*. It was surely intended to mean "impressive." In *Lycidas*, however, there is no "long," and unless one supposes Coleridge used the word carelessly as a meaningless rhyme, one must suppose he actually envisaged a long poem.[14]

It does not do, though, to speculate too far upon the intentions of Coleridge, for he is quite likely to have begun with only the vaguest plan in mind or even none at all. He may have begun the piece, as painters and other poets sometimes do, as a kind of glorified doodling—an accurate enough name for "daydreaming" with pen or brush—

which might or might not develop an intention as it
proceeded.

However much or little of a plan Coleridge may have
had, the fragment as it stands perhaps carries within itself
the seeds of its own early collapse. The texture is exceedingly rich and concentrated for the opening of a long poem.
The author could hardly sustain it, one feels, and if he
could the reader could not. A narrative poet almost of
necessity lets the reader into his tale more thinly, with his
matter spaced more widely; or if the opening texture is
extremely rich the pace will be slower, more leisurely or
more dignified, as in *Paradise Lost* and *Lycidas*. The movement of *Kubla Khan* is rather swift, yet its texture is fully
as elaborate as that of *Lycidas*, without the retarding
gravity and the uncrowded, fully explored imagery with
which that poem opens. I question whether Coleridge or
any poet could have continued it without producing either
anticlimax or surfeit. It is impertinent, however, to suggest what a poet could or could not do; and it is idle any-
how to worry the question of whether *Kubla Khan* is unfinishable or merely unfinished. Such speculations are unprofitable about most poets but particularly so about
Coleridge, whose progress through the world was marked
by many more fragments than this one. The poem, at any
rate, must surely be thought of as a fragment that has
been brought to a close of sorts but not wrought into a
poetic whole—perhaps, more exactly, as a fragment with a
poetic postscript.

3. SYMBOLS AGAIN: COLERIDGE AND "TRANSLUCENCE"

Not until the present century, apparently, has *Kubla
Khan* been found to mean more than it says, though when
symbolic criticism once seized upon the poem it made up
for lost time. I have already spoken of the meanings Mr.
Robert Graves found, and should like to return to that
and other symbolic interpretations of the poem to inspect

them not only in the light of the criterion discussed in the opening chapter. It should be revealing also to examine them in the light of Coleridge's own theory and practice. How did he express symbolic meaning in poems that indubitably have it, and what were his criteria for symbolic writing if he had any? These questions should at least be looked into. If the critic chooses to draw conclusions that would have surprised the poet, he ought at least to take that surprise into account.

Apart from Mr. Graves's analysis of the poem, the best-known interpretations are those of Miss Maud Bodkin and Professor Wilson Knight. Miss Bodkin writes of the garden, the fountain, the caverns, the subterranean river, and the sunless sea, and asks what the emotional significance of these may be to their author, to us, and to all those predecessors of Coleridge who made the mythical language from which they come. She traces the pattern of contrast between the symbols of Paradise mount and Hades cavern through Milton to Greek, Hebrew, and more primitive traditions; then suggests further for these images an emotional coloring derived from primary functions of the human body associated with the breast, the womb, and the excretory organs. Though her account is too complex and subtle to be fairly summarized, this is its drift.

Professor Knight analyzes the "little Paradiso" most elaborately. The sacred river that runs into caverns he thinks is a symbol of life running through nature to death. The origin of the river in a savage, holy, and enchanted place blends "romantic, sacred, and satanic suggestions." The maze, he believes, may refer to the "spiritual complexities of human life," which finally bring man to the measureless caverns of infinity and nothingness. The "voices prophesying war" in the poem are the symbol of the destructive forces that bring man to death, and the fact that the voices are "ancestral" suggests to him the school of psychoanalytic thought that would find a place for "unconscious ancestor worship" (i.e., I suppose, the psychology of Jung). Kubla himself may be God—or nearly God. The pleasure-dome represents the true immortality, not merely an immortality after death but something beyond the dimensions of time. The "mingled measure" suggests the blending of "fundamental oppositions": the masculine principle, which is life or creation, and the feminine, which is death or destruction. These oppositions "mingle under the shadow" of the immortality-dome. Sexual symbolism pervades this *Paradiso* throughout the garden, river, and fountain passages: fountain and cave are male and female. On this plane the pleasure-dome is the union of the "great contesting" He and She; it is also "some vast intelligence" enjoying that union of opposites. In the final lines of the poem the dome becomes the "mystic music," a "spiritual dome." Or—the author presents an alternative—the dome may here be the poet: "he would become himself the domed consciousness of a cold, happy, brilliance, an ice-flashing, sun-smitten, wisdom." Professor Knight offers, finally, the suggestion that the very names in the poem are "so lettered as to suggest first and last things"—Alph, Abyssinian, Abora, and Xanadu, with Kubla Khan in the middle. He sees the poem as a complete and perfect whole.

I think it will have to be agreed that this mode of thought was never in accord with Coleridge's conscious practice, and probably not with his theory either. His mind seems to have worked differently. Perhaps it was the preacher in him, which Lamb more than once remarked upon; at any rate, his habit was to expound his interior meanings outright. Often enough he conferred upon images of nature some deep significance, but he regularly made that explicit. In an early poem, *A Wish*, he wrote of a stream that meandered through hills and vales to the ocean. Two of the four stanzas described the stream's progress; the other two presented the parallel: "Thus thro' its silent tenor may my Life [flow]."[15] His manner of saying this kind of thing grew more flexible as he drew further away from neoclassical methods, but the explicitness remained. In *The Eolian Harp* the "white-flower'd Jasmin, and the broad-leav'd Myrtle" about his cottage are "meet emblems" of "Innocence and Love." The more important symbolism of the Aeolian harp itself is expressly described.[16] In verses addressed to Charles Lloyd in 1796 he again dots the *i*. "Thus rudely vers'd in allegoric lore, The Hill of Knowledge I essayed to trace," he explains and continues matching up his scene with its significance.[17]

These illustrations are from poems earlier than *Kubla Khan*, but they can be matched in the later writings and there is no counterweight that I know of from poems one naturally feels to be symbolic, in which no specific meaning is avowed. The image of the Aeolian lyre that Coleridge liked so well is never, so far as I recall, a silent symbol but is always offered with clear indication of its double meaning. And when he uses snakes to represent insidious evil he says so:

> Hence, viper thoughts, that coil around my mind,
> Reality's dark dream!

The snake images in *Christabel* are patently evil; the reader does not have to guess.[18] Occasionally Coleridge makes his meaning explicit only by the title, as in the lines *To an Unfortunate Woman Whom the Author Had Known in the Days of Her Innocence*. Throughout, the lady is a myrtle leaf blown about by the wind; but even without the title the reader is given plenty of clues. By the time the "foolish" myrtle leaf has "gaily" left its "mother-stalk" and "fluttered" to the "sighs" and flatteries of the wooing wind, only to be "flung to fade, to rot and die," even a dull reader can scarcely miss the analogy of seduction.[19]

The critic nourished on Donne, Yeats, and Mr. Eliot may be repelled—but, whether one likes it or not, this is the way Coleridge actually wrote. He often wrote much better but always in the same kind. Undoubtedly he was very modern in some ways; but he was neither modern nor medieval enough, he was still too close to the earlier eighteenth-century habits of thought, to transform symbol or allegory altogether into pure metaphor in such a way that the relation between different levels of meaning is wholly implied and not explicit. This open symbolism, with its obvious reference to the moral world, is the only kind that we are sure Coleridge practiced. We should have an exceptionally good reason before we suppose that in *The Ancient Mariner*, *Christabel*, and *Kubla Khan* he departed from it, yet at the same time departed so invisibly that posterity has required a hundred and some years to uncover the true meaning.

Not only as a poet but as a critic also Coleridge naturally thought in other terms than those of dark symbol. His opinion of the poetry of his contemporary Blake suggests as much, for it shows him imperfectly at home with those poems in which the symbolism is implied rather than expressed. Introduced to the *Songs of Innocence and Experience* in 1818, Coleridge recognized them as the work of genius but clearly preferred the simpler to the more complex poems. His first choice was *The Little Black Boy*, and next to this were the relatively conventional and simple *Night* in the *Songs of Innocence*, and *The Divine Image*. *The Tyger* was much farther down on his list, below *Infant Joy* and *The Schoolboy; The Poison Tree* was at the bottom; *Ah! Sun-Flower* was not mentioned.[20] It is no discredit to Coleridge that he should have failed to recognize fully a merit that others in his day also missed; but I think the taste exhibited in his list bears out what his own poems have already seemed to show, that concealed symbolism was foreign to his habit of mind.

His theory was, on the whole, consistent with his practice and taste, though his remarks on symbolism and allegory are somewhat mixed. Commonly, he used the word *allegory* as a lump term for almost all that was not literal. Twice, however, in 1816 and 1818, evidently under the influence of his later studies in German philosophy, he drew a distinction between allegory and symbol. On the first occasion, writing not of literature but of religious faith, he remarked that symbols stand somewhere between the literal and the metaphorical. An allegory merely translates abstract ideas into a "picture-language." A symbol, on the other hand, is characterized by a *translucence* of the special in the individual, or of the general in the special, or of the universal in the general; above all by the translucence of the eternal through and in the temporal. *It always partakes of the reality which it renders intelligible;* and while it enunciates the whole, abides itself as a living part in that unity of which it is the representative." The "flowering meadow" that lay before him, he said, stirred a feeling of awe, "as if there were before my eyes the same power as that of the reason—the same power in a lower dignity, and therefore a symbol established in the truth of things." This was so because Nature does literally "declare the being and attributes of the Almighty Father."[21] The same definition Coleridge afterwards applied to literature in a lecture on *Don Quixote*, distinguishing the symbolic from the allegorical by its being "always itself a part of that, of the whole of which it is the representative." His illustration suggests, however, merely the rhetorician's distinction between synecdoche and metaphor. "Here comes a sail" (= a ship), Coleridge said, is symbolic; " 'behold our lion!' when we speak of some gallant soldier, is allegorical." The sail is part of the ship, the lion entirely separate from the soldier. The allegory, Coleridge said further, must always be conscious, but in the symbol "it is very possible that the general truth represented may be working unconsciously in the writer's mind during the construction of the symbol."[22] Symbolism unconsciously arrived at he thus recognized; he did not, however, imply that the poet remains ignorant of the symbol he has been constructing, nor did he give up his provision that the symbol, to exist at all, must be translucent," that it must "enunciate" and "render intelligible" the reality it represents, and that it must actually be a *part* of the larger meaning. By Coleridge's definition, most modern interpreters of *The Ancient Mariner* and *Kubla Khan*, and perhaps of *Christabel*, would have to be called allegorists rather than symbolists, for he appears to confine symbolism to passages in which an expression of a specific love, for example, or fear, or power, becomes symbolic of the same feeling generally or universally.

In the lectures of 1818 Coleridge had a good deal to say of allegory. There too intelligibility—the equivalent of "translucence" in symbols—he held to be essential. The difference between the thing said and the thing meant must be "everywhere presented to the eye or imagination while the likeness is suggested to the mind; and this connectedly so that the parts combine to form a consistent whole."[23] Here Coleridge did not maintain the distinction between allegory and symbol but seems to have lumped them both under the first term, as he customarily did. Prophetically, he wrote his own derisive comment on his unborn symbolic interpreters, though at the time he thought he was only writing of Tasso:

The most decisive verdict against narrative allegory is to be found in Tasso's own account of what he would have the reader understand by the persons and events of his Jerusalem. Apollo be praised! not a thought like it would ever enter of its own accord into any mortal mind; and what is an additional good feature, when put there, it will not stay, having the very opposite quality that snakes have—they come out of their holes into open view at the sound of sweet music, while the allegoric meaning slinks off at the very first notes, and lurks in murkiest oblivion—and utter invisibility.[24]

Toward Milton's allegorizing, nevertheless, he was sympathetic. " 'Where more is meant than meets the ear,' " he said, "is true of [Milton] beyond all writers. He was so great a man that he seems to have considered fiction as profane unless where it is consecrated by being emblematic of some truth." He proceeded to read into one passage of *Comus* more, certainly, than the surface of the lines conveys and cited "Milton's prose works" in defense of the "allegorising of poets." But of course *Comus* as a whole is "allegorised" in the explicit fashion that Coleridge himself used. These remarks in a letter of 1802 followed others of a contrary tendency. Of some poems of Bowles he said:

There reigns through all the blank verse poems such a perpetual trick of moralizing everything, which is very well, occasionally, *but never to see or describe any interesting appearance in nature without connecting it, by dim analogies, with the moral world proves faintness of impression.* Nature has her proper interest, and he will know what it is who believes and feels that everything has a life of its own, and that we are all *One Life*.[25]

These statements on symbolism and allegory are not perhaps wholly consistent, and the distinction Coleridge once took pains to draw between the two never became his actual habit of thought. Always, however, he insisted upon "translucence" or intelligibility, and he never seems to have regarded symbolism as in any way essential to good poetry.

Apart from his theoretical views on the subject, there is nothing in his attitude toward his three most multifariously interpreted poems to suggest that he felt in them any hidden meanings. He does not seem to have quoted or referred to them in later years to illustrate truths other than apparent ones, though he was generally fond of quoting his poetry to illustrate his prose discourses and did not ordinarily minimize the depth of its poetic meaning. In *The Ancient Mariner* the verse itself seems more consonant with Coleridge's own remark that the poem had too much moral than with any elaborate cosmic interpretation: its movement does not strike my ear as sufficiently grave to bear the weight of all the meanings that have been bestowed upon it. When he planned to write on great or cosmic themes Coleridge never seems to have thought of inclosing them in the small packets of minor poetic forms; on the contrary, he would plan an epic on "The Origin of Evil" or "The Destruction of Jerusalem," or a "Poem in one [or three] Books in the Manner of Dante on the excursion of Thor." On such works he would expect to bestow not less than twenty years.[26]

If one proceeds upon the belief that a man cannot open his mouth without being symbolic, perhaps one can do no better than accept for *Kubla Khan* some such interpretation as Professor Knight's or, a better choice, I think, Miss Bodkin's, and Professor Warren's of *The Ancient Mariner*. To the critic who maintains that a poem has a meaning of which the poet was unconscious there is no answer. And indeed I do not doubt that this sometimes occurs. There is no question, I think, that unconscious and subconscious forces lurk beneath the surfaces of our thought and feeling and that the appeal of a work of art may derive partly from a secret correspondence with these forces. But that it always does so in the sense usually supposed is far from being established; and that the conscious symbol-seeking of critics or psychoanalysts often succeeds in salting the tail of this invisible bird is a matter of very considerable doubt. If *Kubla Khan* naturally conveys to a reader one or another of the various meanings of sexual opposition or immortality or the life of man—or of King Oedipus and incest—perhaps they are there. But to me—except for Miss Bodkin's Paradise-Hell contrast, which very naturally comes to mind though Coleridge purposely diminished it by altering "Mount Amara," a really traditional earthly Paradise, to "Mount Abora"—except for that meaning, which I think of in this poem as rather associative than symbolic, such elaborate interpretations as have been made of *Kubla Khan* thus far seem more ingenious than compelling. They do not coalesce naturally with what Coleridge actually wrote; on the contrary, the thought of these meanings drives the poem itself out of one's mind.

The means by which symbolism is conveyed, whether we suppose the process conscious or not, have been discussed at length earlier. Symbolic meaning becomes "translucent" when the poet alters the course of nature or heightens or distorts certain features of his subject in ways not accounted for by the surface meaning alone, when a particular emphasis not otherwise explicable is laid upon a word or image, or when his verse form takes on a special character that is intelligible only through a symbolic meaning. This may come about unconsciously, so that the poet betrays rather than conveys his meaning without knowing even afterward that he has done so—though I suspect this last does not occur often in the greatest poetry. Generally, I think, the process is partly conscious and partly not, but the poet in the end usually comes to have at least some inkling of what he has said. Regardless of what he knew or did not know he was saying, however, the poem itself can be symbolic only if the ulterior meaning has actually stamped its impress upon the poem, only if it has done something to the language, form, images, incidents, that the ostensible meaning would not do. A meaning that may actually have existed in the poet's mind, conscious or unconscious, is still—"Apollo be praised!" as Coleridge said—not a meaning *in the poem* unless it has done this. No doubt there are borderline instances where the impress of a second meaning is so lightly marked that one wonders if it is there at all, or where the whole is so complex that we find it difficult to decide whether the meaning is single or double or merely associatively rich as it is in any good poem.

Of *Kubla Khan* it is perhaps less easy to say than of some poems, categorically, that everything is explicable in terms of a primary meaning. The fragment is too brief for

its full intention to have become evident, and its division
into disparate parts leaves unanswered questions. The
symbolic interpretations presented in the past, however,
have not been offered as healing the split in the poem;
they have not pretended to show that on a symbolic level
the division is bridged or is necessary to the form and
meaning of the whole. They do not, in fact, solve any of
the problems that the poem really presents.

4. PARADISE, AND THE MILTONIC ECHOES
THE MUSICAL PATTERN

Something nevertheless remains. Though *Kubla Khan*
may have no great depths of symbolic meaning, may tell
us nothing we did not know about the unconscious mind of
genius, and may not even be a "psychological curiosity"
at all, it is still unlike anything else; and for those who
have felt it to be the quintessential romantic poem, something of a point remains, for it lies squarely upon a cross-
roads where two or three main romantic traditions meet.

In *The Road to Xanadu*, neglecting almost entirely
Coleridge's world at the close of the eighteenth century,
Lowes wrote as if Coleridge had existed in eternity but not
in time. Actually, however, most of the imagery of *Kubla
Khan* may be found, not merely in the old travelers' narratives, and not in merely minor literary sources, but in a
major line of poetry that was thoroughly familiar to every
reader in the 1790's and not only to a library cormorant
like Coleridge. As I have said earlier, there was nothing
novel and nothing dreamlike about the combining of material from widely separated geographical regions. The
synthesis of this matter had been created by the literary
tradition itself, running back through Milton to Spenser,
Ariosto, and the other Renaissance romancers who grafted
these new trees upon medieval stock. The *Orlando Furioso*,
for example, is full of "domes"; there is, in fact, a project
for a golden dome (it is the Western writers, spicing their

writing with Eastern flavors, more often than the Eastern writers and travelers, who deck their scenes with domes); Ariosto's Angelica is the daughter of the Khan of Cathay; there is an earthly Paradise and a mingling of Egypt, the Nile, Nubia, Cathay, India, and other far places. The later travelers and geographers themselves often took their descriptive language from this and other literary sources. In Milton, as in Ariosto, all the strands are united. Afterward they sometimes descend separately, through Gray and Collins, through Addison and Johnson. By 1790 the oriental tale in prose or verse had lost much of its freshness but was far from dead. Coleridge was not likely to have forgotten Addison's "Vision of Mirzah" when he suggested to Godwin Myrza's death as a subject. The imagery of many of these pieces of literary orientalism bears a family resemblance. Addison not only wrote his as a "vision"; he spoke of life itself as a "dream." His "vision" presented to the ear magical music "inexpressibly melodious," like the "heavenly airs" that greet the soul entering into Paradise, and to the eye valley, river, fountains, and all else that belongs to the Paradise garden.[27] And in Johnson's opening paragraphs of *Rasselas, Prince of Abyssinia* the same geographical properties are disposed even more as they are in *Kubla Khan,* for the sources of the Nile, Amhara, and Abyssinia furnish the background for the palace and gardens in a vale to be entered only through a cavern, with a lake discharging waters through another cavern full of broken rocks, with rivulets that fill all the valley "with verdure and fertility," and a "dark cleft of the mountain" through which a stream falls "with dreadful noise from precipice to precipice till it was heard no more."[28]

The last paragraph of *Kubla Khan* is about poetic inspiration. Though I think Greek thought, as focused in the *Ion* and elsewhere, is at the root of Coleridge's imagery, the inheritance descends through the only superficially more northern bardic figures in Gray and Collins. Gray's inspired poet-prophet stood "on a rock" with "haggard eyes" while his "hoary hair Streamed, like a meteor, to the troubled air" as he struck his lyre; Gray's poet was associated with a cave, a "torrent's awful voice," a "magic song," and (in the companion piece) "a thousand rills" in "mazy progress" and the whole line of familiar furniture and epithets: vales, steep hills, rocks, groves, "odorous shade," "savage" youth (*savage* in the favorable sense merely of *wild*, for he sings his love song in numbers "wildly sweet"), "enchanting," "holy," the stream Maeander himself, and the rhyme of "measures" with "pleasures."[29] Collins's *Ode on the Poetical Character* and *The Passions: An Ode for Music* belong to the same family. The poet must always by tradition have notable hair; "haunted" is associated with "holy"; "measure" again rhymes with "pleasure"; a "war-denouncing trumpet" is blown with "prophetic sounds"; and the phrase "mingled measure" anticipates exactly Coleridge's phrase.[30]

All this merely takes us back once more to Milton, who hovers over Coleridge's poem as he does over so much other romantic poetry. Everything is there, from the archaic use of *savage* and the *measure-pleasure* rhyme, to the meters and the theme of Paradise. Coleridge himself once commented emphatically upon Milton's mingling of Eastern and Western materials;[31] and Milton's topography is clearly implied in the laying-out of Kubla's more indefinite garden. In the fourth book of *Paradise Lost* Satan beholds the earthly Paradise in one of the scenes to which Coleridge referred more than once:

> So on he fares, and to the border comes
> Of *Eden*, where delicious Paradise,
> Now nearer, Crowns with her enclosure green,
> As with a rural mound the champain head
> Of a steep wilderness, whose hairie sides
> With thicket overgrown, grottesque and wilde,

Access deni'd; and over head up grew
Insuperable highth of loftiest shade,
Cedar, and Pine, and Firr, and branching Palm
A Silvan Scene, and as the ranks ascend
Shade above shade, a woodie Theatre
Of stateliest view. Yet higher then thir tops
The verdurous wall of Paradise up sprung:

. . . .

And higher then that wall a circling row
Of goodliest Trees loaden with fairest Fruit,
Blossoms and Fruits at once of golden hue
Appeerd, with gay enameld colours mixt:
On which the Sun more glad impress'd his beams

. . . .

and to the heart inspires
Vernal delight and joy, able to drive
All sadness but despair: now gentle gales
Fanning thir odoriferous wings dispense
Native perfumes, and whisper whence they stole
Those balmie spoiles [ll. 131–59].

Paradise is thus outlined. Gardens, at least Paradise ones, are always fragrant or "odoriferous." But Coleridge applied an unusual epithet, "incense-bearing," to his trees, remembering, I feel sure, the odors of that "spicie shoare" for the sake of which Milton momentarily interrupts the description of his inland Paradise to embark upon a long voyage in a simile. For at the point where my quotation leaves off, the "native perfumes" of Paradise waft Milton around the whole of Africa, to delight sailors at sea with the breeze-blown odors from Saba (Sheba), traditional source of frankincense and spices:

As when to them who sail
Beyond the *Cape of Hope*, and now are past
Mozambic, off at Sea North-East windes blow
Sabean Odours from the spicie shoare
Of *Arabie* the blest, with such delay
Well pleas'd they slack thir course, and many a League
Cheard with the grateful smell old Ocean smiles.
So entertaind those odorous sweets the Fiend
Who came thir bane . . . [ll. 159–67].

Southey made off with this same image for *Thalaba*.
"Odours diviner than the gales of morning Waft from
Sabea" accompanied fruit that one of his damsels brought
"from the Bowers of Paradise" (XI, 8–9). And as Milton
followed his Sabean excursion immediately by a comparison of Satan to the demon Asmodeus in the Book of
Tobit—who was a demon-lover of sorts—it does not seem
fanciful to suppose that Coleridge's incense-bearing trees
too were a telescoping of Milton's preceding simile.[32]

Milton located the true earthly Paradise somewhere in
the region roughly between Damascus and Babylon. His
description of it, however, mingles the Cape of Good
Hope, the east coast of Africa, Arabia, Media, Egypt,
Abyssinia, Mount Amara, and the sources of the Nile, as
well as traditional Greek place names and myths—almost
everything, indeed, except Xanadu itself. After the digres-
sions to the spicy odors of Arabia and the demon Asmodeus, Satan's first general view of Paradise is filled in. In
the celebrated passage beginning with "that steep savage
Hill," Satan's leap over the wall, the great prototype of all
intrusions, is embroidered by a set of variations—other
leaps over other walls—and Satan is brought to rest "like
a Cormorant" to view the Garden that God had "or-
daind" in "fertil ground," as Kubla "decreed" his in the
inclosure of ten miles, also of "fertile ground." Milton's
Paradise mount had been raised astride the River Tigris,
which consequently "at the foot of Paradise Into a Gulf
shot under ground," "ingulft" beneath the "shaggie hill,"
till part was drawn up through the earth and rose "a fresh
Fountain" by the Tree of Life. "With many a rill" that ran
"with mazie error" it watered the Garden and the plants
growing in profusion "on Hill and Dale and Plaine," then
"united fell Down the steep glade, and met the neather
Flood" (IV, 223–43; IX, 71–73). In much the same way,
Coleridge's "sacred river" rose from the earth in a fountain. Diversified by "sinuous rills," it flowed on, "meander-

ing with a mazy motion Through wood and dale," until it likewise fell back beneath the earth to nether Flood or "sunless sea." Milton's scene is distinguished by the "insuperable highth of loftiest shade" of cedar and pine mentioned earlier—a "stateliest view"; the "enclosure green"; "lawns, or level downs"; "umbrageous grots and caves of coole recess"; and other "slope hills" besides the particular "steep savage Hill." These are matched by Coleridge's ancient forests "enfolding sunny spots of greenery," caverns, and the deep "chasm which slanted Down the green hill athwart a cedarn cover! A savage place." Milton overlays his Paradise with other associations, the "inspir'd *Castalian* Spring" and the false Abyssinian Paradise of "Mount Amara" "where *Abassin* Kings thir issue Guard." His scene, too, had its image of "rumord Warr." In "this Assyrian Garden" of Paradise, "the Fiend Saw undelighted all delight" (IV, 273–86, 817). I think there can be no question that Coleridge, who also had lost the "deep delight" that would have enabled him to create his dome in air, nevertheless had sat to very good purpose, like the prospecting Cormorant, upon the tree of Milton's knowledge.

Milton's subterranean Tigris is appropriately translated into the subterranean Alpheus with its Sicilian fountain of inspiration, since the Paradise river is by tradition also the first of rivers, "Alph." The "loud" music of the Muses by the "sacred" well from *Lycidas* mingles with the rest,[33] and I think the water-haunted lines of *Lycidas*, so full of streams and fountains and the dark depths of ocean, lent something of their spirit to *Kubla Khan*. The "sounding seas" that hurled Lycid "under the whelming tide" to "the bottom of the monstrous world" are not remarkably far from the "sunless sea" into which Coleridge's river sinks through its measureless caverns with their sound of "tumult." Lycidas knew how to "build the lofty rhyme" (Coleridge had consciously used this phrase of Milton's elsewhere); Coleridge wished he might "build that dome in air" in his own rhymes. But the meter of *Kubla Khan*, appropriately for its lighter theme, takes us back, as we saw earlier, to *L'Allegro* and *Il Penseroso*.

Here, as in other poems, Coleridge showed himself exceedingly sensitive to the music as well as the imagery of Milton's poetry. His ear retained and reproduced many of Milton's grammatical and rhetorical patterns and cadences. The shift of tempo, accompanying the shift of subject in *Lycidas*,

> And old *Damaetas* lov'd to hear our song.
> But O the heavy change, now thou art gon,

probably had something to do with Coleridge's

> But oh! that deep romantic chasm which slanted,

which accelerates after a tapering cadence with much the same movement. This parallel might seem of the dimmest and most accidental sort if it were not reinforced by other analogies and by Coleridge's own technical comments on these very lines of *Lycidas*, which I shall notice presently.

Years earlier, Milton's metrical effects had become audible in Coleridge's poetry with echoes that are at once verbal, grammatical, and assonantal. His lines on *Music* made no bones of beginning with "Hence, soul-dissolving Harmony," in which more sounds than the "Hence" recall the "Hence loathéd Melancholy" of *L'Allegro*. The first words of *The Wanderings of Cain* may have been written with the first words of *Samson Agonistes* hovering in the air.

"A little further, O my father, yet a little further, and we shall come into the open moonlight." Their road was through a forest of fir trees . . . [*Cain*, ll. 1-3].

> A little onward lend thy guiding hand
> To these dark steps, a little further on;
> For yonder bank hath choice of Sun or shade
> [*Samson Agonistes*, ll. 1–3].

Coleridge's Cain is led by a child, who describes the scene to him so entirely as if he were blind, like Samson, that the reader half-forgets he is not.

Your true poet is an imitative animal, and why should he not be? Words, phrases, tunes, and even atmospheres may run like quicksilver from poet to poet. Shakespeare's discovery, in *Lear*, of what lay hidden in the word *hang*— "half-way down Hangs one that gathers samphire, dreadful trade!"—sends Milton's Satan, like a fleet that "hangs in the clouds," upon his flight through Chaos. Coleridge tamed the image to "hanging woods" in *Osorio*, after which it sank into the morasses of the *Monthly Magazine* through the "hanging forests" and "hanging groves" of the River Wye in descriptions by John Thelwall but was raised aloft once again in Keats's composite Miltonism, "Forest on forest hung above his head Like cloud on cloud." This history of *hang* is not imaginary, or at least would not have been thought so by Coleridge; Wordsworth commemorated the early part of it (tracing it, in fact, further back to Virgil) when he wrote of words and the poetic imagination.[34] And Cowper's use of "slant hills" in *The Task*, or perhaps some earlier use of the word that I have not noticed, revealed a way of looking at the world, through a single word, that promptly scattered "slant" through the vocabulary of romantic observers of nature until it died away from overuse.

Subtle inflections and brief strains of music are blown about from pen to ear in the same way: Keats's *Ode to a Nightingale* and a ship of Wordsworth's drift into Robert Bridges' description of a ship; Hopkins's *Spring* and *Heaven-Haven* and the same ship of Bridges counterpoint their way into one of Mr. Auden's most poetic pieces. The tracing of these echoes may seem—may be—mere academic pedantry. The hearing of them, however, with the mind's ear adds immeasurably to the charm of the poetic effect. Bridges' ship trails its own beauty into Mr. Auden's stanzas, where it meets not only the bay of Hopkins but the ghost, too, of Lear's samphire gatherer, in the gull that just does not "hang" upon the sheer side, but "lodges." From the standpoint of the poet, these exchanges are the freemasonry of the craft; from that of the final effect, they are the invisible linking of one beauty with another, enriching both. The work of art—like its maker, the individual man—is both self-contained and not self-contained. Its aesthetic effect, indeed, derives in large part from this very fact, that it can be harmoniously both, a principle insufficiently recognized by certain of our otherwise admirable modern critics. But that is a subject in itself.

Often, if not always, Coleridge was fully aware how subtly Milton's voice had invaded his own poetic ear. His variations upon the Miltonic music were one notable aspect of his deliberate, tireless interest in metrical problems to which Wordsworth many years later bore emphatic testimony. When intent on a new experiment in meter, Coleridge bestowed, he said, "inconceivable" time and labor, was indeed "an epicure in sound."[35] Poems, notebooks, and letters easily bear out Wordsworth's assertion. Coleridge discussed feminine rhyme and hexameters with Southey, sent experimental hexameters—pretty bad ones, to be sure—to the Wordsworths in Germany. Some fragments of metrical experiments survive, and, besides the celebrated venture in the verse of *Christabel* and the variations of ballad stanza in *The Ancient Mariner*—departures from standard practice in the direction of greater freedom—there was the contrary experiment in the extremely elaborate and rigidly fixed pattern of *France: An Ode.*

During one early period, roughly between 1792 and 1795, Coleridge was writing very obviously under the spell of both Spenser and Milton. In *To the Nightingale* he quoted from *Il Penseroso*, "Most musical, most melancholy Bird!"; in the Spenserian stanzas of *To the Author of*

Poems he quoted *Lycidas;* he wrote avowed *Lines in the Manner of Spenser.*[36] Here, besides the array of obvious archaisms—lines decked with *y-pluckt, wight, Elfin, withouten*—he practiced all sorts of musical devices of alliteration and assonance. He played, for one thing, with a trick of foreshadowing his terminal rhyme or other terminal sounds by a preparatory echo in the preceding words.

> O Peace, that on a lilied bank dost *love*. . . .
> For O! I wish my Sara's *frowns* to *flee*. . . .

This device he worked and overworked. Or he combined this with a sort of concealed double or triple rhyme: "*head did pillow*" rhyming with "herself *with willow*," "*wile, I ween*" with "*smiles* hath *seen*," "*blossom's bloom*" with "*soft perfume*." These are like the rhyme of "nĕver-sēar . . . mĕllowing yēar . . . lĕft his pēer" in the opening lines of *Lycidas*. Coleridge toned down his experiments somewhat in the *Lines at Shurton Bars*, but he was still weighting the latter half of his lines with redoubled sounds: "*gentler sense*," "*blossom's bloom*," "*viewless influence*," "*rolling stones*," "*tides supply*" are five out of eight successive line endings.[37] In *The Eolian Harp* these devices are modified to fit the blank-verse pattern, but in that too Coleridge's great concern for musical effect is evident. Never again did he make himself and his readers quite so dizzy with reduplicated sound as in that early and prolonged orgy. Interlaced alliteration and assonance occur often later, notably and most effectively in *Frost at Midnight*. Only in *Kubla Khan*, however, and in two or three other poems written late in 1799 do we find again a pattern as elaborate as in those early verses. The word-for-word dream of *Paradise Lost* that he said he dreamed that winter; his use in the *Ode to the Duchess of Devonshire* of the series of *o*-rhymes like those of Milton's sonnet *On the Late Massacre in Piemont* and certain other considerations suggest that it was again Milton who inspired Coleridge's

return to those sound patterns. In *Kubla Khan* the design
is even more complex, but it is also freer and more subtle.

It is difficult not to suppose that the effect of free or imperfect rhyming in *Kubla Khan* was in part a deliberate
reflection of *Lycidas*, for in later years Coleridge described
that very feature of *Lycidas* in words that fit his own poem
quite as well. Discussing a not very important question,
whether Milton intended the *hill-rill* couplet of lines 22–23
to close one paragraph of *Lycidas* or to open the next,
Coleridge argued for the first choice on grounds that, he
thought, must be "for a poet's ear convincing." The
eighth line of the preceding paragraph ("And bid fair peace
be to my sable shrowd"), like the first ("Begin then,
Sisters of the sacred well"), "is *rhymeless*, and was left so,
because the concurring rhymes of the concluding distich
were foreseen as the compensations." In other words,
Coleridge was arguing that Milton had deliberately
opened a paragraph with an unrhymed line but would not
have closed it so. He went on to make further comments
upon the rhymes of the fourth paragraph of *Lycidas* ("But
O the heavy change," etc.). "There is a delicate beauty of
sound produced by the floating or oscillation of assonance
and consonance in the rhymes *gone, return, caves, o'ergrown, mourn, green, seen, lays.* Substitute *flown* for *gone*
in the first line: and if you have a poet's ear, you will feel
what you have lost and understand what I mean."[38] The
off-rhymes *gone-o'ergrown* and *return-mourn* are precisely
the kind of imperfect rhyme exhibited in *Kubla Khan*
more often than in most of Coleridge's poetry. Coleridge
rhymed "b*u*rst" with "f*o*rced" (". . . momently was
forced: Amid whose swift half intermitted burst"), an off-
rhyme that exactly duplicates the vowels and the *r* of one
of those he remarked upon as especially poetic in Milton,
"ret*u*rn" and "m*o*urn." The off-rhymes of *Kubla Khan*
include *ever-river* (not uncommon in English poetry), *far-
war* (also not uncommon), and perhaps *saw-Abora.* His

remark upon Milton's use of an unrhymed line *at the be-ginning of a verse paragraph* might equally well have referred to the *first line* of his own final paragraph, "A damsel with a dulcimer." I do not suppose Coleridge thought of *dulcimer* as even an off-rhyme to *once I saw* or *Abora*. His rhymes, in fact, follow so precisely not merely the rhyming of *Lycidas* but what he later particularly pointed out in that rhyming—that one does not readily imagine them to have been produced unconsciously.

However much it owes to Milton, Coleridge's poem has its own quite un-Miltonic individual identity of music. A particular tone is given to the whole by a predominance of *æ*- and other modified *a*-sounds that set the poem distinctly apart from any music characteristic of Milton. The sound is common in Eastern names, particularly as anglicized in Coleridge's day, and is very noticeable in *Thalaba*, where, besides the hero's own name and the staples Allah, Mohammed, Arabia, Bagdad, Babylon, Ali, the stanzas are dotted with Lobaba, Abdaldar, Dom-Daniel, Okba, Naÿd, Moath, Saleah, Haruth and Maruth, Al-Maimon, Aloadin, Mohareb, Zohak, Ararat, Laila, Bahar-Danush. These names spring out from the pages as one turns them quickly, and their number might easily be doubled. Southey was conscious of their prominence and attempted, like Coleridge, to play his tune upon them. So his maiden is usually a "d*a*msel" and she plucks fruit from the "t*a*marind" tree. "C*a*mels" and "c*a*verns" and "P*a*radise" and "m*a*gic" follow as automatically as a string of beads, often like a reflex motion of the voice when the mind has gone off elsewhere.

The pattern of *Kubla Khan*, however, is not confined to the *æ*-sounds. The rhyme, with all its freedom, its shiftings and *Lycidas*-like "oscillations," has elaborate hidden correspondences. The rhyme scheme of the opening seven lines, for example, is exactly repeated in the first seven lines of the second paragraph. The extraordinary elabora-

tion, also, of the assonance keeps the music of this poem
fresh through many rereadings. Even when one knows it
well, it is still full of half-caught echoes, correspondences
of sound felt but too complex to be anticipated or to remain tabulated in the mind even after they have been
analyzed. And so they retain a subtle, secret harmony.

The most obvious of the patterns in the opening lines,
apart from the ubiquity of the *æ*-sounds, is the alliteration
that closes each of the first five lines: "*Kubla Khan,*"
"*dome decree,*" "*river ran,*" "*measureless to man,*" "*sunless
sea*"—a revival of the device Coleridge had practiced so
conspicuously in his Spenserian-Miltonic verse of 1795.
Here, however, it is only a small part of his effect and is so
well subordinated to the whole pattern that one might
know the poem for a long time without becoming conscious of the obvious and somewhat mechanical device.

The opening line, "In Xa'nadu' did Ku'bla Kha'n," receives its primary shape from the inclosed assonance of its
four stresses, *a—u—u—a*, which swings the sound as if in
a shallow curve, the symmetry being still further marked
by the full rhyme of the inclosing syllables, *Xan-* and
Khan (Coleridge undoubtedly pronounced *Khan* as it was
often spelled, *Can*) and the embellishment of minor
echoes, *d*'s and short *i*'s binding together the first part and
k's the end of the line:

In Xanadu did Kubla Khan

Two of the next three lines are given the same outer shape
by means of the same inclosing assonance, "Alph . . . ran"
and "caverns . . . man"; but the extremely symmetrical
swing of the first line is broken and varied afterwards.

In the first four lines only one sound stands out alone,
without an echo; it is the most resounding syllable in the
poem—*dome*. The word resounds naturally of itself, but

its intrinsic length and weight are here increased by its
isolation and its contrast against the background of the
lighter vowel sounds that precede it:

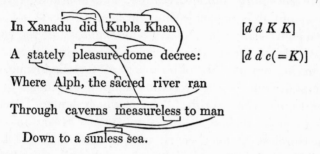

The *dome* stands alone, though it is tied into the verse by
its focusing of the *d*-sounds before and after. In contrast
with the self-contained symmetry of the first line, the
second has a freewheeling sound, for it has little internal
pattern to give it a shape of its own beyond the inflectional
shape determined by its meaning. Its sounds, all but
dome, dissolve into the general fabric. The closing word,
decree, unites in its two chief consonants the two minor
alliterations of the first line, the *d*'s ("-du did") and the
k's ("Ku- Kha-"). *Stately* disappears into *sacred* in the
next line, and *pleasure* has its full double rhyme in *measure*
in the line after. This absorption of the other elements of
the line lends still greater prominence to *dome*.

The tune and variations to be played upon the *æ*-sound
are established by the first sentence, in which three of the
five lines begin and end with stresses upon it. But this
effect is overlaid or interwoven with an elaboration so
intricate that one could scarcely point to its mate in English poetry if we except the more subtle harmonies of Milton and Bridges. It would be both useless and impertinent,
however, to point out in detail the almost innumerable
linkings of sound in *Kubla Khan*. Anyone can do it for
himself who cares to, though the maziness of the design is
remarkable. After the initial sentence the pattern becomes

more flexible and varied. The *æ*-sounds recur, but less regularly, and often lengthen or shade into the broader *a*'s. Exactly what sounds Coleridge thought or heard when he wrote *enchanted, haunted, chaffy,* and *dance* we do not know, but it is probable that he heard at least some of them equivocally as both *hænted* and *hānted,* like the variegated *a*'s of the Eastern names. Often throughout the poem he repeats his old device of foreshadowing the terminal rhyme by a preceding echo of assonance or alliteration—"sinuous rills," "chasm which slanted," "ceaseless turmoil seething," "mazy motion," "river ran" and "measureless to man" each used a second time, "from far," "mingled measure," "loud and long." This device, used skilfully as it is here and partly concealed by the interlacing of other patterns, contributes something to the floating effect of the whole, for the assonance softens the impact of the rhyme and so lessens its tendency to bring the line to earth at the close: the terminal rhyme does not settle so heavily upon the mind when its emphasis has been partly stolen by its preceding shadow. The forward movement is made to pause and "oscillate" further at times by the considerable number of lines in which the meaning looks forward while the rhyme looks back. One finds this often elsewhere as the closed couplet of the eighteenth century broke down, but it seems to be used in *Kubla Khan* with a somewhat special effect.

To my mind, none of this bears the marks of dream-composition, though it has co-operated with Coleridge's story of a dream by contributing to the floating effect. It does not sound, either, like any other sort of fully automatic composition. The intense concentration of the act of composing does indeed bear some likeness to reverie; it is, in fact, reverie in one of Erasmus Darwin's senses, "the poet's reverie" in which the will is active though attention is detached from the outside world. But it is creative *will* that is at work and not the *wish*-fulfilment reverie of certain psychologico-aesthetic theories. That will is felt in *Kubla Khan*, I think, even though its aim may be only vaguely determined.

5. THE "LAOCOÖN," PERHAPS

The poem does, however, have a quality that is different from Coleridge's other work; and it is possible that this may have had something to do with Lessing. When Coleridge wrote his series of long descriptive letters from Germany, with their accounts of the snowy cavern roofed with summer leaves, he twice remarked ruefully upon his own inability to describe. What could account for his being "so miserable a Describer?" he had asked. "Is it that I understand neither the practice nor the principles of Painting?" His answer is almost directly out of the mouth of Lessing. "I could half suspect that what are deemed fine descriptions, produce their effects almost purely by a charm of words, with which and with whose combinations, we associate *feelings* indeed, but no distinct *Images*."[39]

It was a few months earlier (the account was later published in *Satyrane's Letters*) that Coleridge had first come to know the work of Lessing. The attraction had been instantaneous and personal; the mere sight of a portrait had aroused in him a sense of kinship. "I saw there," he wrote of his visit to Klopstock's brother, "a very fine portrait of Lessing, whose works are at present the chief object of my admiration."[40] By January, 1799, he had matured a plan for a life of Lessing, which was to occupy his intentions, if not his time, for two years or more; he was already collecting material and writing a preliminary sketch. From this time until at least the end of 1800 the work on Lessing was officially, if not always in fact, Coleridge's Work-in-Progress. He mentioned it often, once in this very letter that deplored his own weakness as a describer.

I suspect—but this can be so only if *Kubla Khan* was composed in 1799 or 1800—that a part of what under the dazzle of Coleridge's preface we have interpreted as a kaleidoscopic dream-quality may have originated in a deliberate effort to write descriptive poetry by this new light, by giving over the attempt to "paint" a scene and securing his effect instead "by a *charm of words*, with which *and with whose combinations*, we associate *feelings* indeed, but no distinct *Images*." That is what the poem *Kubla Khan* actually, I think, does. Despite the image-making words, I do not find myself really picturing Kubla's pleasure-grounds. Miss Maud Bodkin, who approached the poem from a quite different angle and with neither Lessing nor Coleridge's theories of description in mind, remarked upon this effect. The "meaning and value" of the description for her, she wrote, "is hardly at all in the faint visual images aroused: it is in the far-reaching suggestiveness, so much harder to explore, that belongs to the words, and clings also about these image fragments."[41] I suspect this is the effect of the poem upon most other readers. The notion of substituting "charm of words" for a clearly "painted" scene may have been the impulse that sent Coleridge back in *Kubla Khan*, as in other poems known to have been composed late in 1799, to the elaborate sound patterns of his early Spenser-Milton period. Certain of his later comments on Milton lend weight to that possibility.

In the familiar twenty-first chapter of the *Laocoön*, Lessing discussed two methods by which the poet, working within the limitations of his temporal medium and so avoiding complete description, may produce an impression no less powerful than that of a painting. One means is that of showing the effect of the object upon others. He used the perennial illustration for this, Homer's presentation of Helen's beauty through its effect upon the old men of Troy. "Let the poet paint us the delight," Lessing wrote, "the affection, love, and rapture, which beauty produces, and he has painted beauty itself."[42] The other method, he said, is that of transforming beauty into *charm* (*Reiz*).

"Charm is beauty in motion, and is, for this very reason, less suitable to the painter than to the poet." Charm "comes and goes; and since we can generally recall to our minds a movement more easily and vividly than mere forms or colours; charm necessarily, in the same circumstances, produces a stronger effect upon us than beauty." The beauty of Alcina (in the *Orlando Innamorato* of Boiardo) is shown by the movement of her features. Her mouth is formed into "that lovely smile, which in itself already opens a paradise upon earth; . . . Her bosom charms, less because the images of milk, and ivory, and apples, are called up . . . than because we see it softly swell and fall, as the waves upon the extreme edge of the shore."[43] These remarks are an extension, with emphasis upon "charm," of Lessing's earlier account of the poetic method illustrated from Homer, who "describes nothing but progressive actions," a statement that Lessing expanded by means of that other familiar instance, Homer's presentation of Hera's chariot not by describing it ready-made but by building it "piece by piece, before our eyes." So too with the apparel of Agamemnon: we see him putting it on.[44]

Though some of these ideas of Lessing had been voiced earlier by Burke and Lord Kames, Coleridge's observation on descriptive writing in the letter of May, 1799, that also refers to Lessing is phrased as if the idea were then new to him. The *Laocoön* undoubtedly made him more conscious than before of the problems of descriptive writing, as well as more self-critical; it apparently also suggested his phrase "charm of words," though—whether purposely or from imperfect comprehension of the German —he did not reproduce Lessing's idea quite exactly.[45]

This Lessing-like conception never became a central tenet in the critical thought of Coleridge, but neither was it a mere passing notion. In the lecture on Milton in 1818, in which he spoke of Milton's fusion of Christian, Jewish, and Mohammedan materials in *Paradise Lost*—a lecture that in several respects seems to hark back to the time of his sojourn in Germany and shortly after—Coleridge introduced a definition of "high poetry" unlike any of his better-known definitions and apparently reminiscent of the central thesis of the *Laocoön*. "High poetry," he said, "is the translation of reality into the ideal under the predicament of succession of time only." And though he praised the Paradise scene of *Paradise Lost,* in which he thought Milton's "descriptive powers are exercised to the utmost," nevertheless "Milton is not a picturesque, but a musical poet," he said.[46] "Adam bending over the sleeping Eve, in the Paradise Lost," he added still later, "and Dalilah approaching Samson, in the Agonistes, are the only two proper pictures I remember in Milton."[47] These remarks belong to a single thread of thought and apply accurately also to *Kubla Khan*, bulging as it is with reminiscences of Milton's Paradise scene, which, he said, displayed "Milton's sunny side as a man." Again one is reminded of that occasion in 1800 when he dreamed (or said, or thought, or dreamed he dreamed) the whole of *Paradise Lost*, as fifteen years later he was to say he had dreamed *Kubla Khan*. But, Coleridge said, though he will "admit the prerogative of poetic feeling, and poetic faith," he "cannot suspend the judgment even for a moment. A poem may in one sense be a dream, but it must be a waking dream."[48] Surely with these words Coleridge himself denied by implication either the dream or else the poetry of *Kubla Khan*.

Whether or not Coleridge did compose *Kubla Khan* in accordance with a new notion, for him, of how poetic description might be written, it is undoubtedly "musical" rather than "picturesque" to an even greater degree than Milton's account of Paradise, but in the same sense. Especially, Coleridge foregoes any topographical outline such as even Milton provided for his Eden and Paradise.

One is not told where anything stood with reference to anything else; the dome, the caves, the chasm, and the gardens remain unmapped, a circumstance that undoubtedly contributes much to the "dream"-effect. The whole is "compounded" of what in another connection Coleridge called "half-verbal, half-visual metaphors."[49] The handling of both time and space is what we should expect if a poet were writing with the observations of the *Laocoön* in mind. Though the material of the fragment is essentially descriptive, it is rendered as far as possible in narrative terms quite unlike Coleridge's more static earlier descriptive poetry. As in Homer's description of Hera's chariot, the scene is first presented through progression in time: Kubla *decreed* the dome, *so* the walls and towers *were built* to *encircle* the five miles of fertile ground. That, however, is the end of the building process, for in the remainder of the first two paragraphs the building is assumed to be complete. Finally, in the postscript, it is again undone—in a different sense—by the equivocation of a metaphor identifying palace with poem, the subject of the verse with the verse itself. So the poem oscillates between the done and the undone. Both states, however, are represented as far as possible through activity and motion. After the building process is dropped, movement is taken over by nature itself. The hills *enfold*, the chasm *slants;* the fountain *seethes* with *ceaseless turmoil* and, *breathing* in *fast thick pants, is forced* upward in *swift half-intermitted bursts;* the rocks *vault, rebound, dance* as if from a thresher's *flail.* And so on. Here is the "charm," not only of words but of Lessing's "beauty in motion." The shiftings of time and place, however, are not genuinely dreamlike or kaleidoscopic. Those of place are logically or at least conventionally presented as comparison or reminiscence; the central Paradise scene has the air of shifting only because explanation of the topographical disposition of its features is omitted. The apparent shifting of time, too, is no more than a rhetorical device; whether conscious or not, whether under the influence of Lessing or not, it is hardly more truly dreamlike than the chariot of Hera or the shield of Achilles in Homer. There is no phantasmagoria whatever; only, the method here is to flit and not to dwell; space is deployed through action and time.

It would be an interesting and curious point in literary history if the familiar, baffling fragment of *Kubla Khan* should actually prove to be the first poetic godchild in England of the *Laocoön*. Without certainty about the dates, however, this can be but a speculation. Though the poem departs from the earlier work of Coleridge in a direction that might, certainly, have been determined by the ideas of Lessing, the change is not so revolutionary that one is obliged to presuppose a theory imported from outside the poet's own spinning brain.

6. THE SPIRIT OF OSCILLATION

Whatever proportions of this and that went into the making of *Kubla Khan*—perhaps a statistical critic will come along and assign percentages to Milton and Purchas —we end, as we began, with an awareness of its special character. It may not be the unique and novel synthesis of geographical elements that Lowes thought it, and it may not carry a great weight of specific symbols or tell us anything we did not know about unconscious genius. It may not be—and in fact I think is not—among the very greatest achievements of English poetry. Still, it has perfection in its kind; we do not forget it, and we never mistake it for anything else. And some things about the essence of poetry can be perceived more easily, perhaps, in the lesser than in the greater masterpieces.

In part, the special "witchery" of *Kubla Khan* is owing to its odd union of Miltonic verse texture with rather ordinary, conventional Gothic–oriental- tale matter. When Milton himself used Eastern material it succumbed, like all his other sources, to his own severe logic and the firmly organic continuity he gave it. But between his use of it and Coleridge's there intervened the epidemic of oriental and pseudo-oriental tales, which exhibit the wayward structure almost of improvisation. The tales of the *Arabian Nights* themselves seem to Western habits of mind a fabulous sequence of nonsequiturs. Their wilful inconsequence, their flitting logic (annihilating cause and effect) reappear in Western pseudo-oriental tales as mere structural laxness and irresponsibility. A similar laxness of structure and style characterized the Gothic romance (with the partial exception of Mrs. Radcliffe's) and the verse romances, whether Gothic or Eastern. Southey composed *Thalaba* as if with a dump truck; despite all the pains bestowed upon his work, the final impression upon the reader is of an indiscriminate pouring-out of large lumps of inert matter animated by no living breath, held together by no structure in the design and no texture in the writing. In *Kubla Khan* the materials are the same. But the Miltonic texture transforms the whole into something altogether different, something that is neither Milton's nor Gothic-oriental. The intricate complexities and unifications of the verse pattern here produce a subtle music that bestows upon ordinarily chaotic—and also stale—material an air of mysterious meaning. It is a new tune; though the texture is Milton's, the voice is the voice of Coleridge.

I do not know any other poem in which the pattern is played primarily with *æ*-sounds. The outlandish proportion of these, along with the Eastern names, is in some measure responsible for the particular flavor of the poem. They are intersprinkled with a good many other short vowel sounds, and most of the long vowels are rather light —either without depth of tone or carried quickly by. Even the other *ō*-sounds, except for the *dome*, are mostly light passing ones that can scarcely be dwelt upon—*momently*, *holy*, *float*. Throughout the poem many of the syllables carrying the nominal verse stress are but lightly touched. In the midst of them the "dome" stands out, dominating the poem by pure frequency as well as contrast. This dwelling upon the dome might be thought to justify reading into it such profound symbolic meanings as the "immortality" or the union of male and female opposites of Professor Knight's theory, for the word is not as natural in its setting as one might suppose. Most of the Eastern travelers described such buildings as either palaces or pleasure-houses; nor are domes notable in the Milton-Gray-Collins tradition. Coleridge brought it in from somewhere else, and in the poem it indubitably sounds important. Even so, its resonance does not seem to me quite symbolic in any specific sense. The word, I suspect, was running through his head as part of a verse tune, probably owing to personal or chance associations. The Royal Pavilion at Brighton, with its shallow central dome and its associations with idle pleasure, might have suggested it, though the Royal Stables, actually known as "the Dome," were not yet in existence.[50] If the date was 1799 or later, there would have been the Dom-Daniel caverns beneath the roots of the ocean luring him to do something more poetical than Southey could do; and the Dome Church at Goslar would have come to mind mingled with cavern scenery when he reread his letters from Germany. According to his own account, two lines of poetry in which the sound, without the meaning, of *dome* is peculiarly prominent were haunting him when he wrote the second part of *Christabel* (i.e., in 1799 or 1800). They were from Crashaw's hymn to St. Theresa:

> Since 'tis not to be had at home,
> She'll travel to a martyrdome.[51]

Coleridge said these lines had perhaps suggested to his mind the whole poem of *Christabel*. The effect of Crashaw's rhyme in distorting *martyrdom* is compulsive, rather as a sore tooth is to the irresistibly exploring tongue, and Crashaw used it in the poem not once but twice. The reader's mind keeps altering the sound over and over, for the violence done to it by the tyrannical rhyme causes the final syllable to haunt the ear until the suffix takes over the whole word. The word *dome* may have had an emotional richness for Coleridge that led him in *Kubla Khan*, half intentionally and half by the accidents of a developing sound pattern, to give it a prominence not fully deserved by its actual meaning within the poem. Set aloft by itself as it is in the opening lines, *dome* is bound, I suppose, wherever it came from, to carry a hint of its cousin *doom*, as it does also in Crashaw's lines.

This air of importance without visible foundation contributes to the suggestion of mystery about the poem that is part of its charm. A severe critic may object that such charm is factitious and the imputation of it an insult to the poet, but that is not really so. It occurs often enough elsewhere, whether in life or art. An accident of light or shadow along a street may lend an air of mystery to a scene not at all mysterious, transforming an ordinary house front into something as final or portentous as doomsday. And in a painting by Manet, a dead fish and a white tablecloth painted white by means of a good deal of black may take on a look of permanence that is like eternity itself. Even in the greatest poems, though the major elements of their greatness will no doubt have other foundations, there are moments in which this kind of charm, an *air of meaning* rather than meaning itself, affects the reader. That mysterious air, if its form is rich enough, is capable of housing whatever may be the besetting mysteries of each reader. Undoubtedly there are reasons why these things affect us as they do, but the reasons are not usually those furnished by the relatively simple equivalences of the symbolic criticism that has developed hitherto. They are probably too subtle and too complex to be traceable, at least in the present state of man's knowledge and consciousness; and they are certainly more inextricably bound up with the elements of form than we are in the habit of supposing.

I sometimes think we overwork Coleridge's idea of "the balance or reconciliation of opposite or discordant qualities." I have to come back to it here, however, for the particular flavor of *Kubla Khan*, with its air of mystery, is describable in part through that convenient phrase. Yet the "reconciliation" does not quite occur either. It is in fact avoided. What we have instead is the very spirit of "oscillation" itself. One could scarcely find words better than those Coleridge used of *Lycidas*, "the floating or oscillation of assonance and consonance," to describe the effect not of the terminal rhymes alone but of the whole sound pattern of *Kubla Khan* and, beyond that, of its imagery, its movement, and, in the end, even its meaning. The poem is the soul of ambivalence, oscillation's very self; and that is probably its deepest meaning. In creating this effect, form and matter are intricately woven. The irregular and inexact rhymes and the varied lengths of the lines play some part. More important is the musical effect in which a smooth, rather swift forward movement is emphasized by the relation of grammatical structure to line and rhyme, yet is impeded and thrown back upon itself even from the beginning by the x-inclosed line units. Like the Mariner's ship at the Equator, the verse moves "backwards and forwards half her length," or like tides rocking in a basin. In the middle of the poem the slightly stronger forward movement loses itself altogether in the floating equivocation between backward-turned trochaic and forward-leaning iambic movement. One hears the texture of Milton, whose great will and drive, even in his discursive moments, gives to all he wrote an air of power and singleness of direction, however elaborate and circuitous his form may be. But in *Kubla Khan* one hears this elaboration almost wholly deprived of such will or with only enough will to keep it afloat. Its spirit is "to care and not to care," but not in Mr. Eliot's sense.

In this forward-flowing movement counterpointed against a stationary-oscillating one, form and meaning are almost indistinguishable. The pleasure-dome is built, then it is unbuilt. The poem is about Kubla, then it is not about him. The oppositions of image are not only the obvious ones of light and darkness, sunny dome and sunless sea or caves of ice, Paradise garden and hints of hell. In the elaborate opening passage *stately, dome, decree, sacred, caverns, measureless,* and *sunless* are all rather solemn words and, except for *stately,* not cheerful-solemn but awful-solemn. Yet the dome is a pleasure-palace; the movement and music of the verse are light rather than solemn. The central statement, through the first half of the poem, is one of bright affirmation. The talk and activity are of building, the pleasure-dome and a delightful Paradise materialize. But even as the words give they take away with half-Miltonic negatives. *Pleasure* itself is rhymed with one of them—*measureless*; deprivation haunts the language. The negations recur in *sunless, ceaseless, lifeless,* a second *measureless*. The demon-lover is not in Paradise; he is an *as-if* brought in to cast his shadow. Images of awe and mystery underlie Paradise in the subterranean river and ocean, and the ancestral threat of war is heard far off. The whole poem oscillates between giving and taking away, bright affirmation and sunless negation, light flowing music that nevertheless stands still and rings the portentous sound of *dome* time after time.

The spirit of the poem, moreover, is cool and rather nonhuman. One feels no real warmth even in the sunny garden. And though the verse is nominally well peopled, Kubla, the wailing woman, and the Abyssinian maid are not really there, and their half-presence leaves the place less human than if the theme were a poetic scene of nature alone. Even

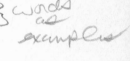

the poet, who is half-present in the end, is dehumanized behind his mask of hair and eyes and magic circle and is only present as mirrored in the exclamations of nebulous beholders—or rather, he *would* be mirrored *if* he had built his dome and *if* there had been beholders. Nor is there any human or personal feeling in the poem; the poet's "deep delight," impersonal enough even if it were there, exists only to be denied.

Here in these interwoven oscillations dwells the magic, the "dream," and the air of mysterious meaning of *Kubla Khan*. I question whether this effect was all deliberately thought out by Coleridge, though it might have been. It is possibly half-inherent in his subject. Paradise is usually lost and always threatened, in Genesis and Milton, in the Paradise gardens of Irem, of Aloadin, of Abyssinian princes. The historical Cubla did not apparently lose his in the end, but it too was threatened with war and dissension and portents. The Paradise of Coleridge's poem was not exactly lost either. What was lost, the closing lines tell us, was the vision of an unbuilt Paradise, an unwritten poem. His Paradise in that sense was truly enough a dream. What remains is the spirit of "oscillation," perfectly poeticized, and possibly ironically commemorative of the author.

Professor Heeren of Göttingen and the "Monthly Magazine"

Within little more than a month of Coleridge's return from Göttingen, a "Professor Heeren of Göttingen" published in the *Monthly
Magazine* the first of several communications on Bruce, Mungo Park,
Herodotus, the course of the Nile, and related subjects. It was a small
item in the compilation of "Literary and Philosophical Intelligence" in
the issue published September 1, quoting a report from "Professor
Hornemann" of "an Abyssinian bishop" who had told of Bruce's
presence in Abyssinia and had corroborated Bruce's claim to have
approached the sources of the Nile.[1] This was a mere note. But the
number published in the beginning of January, 1800, contained two
articles from the pen of Professor Heeren.[2] The first was "On Transplanting the Camel to the Cape of Good Hope; and on the Advantages
To Be Thence Expected in Facilitating the Exploring of Southern
Africa, and Opening a Commercial Intercourse with the Natives."
Despite the authoritative air of the title, the article itself was apparently thrown off casually. Its tone is jaunty, and it betrays no particular
knowledge of either Africa or camels. Professor Heeren's second article
in that number is an "Inquiry whether Herodotus Was Acquainted
with the River Joliba." It opens with general remarks upon the current
interest in African exploration and on the rich treasure of the accounts
left by Herodotus. As the recent travels of Mungo Park had confirmed
some of Herodotus' statements, the professor undertook to "translate
the passage of his History . . . which relates to this subject," and to
illustrate it from Park's work, which had just been published with a
geographical appendix by Major Rennell. The translation from Herodotus follows, and the author goes on to the question of whether the Nile
has a western branch and whether the "great river" of Herodotus was
the Niger (Joliba). He comments on the remarkable confirmation of
many of Herodotus' statements by modern explorers. For this he turns
to Rennell's geographical portion of Park's *Travels*. In the "Literary
and Philosophical Intelligence" of the next issue, "Professor Heeren's"

previous remarks upon Herodotus and the Nile are referred to briefly.[3] And that is the end, so far as I know, of the professor's connections with the *Monthly Magazine*.

I must confess that when I first encountered "Professor Heeren of Göttingen" in English dress—very native English too—in a magazine with which Coleridge had connections and within about six weeks of his return from the same German university, I was somewhat suspicious of the professor's identity. Several circumstances encouraged the speculation that behind the professor might lurk S. T. Coleridge, abetted perhaps by Southey while the two were working at the same table in Stowey or in Exeter. I find, however, that there was in fact at Göttingen a Professor Arnold Hermann Ludwig Heeren and that he was actually a student of the history, geography, and political thought of antiquity. This discovery does not lessen the mystery much. Though we must— perhaps—suppose that the Heeren of the *Monthly* was no hoax and that the German scholar actually wrote the articles, a doubt persists. The autobiographical introduction to Heeren's *Historischen Werke* makes plain that he knew very little, if any, English—possibly enough to make out prose accounts of travel but certainly not enough to write the language.[4] He must have had a translator, for his contributions to the *Monthly* are perfectly easy and idiomatic. And a large portion of one of the articles would not have passed through the German language at all, for it is a direct translation from Herodotus into English. If the professor had something significant to offer English readers, a translation or polishing by another hand would be natural enough; but these contributions have too little substance, one would think, to have crossed the North Sea self-propelled. They betray no particular learning; they sound like nothing more than casual pieces tossed off in an hour with the expectation of gaining a guinea or two and are not conceivably worth translating. The proposal for transplanting the camel to the Cape, which occupies less than a page, is merely an improvisation, apparently inspired by some comments of Mungo Park on elephants and camels.[5] Heeren's remarks are both vague and lighthearted—"how trifling would be the expence of transporting a couple of camels from Mogador, or any other convenient place"—and are pieced out with irrelevant decoration—"the inhabitant of Jamaica, reposing under the shade of his bread-fruit tree. . . ." Everybody was reading Mungo Park's new book, including Southey, who used it in his notes to *Thalaba*. Southey also, rather curiously, cited Heeren's article. Though his other sources for *Thalaba* are serious and more or less relevant to the poem, he lugged Heeren's camels into the notes by the thinnest of threads and then proceeded to demolish them, noting from a different authority that the camel is suited only for level countries and is " 'very ill qualified to travel upon the snow or wet ground.' "[6] His authoritative answer to Heeren came as readily to hand as if both had been prearranged.

The other article by Heeren, on Herodotus, wears a weightier and more learned air until the reader discovers that all of it, too, comes from Major Rennell's appendix to Park. The article on camels had, however irresponsibly, at least propounded one suggestion that was not from Park. This article does not do so much as that. Rennell's appendix refers to the thirty-second chapter of the second book ("Euterpe") of Herodotus. Heeren simply translates this and the thirty-third chapter and then comments upon them. And the comments are little more than a brief rehash of Rennell's own observations. These chapters of "Euterpe" are part of the section that Lowes in *The Road to Xanadu* thought must have influenced *Kubla Khan*. Though he could not show when Coleridge read them, he did not doubt that they entered into the "dream"-poem.

Professor Heeren, then, would appear to have sent over from Germany for translation or revision a couple of articles that any English reader of travels after a perusal of Mungo Park might have tossed off in a leisure hour. It is perhaps not impossible that a mildly lucrative hoax should have been perpetrated in England at the expense of the professor's name. Southey and Coleridge were in the mood for horseplay, as their joint poem, *The Devil's Thoughts*, shows. In later years Coleridge expressed the two main views put forth by Heeren, the defense of Bruce against imputations of his having made false claims and the modern corroboration of Herodotus.[7] Neither view was particularly unusual, but the identity of both with two of Heeren's three incursions into the *Monthly* tempts one to guess.

I do not know whether bishops multiply like blackberries in Abyssinia or not, but I find an additional cause for trifling surprise in meeting here again an anonymous "Abyssinian bishop" so soon after he or another like him had figured in William Taylor's verses *The Devil in Ban*, which had appeared in the February number of the same magazine (as well as in Taylor's "magic palace" letter to Southey) and which had inspired Southey and Coleridge's *The Devil's Thoughts*. Taylor's verses had contained an episode about the Devil, a girl, and an "Abyssinian bishop," quite properly in that context left nameless. When one hopes, however, to authenticate such a well-known historical claim as that of the traveler Bruce, one is ordinarily expected to name one's bishop. Professor Heeren did not. Taylor's poetical Abyssinian bishop must have lain before the eyes of Coleridge and Southey at precisely the same time as Heeren's bishop was making his way into the pages of the *Monthly*.

Whatever Coleridge might or might not have known about the

contributions of Professor Heeren before they appeared, he as well as Southey surely read them afterward. They presumably brought together before his conscious eye certain associations of Bruce, Abyssinia, and Herodotus, which Lowes thought had floated to the surface of his dream from the dim and scattered repositories of past reading. Bruce, Abyssinia, Herodotus, and Mungo Park, as well as Heeren, all were busily dovetailed, too, into the notes for *Thalaba*.

Coleridge read the *Monthly* regularly and occasionally wrote for it. His best-known contribution was the series of sonnets published (in November, 1797) under the name of "Nehemiah Higginbottom," in which he had parodied the style of Charles Lamb, Charles Lloyd, and himself.[8] At times the journal reads almost like a family affair of Coleridge's and Southey's circle, echoing even their quarrels and reconciliations. In the half-yearly "Retrospect of Domestic Literature" in the supplementary number dated July 20, 1799, Charles Lloyd's *Lines Suggested by a Fast* was briefly reviewed. The reviewer abused Lloyd violently and accused him of copying "the rich poetry of Mr. Southey." There was also brief praise of Lamb's *Rosamond Gray*.[9] I do not know who wrote this "Retrospect," but it would not be surprising if its abuse of Lloyd, joined with the praise of Southey and Lamb, had something to do with the reconciliation between Coleridge and Southey that took place about a fortnight later. On the twenty-ninth Coleridge wrote a letter to his brother-in-law that opened the way to a resumption of their friendship. Blame for the quarrel was laid upon Lloyd.[10]

Six months earlier the "Retrospect" had been airing what looks like some malice toward Coleridge. It singled out *The Ancient Mariner* in the *Lyrical Ballads* for condemnation and praised Lloyd's *Edmund Oliver* for the very thing that touched Coleridge, its portrayal of character[11] (the portrayal, it will be recalled, had included Coleridge's use of laudanum to drown his troubles, his unsuccessful first love, and the military aberration of his youth). But six months before that the attitude is again reversed. The "Retrospect" found the volume of "Blank Verse" by Lloyd and Lamb "childish" and "ludicrous."[12] This was in July, 1798, two or three months after the appearance of *Edmund Oliver*. It all sounds rather like a private battle waged publicly behind the impersonal front of the "Retrospect," which was, in fact, not always written by the same person.

The authorship of articles in the *Monthly Magazine*, at least for the years 1797–1800, should be explored further by someone who knows more of Coleridge than I do.[13]

⇝ Appendix II ⇜

The Gutch Memorandum Book, 1799

The notebook of Coleridge known as the "Gutch Memorandum Book," which on the whole certainly belongs to an earlier period, was formerly believed to contain no entries written later than 1798.[1] That was a mistake; it was in use again after Coleridge's return from Germany. Indirect evidence had suggested as much to me in reviewing the events of 1799 and 1800; and now, as this appendix goes to press, Miss Coburn tells me that an entry relating to Godwin, hitherto supposed to refer to *Political Justice* and to have been written in 1796 or 1797, actually refers to *St. Leon*, which was not published until the beginning of December, 1799. The entry was written during that month or the next. Miss Coburn's discovery establishes the most essential point for my purpose. As the Gutch notebook, however, has been closely associated with *Kubla Khan* by Lowes and others and as it has certain connections with Southey and *Thalaba*, I shall run through the other entries that appear to have sprung to life during the latter part of 1799. The notebook had probably remained at Stowey during the absence of Coleridge in Germany and was taken out again while he and Southey were collaborating at the same table in August, 1799. Whether any new entries were made just at that time I cannot say. But as there were many blank and many partly filled pages, Coleridge's ready pen is likely to have added at least an occasional note here and there.

Among the jottings on Godwin, Coleridge had written: "Why must every Man be Godwin—'tis the pedantry of Atheism." It has been assumed that this, as well as the comments on *Political Justice*, belongs to 1796 or 1797, for at that time Coleridge was planning a reply to Godwin's ethical system. Two circumstances, however, in addition to the unquestionably later date of the entry on *St. Leon*, suggest either a later writing or a later use of these notes. On December 19, 1799, Coleridge used the same phrase in writing to Southey from London about the conversation of Godwin, with whom he had recently become friendly: "The pedantry of atheism tickled me hugely."[2] The project of an attack on Godwin's system had also been revived that autumn. The late Professor Harper described a manuscript discourse by Coleridge in which the ideas of Godwin were criticized, though Godwin was not specifically named. This manuscript, preserved in the British Museum, bears Coleridge's own date: "Oct. 6, 1799." An additional comment was dated October 8, 1799, at Stowey.[3] The Gutch entry would thus seem to be even more closely connected with the later than with the earlier dates, though the connection might have grown partly out of a rereading in 1799 of his old notebook.

Then there is the entry that Lowes perhaps intended to connect with the woman wailing for her demon-lover in *Kubla Khan*, though in tracing the ramifications of the tale he apparently lost the thread and did not finally draw the parallel: "Dioclesian King of Syria / fifty Daughters in a ship unmann'd—same as Danaides—land in England—commit / with Devils."[4]

Diocletian's fifty adulterous daughters and their devil-lovers went the rounds of Coleridge's circle between August and October, 1799. Who raised the specters first I cannot tell, or whether they rose in more than one poetical mind independently. Southey inserted them into his dazzled accounts of the Valley of Stones, which he had visited just before joining Coleridge at Stowey. That scene he found so remarkable that he was impelled to "hypothesize" a legend for it. So he conceived the place to be "the ruins of some work erected by the devils who concubinated with the fifty daughters of Diocletian." This first statement of Southey may have been written before he reached Stowey and hence before he could have been reading Coleridge's notebook, but it may equally well have been written afterward. At any rate, he liked the fancy so well that he repeated it more than once in letters written after he joined Coleridge. By October, Humphry Davy was planning to use the tale or at least the story of Brutus that stems from it, as the subject for a poem. Southey conveyed his approval of the theme on grounds especially of its being so little known—its "utter obscurity" was an advantage, he thought.[5]

As Lowes pointed out, the source of Coleridge's version of the tale is Milton's *History of Britain*.[6] Beyond the implication of the "Dioclesian" note itself, we have no knowledge of when Coleridge may have read this. What we do know is that at the end of September, 1799, Coleridge asked Southey to buy Milton's prose works for him in Exeter, and that both Southey and Davy at about this time were referring to the daughters of Diocletian, the story of Brutus to which they serve as introduction, and Milton's argument for introducing legend into history. The opening pages of Milton's *History of Britain*, containing both the daughters and the author's excuse for admitting their fabulous kind, were obviously a topic of conversation in Coleridge's circle just then. Davy's sketch for his poem made use of the Brutus portion of the story and quoted Milton's argument that legend should be made a part of history for the sake of future poets. Dating the note of Coleridge, even if we could do so positively, would obviously not date *Kubla Khan*, for though the multiple princesses and their multiple demon-lovers may have been in his mind when he wrote the poem, they need not have been, since we know of one woman who not only had, but longed and wept for, a demon-lover in the tale of Maugraby, which Coleridge must have been reading or hearing about from Southey in 1799 if he did not know it earlier. All we can be sure of is that Southey had the Diocletian story in mind just *after* he joined Coleridge in August (perhaps also just before) and that Davy was thinking of the same material in October at about the time Coleridge saw him in Bristol.[7]

Several items from the Memorandum Book seem to have been used in Coleridge's poems of 1799. One note runs thus: "A Maniac in the woods—She crosses (heedlessly) the woodman's path—Scourg'd by rebounding boughs—." Campbell and E. H. Coleridge both remarked upon the use of this note in the *Introduction to the Tale of the Dark Ladie* (the original version of *Love*), written in November or December, 1799·

> "...
> That craz'd this bold and lovely Knight;
> And how he roam'd the mountain woods,
>   Nor rested day or night;
> "And how he cross'd the Woodman's paths,
>   Thro' briars and swampy mosses beat;
> How boughs rebounding scourg'd his limbs,
>   And low stubs gor'd his feet."

The image of scourging boughs, along with some other elements in the scene, may owe something to a passage near the beginning of Wieland's *Oberon*, more particularly to Sotheby's English version of it, published in 1798. Stanzas 12–15 of Sotheby's first canto contain "many a *pathless wood*, and *boundless* plain . . . . wand'ring step . . . . he speeds thro' storm and rain To right and left the livelong day . . . . bush and *briar* . . . . steep ascent . . . circling forest,—far and wide, As *roams* his *boundless* eye . . . . How fares he in the wilderness (by day Where scarce the *forester* had found his way) . . . . night . . . . Where, at each *wilder'd* step, thick *boughs his forehead smite* . . . . Tones . . . *rebound*. . . ." (In the original German there is bush but no briar, there is no woodman or forester, no bough that smites the wanderer—who merely bumps his head on a tree—and none of the "bound" or "rebound" sounds). Coleridge's note could scarcely have been suggested by the German lines (Stanza 14):

"Er führt sein Pferd so gut er kann am Zaum,
   Und stösst bey jedem Tritt die Stirn an einen Baum."[8]

An apparent echo of the notebook occurred earlier, in the verses composed with Southey, *The Devil's Thoughts*. It consists of a reference to Archbishop Randolph's consecrating the Duke of York's banners, an event that had occurred in November, 1795. Apart from the entry in the Gutch Memorandum Book, nothing more is heard of this minor historical event until *The Devil's Thoughts* of 1799, where the episode was inserted cryptically without any necessity or even much relevance.[9]

In the notebook this last entry is No. 18 in a series of twenty-seven items listed and numbered by Coleridge as prospective subjects for literary works. Two other items in the list have a connection with *Thalaba*, as does one other observation from another part of the notebook. Number 7 in the list is "Burnet, de montibus in English Blank Verse."[10] Both Southey and Coleridge had long known Thomas Burnet's *Telluris theoria sacra* in both its Latin and its English form. It underlay certain portions of *Thalaba* and no doubt, as Lowes believed, lurked somewhere beneath the imagery of *Kubla Khan*. Almost anyone who had ever read it would be bound to recall it when he saw or read of caverns and underground rivers. Despite the existence of Burnet's own English version in somewhat poetic prose, Coleridge thought it fit matter for blank verse, particularly the chapter "De montibus." That same chapter Southey also singled out for a brief adaptation of a few lines into the irregular "blank verse" of *Thalaba* and for special comment in his notes, where he praises the poetic power of the Latin and decries the English version.[11] Thus in late 1799 or early 1800 Southey carried out a minor bit of Coleridge's undated project in the Gutch Memorandum Book. And in his notes to the poem, Southey's comments upon this chapter of Burnet are followed almost at once by other matter that has been associated with *Kubla Khan*—the accounts of the Paradise of Aloadin, quoted from Sir John Mandeville, Odoric, and Purchas. On Coleridge's memorandum list, Burnet's "De montibus" is No. 7; No. 9 is the brief note, "Cavern-candle," which recalls that most gruesome of all cavern-candles with the dead hand for candlestick that lights the cavern scene of Book V in *Thalaba*. Southey's candle "burns clear, but with the air around, Its dead ingredients mingle deathiness."[12] And in the same scene, Southey appears to have borrowed another image (which I mentioned earlier, in chapter iv) from Coleridge's entry "A dunghill at a distance sometimes smells like musk, and a dead dog like elder flowers."[13]

Several other notes in the Gutch Memorandum Book may belong to the year 1799 or 1800. One that puzzled Lowes, a cryptic item containing the word *Duppe* (or, Lowes suggests, *Dappe, Dupper,* or *Dapper*) almost certainly refers to Richard Duppa, whom Southey had met at Balliol in 1793 but who appears to have been abroad during most of the time that the Gutch notes are generally supposed to have been made. He was in England again in 1799, however, and his name is mentioned by Southey several times between August and the following February as a source of information about facilities for travel in Italy, when he was trying to persuade Coleridge to go with him and cited Duppa's usefulness for direction and advice.[14]

Another entry, "J Hucks—N 9—Inner Temple Lane," evidently refers to Joseph Hucks, with whom Coleridge had made a tour in Wales in 1794. I know of no correspondence between the two subsequent to this tour, and they had parted company before the notebook was purchased. The entry is not in Coleridge's hand; Miss Coburn thinks it is in Hucks's own. The only later reference I know of that Coleridge made to Hucks occurs in 1799. The two met again in Exeter, perhaps for the first time since those early days, and Hucks then promised to contribute verses to the *Annual Anthology*. It seems likely that the address was written into the notebook either then or in the following winter.[15]

Projects for the Upas Tree appear in the notebook,[16] and an episode involving the same gruesome matter was inserted in the first edition of *Thalaba*. This might well be an accidental association, however, since the subject is featured in Darwin's *Botanic Garden* and was discussed from time to time in periodicals of the day.

These connections of the Gutch Memorandum Book with the late summer, autumn, and winter of 1799 came to my attention rather incidentally. They are trifling enough; but as the notebook has so often been associated with *Kubla Khan*, they appeared to be worth recording.

❧ Appendix III ❧

Dorothy Wordsworth's "Kubla"

The German journal of Dorothy Wordsworth opens with a retrospective summary of events from September 14, 1798, when she left
London, to her arrival with William, Coleridge, and John Chester at
Hamburg. From September 20 she continued the account at Hamburg with almost daily entries, closing the final one on the evening of
October 1 (or possibly later) with "Drank tea."[1] So much of the
manuscript journal was written into one notebook. Though this was
not filled, the remainder of the journal as we now have it is in another
notebook and was written evidently at some later time. The narrative is
retrospective. It records her journey with Wordsworth from Hamburg
through Brunswick to Goslar, October 3–6, and there leaves off for good.

Both portions of the German journal are objective and factual, unlike the more personal ones of Grasmere and even of Alfoxden. This
one is full of typical travelers' details of the accommodations at each
inn, the cost of meals, the character of the country, the discomforts of
vehicles, the Germans' habit of cheating foreigners. At the close of the
retrospective narrative, after describing the inn at Brunswick with its
"excellent" beds and blankets, Dorothy wrote: "We had taken places
in the Goslar diligence, and were to set off at 8 o'clock in the morning,
so we rose at a little after seven." Here she broke off for a brief description she had neglected to put in about the town as they had seen it the
evening before, after which she resumed: "When we left our inn Wm.
carried the portmanteau, and I the small parcel. He left them under my
charge and went in search of a baker's shop. He brought me his pockets
full of apples, for which he paid two bon gros, and some excellent bread.
Upon these I breakfasted and carried *Kubla* to a fountain in the neighboring market-place, where I drank some excellent water. It was on
Saturday the 6th of October when we arrived at Goslar at between 5
and 6 in the evening."[2]

The context in which the word "Kubla" appears led me at first to
question the correctness of the printed version; I wondered whether
Dorothy might have tried out her weak German on *Kuche(n)* or written
something else. The judgment of Miss Helen Darbishire and an inspec-

tion of photographs of the manuscripts, however, put an end to that surmise.[3] Dorothy wrote "Kubla" unmistakably at least once, in a fair copy of which only fragments survive, and presumably also in the surviving notebook that forms the chief basis of the printed text, though the reading there is not quite so plain.[4]

There is no doubt that the word is odd where it stands; no obvious explanation can make it seem natural. Its presence might be accounted for in any one of three ways, but they are all somewhat improbable: when Dorothy wrote that she carried "Kubla" that morning, she might actually have referred to the poem; she might have referred to some other object that she carried, using a nickname for some possession; or her pen might have slipped. There are obvious objections to each of these possibilities, but if there is a fourth, it escapes me.

Although the first is the simplest explanation, it does not hold up well under scrutiny. As we can hardly suppose *Kubla Khan* written while Coleridge was in Germany,[5] the poem, if it was in existence, must already have been familiar to Dorothy for some time. It could not very well be something she had just received from Coleridge by letter. He and Chester had left for Ratzeburg on Sunday, September 30; the Wordsworths left Hamburg on Wednesday, October 3. There was hardly time, either Coleridgean or German postal time, for Coleridge to have sent back a poem. Even if he had, it would have been part of a letter, and Dorothy would presumably have referred to it as that in her journal rather than as "Kubla." Coleridge's poems when sent in letters were customarily written in, not on a separate sheet, but as part of the letter itself.

Reconstructing the events of that morning in Brunswick, we have to imagine Dorothy Wordsworth rising on the last day of her journey, after three nights en route, and, in preparation for a day-long ride in a jolting diligence, taking out from her luggage in order to carry it separately a sheet or two of paper containing a short poem of Coleridge which, if she cared as much as that for it or its author, she probably knew by heart. She and Wordsworth set out from the inn, he carrying the portmanteau (purchased a few days earlier for seven marks) and she the "small parcel." She guarded the luggage while he went to buy bread. He returned with this and apples, which she ate. And then in the same sentence that records this breakfast she inserts "Kubla," with an apparent incoherence such as her journals do not elsewhere show. She had not mentioned it among things she carried when they set out from the inn; but here, between the bread and apples and the drink of water, where it is irrelevant if it is a poem, she speaks of it: "Upon these I breakfasted and carried *Kubla* to a fountain in the neighboring market-place, where I drank some excellent water. It was on Saturday the 6th"

—and so on. Even though we suppose that an attachment to Coleridge might have induced her to carry the poem separately, we still must wonder at her wishing to record the fact in a journal that contains elsewhere nothing confidential and that expresses or betrays no hint of personal intensities, a journal, furthermore, that was not written spontaneously when the events were fresh but at some later date. It is worth remarking, too, that neither she nor Wordsworth mentioned the poem in any of their surviving letters to Coleridge at that time. Finally, still supposing she carried the poem and later wished to record that she had done so, there remains the awkwardness of explaining the unnatural position of the statement, which rather seems to make nonsense of it. This first alternative for the reading of the passage—that on the morning of October 6, 1798, Dorothy actually carried a manuscript copy of *Kubla Khan* from Brunswick to Goslar—is possible but does not seem very probable.

The second alternative has, I think, a little more to recommend it. Here we must suppose that some article possessed by the Wordsworths was known in the family, either at the time or later when the journal was written, by the name of "Kubla." The improbability of this needs no elaboration. But it is possible.

The third alternative, that the word was an absent-minded slip, raises a number of difficult questions; but first it must be said that it too is not probable, chiefly because the word seems to have been written twice, not just once. Slips in themselves are not unusual with most people and were certainly not infrequent in Dorothy Wordsworth's writing; they are not so common, however, as to coincide often with the crux of a mystery. The commonest error of this kind appears to be the writing of one word in place of another with the same initial letter and often with other similarities of sound. I do not speak here of Freudian slips, though I suspect the axles of even these may be greased by auditory resemblance. In editing the journals of Dorothy Wordsworth, de Selincourt noted that she had written *far* when she meant *fast, sent backward* for *sent back word, Murray* for *Mary, point* for *pint, Place Dame* for *Place d'Armes* (possibly a different sort of error), and perhaps *fish* for *fuel*.[6] These were miswritings that she herself did not catch. In the manuscript notebook, the passage containing the word "Kubla" shows several cancellations, one of which looks like the same kind of slip, the beginning of another word with *di-* when she meant to write *dismal.*

Explanation of "Kubla" as either a slip or a nickname is scarcely imaginable, however, except on the supposition that Coleridge's poem was in existence before the word was written. One can hardly suppose the Wordsworths, independently of the poem, to have had the Tartar

king so familiarly in mind as to name their possessions after him or
write his name in absence of mind. This being so, it would be immaterial
for the date of *Kubla Khan* to determine whether Dorothy's "Kubla"
was a poem, an object, or an error if we knew the word was written
while the Wordsworths were still at Goslar. But we do not know that
Dorothy wrote the passage then, and there are reasons for thinking she
may have written it a good deal later. One point is certain: the passage
(at least in the form that now survives) was not written immediately
after the incident itself occurred. So much the retrospective language of
the narrative reveals. It may have been written before the Wordsworths left Germany, or, for all we can tell, it may have been written as
late as 1802 at Grasmere.

The circumstances under which a slip might have occurred are
worth exploring. If Dorothy wrote the passage after her return to England, she is likely to have done so with Coleridge and his works vividly
in mind. At times during the year or two that began with his visit at
Sockburn in November, 1799, the notebooks, conversation, and recollections of Germany of all three travelers were so intertwined that
Dorothy's pen might well enough have slipped his title into her journal
by mistake. Coleridge had bestowed care upon his descriptions of the
Harz region with its palace-like, summer-snowy cavern, its chasms and
underground stream and all the rest, concluding with his account of the
Dome Church at Goslar. After his return to England he assembled
those and other letters he had written, pondering the advisability of
publishing them as a book. Sometimes he thought he would, sometimes
he would not publish; but at one point he wrote to Longman, who expected to bring them out, that the work was practically completed.
Wordsworth had offered him the use of his journal, and he was going
to incorporate that.

It is likely that the Wordsworths' material actually was turned over
to Coleridge at this time. We know he used it some years later in *The
Friend*. At any rate, as Dorothy was her brother's chief copyist, she was
very likely going through their German notes and copying out portions
of them with Coleridge's book in mind at some time between October,
1799, and the end of 1800. The mingled associations would have been
strong: her journal ended at Goslar, as his letter did. Coleridge was
evidently making some of his preparations for the volume while he
stayed with them in the summer of 1800, for he wrote to Poole at that
time, asking for a copy of one letter that was missing.[7]

The physical makeup of the surviving manuscripts of the journal
yields a few clues to their dates.[8] Notebook 1 (as for the sake of convenience I shall call the book containing the first German entries) was
unquestionably used in Germany in 1798: it contains apparently the

only day-by-day entries that remain from the expedition, the last one dated October 1 at Hamburg. It was in use again later in England sometime after November 12, 1799—probably at Grasmere between late December and the following February—for it contains part of *The Brothers*, which Wordsworth was writing at that time; and it was used again for Dorothy's Grasmere journal from October 10, 1801, to February, 1802.[9] This filled the book.

Notebook 2 may or may not have been used in Germany. Nothing that I know places it there, for though it contains two narratives of events from that period, both are written retrospectively. The first is Wordsworth's account of conversation with the poet Klopstock. This narrative was eventually published by Coleridge in *The Friend* along with his own German letters; a copy of it may have been made for him in late 1799 or 1800 when the publication was first projected. In the notebook this matter is immediately followed by the other retrospective account by Dorothy of the journey from Hamburg to Goslar. It opens: "We quitted Hamburgh on Wednesday evening, October 3, at 5 o'clock, reached Luneburg at breakfast on Thursday," and proceeds by consecutive narrative to the breakfast of bread and apples at Brunswick, the carrying of "Kubla," the drink of water in the market place, and the arrival on the evening of the sixth at Goslar. There it ends. The page following this and lying opposite it when the book is open bears notations that at first one would guess had been made in Germany. Instead, however, they were probably written at Grasmere in 1802. They are notes of German words and phrases, apparently to be looked up or inquired into, and were copied, as the notations indicate, from the *Fables* of Lessing. After this follows some German grammar, and after the grammar a continuation of the Grasmere journal from February 14 (where Notebook 1 ended) to May 2, 1802. Next comes an extended note by Wordsworth attacking Godwin and Paley, then a bit more from Lessing's *Fables*, and some portions of *The Prelude*.

We do not know whether Dorothy read anything of Lessing while she was abroad or not. We know, however, that during February and March, 1802, when she was using both these notebooks for her Grasmere journal, she was also working more or less systematically on Lessing's *Fables* and German grammar. On February 6 she "translated two or three of Lessing's *Fables*" and two days later "read a little in Lessing and the grammar." She may have hoped to produce a publishable translation, for she continued to refer to the work now and then through most of March.[10] Because of the spacing, the presence of blank leaves, and the fact that the book was used part of the time upside down, progressing in the opposite direction, it is not possible to determine the order in which all the batches of material were written down. The

"Kubla" passage does appear to have been written, however, before the notes of Lessing's *Fables*, hence before about February 6, 1802. The attack on Godwin and the portions of *The Prelude* would not likely have been written before the autumn of 1799.[11]

The important points may be reconstructed in summary. Notebook 1 was in use in September, 1798, at Hamburg, again early in 1800 (or the very end of 1799), and from October, 1801, to February, 1802. Of Notebook 2 we can say with assurance only that it was in use from February to May, 1802, that the page of Lessing immediately following the "Kubla" passage and the German grammar were almost certainly written early in the same year, and that the Hamburg-Goslar narrative must have been written before the Lessing notes. From the physical makeup of the two notebooks and their relation to each other, it would appear quite possible that Notebook 2 was not used in Germany at all but only later, perhaps at the end of 1799 and 1800 as well as in 1802.

This possibility is considerably strengthened by two or three bits of internal evidence that suggest a longish rather than a brief lapse of time between the actual journey to Goslar and the account we have of it. One of these is a comment about German diligences. Writing of the one in which she traveled as far as Brunswick, Dorothy said it had seemed to her at the time a poor conveyance. Its covering and lining, however, she added, were "luxuries which I have since found are not often to be met with in a German diligence."[12] If she was speaking from experience, as her words rather suggest, she might not have been in a position to generalize about German diligences before her final departure from Germany. Only one other vehicle took the Wordsworths from Brunswick to Goslar, and when they left that city some four months later they traveled on foot. Though there might have been unrecorded rides in diligences thereafter, we know of none until their final return by that conveyance to Hamburg when they sailed for home in the spring. Dorothy's comment therefore sounds—though not conclusively, for she might have collected secondhand information about diligences—as if it might have been written after the whole German expedition was behind her.

The second circumstance that hints at some lapse of time between the journey and the journal is that the latter conflicts on one point with the surviving fragments of a letter that was certainly written at the time. Writing shortly after her arrival in Goslar (perhaps to Mary Hutchinson), Dorothy ended her account by saying that the diligence arrived at Goslar "at eight at night." In the journal she reported the time as "between 5 and 6 in the evening." The discrepancy is minor but is most easily accounted for—since the phrasing of this part of the letter seems to indicate that it was written soon after the journey—by suppos-

ing the journal written long enough afterward for Dorothy to have forgotten the hour.[13]

Finally, there are indications that the journal as it survives in Notebook 2 may be a composite, put together from more than one source, of
which this same letter may be one. For though the time of arrival is
different, the beginning of the letter and of the narrative in the journal
correspond practically word for word except that in the latter a date is
inserted—a difference that makes the letter sound current, as the
journal certainly is not.[14] The description of Brunswick, as far as it is
preserved in the fragmentary letter, coincides also with a passage inserted out of its proper order in the final paragraph of the journal.[15] It
looks as if the journal as we have it may have been partly copied at
some later date either from this letter or from notes made at the same
time as the letter. My impression that the journal has a composite
origin comes in part from the discrepancy in the hour of arrival, in the
face of the other word-for-word correspondences.[16] More especially,
however, it derives from the way in which the journal itself back-tracks
so that Dorothy brings herself and William into Brunswick on Friday
"between 3 and 4 o'clock" twice, some two printed pages apart. There is
a second back-tracking toward the end that might also have been due
to a combining of material from two sources, though this one sounds
more like a common omission by oversight. She introduced it by saying,
"I ought to have mentioned that we walked about the city of Brunswick after we had dined." What follows is one of the two passages that
correspond closely to the letter.[17]

If, as de Selincourt suggested, the letter was to Mary Hutchinson
and if it was one direct source of the narrative in the journal, the latter
must certainly have been composed after Dorothy returned to England,
when she could have referred to her own letter again at Sockburn or
Grasmere. Even if there were an intervening source in the form of early
notes that employed the same language as the letter and that later were
copied into the present notebook, the impression one gets of there being
more than a single source and more than one time of writing behind the
present form of the journal, together with the comment on what she
had "since" found about German diligences, still suggests the likelihood
of a date after the travels were over. On the whole, then, the internal
evidence of the Hamburg-Goslar journal seems to point to some later
date; a survey of the other contents of the two notebooks does not discourage but rather mildly encourages that view; and the known circumstances of one or two later periods—late 1799–1800 and possibly early
1802—favor it. Sometime during the first of these, the Wordsworths'
German notes were almost certainly being gone over for the sake of
Coleridge's projected book; copying and perhaps some rewriting were

done; and Notebook 1 seems pretty clearly to have been used then. The Goslar narrative may have been written into Notebook 2 at that time. If it were written at the still later date, 1802, when we know that both notebooks were in use consecutively, that too was a time when Coleridge and his poetry were haunting Dorothy Wordsworth's mind. Her journal of that time shows the deepest concern for his domestic unhappiness and his health, and during the early days of her work on the *Fables* and German grammar his poetry was running in her mind so that she described the moon and stars in words from *The Ancient Mariner*.[18] At either of these times a cross-current from Coleridge's poetry would have been as likely as anything else to lead her pen astray.

This still, however, leaves us with a slip of the pen on our hands, or else with an object that had come to be known as "Kubla." Professor Bald has said he inclines toward the latter explanation; he reminds me of the "spirit of fun" that transformed a small cataract into a "kittenract" in Coleridge's and probably also Dorothy Wordsworth's private language. Independently of this, Professor Irwin Griggs suggested that "Kubla" Can might very well have been a drinking-Can—a pun not much beyond the bounds of "kittenract." As this appendix was about to go to press, the same guess appeared from another quarter: Mr. H. M. Margoliouth, in his new book *Wordsworth and Coleridge: 1795–1834*,[19] takes for granted that the Wordsworths had named their drinking-can in honor of Coleridge's poem. On the whole, I think this is perhaps the most likely explanation of the passage. A can or cup would at any rate have been the most natural object for Dorothy to carry to the fountain, and the fun of using the word would account for her recording the trivial circumstance. This explanation, however, does nothing to establish a date for Coleridge's poem, since the nickname may go back only to the date of Dorothy's writing and not to the morning of her drink in Brunswick. As the Wordsworths were not apt to throw away even trifling possessions, a drinking-can carried in Germany would very probably have gone upon other journeys afterwards; it might have accompanied William and Coleridge on their tour of the Lakes in November, 1799. The pun could have struck them at any time. Thus, only if the "Kubla" passage were known to have been written *as it now stands* while the Wordsworths were still in Germany or before Coleridge returned to Stowey in July, 1799, would it constitute evidence for the composition of *Kubla Khan* in 1797 or 1798. We have no such knowledge, and, as we have seen, a number of circumstances suggest that the passage was written later.

This is the end of the morass of *ifs* and *perhapses* relating to the "Kubla" of Dorothy Wordsworth's journal. We are left pretty much where we began, for it provides no decisive evidence either way.

Notes

CHAPTER I

1. *The Road to Xanadu* (Boston, 1930), pp. 56, 91–92, 102–3, 376. I use the "revised" edition, but the page references will be found, I think, to fit the 1927 edition as well. The "revision" appears to consist of an additional brief preface and a series of "Addenda and Corrigenda" inserted within the original pagination.

2. Dr. I. A. Richards expressed the view that, far from being absurd, the claim of Coleridge to an epoch-making discovery was justified, that he had "glimpses of a new possible theoretic order." For the account of this see his *Coleridge on Imagination* (New York, 1935), pp. xiv, 20–21. Some other writers also, with whom I hesitate to differ, are convinced that Coleridge developed a fully satisfactory poetic theory. I find brilliant insights but can find no coherent aesthetic philosophy or psychology and none that seems to me satisfactory as a whole.

3. *The Rime of the Ancient Mariner*, with an Essay by Robert Penn Warren (New York, 1946), pp. 70–71.

4. *Ibid.*, p. 75.

5. G. Wilson Knight, *The Starlit Dome* (London, 1941), chap. ii; Robert Penn Warren, *The Ancient Mariner*, Secs. IV, V, and *passim;* Kenneth Burke, *The Philosophy of Literary Form* (1941), pp. 96–97; Robert Graves, *The Meaning of Dreams* (London, 1924), pp. 145–58. Maud Bodkin, *Archetypal Patterns in Poetry* (London, 1948; originally published in 1934), chaps. ii and iii. Roy P. Basler, in *Sex, Symbolism, and Psychology in Literature* (New Brunswick, N.J., 1948), chap. ii, discusses *Christabel* from the psychoanalytic point of view.

6. See Arthur H. Nethercot, *The Road to Tryermaine* (Chicago, 1939), especially Book IV, for what is essentially this view with but slight modifications. It is impossible to refer to the contents of any critical works without oversimplifying them. For this I apologize, though I have tried to avoid misrepresenting them needlessly.

CHAPTER II

1. Coleridge, *Complete Poetical Works*, ed. E. H. Coleridge (Oxford, 1912), I, 295–97. Unless otherwise indicated, references hereafter are to this edition under the abridged title *"Poems."*

2. *Memoir and Letters of Sara Coleridge* (London, 1873), II, 21–22.

3. Charles Lamb, *Letters*, ed. E. V. Lucas (New Haven, 1935), II, 190.

4. August 2, 1934, p. 541. Cf. also its rediscovery in *TLS* in 1951: January 12, p. 21; January 26, p. 53; February 9, p. 85.

5. E. K. Chambers, *Samuel Taylor Coleridge* (Oxford, 1938), p. 102. Cf. also the apparently wide gaps between watermarks and date of entry shown in Miss Kathleen Coburn's notes to *Inquiring Spirit* (London, 1951).

6. Cf. John Livingston Lowes, *The Road to Xanadu* (Boston, 1930), pp. 374-76; and Lane Cooper, "The Abyssinian Paradise in Coleridge and Milton," *Modern Philology*, III (1906), 327-32. Another Miltonic variant in the Crewe MS is "hideous" for "ceaseless" in l. 17. See the discussion of Milton's influence in chaps. iv and v, hereafter.

7. Almost all modern studies of the effects of opium have used morphine, given by injection or, occasionally, by mouth, since this has been much the commonest form of opiate addiction during the present century. Throughout most of the nineteenth century and earlier, opium was regularly taken by mouth either alone or, dissolved in a diluted preparation of alcohol, as laudanum. Morphine is the primary narcotic element in opium. Isolated first in 1803, it did not come into general use until the latter years of the century and was apparently never taken by either Coleridge or De Quincey. As far as is known, there is nothing in opium that would produce effects different from, or beyond, those of morphine. The latter is more concentrated and, when taken by injection, acts more quickly. Otherwise, authorities agree that there is no significant difference between addiction to opium and addiction to morphine. With laudanum the effect of varying amounts of alcohol accompanies that of opium, just as when an addict takes a drink. The effects of opium and alcohol may possibly tend to counteract each other, one being initially a stimulant and the other almost entirely a depressant— at least I have seen this stated, but only by one writer, whose account is not grounded in experimental observation. Apart from this possible slight variation, there is no evidence to suggest that the effect of laudanum is in any respect different from that of other opiates. If anyone wishes to argue that *Kubla Khan* or De Quincey's famous "opium dreams" are expressions of delirium tremens from alcoholism, he may do so. It was opium, however, not laudanum, according to the Crewe manuscript, that Coleridge said he had taken before he composed his poem. In view, at any rate, of modern medical findings on the subject, there seems no reason to doubt that what is found true today psychologically and physiologically concerning the effects of the morphine derivative of opium is true also of opium as it was used earlier. Professor Meyer H. Abrams, it is true, cites a statement by Jean Cocteau that each form of opium has a different effect. M. Cocteau was an opium smoker and insists that the smoker is the aristocrat of addicts;

he makes much of the pleasures of the elaborate ritual attending the use of the pipe. These are understandable but irrelevant to our study. Coleridge and De Quincey did not smoke the drug. M. Cocteau, in any case, does not pretend to write an objective report. See Hugo Krueger, N. B. Eddy, and M. Sumwalt, *The Pharmacology of the Opium Alkaloids* ("Public Health Reports," Suppl. No. 165 [2 vols; Washington, D.C.: U.S. Public Health Service, 1941–43]), I, 2, 728. These volumes report quite fully the modern scientific work on the subject. I shall refer to them hereafter as "Suppl. No. 165." See also Alfred R. Lindesmith, *Opiate Addiction* (Bloomington, Ill., 1947), p. 40; and Meyer H. Abrams, *The Milk of Paradise* (Cambridge, Mass., 1934), p. 66.

8. C. E. Terry and M. Pellens, *The Opium Problem* (New York, 1928), p. 501 and elsewhere. This work is a standard modern treatment of the subject, published under the auspices of the Committee on Drug Addiction with the purpose of assembling all significant modern contributions to the knowledge of opium. It is supplemented but not superseded by the more recent U.S. Suppl. No. 165.

9. T. S. Blair in *Journal of the American Medical Association*, May, 1919, and S. D. Hubbard in 1920, quoted in Terry and Pellens, *op. cit.*, pp. 497, 501, where the general statement is confirmed by Hare and others. Cf. also E. S. Bishop, *The Narcotic Drug Problem* (New York, 1920), p. 47; and Lawrence Kolb, *Pleasure and Deterioration from Narcotic Addiction* ("National Committee for Mental Hygiene Reprints," No. 211 [New York, 1925]), pp. 11–12.

10. George Crabbe, *The Life of the Rev. George Crabbe* (Cambridge and Boston, 1834), pp. 153–54; R. and S. Wilberforce, *Life of William Wilberforce* (London, 1838), I, 173–74. De Quincey's addition in 1856 to the original Preface (1821) of his *Confessions* is but one indication that in the interim some disgrace had come to be attached to the use of opium (*Collected Writings*, ed. Masson [London, 1896], III, 214).

11. *Confessions* (early version), ed. E. Sackville-West (London, 1950), p. 255; T. Wemyss Reid, *Life . . . of Richard Monckton Milnes . . .* (New York, 1891), I, 100.

12. The chief effects are a slight retarding of the pulse, constipation, retarding of some glandular activity, and—of course—a marked dulling of the sense of pain. Slight anemia, loss of weight, neglected teeth, and other evidences of careless personal hygiene occur; but in modern studies these have been ruled out as not being due to the actual physiological effect of the drug but to economic and psychological causes. A few other minor changes have been found by certain experimenters (cf. Suppl. No. 165, I, 729–30; Lindesmith, *op. cit.*, p. 40; and other references hereafter). Some writers maintain that physical impairment does occur as a result of opium; others—including the authors of an in-

tensive study in New York of 318 cases—that there are no uniform physical changes at all other than neglect of personal hygiene. It is notable that the accounts of the first group of writers are more often generalized and undocumented statements that may derive as much from the literary tradition as from scientific observation. The reports founded on experimental procedures all tend in the contrary direction.

13. Arthur B. Light and Edward G. Torrance, *Opium Addiction* (Philadelphia, 1930), reprinted from a long series of studies published in *Archives of Internal Medicine*, Vols. XLIII and XLIV; see especially XLIII, 111-12.

14. Lawrence Kolb, "Drug Addiction—a Study of Some Medical Cases," *Archives of Neurology and Psychiatry*, XX (1928), 178, quoted also in Lindesmith, *op. cit.*, pp. 38-39. Brief case histories of others who have led fully normal and useful lives despite long addiction are given also in Kolb's *Pleasure and Deterioration*.

I have seen two reports of experimental study, possibly significant, though very limited in scope, which indicate that there may perhaps be a slight diminution in physical and mental efficiency under the continued use of opium. Tests of simple muscular co-ordination and word response showed a slightly slower reaction under morphine, and arithmetic problems of continuous subtraction were not quite so well done. Even so, the authors reported that "the effects are not of sufficient magnitude to constitute a serious disruption of general working efficiency." The study, though carefully carried out, is far from being conclusive because only two individuals were tested. As far as it goes, the experiment is consistent with other known effects of the drug—that is, its slowing of the pulse and its general narcotic effect. Even if it is confirmed by fuller studies, however, Crabbe and Wilberforce may still have had reason for thinking that they were better off under opium, for there is some likelihood that the drug produces a narcosis of nerve centers affecting inner emotional conflicts. In that case the gain in efficiency from the calming of those conflicts might well outweigh its minor negative effect on the speed or efficiency of elementary processes. One aspect of these tests suggests that this may be true, for it appeared that when free from opium the individuals were more disturbed or blocked by "disturbing" words than when they were under opiates. But the results of the test as a whole were by no means conclusive even for the two individuals studied. The experiment is mentioned here because it is one of the few that in any way differ from the conclusions of the best recent authorities (Edwin G. Williams, Fred W. Oberst, and Ralph R. Brown, *A Cycle of Morphine Addiction* [Reprint No. 2686 from the "Public Health Reports" (Washington, 1946)], pp. 34-41; D. I. and M. B. Macht, "Comparative Studies of Cobra Venom and Opium Alkaloids on Audition . . . ," *American Journal of Physiology*, CXXVI [1939], 574).

15. These are of course absolute names for what is properly relative and variable; everyone is no doubt unstable in some sense or in some degree. The entirely "normal" individual is a purely hypothetical character; and there is, I realize, a certain odor of arrogance in the way in which we have translated the *moral* and *immoral* of our ancestors into normal-abnormal, stable-unstable, well-adjusted or ill-adjusted, psychopathic, neurotic, or something else. One has, however, to use some terms. And, whatever one's psychological assumptions, the general distinction between *stable* and *unstable* is clear for practical purposes; there would be disagreement only on borderline cases.

16. Terry and Pellens, *op. cit.*, p. 149.

17. Lawrence Kolb, "Types and Characteristics of Drug Addicts," *Mental Hygiene*, IX (1925), 312–13; cf. also studies by the (New York) Mayor's Committee on Drug Addiction reported in *Journal of the American Medical Association*, XCIII (1929), 1297 ff., and *American Journal of Psychiatry*, X (1930), 433 ff.; also cited in Suppl. No. 165, I, 731–32. Terry and Pellens (*op. cit.*, pp. 514–15) consider that the general psychological abnormality of addicts has not been actually proved, though they do not indicate disagreement.

18. Lawrence Kolb, "Clinical Contribution to Drug Addiction: The Struggle for Cure and the Conscious Reasons for Relapse," reprinted from *Journal of Nervous and Mental Disease*, LXVI, No. 1 (July, 1927). Other studies at Lexington involving more than a thousand cases corroborate Kolb's conclusions (see M. J. Pescor, *A Statistical Analysis of the Clinical Records of Hospitalized Drug Addicts* ["Public Health Reports," Suppl. No. 143 (Washington, 1938)], pp. 17–18; cf. also J. R. Rees, "Psychological Factors in the Prevention and Treatment of Alcohol and Drug Addiction," *Lancet*, CCXXIII [1932], 929). Other writers who agree with Kolb and Rees are quoted by Terry and Pellens, *op. cit.*, pp. 493–504. Cf. Alexander Lambert's statement that the craving for opium "is always an emotional impulse," and its victims are "psycho-neurotic" individuals in whom "alcohol and drug addiction is but the expression of the desire for relief from a strain which cannot be borne" (Terry and Pellens, *op. cit.*, p. 148). Lambert recognizes the existence of cases of medical addiction also, however, that are not "psycho-neurotic." More recent presentations of the same view are those by J. B. Miner, *Journal of Abnormal and Social Psychology*, XXVIII (1933), 119–22; H. von Hattingberg, work reviewed in *Psychological Abstracts*, No. 328 (1940); J. D. Reichard, "Narcotic Drug Addiction: A Symptom of Human Maladjustment," *Diseases of the Nervous System*, IV (1943), 275–81; R. H. Felix in *Mental Hygiene*, XXIII

(1939), 567-82; and many others. The last-named, Felix, has had, like Kolb and Pescor, the advantage of observing thousands of drug addicts in the Lexington hospital.

19. A. Andaló, in a study of certain European poets who were addicted to opium, undertook to demonstrate that the unusual elements in their poetry derived from abnormalities in their psyches rather than from the effects of opium ("Studio critico-letterario e medico-psicologico sulle tossicomanie di alcuni grandi poeti," *Annali dell'Ospedale psichiatrico di Perugia*, XXXI [1937], 1-58). This paper I have not been able to see; my report of it is from *Psychological Abstracts*, 1939.

20. For an illustration of the cure of normal persons see the account by Lambert in Terry and Pellens, *op. cit.*, p. 415. There are a few accounts of infants addicted from before birth and later cured (pp. 415-27). An experiment conducted in recent years on chimpanzees tends to bear out the notion that morphinism is genuinely curable when there is no emotional involvement. In these animals the desire for morphine vanished without leaving a trace, as soon as they were physically comfortable without it (the experiment is summarized in Suppl. No. 165, I, 733-34, 739-40). I mention it here, for what it is worth, because a few writers have maintained that no one is ever cured of morphinism. They are convinced that an actual physiological craving outlasts the withdrawal symptoms and sooner or later forces the victim to return to the drug.

21. Light and Torrance, *op. cit.*, XLIII, 33.

22. Charles Lloyd, *Edmund Oliver* (Bristol, 1798), I, 210, 218, 245.

23. Erich David in 1925 (Terry and Pellens, *op. cit.*, pp. 590-95) stated the case for a less psychological theory of relapse. The argument is persuasive but appears to depend wholly on the unsupported word of one addict.

24. Herxheimer and Kost, in 1932, reported in Suppl. No. 165, I, 18.

25. *Pleasure and Deterioration*, pp. 5-6. I have omitted three statements that duplicate, except in wording, the first three quoted.

26. *Ibid.*, pp. 1-7, 20-21 (Kolb records finding a very few cases in which apparently stable persons had experienced euphoria); R. B. Brown, "The Effect of Morphine upon the Rorschach Pattern in Post-addicts,"*American Journal of Orthopsychiatry*, XIII (1943), 339-43. Cf. Lindesmith, *op. cit.*, pp. 22-23, who quotes one addict as specifically noting that opium merely restores one "to a normal, or nearly normal, state of mind and body." The authors of Suppl. No. 165 (I, 17-18) mention the subject briefly and are not convinced that there is a proved connection between instability and euphoria but do not point to any significant studies leading to a different conclusion.

27. Abrams, *op. cit.*, pp. 4, 20. Besides De Quincey, Baudelaire, and

Symons, he cites Roger Dupouy, *Les Opiomanes* (Paris, 1912), pp. 93–94, which see. M. Dupouy leaned rather heavily upon De Quincey, Coleridge, and Poe but also received information directly from addicts. His reports of sensitivity are all subjective; some are, in essence, expressions of the desire to remain undisturbed: the sound of a foot on the stair or of neighbors speaking is disagreeable and even painful. These latter reports are in keeping with recent findings, though not all the others are. M. Dupouy's views as a whole have more in common with recent studies than do most works written as early as 1912 and more than some of his readers have appeared to realize. Discussing the usual "reveries" of opium smokers, he notes that they are "intérieures et mentales" and that the smokers know they are. Opium does not, he says, create a *special kind* of reverie. The reveries are voluntary and not hallucinative. Hallucination may occur occasionally, he says, after an overdose, just before complete torpor occurs. He insists, as De Quincey partly did, that only dreamers dream under opium; and he further remarks that, though opium may give the illusion of greater ease in whatever one is doing, it does not actually increase the individual's powers. He seems also to have some suspicion that there may be a good deal of self-hypnosis in the smokers' reveries: "Surtout que le dilettante toxicomane ne garde pas, s'il l'a puisée en quelque récit fantaisiste, sa croyance en la vertu magique de l'opium donnant au fumeur la puissance d'évoquer à sa guise les tableaux les plus divers." Opium smoking in Paris, and to some extent elsewhere, is a kind of ritual. Smokers go to a specific place for it, the lights are dim, the whole atmosphere is of a sort to encourage passive reverie, no one is in a hurry. All this prepared atmosphere, with its leisure and its provisions for reclining and, as M. Dupouy says, the belief in the magic power of opium to produce visions, is enough in itself to evoke the kind that he describes, the interior cinema that is like ordinary reverie. M. Dupouy emphasizes that the evocation of memory and imagination is voluntary. As to Coleridge, he argues at some length that opium did not inspire his work or lend any special character to it; nor does he take Coleridge's preface to *Kubla Khan* at its face value. Coleridge, he thinks, was of a manic-depressive temperament and had been neurotic from early years; his abnormalities were not attributable to opium (pp. 94–96, 116–22, and, on Coleridge, 229–54).

28. Suppl. No. 165, I, 29–32. See also the statement quoted (p. 730) that "vision, smell and hearing are enfeebled" by opiates. For convenience I have given here the summary of experimental work from Suppl. No. 165. Inspection of the original studies (for example, that of D. I. and M. B. Macht, "Comparative Effect of Cobra Venom and Opiates on Vision," *Journal of Experimental Psychology*, XXV [1939], 481–93),

yields nothing significant beyond the information supplied in the Supplement.

29. Recognition of this kind of automatic imagery goes back at least as far as Hobbes (see *Leviathan*, Part I, chap. ii [Oxford, 1909; W. G. P. Smith's reprint of the edition of 1651]).

30. Lowes, *op. cit.*, pp. 363, 93, 104, 343, 401, 412.

31. *Milk of Paradise*, pp. 4, 46.

32. Lawrence Hanson, *The Life of S. T. Coleridge: The Early Years* (New York, 1939), p. 260.

33. In *Modern Language Notes* for the year 1910. The author shall be nameless. He was, of course, writing in full conformity with the medical as well as literary opinion of that day.

34. See the *Confessions*, the article on "Dreams" in *Collected Writings*, XIII, 333 ff., and other scattered passages.

35. R. C. Bald, "Coleridge and *The Ancient Mariner*," *Nineteenth Century Studies* (Ithaca, 1940), pp. 29 n.–30 n. Cf. the instance noted in Suppl. No. 165, I, 17, and the interesting (though, as Mr. Bald suggests, perhaps not wholly reliable) account of experiences with opium in William Blair's *An Opium-Eater in America* . . . , ed. R. C. Bald (Aurora, N.Y., 1941).

36. Horatio C. Wood, "The Story of the Use and Abuse of Opium," *American Journal of Pharmacy*, CIII (1931), 19; Lindesmith, *op. cit.*, p. 24; C. Edouard Sandoz, "Report on Morphinism to the Municipal Court of Boston," *Journal of Criminal Law and Criminology*, XIII (1922), 13, quoted in Lindesmith, *op. cit.*, pp. 24–25.

37. See especially Kolb, *Clinical Contribution to Drug Addiction*, and Pescor, *op. cit.*, p. 105. The exception, in *Psychological Abstracts* (1944), Item 3469, reported from the *Psychoanalytical Review*, is merely a notice of one case of childbirth in which the mother had been given an opiate and had two dreams in color.

38. Terry and Pellens, *op. cit.*, p. 452.

39. Kolb, *Pleasure and Deterioration*, pp. 13–14; R. L. Mégroz, *The Dream World* (New York, 1939), p. 293. Kolb's dreamer used cocaine as well as morphine.

40. *Pleasure and Deterioration*, p. 6. Kolb does, however, remark that a pleasant sensation of floating seems to be fairly common in early stages of opiate addiction.

41. David Hartley, *Observations on Man*, Part I, chap. iii, sec. v, "Of Imagination, Reveries, and Dreams" (London, 1749), I, 386.

42. To George and Georgiana Keats, February–April, 1819 (*Letters*, ed. Buxton Forman [Oxford, 1931], II, 352; italics mine). Cf. lines that describe waking imagery in Keats's *Isabella*, stanza XLI, and Browning's comments upon them, quoted in de Selincourt's edition of Keats

p. 463. I am indebted to Mr. Bald for drawing my attention to this passage.

43. Abrams, *op. cit.*, p. 3; Terry and Pellens, *op. cit.*, pp. 55–60; D. I. Macht, "History of Opium and Some of Its Preparations and Alkaloids," *Journal of the American Medical Association*, LXIV (1915), 477–81.

44. Crumpe's work will be discussed later. The statement quoted here is from p. 50 of the book.

45. *Psychological Abstracts* (1944), Item No. 2399, and commonly elsewhere in accounts of marihuana, which is essentially the same drug as hashish. Chardin mentions bang (i.e., hashish) in the same sentence with opium and does not appear to have known any difference in the effects of the two (John Harris, *Navigantium atque itinerantium bibliotheca* [London, 1764], II, 894). Coleridge had no doubt read the account of opium and bang in the very work that furnished the opening lines of *Kubla Khan*, Purchas's *Pilgrimage*. Opium is there described as "a dangerous drugge, used much in Asia and Africa, which makes them goe as if they were half a sleepe: they suppose I know [not] what conjunction and efficacie both of *Mars* and *Venus* therein: but being once used, must daily be continued on paine of death, which some escaped in *Acostaes* companie by the help of wine. Bangue is another receit of like use, especially with slaves and souldiers, made them drunke-merrie, and so to forget their labour" (*Pilgrimage*, Book V, chap. xii [London, 1614], pp. 507–8). Purchas was not the only old writer to report the notion—the exact contrary of the fact—that opium stimulates sexual desire. In 1803 Coleridge and Tom Wedgwood became interested in trying out bang (*Unpublished Letters*, I, 245–46, 252–53).

46. Hartley, *op. cit.*, I, 385.

47. *The Botanic Garden*, Vol. II, Canto II, ll. 271–72. Mégroz (*op. cit.*, p. 293) quotes a passage from John Aubrey's *Miscellanies* that implies a belief in some connection between visions and the drug.

48. Southey, *Common-Place Book*, ed. J. W. Warter, Ser. IV (London, 1851), pp. 20–21. I date the list through a reference in it to one poem already written, which he himself elsewhere dated 1799 (*Poetical Works* [London, 1837–38], III, 62–64), and one projected poem in the list, which as "The Pig" (*ibid.*, pp. 65–67), was written on May 12, 1799 (Southey's *Letters*, ed. J. W. Warter [London, 1856], I, 71–72). The "Ode" on his cold is dated December 19, 1799; it is printed in *Letters from the Lake Poets to Daniel Stuart* (London, 1889), pp. 442–44. Cf., however, Southey's expression a few months later, when he took opium to preserve him from fatiguing dreams (*Fragmentary Remains . . . of Sir Humphry Davy*, ed. John Davy [London, 1858], pp. 42–43). There is another brief reference to what may be meant as an influence of

opium upon dreams in the *Arabian Tales* (IV, 167), which provided Southey's starting point for *Thalaba*. As demons, black magic, and other supernatural elements are involved, one cannot be sure, among all the ambiguities, how the various properties and powers are intended to be assorted. For an account of this work see chap. iii.

49. Albert H. Buck, *The Growth of Medicine* (New Haven, 1917), p. 424; Samuel Crumpe, *An Inquiry into the Nature and Properties of Opium* (London, 1793), pp. 48–53, 177–79. For other accounts of opium derived from travels in the East, some of them grossly inaccurate on other matters than dreams, see Harris, *op. cit.*, I, 771; II, 818, 894; and *Memoirs of the Baron de Tott*, translated by "an English Gentleman at Paris" (London, n.d.), I, 176–78. In several accounts opium is associated with bang. Coleridge knew Harris's collection in 1800 and probably earlier. It contains narratives of Mandelslo, Chardin, Thevenet, Tavernier, and others that Southey was reading in connection with *Thalaba* in 1799.

50. *Zoonomia* (Dublin, 1800), Part III, Art. II. I. 1.

51. It is now known that there is or may be a brief and slight effect of stimulation preceding the main effect, which is the reverse. For an account of this controversy in the eighteenth century see Terry and Pellens, *op. cit.*, pp. 59–60.

52. *Zoonomia*, Part I, Sec. XII, 3. 1–2, and Sec. XXXIII, 1. 4.

53. *Ibid.*, Part III, Art. II. 2. 1. 9–10; Part I, Sec. XII, 7.

54. The authors of Suppl. No. 165 imply that "addiction as such" was not recognized until sometime after 1870 (I, 728). They mean by this, however, a fairly accurate understanding of it; Coleridge became acutely, if inaccurately, aware of his own addiction at least as early as 1802 or 1803.

55. *Op. cit.*, pp. 177–79.

56. E. Levinstein, *Die Morphiumsucht*. An English translation by Charles Harrer appeared in 1878. The account of withdrawal symptoms is reprinted in Terry and Pellens, *op. cit.*, pp. 431–34.

57. W. M. Kraus, "An Analysis of the Action of Morphine upon the Vegetative Nervous System of Man," *Journal of Nervous and Mental Diseases*, XLVIII, No. 1 (July, 1918); quoted in Terry and Pellens, *op. cit.*, pp. 460–62.

58. Kolb, *Clinical Contribution to Drug Addiction*, pp. 7–8; Light and Torrance, *op. cit.*, p. 211; Suppl. No. 165, I, 736. Correlation between emotional stability and acuteness of withdrawal symptoms is not regarded by all authorities as proved.

59. Maguin and Kraus in Terry and Pellens, *op. cit.*, pp. 442–44, 460–62; Kolb, *Pleasure and Deterioration*, p. 12. Cf. the same author's *Clinical Contribution*, p. 17, and elsewhere.

60. Jean Cocteau, *Opium: The Diary of an Addict*, trans. Ernest Boyd (New York, 1932), pp. 9–10.

61. I wonder a little whether Coleridge's determined conviction that his disease at this time was atonic gout may not have been in part a rationalization. The standard prescription for that ailment was opium (cf. Crumpe, *op. cit.*, p. 183, citing the more influential *Materia medica* of Cullen; and Darwin, *Zoonomia*, Part II, 1. 2. 4. 6).

62. Miss Coburn reports a family tradition that Coleridge was given opium as a baby. Probably very few children at that time grew up without benefit of at least occasional doses of laudanum. The habit itself Coleridge may have established in 1796, either temporarily or permanently, and either during the spring, when he was taking laudanum for a time "almost every night" because of worries and other emotional disturbances, or at the close of the year, when he used the drug for acute pains, apparently neuralgic (Coleridge, *Letters*, ed. E. H. Coleridge [Boston, 1895], I, 172–76, 193; *Unpublished Letters*, ed. E. L. Griggs [New Haven, 1933], I, 3, 45–47). Coleridge's early references to opium have been surveyed by E. H. Coleridge (*Letters*, 173 n.–74 n.), Bald (*op. cit.*, pp. 25–30), and others. Professor Abrams thinks Coleridge certainly became addicted in 1796. This seems likely, but I do not believe we can be at all sure.

63. *The Pains of Sleep, Letters*, I, 435–37. I quote from the version sent to Southey on September 10, 1803, with the comment: "I do not know how I came to scribble down these verses to you—my heart was aching, my head all confused—but they are, doggerel as they may be, a true portrait of my nights." On October 3 a portion of the poem was sent to Poole along with a prose account of his sufferings (*Unpublished Letters*, I, 286–87). On September 22 he told Sir George and Lady Beaumont that the poem had been composed nine years earlier during an attack similar to that of 1803 (*Memorials of Coleorton* [Edinburgh, 1887], I, 7). The date of 1803, however, is undoubtedly correct. The experiences described in the poem correspond in practically every detail with the numerous accounts of night horrors in the letters of 1803. Even to Southey, Coleridge wrote deprecatingly of the verses as "doggerel." He was obviously eager at this time to make a favorable impression upon the Beaumonts, who were recent acquaintances, and was probably unwilling to own the poem as a product of his mature years. He was no doubt merely protecting his poetic flank with the date "nine years ago."

64. *Letters*, I, 435; *Unpublished Letters*, I, 280.

65. *Letters*, I, 434 (the portion in brackets supplied by the editor); *Unpublished Letters*, I, 272–73. What immediately preceded these latter words we do not know, for the original (or transcript?) the editor reports has been mutilated.

66. *Zoonomia*, Part II, I. 3. 1. 8 and 10 and IV. 3. 1. 8. Darwin also described a *hysteria a timore*, which also affects the stomach and bowels (Part II, IV. 3. 1. 8).

67. *Unpublished Letters*, I, 274.

68. *Memorials of Coleorton*, I, 8–9.

69. *Letters*, I, 430–42; *Unpublished Letters*, I, 268–97; *Memorials of Coleorton*, I, 4–17; and elsewhere.

70. Much has been made, in extenuation of Coleridge's weaknesses, of the report of a post mortem examination that found abnormalities in the heart and chest, though the report is insufficient by modern standards to warrant any significant conclusions.

71. *Unpublished Letters*, I, 275, 280.

72. Light and Torrance, *op. cit.*, XLIII, 209–10; XLIV, 11–14.

73. He could not have known much about the problem, but he must have picked up a piece or two of information from one source or another. For a time, when he awoke screaming at night, he tried taking tea or coffee with an egg "and a good deal of cayenne pepper," though he was allowing himself little other stimulant—only "one tumbler" of brandy and water a day. Crumpe had reported from an Eastern source that wine with the addition of pepper and other aromatics could be made to substitute for accustomed opium (*op. cit.*, pp. 178–79). Pepper may have been a common prescription for the purpose; I have seen a reference to its use as late as 1874 (Terry and Pellens, *op. cit.*, p. 522).

74. *Unpublished Letters*, I, 297. For the information from the notebooks I am indebted to the kindness of Miss Kathleen Coburn, who is editing them.

75. Euphoria is occasionally recaptured also in the midst of addiction by means of an unusually large dose. Coleridge was clearly one of those persons (according to Kolb and others, nearly always the unstable) who experience a marked euphoria from opiates. In later years he denied ever having received pleasure from the drug. His memory, however, must have grown dim on this point, for at least twice in the earlier years when it was occurring and before he came to feel any sense of guilt about the drug, he mentioned it. In April, 1798, he wrote to his brother George an account of a recent illness: "Laudanum gave me repose, not sleep; but you, I believe, know how divine that repose is, what a spot of enchantment, a green spot of fountain and flowers and trees in the very heart of a waste of sands! . . . I am now recovering apace, and enjoy that newness of sensation from the fields, the air, and the sun which makes convalescence almost repay one for disease." On another occasion he referred to "a sort of stomach sensation attached to all my thoughts, like those which succeed to the pleasurable operations of a dose of opium" (*Letters*, I, 240; H. A. Bright [ed.], "Unpublished Letters . . .

Coleridge to . . . Estlin," *Miscellanies of the Philobiblon Society*, XV [1884], 102–4; G. H. B. Coleridge, "Biographical Notes" in *Coleridge: Studies by Several Hands*, ed. E. Blunden and E. L. Griggs [London, 1934], p. 49).

76. Unpublished notebook No. XVI, pp. 50–51. The passage is printed in Bald, *op. cit.*, p. 41, and there dated "early in December 1803."

77. Unpublished notebook No. 21, p. 102. I print from Miss Coburn's typescript. Bald prints it (p. 36) with an interpretation that connects it with the creative imagination and *Kubla Khan*. I am indebted to this study of Professor Bald for directing my attention to several of Coleridge's statements and regret having to dissent from his conclusions.

78. Letter to Southey, August 7, 1803 (*Letters*, I, 427–28; cf. also Hartley, *op. cit.*, I, 380, "Of Memory"). But cf. especially the belief set forth in Darwin's *Zoonomia* that many of our ideas originally deriving from external stimuli are produced in us again later by our "sensations of pleasure or pain." These then become "ideas of imagination." "Thus when any painful or pleasurable sensations possess us, as of love, anger, fear; whether in our sleep or waking hours, the ideas, that have been formerly excited by the objects of these sensations, now vividly recur before us by their connection with these sensations themselves. So the fair smiling virgin, that excited your love by her presence, whenever the sensation recurs, rises before you in imagination" (Part I, VIII. 1. 2). Cf. also Darwin's *Temple of Nature*, published in 1802, note to Canto III, l. 72 (New York ed. [1804], p. 73). Darwin's accounts would already have caused Hartley's system to totter in the respect suggested by Coleridge. Cf. also, under "Classes of Ideas": "Our identity is known by our acquired habits or catenated trains of ideas and muscular motions; and perhaps, when we compare infancy with old age, in those alone can our identity be supposed to exist" (*Zoonomia*, Part I, Sec. XV, 3. 5; cf. also Part II, III. 2. 2. 1 and IV. 2. 3. 8). For indications of Darwin's influence on Coleridge see pp. 91–105, below.

79. Unpublished notebook No. 21½, pp. 11–12. Printed in Bald, *op. cit.*, p. 36, and there dated 1808.

80. Kathleen Coburn (ed.), *Inquiring Spirit: A New Presentation of Coleridge from His Published and Unpublished Prose Writings* (London, 1951), p. 37. The note is undated.

81. *Ibid.*, p. 56, undated.

82. *Collected Writings*, I, 42, 47–48, and elsewhere.

83. *A Diary of Thomas De Quincey: 1803*, ed. H. A. Eaton (New York, 1927), pp. 154–55.

84. *Ibid.*, p. 155. I use De Quincey's titles. The last two tales are by Mrs. Radcliffe and Clara Reeve. See Eaton's notes on the reading.

85. *Ibid.*, pp. 156–57.

86. *Ibid.*, pp. 155, 158, 162–65, 177, 181–84, 187.

87. *Poetical Works*, II, 129–31.

88. *The Monk*, ed. E. A. Baker (London, 1922), pp. 17–18.

89. See Paula Ritzler, *Der Traum in der Dichtung der deutschen Romantik* (Bern, 1943).

90. Jean Paul Richter, *Levana* (London, 1876), pp. 269, 215, 205. For De Quincey's relation to Jean Paul see his own accounts in the *Collected Writings*. How much he owed to the German for the conception of prose as music and for the wayward discursive structure or *un*structure of his writing would not be easy to determine. It must have been a great deal.

91. Passages in Crabbe's poetry that have to do with dreams, cited by Professor Abrams (pp. 14–20) as opium visions, seem to me merely a part of this stream of writing on the subject. Crabbe, like the others, had read Monk Lewis and Mrs. Radcliffe and was not above trying their vein once or twice, however foreign they were to his ordinary temper.

92. *Unpublished Letters*, I, 170.

93. *Poems*, I, 213; *Wordsworth and Coleridge: Studies in Honor of George McLean Harper*, ed. E. L. Griggs (Princeton, 1939), p. 177, a passage in a review of *Christabel* in which Coleridge may have had a hand.

94. Many letters of Coleridge remain unpublished. I am indebted to Professor Earl Leslie Griggs, who is engaged in editing a full edition of the letters, for his kindness in looking out for evidence bearing on this as well as one or two other points. Thus far, at least, nothing has been found.

95. *Unpublished Letters*, I, 281.

96. Through the kindness of Miss Coburn I have read photographs or typescript copies of the notebooks for the period that concerns *Kubla Khan*. Miss Coburn tells me that she has seen no reference to that dream elsewhere either.

97. Lamb, *Letters*, II, 90.

98. Clement Carlyon, *Early Years and Late Reflections* (London, 1856–58), I, 198–240. Carlyon gave the time as autumn, 1803, but Coleridge was not in London then. He visited London in the spring of 1803 and again early in 1804. Carlyon seems to have been describing the first of these occasions. Though the book was written long afterward and is not wholly free of errors, Carlyon described this conversation from notes made at the time (see p. 235), and his account of it is probably on the whole reliable. For Davy's brief account of Coleridge's visit, see Chambers, *op. cit.*, p. 169.

99. Coleridge, *Lectures and Notes on Shakespeare* . . . , ed. T. Ashe (London, 1897), pp. 17–18. Lowes (*op. cit.*, p. 586) quotes part of the

passage. The entry as printed has no date but must have been made before publication of the poem in 1816; the context of the passage and other circumstances point to 1811 or 1812.

100. Unpublished notebook No. 10, p. 102. I am indebted to the kindness of Miss Coburn for permission to quote this entry from her typescript. It is undated but appears among other entries that she dates between February and May, 1800.

101. *Memoirs of the Late Mrs. Robinson, Written by Herself* . . . (London, 1801), II, 129-32. The poem may be found in *The Poetical Works of the Late Mrs. Mary Robinson* . . . (London, 1806), II, 298-303. For an account of this friendship see E. L. Griggs, "Coleridge and Mrs. Mary Robinson," *Modern Language Notes*, XLV (1930), 90. See also chap. iv, below.

For some years it had been supposed that Coleridge wrote the review of Mrs. Robinson's *Hubert de Sevrac* that appeared in the *Critical Review* in 1798. Charles I. Patterson (*Journal of English and Germanic Philology*, L [1951], 517-21) has given persuasive reasons for rejecting the attribution of this review to Coleridge. His conclusion, however, leaves unexplained the story told by Carlyon (*op. cit.*, I, 175) of Coleridge's first communication with Mrs. Robinson, which had originated, according to Coleridge, in his (apparently published) disapproval of one of her works.

102. In a letter to Miss Robinson written in 1802, not long after publication of the *Memoirs*, Coleridge said he had not seen it (*Unpublished Letters*, I, 233). He would probably have read it in the course of time, however; his friendship for "Perdita" had been enthusiastic, if not long, and the volumes contained, among other tributes, a poem of his own addressed to her, *A Stranger Minstrel*.

103. If Coleridge was accurate in saying that he had taken "two grains" of opium, the amount was not large. From one to two grains seems to have been a common prescription during the eighteenth century (Darwin, *Zoonomia*, Part I, Sec. XII, 3. 1 and 2; and elsewhere; Crumpe, *op. cit.*, p. 217, recommending one grain; Bald, citing others [*op. cit.*, pp. 30-32]). Asked whether Coleridge's two grains would have been likely to produce a "profound sleep" in his chair for three hours, two modern professors of medicine (not specialists on opium) gave different replies. According to one, it was quite possible. According to the other, it was very improbable: any effect beyond a slight euphoria, he indicated, would be unlikely even in one who had not built up tolerance. Nothing can be stated with certainty, however, on this subject, for natural crude opium varies greatly—from less than 1 to nearly 25 per cent —in its morphine content. Though prepared opium in Coleridge's day

did not vary to anything like that extent, it still was not uniform; legal standardization did not take place until many years later.

It is quite possible, of course, that Coleridge woke up from an opium-induced sleep with a bit of Purchas versified, enough to start his poem off. Because of the Crewe note, however, this seems unlikely.

104. *Unpublished Letters*, I, 62.

105. Ernst Krause, *Erasmus Darwin*, trans. W. S. Dallas (London, 1879), pp. 111, 118–24.

106. *The Eolian Harp* (*Poems*, I, 101). The phrase occurs in a passage added after 1797.

107. The interdependence of mind and body was, of course, no news; it had been discussed by many writers before Darwin. Burke made a special point of it in the *Essay on the Sublime and Beautiful;* and it was recognized, at least nominally and within the limits of his theory, by Hartley. Darwin's handling of the subject, however, is more modern in spirit than that of others who preceded him, so far as I know them.

108. *Zoonomia*, Part I, Sec. XVI, 6–8; Part II, IV. 3. 1. 3.

109. Letters to Josiah Wade, January 27, 1796, and to Thelwall, February 6, 1797, *Letters*, I, 152, 215; Gutch notebook, fol. 25b (*Archiv für das Stud. der neu. Sprach.*, XCI, 354); cf. also the connection with Darwin marked in n. 78, above. For other evidence of Coleridge's familiarity with the work of Darwin, see the brief résumé in Lowes, *op. cit.*, p. 473; and James V. Logan, *The Poetry and Aesthetics of Erasmus Darwin* (Princeton, 1936), pp. 19–20. Cf. also *The Philosophical Lectures of Samuel Taylor Coleridge*, ed. Kathleen Coburn (London, 1949), pp. 213–14, 419; *Coleridge the Talker*, ed. Richard W. Armour and Raymond F. Howes (Ithaca, 1940), pp. 211–12 (from the Farington Diaries); Carlyon, *op. cit.*, I, 88. Anna Seward's life of Darwin (1804) contains accusations of plagiarism.

There is no doubt that Coleridge knew the *Zoonomia*, as well as the *Botanic Garden*, early. Wordsworth borrowed it from Cottle, apparently just after a visit from Coleridge to Racedown in 1797 and founded his poem *Goody Blake and Harry Gill*, written while he was Coleridge's neighbor at Alfoxden in 1798, on an incident in it. The account of dreams in the *Zoonomia* may have been discussed at Carlyon's dinner party in 1803; Carlyon (*op. cit.*, I, 210) at least refers to it in that passage, though without saying it was discussed.

110. *Coleridge's Shakespearean Criticism*, ed. T. M. Raysor (London, 1930), I, 127–30.

111. A. W. Schlegel, *Lectures on Dramatic Art and Literature*, trans. John Black (London, 1846), p. 246. "Die theatralische Täuschung wie jede poetische ist eine wache Träumerey, der man sich freywillig hingiebt," are Schlegel's words (*Vorlesungen . . .* , ed. G. V. Amoretti

[Bonn and Leipzig, 1923], II, 16). For the best condensed account of the evidence for and against Coleridge's debt on this point, see Professor Raysor's Introduction and notes in *Coleridge's Shakespearean Criticism*, I, xxxviii–xl, 200–201; see also A. C. Dunstan in *Modern Language Review*, XVIII (1923), 190–99, and D. I. Morrill in *Modern Language Notes*, XLII (1927), 436–44. Schlegel's lectures were delivered in 1808. Coleridge had formulated his ideas on dramatic illusion earlier than the lectures of 1818, but the precise date has not been determined.

112. *Zoonomia*, Part I, Sec. XVIII, "Of Sleep." My quotations from Darwin hereafter are from this chapter or section except when otherwise noted.

113. Part I, Sec. XVII, 3. 7. The claim of Coleridge seems to have been generally allowed; certainly he met the term in the elder writers and quoted their use of it (*Biographia literaria*, ed. J. Shawcross [Oxford, 1907], I, 108–9, 249, 166–68; II, 229–30). He wrote that he had "followed Hooker, Sanderson, Milton &c., in designating the *immediateness* of any act or object of knowledge by the word *intuition*." Darwin, however, had preceded him. Coleridge said nothing of Darwin's prior use of the term *intuitive analogy*, though it occurred in the midst of a statement he appears to have used in his account of dreams. Yet in two of three passages on intuition he cited Darwin's revival of old terms in support of his own practice; in the third he elaborated his own use of the term through illustrations drawn from insects—and the insects, in turn, may have owed something to Darwin's *Temple of Nature*. In this latter work Darwin had inserted a passage on sleep and dreams, repeating his earlier statement about "intuitive analogy" and referring back to the *Zoonomia* for the fuller account (*Temple of Nature*, Canto III, ll. 79–84 and note; also Additional Note XIII). In the *Zoonomia*, on the page or two preceding the chapter on sleep, Darwin had said that in our waking hours, "whenever an idea occurs, which is incongruous to our former experience, we instantly dissever the train of imagination by the power of volition, and compare the incongruous idea with our previous knowledge of nature, and reject it. This operation of the mind has not yet acquired a specific name, though it is exerted every minute of our waking hours; unless it may be termed INTUITIVE ANALOGY. It is an act of reasoning of which we are unconscious except from its effects in preserving the congruity of our ideas" (*Zoonomia*, Part I, Sec. XVII, 3. 7). Coleridge poured a certain amount of transcendentalism into the terms *intuition* and *intuitive*, and their equivalent undoubtedly cropped up in his German readings. But he could not have missed it in Darwin either.

114. Part I, Sec. VIII, 1. 2, "Of Sensitive Motions."

115. Of Coleridge's three extended accounts of dramatic illusion, I

have quoted the latest. The longest one, of undetermined date but probably much earlier, is printed by Professor Raysor (*op. cit.*, I, 199–207);
the other appears in a letter to Daniel Stuart of May 13, 1816 (*Letters*,
II, 663–64). Here Coleridge's argument follows the same order of ideas
as Darwin's, beginning with dreams and proceeding to Shakespeare and
the unities. In the lectures the order was reversed. A much briefer account of the subject is preserved from the lectures of 1811–12 in Raysor,
op. cit., II, 83–84.

116. Interludes between the first and second and between the second
and third cantos, *The Botanic Garden* (4th ed.; London, 1799), II, 69, 71,
116, 119. For Kames's discussion of "ideal presence" see the *Elements
of Criticism*, chap. ii, Part 1, Sec. 7.

117. *Botanic Garden*, II, 72–73, 115. Cf. *Coleridge's Shakespearean
Criticism*, I, 21, where among his famous comments on the opening
scene of *Hamlet* Coleridge wrote: "Hume himself could not but have
faith in *this* Ghost dramatically, let his anti-ghostism be as strong as
Samson against ghosts less powerfully raised." Cf. also Darwin's Second Interlude, pp. 116–17, with *Coleridge's Shakespearean Criticism*, I,
204.

118. Hobbes, for example, had written of the absence of surprise in
dreams and of their vividness. Miss Coburn has drawn my attention to
the long discourse on dreams by Andrew Baxter, which Coleridge had
read and admired, and in which the absence of surprise is discussed
briefly. Other writers had commented on the inconsistency and incoherence, the superior vividness, and various other characteristics of
dreams. But the particular points emphasized by Darwin and Coleridge
in the passages discussed here—the emphasis upon volition and powers
of comparison, the particular definitions of nightmare and reverie, and
the bearing of all these upon literary theory—of this, which constitutes
the main line of thought on the subject by both men, I have seen nothing elsewhere. In 1799 at Göttingen, Coleridge attended the lectures of
the famous Blumenbach on physiology and later thought of translating
them. But Blumenbach's account of sleep and dreams as published in his
Institutions of Physiology (Sec. XX) bears no resemblance at all to
Coleridge's ideas. Thomas Hobbes, *Elements of Philosophy* and *Human
Nature*, chap. iii, *The English Works*, ed. Molesworth (London, 1839),
I, 400–402; IV, 13–14 (cf. also *Leviathan*, Part I, chap. ii); Hartley, *op.
cit.*, Part I, chap. iii, sec. 5; Baxter, *An Enquiry into the Nature of the
Human Soul; Wherein the Immateriality of the Soul Is Evinced from the
Principles of Reason and Philosophy* (3d ed.; London, 1745).

119. Second Interlude, p. 115.

120. Canto III, ll. 50 ff., pp. 126–28.

121. *Coleridge's Shakespearean Criticism*, I, 202–3. As it stands,

Coleridge's passage on nightmare appears to have been introduced without much relevance to the subject of dramatic illusion, but that is perhaps because the fragment is incomplete; it breaks off abruptly at the conclusion of those remarks.

122. *Letters*, I, 110-11.

123. May 13, 1816 (*ibid.*, II, 663).

124. November 15, 1796 (*Unpublished Letters*, I, 62).

125. *Zoonomia*, Part I, Sec. XIX, "Of Reverie"; Part II, III. 1. 2. 2.

126. Hanson (*op. cit.*, p. 149), at any rate, informs us that Lloyd went to Darwin about this illness. For other expressions of Coleridge that parallel those of Darwin, see *Coleridge's Shakespearean Criticism*, I, 203; *Inquiring Spirit*, p. 135; *Zoonomia*, Part I, "Of Sleep"; *Botanic Garden*, II, 127-28.

127. It has been suggested that in defining *nightmare* as oddly as he did, Coleridge was appropriating the term to describe a special kind of opium hallucination occurring in a state between sleeping and waking (Bald, *op. cit.*, pp. 34-35 and note). Coleridge departed from Darwin's definition, however, in but one rather immaterial point. In a note published, with omissions, in *Anima poetae* (p. 206) and more accurately by Professor Bald, Coleridge described the "Night-mair" as something that occurs most often on the fringes between sleeping and waking. He thought the phenomenon should be considered, like somnambulism, a form of reverie rather than sleep because "the volitions of reason, that is, the faculty of comparison, etc., are awake though disturbed." It originates, he believed, in some physical pain or discomfort. After discussing that matter, he recapitulated his first statement: "In short, the Night-mair is not properly *a Dream;* but a species of Reverie, akin to Somnambulism, during which the Understanding & moral Sense are awake, tho' more or less confused. . . ." When he digressed from dramatic illusion to redefine *nightmare*, he repeated that it "is not a mere dream, but takes place when the waking state of the brain is re-commencing and most often during a rapid alternation, a *twinkling*, as it were, of sleeping and waking" (the phrase is reminiscent of Darwin's rapid-alternation notion of theatric reverie). It arises often from derangement of the "stomach or other digesting organs acting on the external skin (which is still in sympathy with the stomach and bowels)" (*Coleridge's Shakespearean Criticism*, I, 202). These last phrases, once again, are not imaginative or wholly autobiographical, for they represent Darwin's conception of physiological association between stomach and skin (*Zoonomia*, Part II, IV. 2. 1. 1. and elsewhere). In the chapter on sleep in the *Zoonomia* and again more fully under "Diseases of Volition" (Part II, III. 2. 1. 13) Darwin had described nightmare as originating from either the body or the mind, though digestive discomforts, he

thought, were an especially potent cause. It is a state of "imperfect sleep, where the desire of locomotion is vehement, but the muscles do not obey the will; it is attended with great uneasiness, a sense of suffocation, and frequently with fear." Volition, though present, can become operative only when the sleeper begins to waken. In *The Loves of the Plants*, as we have seen, Darwin had connected it more specifically with somnambulism, as Coleridge did. "When there arises in sleep a painful desire to exert the voluntary motions, it is called the Nightmare or Incubus. When the sleep becomes so imperfect that some muscular motions obey this exertion of desire, people have walked about, and even performed some domestic offices in sleep; one of these sleep-walkers I have frequently seen . . . this disease . . . seemed to be of the epileptic kind" (*Botanic Garden*, II, 128). Darwin classified nightmare, then, as "imperfect sleep," whereas Coleridge insisted that it should be called "reverie"; but in substance Coleridge departed from Darwin's account scarcely at all. No doubt Coleridge did write with some of his own experiences of appalling nightmares in mind, but these did not lead him beyond the general framework of thought established by Darwin. It is most improbable that he intended his account as a description of exceptional experience confined to opium eaters, though it would quite naturally be read in that sense if Darwin's psychology were unnoticed.

128. *Coleridge's Miscellaneous Criticism*, ed. T. M. Raysor (Cambridge, Mass., 1936), p. 197 (for the dating of the draft, see Professor Raysor's note); *Anima poetae*, p. 46; *Biographia literaria*, I, 225–26; Darwin, *Zoonomia*, Part II, II. 1. 7. 1–4, "Diseases of Sensation," and the section on sleep. See also Note 118 above; and Bald (*op. cit.*, pp. 37–40), who, however, interprets Coleridge's use of some of these terms differently, without reference to Darwin. For other comments by Coleridge on dreams, by no means all mere echoes of Darwin, see Coleridge's *Philosophical Lectures*, pp. 319, 402; *Anima poetae*, *passim*, and frequently elsewhere. Cf. also *Coleridge's Shakespearean Criticism*, II, 185, a Darwinesque comment on madness and delirium (which may, however, have been a commonplace of the time). The writings of Coleridge on dream and reverie have recently been employed in the interpretation of his theory of imagination (see, for example, Mr. Humphry House's Clark Lectures on Coleridge, just published). I question, however, in the light of Darwin's discussions or even, for that matter, of Hobbes's remarks on dreams and "phantasms," whether it is safe to read so much philosophical meaning into Coleridge's statements.

129. Cocteau, *op. cit.*, p. 43.

130. Coleridge's unacknowledged borrowings cannot all have been unconscious, but some of them certainly may have been. I have myself found how fatally easy it can be to forget the origin of one's ideas. Re-

reading for the first time something written a dozen years ago, I now find Coleridge, Aristotle, and Conrad's Preface to the *Nigger of the Narcissus* all more closely paralleled than I think they would have been, without specific acknowledgement, had I recalled their origin at the time. And in revising this present chapter I have discovered that an image I had supposed my own belongs properly to Mr. Sackville-West, writing on De Quincey. As I like it, I have kept it, with only this notice.

131. August 1, 1803 (*Unpublished Letters*, I, 264; italics mine). This confession to Southey expressed not a momentary but a settled feeling. During the last years of his life he recorded in a notebook: "From my earliest recollection I have had a consciousness of Power without Strength—a perception, an experience, of more than ordinary power with an inward sense of Weakness" (*Inquiring Spirit*, p. 40). The entry is dated August 9, 1831.

132. *Letters*, I, 338, 347 (1801). For a different explanation of this assertion of Coleridge, the reader is again referred to Richards, *op. cit.*, pp. 20–21. A single statement in a letter, however interpreted, cannot, of course, alone be relied upon as a proof of "egotism"; but the spirit of Coleridge's letters as a whole seems to me to show almost as much of that as of doubt.

133. De Quincey, *Confessions, Collected Writings*, III, 232–33.

134. For Coleridge's unreliability on dates, see chap. iv, pp. 155–57.

CHAPTER III

1. Coleridge, *Poems*, I, 296 n.; *Purchas His Pilgrimage* (London, 1614), Book IV, p. 415.

2. John Livingston Lowes, *The Road to Xanadu* (Boston, 1930), pp. 364–70, 382–99.

3. Coleridge, *Poems*, I, 298 n.; Lowes, *op. cit.*, pp. 379–80, 385.

4. Lowes, *op. cit.*, pp. 361–62, 373–76, 378; Lane Cooper, "The Abyssinian Paradise in Coleridge and Milton," *Modern Philology*, III (1905–6), 327–32. *Amara* appears also in Purchas, from whom Milton derived it. See also Lowes's notes (*op. cit.*, pp. 589–90), where a link with *Rasselas* is dismissed briefly. As Lowes's book was written before the manuscript of *Kubla Khan* was discovered, he did not know that Coleridge's "Abora" had once been actually "Amara."

5. One gets a hint of that in his book, p. 406. But see further, chap. iv, n. 118, below.

6. See pp. 69–70, above.

7. P. 238.

8. Canto IV, stanza 4. I quote from Sotheby's translation (Boston,

1810), with which Coleridge almost certainly was familiar, a point to be discussed shortly.

9. *Thalaba*, Book I, stanza 19 and note; *Common-Place Book*, Ser. I (1849), pp. 422-23.

10. In the number for September, 1799. For Southey's praise of *Gebir* in letters see C. C. Southey, *Life and Correspondence of Robert Southey* (London, 1850), II, 24, and elsewhere.

11. *Unpublished Letters*, I, 71. He would need to master all sciences and arts first, he thought. He was thinking, of course, of an epic on the Miltonic scale, which *Gebir* did not pretend to be.

12. Preface to the edition of 1798. Landor's *Poetical Works*, ed. Stephen Wheeler (Oxford, 1937), I, 473-74. References to Landor's poetry hereafter will be to this volume of Wheeler's edition.

13. In the list of new publications, October, 1798.

14. I know no method of indicating literary parallels that is not clumsy. Perhaps a marginal gloss (borrowed from Coleridge and Purchas) will serve the purpose of keeping Coleridge's words in sight as the others go by.

15. *Excursion*, IV, 1132 ff. See the notes in Wordsworth's *Poetical Works*, ed. de Selincourt and Darbishire, V, 428-29, and Wheeler's notes to *Gebir*, p. 476.

16. For the image of the sun's wheel in the wave cf. Milton's lines in *Comus:*

> "And the gilded Car of Day,
> His glowing Axle doth allay
> In the steep *Atlantick* stream,
> And the slope Sun his upward beam
> Shoots against the dusky Pole . . ." (ll. 93-99).

Kubla Khan does not echo this version of the image (Housman, incidentally, does, in "the upshot beam").

17. If the reader is faintly reminded here and at l. 173 of Coleridge's *Ancient Mariner* (ll. 193 and 204-5), he need not be puzzled by the identical dates of publication, for Coleridge's "Life-in-Death" and "life-blood" did not appear in the 1798 version of his poem. But the phrases are so natural where they occur that their likeness to Landor's words means little.

18. In the third line from the end I print *roll*, from the edition of 1798, in place of the later reading, *roar*.

19. Letter to Josiah Wedgwood, January 9, 1803 (*Letters*, I, 419).

20. J. W. Robberds, *A Memoir of the Life and Writings of the Late William Taylor of Norwich* (London, 1843), I, 223-24; unpublished letter of October 29, 1798, to C. W. W. Wynn (Professor Curry's transcript; unpublished letters from this source will be referred to hereafter

as "Curry"); letter to Wynn, April 5, 1799 (*Selections from the Letters of Robert Southey*, ed. J. W. Warter [London, 1856], I, 68).

21. ... *newly translated from the Original Arabic into French, by Dom Chavis ... and M. Cazotte, and translated ... into English, by Robert Heron* (4 vols.; Edinburgh, 1792). There was another edition in 3 vols. (London, 1794). I do not know which Southey used, but it seems to have been one of these and not the French original. The existence of the "original Arabic" source is doubtful. My references are to the edition of 1792.

22. *Arabian Tales*, IV, 82-95.

23. *Ibid.*, IV, 141-54, 172-73, 308-36.

24. To Wynn, December 18, 1799 (Curry).

25. Book I, stanzas 11, 12. I quote from Southey's *Poetical Works* (London, 1837-38), Vol. IV, except for an occasional word or phrase in which the first edition is significantly different. In discussing or quoting from the prose notes, I have disregarded all that did not appear in the original edition. Hereafter, references will be made to *Thalaba* by numerals representing book and stanza.

26. *Thalaba*, I, 23; *Memoirs of Peter Henry Bruce ... Containing an Account of his Travels in Germany, Russia, Tartary ...* (London, 1782), pp. 118-19. Bruce described the building of St. Petersburg and the czar's summer and winter palaces: "A fine avenue of large trees, which stand by the side of the river, were dug out of the ground in the winter, with large quantities of frozen earth sticking to their roots, and brought in that condition and planted here, and flourished to the surprize of all who saw them."

27. Sale's Preliminary Discourse, Sec. 1; and the Koran itself, chap. 89 and notes ("Chandos Classics" ed.), pp. 5, 445; *Thalaba*, notes to I, 11 and 19. Cf. the parallels mentioned earlier to the story given by Sale of the man who brought a token of stones from this Paradise.

28. "Tide" and "glory" are the readings of the first edition only.

29. Lowes, *op. cit.*, pp. 361-62.

30. The passage quoted from Burnet is from the chapter "De montibus." For the connection of this with Coleridge's Memorandum Book, see chap. iv and Appendix II.

31. Unpublished letters to G. C. Bedford, October 24, 1799, and to Wynn, November 28 (Curry).

32. Southey, *Life and Correspondence*, II, 22-23; unpublished letter to Wynn (Curry); Hazlitt's "My First Acquaintance with Poets." For connections with the Gutch notebook, see p. 294, below. The description of this in Southey's verse is less vivid than in some of the letters.

33. The Arabian maid is not very far from being an "Abyssinian maid." Sir William Jones, at least some of whose work both Southey

and Coleridge seem to have known, in his account of the origins of the Abyssinian people traced them in part to Arabian stock. Abyssinians (the Ethiopians of Meroe) were the same as the first Egyptians, he said. The same discourse comments on the region of Amara ("Discourse on the Borderers, Mountaineers, and Islanders of Asia . . . ," Jones's *Works* [London, 1799], I, 116–17).

34. *Anima poetae*, p. 14. According to Miss Coburn, this was written two or three years later at Grasmere.

35. For connections between details of this scene and Coleridge's notebook, see chap. iv and Appendix II; cf. also Lowes, *op. cit.*, pp. 274 n., 555–58.

36. *Thalaba*, X, 8–13; *Common-Place Book*, IV, 186–88.

37. *Biographia literaria*, ed. Shawcross, I, 12. Lowes's failure to connect this passage with *Kubla Khan* is odd, since he cites it (p. 473) in discussing Coleridge's early reading of Darwin. Darwin himself has an elaborate description of the great caverns of the saltmines near Cracow that makes them seem almost like an underground cave-palace of ice. He writes of their "crystal walls," "glittering domes," "bright vault," and even their "sculptured ice" (*The Economy of Vegetation*, Canto II, ll. 119–50 and notes).

38. The description of Babylon (V, 8–10), a passage that features the "many-coloured domes," is more successful than most of the poem in creating the atmosphere intended. The second phrase is from XI, 17. Numerous other parallels to *Kubla Khan* might be quoted, particularly from the prose plan and the notes.

39. Letter to William Taylor, February 24, 1799 (J. W. Robberds, *A Memoir of the Life and Writings of the late William Taylor of Norwich* [London, 1843], I, 253). A few months later Taylor urged Southey to read Wieland's "metrical romances" in the original before finishing the "Dom Daniel" (June 23, 1799, *ibid.*, p. 285). But Southey had already begun to think of *Oberon* in relation to *Thalaba*. "Oberon," he had written to Wynn on April 5, "must not stand next to the 'Orlando Furioso.' I shall beg leave to put my own 'Dom-Danael' between them" (Southey, *Letters*, ed. Warter, I, 68).

40. *Biographia epistolaris*, I, 142; Hanson, *The Life of S. T. Coleridge: The Early Years* (New York, 1939), pp. 110, 216, 308; Chambers, *Samuel Taylor Coleridge* (Oxford, 1938), p. 104. Mr. Hanson supposes that Coleridge actually read *Oberon* when he first mentioned the work. On the other hand, Miss Coburn from the evidence of unpublished notebooks confirms my impression that when he went to Germany he had only the very sketchiest acquaintance with the language. When he and Wordsworth visited Klopstock, there were apparently not even stumbling efforts to communicate in German; all had to be said in

French through Wordsworth, though this cut Coleridge entirely out of the conversation. Cf., however, Mr. Werner W. Beyer (*Review of English Studies, 1939 and 1940*), who believed that Coleridge knew German earlier, and traced parallels between *Oberon* and *The Ancient Mariner* and *Cain*. Those in *The Ancient Mariner* seem to me too slight to outweigh Miss Coburn's evidence. Those in *Cain* are stronger; but Coleridge is known to have worked on *Cain* more than once, and we have no proof that the present fragment, which was not published until many years later, is the unrevised first version of 1798. The question is immaterial here, however.

41. I know of no certain evidence. But the translation was talked of when Coleridge and the Wordsworths visited Klopstock. Wordsworth had evidently read it (*Biographia literaria*, II, 177; Knight's *Wordsworth*, I, 175). There is also this passage from a letter of Wordsworth to Coleridge written in Germany (December, 1798, or January, 1799): "You do not say how you liked the poem of Wieland which you had read. Let me know what you think of Wieland" (*Early Letters of William and Dorothy Wordsworth*, ed E. de Selincourt [Oxford, 1935], p. 204). See also Appendix II for evidence that a passage in Coleridge's *Love* (1799) may owe something to Sotheby's version of *Oberon*.

42. *Oberon*, trans. Sotheby, I, 10–15, 39, 42. Cf. also the "savage grot" and "golden halls" in II, 20–21, and other similar passages.

43. See, for example, the quotation from James Bruce (referred to earlier in this chapter) that Lowes cited as a main source of Coleridge's "romantic chasm" lines. Lowes italicized *romantic, cedars, a cover, savage, inchanted, a prodigious cave, the ground slopes* [gently], *earth producing fine grass*. Any significance these might conceivably possess evaporates when one sees from his references that the expressions are scattered through more than seventy of Bruce's solid pages (Lowes, *op cit.*, pp. 377, 591).

44. Cf. the parallels of the flower or token brought from Paradise, in *Anima poetae* and elsewhere, previously discussed. The account of all this occupies much of Cantos III and IV.

CHAPTER IV

1. See chap. ii, Sec. 8, above.

2. Lamb, *Letters*, ed. E. V. Lucas (New Haven, 1935), I, 172; Sir Edmund Chambers, *Coleridge* (Oxford, 1938), p. 233; *Coleridge: Studies by Several Hands*, ed. Edmund Blunden and E. L. Griggs (London, 1934), p. 15 (see also pp. 16, 17).

3. *Christabel*, facsimile edition, ed. E. H. Coleridge (London, 1907), p. 43 n.; *Poems*, I, 13 n., 394 n., 419–20, 78 n., 108, 252 n.; *Biographia*

literaria, ed. Shawcross (Oxford, 1907), I, 2, 203; Hanson, *The Life of S. T. Coleridge: The Early Years* (New York, 1939), p. 104; *Unpublished Letters*, ed. E. L. Griggs (New Haven, 1933), I, 50; *Letters*, ed. E. H. Coleridge (London, 1895), I, 128. For other instances of Coleridge's unreliability on dates and similar points of fact, see the summary and references in Lowes, *The Road to Xanadu* (Boston, 1930), pp. 584, n. 3, 581–82; Chambers, *Coleridge*, pp. 181, 242, 277–78, 280; also *Unpublished Letters*, I, 84, and II, 422; Chambers, "Some Dates in Coleridge's *Annus mirabilis*," *Essays and Studies by Members of the English Association*, XIX (1933), 89–90. In support of one of Coleridge's dates, however, Miss Coburn tells me that the *Monody on the Death of Chatterton* in the Ottery copy book is written in a "round childish hand."

4. Its impersonal tone and the phrasing "in the fall of the year, 1797" suggest some lapse of time, particularly if it was written for Southey (a notation on the manuscript shows that it once belonged to him or Mrs. Southey) (see Alice Snyder and Mr. Meyerstein in *TLS*, August 2, 1934, January 12 and 26, and February 9, 1951; Chambers, *Coleridge*, p. 102; chap. ii, above.

5. *Poems*, I, 295 n.

6. *Letters*, I, 245 n.; Hanson, *op. cit.*, p. 260.

7. Robert Graves, *The Meaning of Dreams* (London, 1924), p. 148 (italics mine). Though Lowes pointed out a number of inaccuracies in Mr. Graves's account of Coleridge, I feel sure there must have been some sort of basis for this very specific statement. Without having learned its source, however, I hesitate to lean upon it, useful as it would be to the theory presented in this chapter.

8. Sir Edmund Chambers, "Some Dates in Coleridge's *Annus mirabilis*," pp. 85–111; "The Date of Coleridge's *Kubla Khan*," *Review of English Studies*, XI (1935), 78–80; and *Coleridge*, pp. 98–103. See also *Letters*, I, 228.

9. George Whalley, "The Bristol Library Borrowings of Southey and Coleridge, 1793–8," *The Library* (Transactions of the Bibliographical Society), September, 1949, p. 124. Coleridge withdrew two volumes of Nash's *Worcestershire* on August 25 and returned them on October 13.

10. Chambers, *Coleridge*, p. 101; Hanson, *op. cit.*, pp. 259–60, 483, 487; *Journals of Dorothy Wordsworth*, ed. E. de Selincourt (New York, 1941), I, 16; Coleridge, *Letters*, I, 246–47. The most likely reason for Dorothy's letter would have been some new development in the Lloyd affair. In that case, if Coleridge went anywhere, it would probably have been to Bristol to seek a meeting with Lloyd. The original of the Alfoxden journal has disappeared, and the only text that appears to have survived is Knight's incomplete printed version.

11. Joseph Cottle, *Reminiscences of Samuel Taylor Coleridge and*

Robert Southey (London, 1848), p. 180; Hanson, *op. cit.*, p. 487. Dorothy Wordsworth, *Journals*, I, 16; Malcolm Elwin, *The First Romantics* (London, 1947), pp. 226–35; Whalley, *op. cit.*, p. 125. I rather doubt that propriety would have kept Coleridge from Alfoxden during Wordsworth's absence. There were apparently at least a part-time servant and little Basil Montagu for chaperons. Dorothy seems to have felt no such hindrance to Coleridge's visits later at Grasmere.

12. At the time of his arrival, Hazlitt said, Wordsworth was away, but his sister was at home. On the third day of his stay, Wordsworth returned to Stowey from Bristol. These circumstances, with some others, indicate that Hazlitt must have arrived some time about May 20. At the end of three weeks, he said, he and Coleridge set out together, he toward home and Coleridge "for Germany." "It was a Sunday morning, and [Coleridge] was to preach that day for Dr. Toulmin of Taunton. . . . I did not go to hear him . . . but we met in the evening at Bridgewater. The next day we had a long day's walk to Bristol." Hazlitt's reference to Germany is inexact but probably originated in the fact that Coleridge was on his way to the Wedgwoods' to make financial arrangements for the German journey. The Sunday morning of Coleridge's preaching and Hazlitt's departure was almost certainly June 10, and the long day's walk together from Bridgewater to Bristol would have been on Monday, June 11. An undated letter from Coleridge to Poole, written after his arrival at the Wedgwoods', tells of having reached Bristol on "Monday evening," which would fit Hazlitt's account and the date June 11 precisely. It could not very well have been a week later, for Coleridge would scarcely then have been able to return in time for the Wordsworths' visit at Stowey after they left Alfoxden on June 25 or 26. If Hazlitt stayed exactly three weeks to the day, he must have arrived at Stowey on Sunday, May 20. In that case there would have been no slightest chance for Coleridge to "retire" to Porlock after the middle of May, for Dorothy Wordsworth's journal and his own note to Poole fix him at Bridgewater, Cheddar, Cross, and Stowey continuously until the twentieth. Hazlitt's "three weeks" may have been only approximate, but even so it is difficult to imagine Coleridge's having made a flying trip to Porlock in such a squeezed interval as might possibly have occurred between the twentieth and Hazlitt's arrival. And there is still the undated visit of Cottle, which must then have fallen wholly within the time of Hazlitt's stay, though neither Hazlitt nor Cottle mentions it (Hazlitt, "My First Acquaintance with Poets," *Complete Works*, ed. P. P. Howe [London, 1930–34], XVII, 116–22; J. D. Campbell, *Coleridge* [London, 1894], p. 91; Mrs. Henry Sandford, *Thomas Poole and his Friends* [London, 1888], I, 271–72; *Early Letters of William and Dorothy Wordsworth*, ed. E. de Selincourt [Oxford, 1935], pp. 192–

93, 195; Abbie Findlay Potts, "The Date of Wordsworth's First Meeting with Hazlitt," *Modern Language Notes*, XLIV [1929], 296–99). Howe dates Hazlitt's arrival at Stowey during "the last days of May," but he was unaware of Dorothy's mistake in dating her entry at Cross May 22 instead of May 17 (P. P. Howe, *The Life of William Hazlitt* [London, 1928], pp. 40–41). Coleridge preached more than once for Dr. Toulmin. The occasion Hazlitt mentions could not have been the same as the earlier one referred to above, when Coleridge went directly home afterwards.

The Bristol Library record indicates that Coleridge borrowed or returned books on May 31 and June 1, 8, and 14. If the last of these dates was entered correctly, Coleridge must have left Bristol for the Wedgwoods' on Thursday instead of Wednesday as his letter said, or must have commissioned someone else to return a book for him the day after his departure. As Wordsworth had been in Bristol again since sometime before the thirteenth, however, he may have borrowed books in Coleridge's name. Two volumes of Massinger's dramatic works were borrowed on the eighth and returned on the fourteenth (Whalley, *op. cit.*, pp. 125–26).

13. The full story may be found in Hanson, *op. cit.*, pp. 215, 221–22, 277–82, 353–62, 397–99, 487–88; Chambers, *Coleridge*, pp. 93–98, 126–27, 134; "Some Dates in Coleridge's *Annus mirabilis*," pp. 104–11, and *Review of English Studies*, *loc. cit.*; Coleridge, *Letters*, I, 246, 249–53, 311–12, 322–23, 344. Southey read proofs of the novel for Lloyd, as appears from Southey's unpublished correspondence. Whether he was in fact responsible for the airing of Coleridge's private life and weaknesses can only be guessed. He evidently supplied the title and probably something of the plot; but it must be noted that his own sketch for a vaguely similar novel gives a wholly favorable picture of the hero (*Common-Place Book*, ed. J. W. Warter [London, 1851], IV, 9–10; cf. Lloyd's *Edmund Oliver* [Bristol, 1798], I, 210, 218, 245, and elsewhere).

14. Chambers, *Review of English Studies*, *loc. cit.* Approximately the first half of the entry is printed, with minor variants, in Hanson, *op. cit.*, p. 483.

15. *Letters*, I, 249. Coleridge had also been affected recently by the death of a certain William Lewis, whom he had formerly known, though not intimately (*Unpublished Letters*, I, 105).

The cryptic entry in Dorothy's journal for May 9, "Wrote to Coleridge," followed the editor's omission of an earlier part of the same day's entry and was succeeded by a gap in the journal (whether Dorothy's or Knight's does not appear) until the sixteenth, when the three went on the expedition that was in part to see Cheddar Rocks but mainly to bring Charles Lloyd back from Bristol, evidently so that Coleridge might confront him. These events all fall within the fortnight mentioned by Coleridge on the twentieth, though he may have seen *Edmund Oliver* a trifle earlier. It is not impossible that what Knight omitted from Dorothy's entry of the ninth was some record of her carrying to Coleridge at Stowey "with tears"—as he remembered it in 1810—the letter from Lloyd. She might well enough have followed this the same evening with a note of afterthoughts or reassurance (*Journals*, I, 16).

16. *Letters*, I, 249–50.

17. *Ibid.*, p. 245 n.

18. Lamb, *Letters*, I, 123, 163, 168, 171. In a letter to Lloyd written between December 10 and 14, 1799, Lamb reported that Coleridge was in town—"but I have seen nothing of him." By the twenty-eighth he had dined and breakfasted with him but was still making clear his loyalty to Lloyd.

19. *Letters*, I, 311–12. Cf. also the close of a letter Coleridge wrote to Poole from Germany. He was pining to be at home, though, he wrote, "in England alone I have those that hate me" (*New Monthly Magazine*, XL [1835], 226). Two unpublished letters of Southey, dated August 20 and October 11, 1799, record from Southey's side Lloyd's troublemaking propensities.

20. Unpublished Notebook No. 5, and *Letters*, I, 322–23. Miss Coburn dates the notebook entry November 20–25, 1799. Other victims of the satire were to be Mackintosh, toward whom Coleridge's animosity was fairly acute in 1799 and 1800, and "Canning & the Anti-Jacobins." *The Beauties of the Anti-Jacobin*, published in 1799, had added to the *Anti-Jacobin's* earlier remarks a really vicious attack on Coleridge.

21. Dorothy Wordsworth, *Journals*, I, 62; Wordsworth, *Early Letters*, p. 249. A few entries from the journal will illustrate what was going on: "Coleridge came on Tuesday 23rd and went home with Jones. Charles Lloyd called on Tuesday, 23rd, and on Sunday 28th we drank tea and supped with him. . . . *September 30*th, on *Tuesday*. Charles Lloyd dined with us. We walked homewards with him after dinner." Or again: "[*November* 24th,] *Monday*. . . . After dinner we went to Lloyd's, and drank tea, and supped. . . . [*November* 26th,] *Wednesday*. . . . The Lloyds drank tea. We walked with them near to Ambleside. . . . [*November* 28th,] *Friday*. Coleridge walked over [from Keswick, evidently to stay the week-end]. . . . Coleridge was very unwell. . . . [*December* 1st,] *Monday*. Coleridge unable to go home for his health. . . . *December* 2nd, *Tuesday*. A rainy morning. Coleridge was obliged to set off. Sara and I met C. Lloyd and P.—turned back with them. I walked round the 2 lakes with Charles. . . . [*December* 4th,] *Thursday*. Coleridge came in just as we finished dinner. . . . [*December* 6th,] *Saturday*. Wm. accompanied Coleridge to the foot of the Rays. . . .

Sara and I accompanied him half-way to Keswick. . . . Charles Lloyd had called" (*Journals*, I, 62, 74–75). There is certainly no sign in the journal that Coleridge was less welcome than Lloyd, but it is evident that the Wordsworths must have had their hands full to avoid embarrassments. This went on for a period of more than two years.

22. *Letters*, I, 310, 313, 317, 337; *Unpublished Letters*, I, 156. For further consideration of the dates of composition of *Christabel* see E. H. Coleridge's Introduction to the facsimile *Christabel* and my "Notes on *Christabel*," *Philological Quarterly*, XXXII (1953), 197–206.

23. In a most pathetic letter written during the years of his greatest wretchedness, Coleridge said: "I have in this one dirty business of Laudanum an hundred times deceived, tricked, nay, actually and consciously *lied*. And yet *all* these vices are so opposite to my nature, that but for this *free-agency-annihilating* Poison, I verily believe that I should have suffered myself to have been cut to pieces rather than have committed one of them" (to John J. Morgan, May 14, 1814, *Unpublished Letters*, I, 45–46; II, 111).

24. *Ibid.*, I, 127; *Letters*, I, 307–12.

25. There are records of boils, inflamed eyes, rheumatism, and fever, running off and on from July, 1800, to February, 1801 (Wordsworth, *Early Letters*, p. 264; Coleridge, *Letters*, I, 341–43, 346–49; *Unpublished Letters*, I, 164, 166–71; *Letters from the Lake Poets to Daniel Stuart* [London, 1889], p. 8; Cottle, *op. cit.*, pp. 435–36).

26. *Unpublished Letters*, II, 108–14, 117–19, 163–64; *Letters*, II, 760; R. C. Bald, "Coleridge and *The Ancient Mariner*," in *Nineteenth Century Studies* (Ithaca, 1940), p. 25; Carlyon, *Early Years and Late Reflections* (London, 1856), I, 278 n. Cf. the following account in "Coleridgeiana," *Fraser's Magazine*, XI (January, 1835), 57: "The origin of this [opium] habit he [Coleridge] has described himself, in a document which we have now before us. After his return from Germany he had an attack of acute rheumatism; on which occasion he was attended by a Mr. Edmondson, from whom he borrowed a load of medical books, in one of which he found a case similar to his own where a marvellous cure had been performed by rubbing in laudanum—at the same time that a dose was administered inwardly. He tried it, and finding it answer was induced to continue it." The "attack of acute rheumatism" might have been that of either September–October, 1799, or December–January, 1800–1801; or it might have been a fusion in memory of both. "Mr. Edmondson" belongs to the Keswick period, though I do not know of Coleridge's having consulted him before the fall of 1803, when the first attempt was made to break away from opiates. This may be again a confusion of a later period with events of October–December, 1800, during which both Coleridge and Wordsworth seem to have been

receiving medical advice not from Edmondson but by letter from Dr. Beddoes and Humphry Davy in Bristol. Coleridge at that time was reading medical works, was translating a medical piece for Davy from a German periodical, and—more important—was asking Davy to tell him "some cure for the rheumatism," though not for himself but for a countrywoman he had found suffering. He himself had been reading about the success of mustard in curing "the most obstinate cases of rheumatism." On January 11 he wrote a letter to Davy full of the symptoms of his own "rheumatic fever" and full of medical terms, of which he remarked "how learned a Misfortune of this kind makes one." He asked about a certain "animal oil of Diphelius" derived from Spirit of Hartshorn, "And is it true what Hoffman asserts, that 15 or 20 drops will exert many times the power of opium both in degree and duration, without inducing any after fatigue?" (*Letters*, I, 336–48; *Unpublished Letters*, I, 168–69, 269, 274, 307). Possibly the "load of medical books" belongs to this episode, though Coleridge's medical reading was not confined to any one part of his life.

27. Edith Morley, "Coleridge in Germany," *London Mercury*, XXIII (April, 1931), 554–65; Carlyon, *op. cit.*, I, 138–43. Cf. also Wordsworth, *The Prelude* (1850), XIV, 399–401, in which *The Ancient Mariner* and *Christabel* alone figure in "that summer" at Alfoxden.

28. Southey's letters of October 11, December 15, December 23, 1799 (Curry). Cf. Coleridge, *Letters*, I, 310, 313, 317.

29. *Letters*, I, 317, 318. No one has attempted, I think, to identify this poem that Davy admired. It does not readily fit any of the known fragments of 1799, and it cannot refer to any of the poems actually published in the *Annual Anthology*, for all these are known to have been finished earlier or are too short to be in question, except for the *Ode to Georgiana, Duchess of Devonshire*, which was apparently not begun until December 20 or 21 (*Poems*, I, 335 n.). The problem is discussed further at the close of this chapter.

30. An unpublished notebook entry which parallels this letter brings together even more strikingly the green trees and snowy cave, and then, immediately after, the exquisite circle of greenery, which Coleridge took the trouble to pace off. "As you stand from below on the huge snow heap," he wrote, the "green arms" of the spreading beeches "contrast beautifully, i.e. with the Snow / The Snow lies on a huge Heap of Rock in the middle of the antechamber. . . . Reascended, left the wood, descending—came to an exquisitely beautiful Rotund of Greenery, 170 strides in diameter." Ascending, then, "a smooth green Hill to the Castle," he looked back and "saw again the beautiful spot of Green, and woody Hills" (Notebook No. 3, pp. 45–46; Miss Coburn's transcript).

31. This scene is described in the notebook in similar terms: it "extremely resembles some parts of the River Wye / & still more the Coombes about Porlock &c., except that here the valley is somewhat broader & the River tho' nothing very great, is yet more than a Brook" (Notebook No. 3, pp. 48–49). The underground river is also in the notebook.

32. Letters to Mrs. Coleridge, May 17, 1799 (*New Monthly Magazine*, XLV (1835, Part 3), 213–19.

33. *Unpublished Letters*, I, 107–15.

34. *New Monthly Magazine*, p. 216; *Unpublished Letters*, I, 109. For the discussion of Lessing see chap. v.

35. In 1796 he had dined on cold meat "in a cavern at the head of a divine little fountain" at Dovedale (*Unpublished Letters*, I, 57). Cf. the account (n. 63, below) of a cavern in the same neighborhood described in Darwin's *Loves of the Plants* and its connections with Southey in the summer of 1799.

36. Coleridge, *Letters*, I, 304; Hanson, *op. cit.*, p. 353; Jack Simmons, *Southey* (New Haven, 1948), pp. 82–83; Southey, *Common-Place Book*, IV, 521, 522; unpublished letters of Southey (Curry).

37. *Fragmentary Remains . . . of Sir Humphry Davy*, ed. John Davy (London, 1858), pp. 42–44; William Haller, *The Early Life of Robert Southey* (New York, 1917), p. 201; C. C. Southey, *The Life and Correspondence of the Late Robert Southey* (London, 1849–50), I, 347; Southey, *Letters*, ed. J. W. Warter (London, 1856), I, 77–78.

38. Southey, *Letters*, I, 78. An unpublished portion of this letter concerns Charles Lloyd. It provides no new information but shows that the Lloyd troubles were still current.

39. Southey, letter to William Taylor, the first part undated, interrupted by his "rambles" and resumed on September 1 at Ottery (J. W. Robberds, *A Memoir of the Life and Writings of the Late William Taylor of Norwich* [London, 1843], I, 292–93); unpublished letter to Tom Southey (Curry); *Poems*, I, 319 ff.; Hanson, *op. cit.*, p. 355.

40. Robberds, *op. cit.*, I, 227 (italics mine).

41. The verses sent in the letter and afterwards printed in the *Monthly* were *The Devil in Ban: An Idyll*, translated from the German of Johann Heinrich Voss. Southey had been fired with the idea upon receipt of Taylor's letter the year before and had written admiring the "diabolic idyll"; the notion delighted him: "It might be made the vehicle of some good satire . . . a meeting of devils might make fine confessions of whom they had been visiting" (Robberds, *op. cit.*, I, 233). Southey's inspiration, however, dropped out of sight until after Coleridge's return to Stowey, when the two were reunited and sat working at the same table. Here the Devil's thoughts were hatched, and the

eleven-month-old idea for the Devil's tour of visits to his earthly friends may have come to life again from a fresh perusal of Taylor's letter. If it did, Coleridge would have seen both the "magic palace" sentence and Taylor's lines about the girl and the "Abyssinian bishop." If he read *The Devil in Ban* only in the old *Monthly*, he would have met the girl and the Abyssinian but not the song-built palace on the site of the Dom. I think it most likely, however, that he saw the letter. It was a long and juicy one, such as a recipient would naturally pass around among friends. Its most striking feature was an account brought back from America by Taylor's father, of his visit to George Washington, an account interesting even today and one that would certainly have enthralled both erstwhile Pantisocrats. It described Washington's daily life and his views on slaves. Other things in the letter touched Coleridge more closely. It contained the first proposal for Southey's *Annual Anthology*, for which Coleridge was now undertaking to produce and solicit contributions. It related news of Coleridge's recent companion in Göttingen and the Harz tour, Charles Parry, and contained praise of Southey's own poetry (which the latter had good reason for wishing Coleridge to see). For these and other reasons more microscopic but no less real, Southey would have been likely to show Coleridge the letter. Taylor almost certainly could not have seen *Kubla Khan* or any other unpublished poetry of Coleridge when he wrote his "magic palace" letter in September, 1798. The two men were not acquainted: almost two years later Coleridge was still only hoping to meet Taylor. Their sole mutual friend seems to have been Southey, whose first meeting with Taylor had occurred only in late May and had been followed by a brief visit in June. As this was after the quarrel with Charles Lloyd had accentuated the long coolness between Coleridge and Southey into an active estrangement, there is little chance that Southey either would or could have conveyed the poem to Taylor. Southey was reticent about his relations with his brother-in-law. His correspondence gives no indication that he himself was familiar with Coleridge's current writing except for the *Lyrical Ballads* after their publication and probably *Osorio*. He happened to mention the fact, for instance, in January, 1799, that he had never seen the poem *Fire, Famine, and Slaughter*, though it had been printed a year earlier. His only reference to Coleridge in his letters to Taylor that preceded the latter's magic palace letter was an inquiry about whether Taylor had seen the *Lyrical Ballads*, which he explained had been written by Wordsworth and Coleridge. That had evidently not been discussed between them before. *The Ancient Mariner*, he added—using almost the words of his own review of the volume in the *Critical*—was "the clumsiest attempt at German sublimity I ever saw." Taylor, it turned out, had not read even this published work, and his reply sounds very much as if he had read nothing at all by Coleridge, published or unpublished. The tenor of the correspondence suggests, altogether, that Coleridge's poetry was a new topic between them (Robberds, *op. cit.*, I, 227-33; *Monthly Magazine*, VII [1799], 139; Haller, *op. cit.*, pp. 199-200; unpublished letters of Southey; Coleridge, *Unpublished Letters*, I, 134; Southey, *Life and Correspondence*, II, 5, and *passim*).

42. Southey, *Letters*, I, 81, 84; *Common-Place Book*, IV, 522-23; *Life and Correspondence*, II, 26; Coleridge, Notebooks Nos. 5 and 21; *Letters*, I, 305.

43. *Common-Place Book*, III, 734, 735. I do not know of any other occasion on which Southey is likely to have gone to see Laywell, and I doubt whether he would have taken down these not very spectacular notes of it from the *Philosophical Transactions*, had he not seen or known something of it. So it is likely Coleridge saw it on this tour.

44. For a fuller account of Coleridge's relations with Sara Hutchinson see T. M. Raysor, "Coleridge and 'Asra,'" *Studies in Philology*, XXVI (1929), 305-24.

45. Cf. this passage in Bruce quoted by Lowes, who thought the correspondence to Coleridge's "five miles meandering with a mazy motion" so close as to "verge on the uncanny": the Nile "makes so many sharp, unnatural windings, that it differs from any other river I ever saw, making above twenty sharp angular peninsulas in the course of five miles" (Lowes, *op. cit.*, p. 372). The correspondence does not seem to me so remarkable; but, for what it is worth, Coleridge may have been reading Bruce in 1799 not long before he described the "peninsulating Tees."

46. Most of these notes have been printed in Hanson, *op. cit.*, pp. 368-73, and in *Wordsworth and Coleridge: Studies in Honor of George McLean Harper*, ed. E. L. Griggs (Princeton, 1939), pp. 135-49. I use these along with additional material from Miss Coburn's transcript of Notebook No. 5 (in one or two instances from the expanded version copied into Notebook No. 21). This, incidentally, is the same notebook that recorded Coleridge's project for a satire that should attack "Lloyd and his Gang."

47. William Knight, *The Life of William Wordsworth* (Edinburgh, 1889), I, 202.

48. *Early Letters*, pp. 240-41. Possibly Wordsworth valued this letter a good deal himself. The editor notes that a draft of part of it survives.

49. Ll. 17-20, 47-51, 151-52; *Early Letters*, p. 237.

50. *Poetical Works*, II, 249-54 (see especially ll. 57-62, 128-32), 514;

IV, 200, *Written with a Slate Pencil upon a Stone, the Largest of a Heap* . . . , ll. 5-6.

51. An ode to the cold in his head (*Letters from the Lake Poets to Daniel Stuart*, pp. 442-44). Cf. Coleridge's *The Wanderings of Cain*, in which the same image is used (*Poems*, I, 289-90). In both *Cain* and Southey's ode, the image is followed by that of a hissing serpent. Something of *Cain* was apparently written in 1798; but as the version we have was not printed until thirty years later and as Coleridge seems to have worked on it more than once in the interim, no date can be safely assigned to any particular passage or even to this version as a whole, since fragments of a different version exist.

52. Letter of January, 1800, Cottle, *op. cit.*, p. 429; *The Annual Anthology*, II (Bristol, 1800), 223 ff.; I (1799), 56. Southey's poem was reprinted as *Ximalpoca* in *Poetical Works*, II, 104-6.

53. The author was pretty certainly not Coleridge, and I doubt its being Southey either, though he was engaged in some periodical employments at that time and sometimes wrote for the *Monthly Magazine* (cf. Southey, *Life and Correspondence*, II, 25; Southey, *Letters*, I, 35, 64).

54. *Lines Composed while Climbing the Left Ascent of Brockley Coomb, Somersetshire, May 1795* (*Poems*, I, 94). The Cheddar rocks he knew also, having visited them in 1794 with Southey and in 1798 with the Wordsworths.

55. *Monthly Magazine*, VII, (June, July, 1799), 366-70, 448-51. This is the same neighborhood and includes almost the same scene as is described in the second *Annual Anthology* by the "Rev. C. H. Sherive," whoever he may have been, in some verses *On Leaving Bristol Wells* that open with the apostrophe:

"Ye rocks and woods o'er Avon's winding stream,
   Sublimely tow'ring (in whose shadowy caves
   Dwells Inspiration, . . .
     . . . honouring thee
   Not less, O! sacred Fount, than ancient Bards
   Their Hippocrene . . ."

over which a little later hangs "that bright dome" the sky (*Annual Anthology*, II [1800], 243).

Coleridge we know was a regular reader of the *Monthly*, as well as an occasional contributor. Whether he received current numbers while he was abroad or read all the back issues after his return I have no idea. The July number was still the current one when he returned. I think it practically certain that he would have read that and the preceding one as well, both for the sake of these Bristol articles, whose author he must have known, and for an article by Goethe in the earlier of the two on the Laocoön, with a plate illustrating the statue—which he would have wished to read in connection with his projected work on Lessing. Other articles in that issue would have attracted him, one by Priestley on the "Doctrine of Phlogiston," one of a series by "J. A." on "Personifications in Poetry," and a characteristic communication from his old friend, George Dyer. But the reunion with Southey would have sent him to the June and July numbers for the Bristol articles alone.

In the letters he wrote to Southey after they parted in Exeter late in September, Coleridge refers now and then to particular articles in the *Monthly*. There may be unidentified writing of his own buried in its files. He evidently undertook to do some hack work for Phillips, its owner, and as late as January, 1801, was in Phillips's debt for work he had not done. That may have been one of the compilations he talked of, however, rather than articles (cf. *Letters*, I, 310, 317, 325, 327; *Unpublished Letters*, I, 167).

56. Wylie Sypher, "Coleridge's Somerset: A Byway to Xanadu," *Philological Quarterly*, XVIII (1939), 353–66.

57. Southey, *Life and Correspondence*, II, 24–25, 58, 64; Coleridge, *Letters*, I, 309, 328; Landor, *Works*, I, 479.

58. *Life and Correspondence*, II, 25; Davy, *Fragmentary Remains*, p. 39; unpublished letters (Curry).

59. The date of Coleridge's first reading of Bartram raises complicated questions, fortunately irrelevant here. The evidence cited by Lowes for an early date has collapsed since the discovery that the first version of what later became Coleridge's *Lewti* was written by Wordsworth. It was probably in the winter or early spring of 1798 that Coleridge copied passages from Bartram into the Gutch Memorandum Book and that he first noticed the account of the "Savanna Crane" that he quoted in the note to *This Lime-Tree Bower*. The phrasing of the note, however, which was first printed in the *Annual Anthology*, suggests that he was copying out the passage from Bartram some time after the discovery—probably therefore in the fall or winter of 1799–1800, when he prepared the poem for the press. Both Coleridge and Wordsworth returned to Bartram from time to time (see, for one instance, *Biographia literaria*, chap. xxii) (Wordsworth, *Poetical Works*, ed. E. de Selincourt [Oxford, 1940], I, 263, and notes; Jane Worthington Smyser, "Coleridge's Use of Wordsworth's Juvenilia," *PMLA*, LXV [1950], 419–26; Chambers, "Some Dates in Coleridge's *Annus mirabilis*," pp. 100–102, 111; Coleridge, *Poems*, I, 297, E. H. C.'s note, 181; *The Travels of William Bartram*, ed. Mark Van Doren [New York, 1940], p. 189; Lowes, *op. cit.*, pp. 367 ff., 513–16; Ernest Earnest, *John and William Bartram* [Philadelphia, 1940], pp. 101–3).

60. *Unpublished Letters*, I, 125, 128–29 (the editor names the works

Coleridge wished to borrow: Herder's *Ideen zur Philosophie der Geschichte der Menschheit* and E. A. W. von Zimmermann's *Geographische Geschichte des Menschen*); *Letters*, I, 310; Cottle, *op. cit.*, pp. 475–76 (Poole to Tom Wedgwood, November 27, 1799); Chambers, *Coleridge*, p. 124; C. Kegan Paul, *William Godwin: His Friends and Contemporaries* (London, 1876), II, 9–16 (letters of September–December, 1800). The "Holstein Ambassador" and other travels in Harris were important sources for *Thalaba*.

61. Lowes, *op. cit.*, pp. 154, 360–61, 499. The gloss to *The Ancient Mariner*, which was not printed till 1817 but which E. H. Coleridge suggests may have been written much earlier, owes a great deal to both works of Purchas (see Lowes, *op. cit.*, pp. 324–25, 282, 575). Other sources for the gloss that Lowes uncovered are also works used by Southey for *Thalaba*. It is quite possible that the urge to annotate his own poem—more briefly and poetically than Southey did—may have come into being through the contagion of Southey's notes and the books both were reading in 1799–1800. There are other reasons too for suspecting that the gloss of *The Ancient Mariner* may have been prepared originally for the edition of 1800 but not used until later.

Southey gave the greatest prominence to the Paradise of Aloadin as described in Purchas (cf. Lowes, *op. cit.*, pp. 360–63; Robberds, *op. cit.*, I, 248; *Thalaba*, notes to Books I and VII).

62. See Appendix II for a fuller account of the connections of this notebook with the year 1799.

63. Letters to Southey, November 10 and December 19 (misdated December 9), 1799, *Letters*, I, 314, 317–18; cf. also Lowes, *op. cit.*, pp. 399–400, 593. The parallels with Collins were first noticed by a writer in the *Nation and Athenaeum*, January 28, 1922, pp. 664–66. Cf. also a passage in Darwin's *Botanic Garden* (*Loves of the Plants*, Canto III, ll. 85–130 and notes), which seems to have been in Southey's mind in the fall of 1799. It follows immediately upon the nightmare passage and Fuseli's illustration, which Coleridge had long known, and describes the cavern called Thor's House in Derbyshire, "where the rivers Hamps and Manifold sink into the earth, and rise again in Ilam gardens, the seat of John Port, Esq. about three miles below." Darwin gives further details of the probable origin of the cavern and rivers:

> "Erst, fires volcanic in the marble womb
> Of cloud-wrapp'd WETTON raised the massy dome;
> Rocks rear'd on rocks in huge disjointed piles
> Form the tall turrets, and the lengthen'd ailes . . .
>
> . . . .
>
> . . . where famed ILAM leads his boiling floods
> Through flowery meadows and impending woods."

64. Southey, *Letters*, I, 69, 71, 87, and *Thalaba, passim.*

65. *Poems*, I, 321. (The version of 1799, quoted here, varies slightly from later versions.) Coleridge had once before described himself as something of a "library cormorant." The reference, of course, is to *Paradise Lost*, IV, 192–96, 218–22.

66. See the discussion in chap. v of the Miltonism of *Kubla Khan.*

67. Letters to Southey, September 25, 30, October 15, 1799 (*Letters*, I, 312; *Unpublished Letters*, I, 125, 128); *Poems*, I, 335–38. In October, 1803, Coleridge transcribed into another notebook the account written in 1799 of his tour of the Lake District with Wordsworth. The transcript contains additional comments. Here, along with descriptions of the "peninsulating Tees" and the "wild turns" in other rivers, he wrote: "At Croft we discussed the question of Polytheism & Monotheism, of Tombs by the Roadside & Tombs in Church yards.—Thought of translating Schiller's Götter des Griechenlandes—& of writing an Antiphony to it.—Better write both myself in the manner & metre of Penseroso & Allegro" (Notebook No. 21, Miss Coburn's transcript). The original account written in 1799 speaks of the visit to Croft and the tombs by the roadside and of the intention to send for Schiller's work, but does not mention Milton. It is not clear whether the thought of using "the manner & metre of Penseroso & Allegro" was a new idea in 1803 or whether Coleridge was filling out from memory his earlier notes. His use, in 1799–1800, of meters allied to those of *L'Allegro* and *Il Penseroso* is discussed below, Sec. V, chap. v. For other references to Milton in Coleridge's correspondence in the following few months see Sandford, *op. cit.*, II, 7, 8.

68. *Poems*, I, 339 (italics mine). For Coleridge's use of *loud* and other words discussed here see the *Concordance* by Sister Eugenia Logan (St. Mary-of-the-Woods, Ind., 1940).

69. *Christabel*, Part II, ll. 485, 499–501, 528.

70. *Poems*, I, 92, 130, 158, and elsewhere; *Coleridge's Shakespearean Criticism*, ed. T. M. Raysor (London, 1930), II, 69.

71. We find a concentration of dream, vision, and daydream in the poetry of this time, possibly in part from the contagion of the conventional dream in German romantic poetry. Coleridge's outbreak of them begins with the *Lines Written in the Album at Elbingerode* and continues, sometimes in translations or adaptations from the German, with "floated away, like a departing dream," "in open-eyed dream," "filled, as a dream, the wide waters," "oft in my waking dreams," "like the murmur of a dream," "light as a dream," "last night . . . to me a vision gave," "my heart has need with dreams like these to strive," "music [and a lady's Harp] . . . moulds the slumberer's dreams" (*Poems*, I, 316, 318, 329, 331, 334, 336, 348, 358). But I doubt whether

the dreams are much thicker here than in some earlier years, especially 1793–94. So I do not think any inferences can be drawn about dates from the presence of the "vision" in *Kubla Khan*. The same thing holds for the use of the word *slant*, though Coleridge used it far more often in 1799 and 1800 than he had done earlier. *Slant* is a highly romantic word, despite the opinion of an eminent modern poet (if I recall his remarks correctly) that only classic art is concerned with shape, line, or mass, while the romantic is preoccupied with color. *Slant*, at any rate, crosses the border and is appropriately expressive of certain romantic ways of looking upon the world. Coleridge used the word occasionally in earlier years—twice in *The Destiny of Nations* (1796), ll. 66, 185, in a natural context referring to the beams of the sun in northern latitudes, once in *This Lime-Tree Bower* (1797), l. 34, also describing the beams of the setting sun, and once in the lines *To the Rev. George Coleridge* (1797), l. 61. It occurs in *Fears in Solitude* too (l. 207), but not in the original version of 1798. Dorothy Wordsworth wrote of "slanting woods" in her Alfoxden journal in January, 1798 (*Journals*, I, 3; cf. Wordsworth's *An Evening Walk* [1793], l. 91). Cowper in *The Task* has "slant hills." But the word is used more strikingly by Landor in *Gebir*, where, along with other more ordinary instances, spring is said to be "urged slanting onward by the bickering breeze" (IV, 57–58). From about the time Coleridge must have been reading *Gebir* to the time of his finest use of the word in the "slant night shower" of *Dejection* (1802), it came constantly to his pen when he described scenery in his note-books and letters. "Perdita" Robinson used it, too, in her poem *The Haunted Beach*, which in February, 1800, Coleridge admired greatly and wished to have included in the *Annual Anthology* and in which, incidentally, *The Ancient Mariner* is more than once fairly audible (*Letters*, I, 331–32). *Slant* occurs of course also in *Kubla Khan*. Though the word became actually a mannerism with Coleridge in 1799 and 1800, it still can hardly be thought to have any important bearing on the date of an individual poem.

72. *Poems*, I, 307. The lines are a translation of the opening of Friedrich von Matthisson's *Milesisches Märchen*. The originals of this and the other German verses are printed in the notes of Campbell's edition of Coleridge's poems and reprinted in *Poems*, II, 1125 ff. A full translation of Matthisson's poem had appeared in the *Monthly Magazine* during Coleridge's absence over the signature "A. P.," in the issue for November, 1798 (VI, 367).

73. *Poems*, I, 308–9. Cf. G. Wilson Knight's comparison of this translated poem with *Kubla Khan* in *The Starlit Dome* (Oxford, 1941), pp. 102–3.

74. *Poems*, I, 328–29; II, 1130.

75. *Ibid.*, I, 310-11; II, 1127. The allusions are all conventionally classical. Earlier poems of Coleridge, of course, speak of the Muses, music, Castalie, and other appurtenances of classical inspiration, but in those the imagery is relatively undeveloped and incidental.

76. *Ibid.*, I, 308. Coleridge's rendering is fairly literal.

77. *The Piccolomini*, II, vi, and *Destiny of Nations*, ll. 7-9 (*ibid.*, I, 132; II, 652); *Gebir*, VI, 139; Schiller, *Werke* (Weimar, 1949), VIII, 129. On all three occasions, Coleridge used the word *symphony* in the then permissible sense of music produced by a single instrument. In *Kubla Khan* and *Wallenstein* it had the additional meaning, still acceptable in Coleridge's day, of an instrumental accompaniment or prelude to a song. Cf. also shortly after the song, Thekla's words:

> ". . . I see it nearer *floating*,
>
> . . . .
>
> And lo! the *abyss*— . . .
>
> . . . .
>
> Yea, shoots his lightnings down from *sunny heights*,
> Flames *burst* from out the *subterraneous chasms*"
>
> (II, vii, 121-28; italics mine).

Most of this corresponds to the original; but there is no hint of "bursts" in Schiller's *fahren*, and *heiter* is not quite "sunny." I make these and other statements about the translation not quite categorically, however, since Coleridge worked from a manuscript not always identical with the later standard text.

78. Hanson, *op. cit.*, p. 360.

79. *Letters*, I, 318; *Poems*, I, 324-25. See E. H. Coleridge's note for the possibility that this poem may have been recast from work dating back as far as 1793. As E. H. Coleridge says, however, "the poem as a whole suggests a later date." For our purpose it does not matter whether there had been a preliminary early version, since we know that the poem was prominent in Coleridge's mind in the autumn of 1799 and was certainly being worked on then. My references are to the version printed in the *Morning Post* (as given by E. H. C.). The tail of the poem was cut off in the edition of 1817.

80. *Thalaba*, IX, 42.

81. *The Piccolomini*, I, iii, 31-32 (*Poems*, II, 609). There is a fairly close approach to these expressions in *The Rose* (1793) and *Religious Musings* (1794-96), l. 355 (*Poems* I, 45, 122).

82. *Poems*, I, 107 (cf. also pp. 48, 90), 335-36 (ll. 5-14); *Gebir*, IV, 180; VI, 151. Except for its appearance in *Kubla Khan* and *Ode to Georgiana*, Coleridge used the word *ancestral* in his poems only three times, once in 1811 and twice (quite conventionally) toward the close

of his life (*Poems*, I, 470, 483; II, 981; cf. also the lines to Sara Hutchinson quoted in Sec. 9, below).

83. *Poems*, I, 330–35; II, 1052–59.

84. *The Piccolomini*, I, iv, 92 (*ibid.*, II, 613).

85. *Gebir*, I, 170–73; IV, 168; VI, 56–57; Wordsworth, *Early Letters*, p. 240. See the discussion of *Gebir* in chap. iii.

86. *Poems*, I, 159, 244; *The Piccolomini*, III, iii, 64 (*Poems*, II, 684). He returned to the prepositional use of *midway* in November, 1800—"midway th' ascent"—and again later in *Zapolya* (*Poems*, I, 350, and II, 931).

87. A similar use of *midway* occurs in Part II of *The Three Graves*, where a woman "stopped midway on the floor." The authorship of Part II has now been assigned to Wordsworth on the ground of a manuscript copy in a notebook, said to belong probably to 1797. It was in the hands of Coleridge, however, in late 1799 or early 1800, for he was attempting to carry on the tale then. Mr. Hanson shows from passages in a notebook of Coleridge that ll. 509–17 (in Part IV) were written after November 17, 1799, though the preceding portion (and, by implication, the whole) has sometimes been assigned to the Alfoxden period of 1798. For further evidence on this see "Notes on *Christabel*," *loc. cit.* What matters here is that the poem was evidently on the worktable during the period I am discussing. For the rest, see Coleridge, *Poems*, I, 267–84; Wordsworth, *Poetical Works*, I, 308–12 (esp. l. 108), 374; Southey to Coleridge, May Day, 1800: ". . . send me your Christabell and your Three Graves [misprinted "Graces"], and finish them on purpose to send them" (Southey, *Life and Correspondence*, II, 65); Hanson, *op. cit.*, pp. 373, 508. Coleridge's own date of about 1797, i.e., "more than twelve years ago" in 1809 (the years still remained "twelve" in 1817), must be wrong for at least a portion of Part IV.

88. *The Piccolomini*, I, iv, 173 (*Poems*, II, 616); *Letters*, I, 307; *Wordsworth and Coleridge*, p. 143.

89. *Poems*, I, 335–38 (esp. ll. 54–75). For the uncertain date of Coleridge's thought of employing "the manner & metre of Penseroso & Allegro," see n. 67, above.

90. *Ibid.*, pp. 345, 347–49, 350–52, 40–44, 92. Cf. *Ver perpetuum* (1796) (*ibid.*, p. 148); also *A Christmas Carol* (December, 1799), in the stanza of which a tetrameter quatrain is followed by a pentameter couplet (*ibid.*, pp. 338–40). The combining of four- and five-stress lines, with the former predominating, is characteristic of Coleridge's verse of 1799–1800 and not of 1797–98.

The mixture of iambic and trochaic lines occurs in other poems and fragments of 1799–1800, particularly in the translations and adaptations from German poetry (see *ibid.*, pp. 308–10, 318–19, 326). The practice is most characteristic of those years, though it appears now and then in earlier poems, particularly *Fire, Famine, and Slaughter* and *Lewti*. The verse of *Fire, Famine, and Slaughter* superficially resembles the later meter of shifting acccents but is actually quite different. The prosodic, as well as probably the poetic, ancestors of these blood-thirsty sisters are obviously Macbeth's Witches; they have nothing to do with Milton.

As for *Lewti*, its meter was first established by Wordsworth, whose early fragment *Beauty and Moonlight* Coleridge rewrote and expanded into his own poem. Several other passages of verse, found written adjacent to *Beauty and Moonlight* in an early notebook of Wordsworth, had been found previously among the papers of Coleridge and were attributed to him by editors, though he had never claimed them. They are written in four-stress couplets with an occasional variation in the rhyming and frequent use of initial monosyllabic feet. The meter of *Lewti*, which does not depart from the four-stress line, is essentially the same. It may also be related to the swiftly moving tetrameters, with their often only lightly end-stopped lines and varied rhymes, of *The Idiot Boy, Her Eyes Are Wild*, and certain other of Wordsworth's contributions to *Lyrical Ballads*, for which *Lewti* also was originally intended. Coleridge's poem is distinguished from these by its lighter weight, its grace, its avoidance of clogging consonants, and its quite different unhomely vocabulary and theme. Metrically, however, it is related to this work of Wordsworth as *Kubla Khan* is not. For the confusion of authorship in the early poems, see Coleridge, *Poems*, I, 60–62, 253–56; II, 1049–52; Wordsworth, *Poetical Works*, I, 263–64, 306, 366–74; II, 531; Smyser, *loc. cit.*

One poem of 1796, the *Ode to the Departing Year* (*Poems*, I, 160–68), has superficially an appearance of free form that might seem a hint of later developments, but it too is on the whole quite different. In the editions before 1817 it was printed as a Pindaric ode with the stanza headings "Strophe I," "Strophe II," "Epode," "Antistrophe I," "Antistrophe II," "Epode II." This arrangement somewhat suggests the form of Collins's odes, with the epode between strophe and antistrophe. Coleridge may have intended at first to follow the strict Pindaric form, for his first antistrophe corresponds exactly in meter and rhyme to his first strophe. Cf. also the *Monody on the Death of Chatterton* (1790, 1794, and altered from time to time afterward), in which the pentameter meter is varied by lines ranging in length from three to six stresses.

91. *Poems*, I, 252.

92. *Ibid.*, pp. 243–47, 169–71. The stanzas of *France: An Ode* consist of 21 lines, each arranged in a fixed order: eight five-stress, followed

by three four-stress, one five-stress, one four-stress, one six-stress, seven five-stress. The rhyme pattern is equally complex and equally fixed. There is only one metrical variant, an Alexandrine in the final line of the third stanza.

93. *Christabel* furnishes little evidence for the date of other poems of 1797–1800 because of the obscurity of its early history. Part I has usually been assigned to 1797 or 1798, the Conclusion of Part I and all of Part II to various dates after October, 1799. Even Part I may not have been fully completed in its present form, however, until the later period. See "Notes on *Christabel*," *loc. cit.* In any case, it is only in the portions ascribed by E. H. Coleridge to the later dates that we find a metrical likeness to *Kubla Khan*.

94. The unrhymed line in *Kubla Khan* is l. 37. Cf. also the off-rhymes in ll. 19–20, 38–41, as well as other more conventional imperfect rhyming. The blank lines in verse written before 1799 are as follows: *Monody on the Death of Chatterton* (first version, composed in 1790 or, if Coleridge's date be accepted, 1788), ll. 56, 80 (the first remained in the published version of 1794 in l. 79; the passage containing the second was dropped); *Monody on a Tea-Kettle* (composed in 1790; not published in Coleridge's lifetime), l. 30; *Christabel*, Part I, ll. 94, 173 (but individual lines in this poem cannot be assigned with assurance to the earlier period). Blank lines in 1799–1800 are these: *Christabel*, Conclusion to Part I (1800, according to E. H. Coleridge), l. 284, perhaps l. 282 (*shadows* being scarcely even a spelling rhyme to *vows*), and the off-rhyme *lids-sheds*, ll. 315–16; *The Visit of the Gods* (?1799), ll. 1, 2, 8, 10, 11, 17, 19, 20, 26; *Something Childish, but Very Natural* (April, 1799), ll. 2, 7, 12 (recurring regularly in the second line of each five-line stanza—a pattern roughly similar to that of the original German); *Lines Composed in a Concert-Room* (1799, probably September), l. 34 and conspicuous half-rhymes in ll. 6–8, 14–16; *Ode to Georgiana, Duchess of Devonshire* (December, 1799), ll. 52, 61, 68; *A Stranger Minstrel* (November, 1800), l. 63; *The Snow-Drop* (1800), ll. 5, 7, 10, 13, 21, 23, 29, 31, 37, 39, 45, 47, 53, 55, 61, 63 (recurring almost regularly throughout, but not quite); Epigram 27 ["A Liar by Profession"] (1799 or early 1800), l. 5 (*Poems*, I, 298, 14, 15, 128, 129 n., 19, 219, 222, 225–26, 310–11, 313, 324–25, 337, 352, 356–58; II, 960; and E. H. Coleridge, Introduction to facsimile ed. of *Christabel*). See also the discussion of the rhymes of *Lycidas* in chap. v. There are obvious chances of error in my account of Coleridge's unrhymed lines, both from my own possible oversight and from the possibility that E. H. C. may have misdated some poems. I do not think, however, that either type of possible error could materially alter the fact of a marked change in Coleridge's rhyming practice beginning at some time between the spring and fall

of 1799. Saintsbury attributes the appearance in English of unrhymed verse (other than decasyllabic) in large measure to the influence of German poetry, and names *Thalaba* prominently in this connection. He was referring not to occasional blank lines, however, but to wholly unrhymed verse (*History of English Prosody* [London, 1923], III, 38). After his return from Germany in 1799, Coleridge was no doubt discussing the entire question of rhyme with Southey.

95. The *Ode to the Duchess of Devonshire* was written as a kind of reply to a poem by the duchess herself, which had appeared in the *Morning Chronicle* of December 20 and the *Morning Post* of December 21. Coleridge published his ode in the latter paper on the twenty-fourth. It is not impossible that he may have had a little more time than these dates suggest for his composition. The duchess some years earlier had been a kind and hospitable friend to Mrs. Robinson, who herself wrote some "lines to the Duchess of Devonshire" in late 1799 or 1800. She and, through her, Coleridge may possibly have seen the duchess's verses before their publication (E. H. Coleridge's note in *Poems*, I, 335; the *Memoirs of Mrs. Robinson* for the period of her husband's imprisonment, and the list, at the end of Vol. II, of poetical pieces written during the last year of her life; Coleridge, *Letters*, I, 322, 331–32).

96. *Memoirs of the Late Mrs. Robinson*, IV, 145–49; cf. also Lowes, *op. cit.*, pp. 353–55.

97. By Professor Irwin Griggs and Mr. H. M. Margoliouth. See Appendix III.

98. Robberds, *op. cit.*, I, 292–93, 299, 324; Southey, *Life and Correspondence*, II, 21, 24, 36–39, 58, 88, 95; Southey, *Letters*, I, 97, 122–23, 130; Simmons, *op. cit.*, pp. 81–83, 85, and 235, n. 117; unpublished letters of Southey (Curry); Coleridge, *Unpublished Letters*, I, 124–26. The notes and other essential material for the whole were certainly prepared in England, for Southey took with him no books that would have been of service for the purpose (cf. *Life and Correspondence*, II, 56).

99. Cf. Southey, *Letters*, I, 135, and, more particularly, Southey's statement in the Preface to *Thalaba* (p. xiii) that the dissatisfaction of his friends in England induced him to rewrite the first part of Book XII. This was after Coleridge had removed to Keswick, however, and it is unlikely that he was one of the critical friends. In any case, it was after the latest possible date for *Kubla Khan*.

100. From Exeter, Southey went early in October to Christchurch, then in December back to Bristol, where he remained until April. Before and during the stay in Bristol he talked of going to London (Simmons, *op. cit.*, pp. 83–85; Southey, *Letters*, I, 86, 89, 97, 102–3; *Life and Correspondence*, II, 95–96; Coleridge, *Letters*, I, 326; and unpublished letters of Southey). Meanwhile Coleridge was in London. In

February he was out of town briefly but was not with Southey (*Letters*, I, 326–27; *Letters of the Lake Poets to Daniel Stuart*, pp. 4–5). When Southey passed through London on his way to Lisbon in April, Coleridge was absent on a visit to Wordsworth. However, there was evidently more communication between the two, direct or indirect, than has been published.

101. Irvin Ehrenpreis, "Southey to Coleridge, 1799," *N & Q*, CXCV (1950), 125; *Life and Correspondence*, II, 36–39; *National Review*, XIX (1892), 704–6 (I owe this reference to the as yet unpublished editorial work of Mr. Curry); Coleridge, *Letters*, I, 319, 328–29; *Unpublished Letters*, I, 130; Mr. Curry's transcripts of unpublished letters.

102. Southey, Preface to *Thalaba*, p. xiii; *Letters*, I, 100, 103; *Life and Correspondence*, II, 53–54; unpublished letter of April 8. Coleridge was delegated to look after some of Southey's other literary projects as well. In the end, however, it was John Rickman who arranged with Longman for the publication of *Thalaba;* by that time Coleridge had left London and was settled at Keswick.

103. Notebook No. 10 (Miss Coburn's transcript), entry dated May 7, 1800. Southey left his manuscript of *Madoc* with Danvers and apparently some other things.

104. *Thalaba*, XI, 17, 34; *Paradise Lost*, IV, 216. The stress that Lowes (*op. cit.*, p. 378) laid upon a single instance of floating hair in Bruce seems to me much mistaken.

105. *Common-Place Book*, IV, 186–87. Coleridge could not have seen this sketch during his earlier friendship with Southey. In the Preface to *Thalaba* in the edition of 1837, it is true, Southey said that he had "fixed upon the ground, four years before [i.e., before 1799], for a Mohammedan tale" and had formed a plan and collected materials in the interim. It is evident from his letters, however, that, though he had had in mind earlier some of the materials, the plan was not actually made until the latter part of August, 1798, when he first put together the two main themes, those of the Dom-Daniel and the garden of Irem. The notes in the *Common-Place Book* were clearly made after that, and the meter was not decided upon until the following summer (*Life and Correspondence*, I, 346, 347; Robberds, *op. cit.*, I, 223–24; Cottle, *op. cit.*, p. 218; unpublished letters of October 5 and 29, 1798 [Curry]).

106. *Poems*, I, 325 n. This portion was omitted in later versions of the lines.

107. Cf. *Common-Place Book*, IV, 185–89, *passim*.

108. Coleridge, letter of December 19, 1799 (misdated December 9), *Letters*, I, 318; *Life and Correspondence*, II, 36.

109. See especially *Common-Place Book*, IV, 187–88. There were obviously also notes and outlines more detailed than those published,

and there were apparently passages of verse composed or sketched ahead of their turn.

110. Hanson, *op. cit.*, pp. 410–12; Chambers, *Coleridge*, p. 131; R. B. Litchfield, *Tom Wedgwood, the First Photographer* (London, 1903), p. 93. The visit to the Porlock neighborhood is recorded in a letter of Coleridge to Josiah Wedgwood. Litchfield summarizes but does not print the passage referring to Coleridge's "fruitless house-hunting about Porlock."

111. *Unpublished Letters*, I, 124, 127; *Letters*, I, 308.

112. *Letters*, I, 309–10. If Coleridge had chosen to go off to Porlock on his way home from Upcott, he might have been silent on the matter to his wife (and hence to his brother-in-law, too), merely to save trouble and argument.

113. *Ibid.*, p. 305; Southey, *Poetical Works*, II, 98.

114. *Letters*, I, 307–8 (italics Coleridge's).

115. Since this passage was written Mr. Margoliouth's new book has appeared. I find that he too recognizes the awkwardness of getting Coleridge to Porlock with a folio of Purchas (*Wordsworth and Coleridge: 1795–1834* [Oxford, 1953], pp. 18–19).

116. *Letters*, I, 307–13 (italics Coleridge's in the reference to *Gebir*).

117. The October, 1799, date would also mean that unless Coleridge knew something about the article before its publication, Professor Heeren's account of Herodotus and the sources of the Nile in the *Monthly Magazine* would be out of the picture. It was not, in any case, very material. Heeren's communication relating to Bruce and the Abyssinian bishop in the September issue he would no doubt have seen. On October 15, he commented upon William Taylor's article in that issue (*Letters*, I, 310).

118. T. O. M. in *Explicator*, October, 1948 ("Why Did the 'Abyssinian Maid' Sing of 'Mount Abora'? "), writes: "In a conversation in which he brought the matter up, the late Professor Lowes told me he was not satisfied with his own comments on the subject."

119. *Poems*, I, 375.

120. *Ibid.*, p. 361.

121. *The Picture, Separation*, and *Recollections of Love, ibid.*, pp. 369–74, 397–99, 409–10. See Raysor, "Coleridge and *Asra*," p. 324; see also n. 122, below.

122. The mysterious unfinished poem may, of course, have perished or may have been completed at some later date. *The Picture: Or the Lover's Resolution*, for instance, which was no doubt completed later (E. H. C. dates the whole 1802, the year of its publication; *Poems*, I, 369–74) might have been partly written earlier, as far as one can tell from published evidence. Some of it is founded on Gessner's idyll, *Der*

feste Vorsatz ("The Fixed Resolution") and might belong to the group of translations made or begun after Coleridge returned from Germany (he translated Gessner's *Erste Schiffer* at Sotheby's request in 1802 but knew Gessner's work much earlier). One passage in it harps upon the words *slant* and *stately* and adds *ceaseless* and *bright*.

CHAPTER V

1. Robert Graves, *The Meaning of Dreams* (London, 1924), pp. 145–58; John Livingston Lowes, *The Road to Xanadu* (Boston, 1930), pp. 593–96.

2. Lowes, *op. cit.*, p. 343 (Lowes's italics).

3. *Ibid.*, pp. 401, 412.

4. Mr. E. H. W. Meyerstein explained the poem much as I have done, except for his contention that it is not a fragment at all but a complete poetic whole, a contention that does not seem to me sound (*TLS*, October 30, 1937, p. 803). Miss Maud Bodkin also evidently reads the surface meaning in the same way (*Archetypal Patterns in Poetry* [London, 1948], pp. 94–96). Professor N. B. Allen suggested a slightly different one. He described the latter part of the poem as an expression of the poet's regret at having forgotten the dream. He also found the source of the final description in Coleridge's own physical appearance (*Modern Language Notes*, LVII [1942], 108–13). Coleridge was, of course, in one sense writing of himself; but it was himself in the person and with the trappings of the traditional poet-seer—himself, in other words, transformed, not merely S. T. C. in the mirror.

5. Stanzas 5 and 6 (*Poems*, I, 365–66; italics mine).

6. Kenneth Burke, *The Philosophy of Literary Form* (Baton Rouge, 1941), p. 97.

7. *Dialogues of Plato*, trans. Jowett (3d ed.; Oxford, 1924), I, 501–2. I regret not having known Miss Maud Bodkin's *Archetypal Patterns* when I first published some account of this without mentioning her work. As early as 1934, discussing the final lines of *Kubla Khan*, she said they "half recalled" to her mind the sayings of Plato about "the divine insanity of the poet." The connection must, I suppose, have occurred to other readers in the past, but I have not seen any reference to it in print earlier than Miss Bodkin's. Coleridge had used this traditional picture of poetic inspiration earlier, in the *Ode to the Departing Year:*

> "Then with no unholy madness,
>
> . . . .
>
> I rais'd the impetuous song, and solemnis'd his [Time's]
> flight" (*Poems*, I, 161).

8. See the discussion of experiments of this sort in the work of several German writers, especially Tieck and Brentano, by Margaret E. Atkinson, "Musical Form in Some [German] Romantic Writings," *Modern Language Review*, XLIV (1949), 218-27.

9. Professor Earl Leslie Griggs discovered a manuscript review of *Christabel* that he believes was written by Coleridge's friend John J. Morgan. Many of the ideas were Coleridge's, and certain portions, Professor Griggs thinks, many even have been dictated by him. Certainly the reviewer speaks with unusual authority of the poet's unfulfilled intention; see "An Early Defense of *Christabel*," in *Wordsworth and Coleridge: Studies in Honor of George McLean Harper*, ed. E. L. Griggs (Princeton, 1939), pp. 174-79, 184, 190 (italics mine).

10. G. Wilson Knight, *The Starlit Dome* (London, 1941), pp. 93-94. Professor Knight places the turn from "octave" to "sestet" not where the scene changes but earlier, where "the shadow of the dome of pleasure" appears (l. 30) in an altered meter, "a lilting happy motion." It is not easy to accept this as the main division of the poem in defiance of Coleridge's own paragraphing as well as of the sense of the whole. The author afterward half-changes his mind and tries a three-part division (p. 95).

11. Some of the prose romances on oriental and Gothic themes belong almost to the same class—*Rasselas*, for example. Isaac d'Israeli's tale of *Mejnorin and Leila, the Arabian Petrarch and Laura*, published in 1797 and again in a volume of *Romances* in 1799, is typical of these tales. It contains most of the generic scenery of odorous gardens, etc., and a poem on "The Land of Cashmere" in which are wild music, palaces, domes, and "a high cascade's romantic fall." It is overloaded with lush sensual imagery in the worst possible taste. There is some reason to think Southey probably read this before he wrote *Thalaba*, and Coleridge may also have known it.

12. Purchas, *Pilgrimes*, Vol. XI, chap v; Barthélémi d'Herbelot, *Bibliothèque orientale* ... (Maestricht, 1776), under "Cobla & Cubla Khan." D'Herbelot was being used by Southey in 1799 for *Thalaba*.

13. C. Kegan Paul, *William Godwin* (London, 1876), II, 16; Notebook No. 3½ (Miss Coburn's transcript). Miss Coburn dates the entry (uncertainly) as April or May, 1799. Incidentally, the seat of the earthly Paradise was located by some writers in Cathay (Sir Henry Yule, *Cathay and the Road Thither*, ed. Cordier, Hakluyt Society [London, 1914], III, 198).

14. I have perhaps devoted more space to the question of the completeness of the poem than the debate merits. To me its incompleteness seems perfectly self-evident. But the opposite view has been maintained by a good many writers, some of them eminent. In deference to

that body of opinion I have said more than I believe the subject alone would warrant.

15. *Poems*, I, 33, written in 1792.

16. *Ibid.*, pp. 100–102; cf. also *The Destiny of Nations*, ll. 18–26 (*ibid.*, p. 132).

17. *To a Young Friend* (*ibid.*, pp. 155–57).

18. *Dejection*, stanza 7; *Christabel*, ll. 541–95; cf. also *What Is Life? Psyche, A Tombless Epitaph, Limbo*, etc.

19. *Poems*, I, 172–73 (1797).

20. *Letters*, II, 686–88; *Unpublished Letters*, II, 233.

21. *Statesman's Manual, Complete Works*, ed. Shedd (New York, 1856), I, 437–38 (italics mine), 461–62 (Appendix B). My attention was drawn to the first of these passages by Professor Robert Penn Warren's use of it in his study of *The Ancient Mariner* (pp. 73–74, 125) and to the second by Professor I. A. Richards.

22. *Coleridge's Miscellaneous Criticism*, ed. T. M. Raysor (Cambridge, Mass., 1936), p. 99.

23. *Ibid.*, p. 30.

24. *Ibid.*, pp. 31–32.

25. Letter to William Sotheby, September 10, 1802, *Letters* I, 406–7, 403–4 (italics mine except for the last two words).

26. Gutch Memorandum Book, fols. 21*a*, 23*b* (for references to the printed version of this notebook see Appendix II); *Miscellaneous Criticism*, pp. 408–9; *Unpublished Letters*, I, 71.

27. *Spectator*, No. 159.

28. There are a great many other parallels between *Rasselas* and *Kubla Khan*, including "subterranean passages" in the palace, a contrast between peace and "delight" within the garden and reports of discord or war without. Lowes's attention was called to these parallels, possibly after his theories about the sources of *Kubla Khan* had already crystallized. He referred to the matter only briefly in a note (p. 590) that minimizes the resemblances a good deal.

29. *The Bard* and *The Progress of Poesy, passim*.

30. For some remarks of Coleridge on Gray and Collins see *Letters*, I, 196–97, 318; *Biographia literaria*, I, 12, 26–27, 215; *Miscellaneous Criticism*, pp. 306–11, 355, 431, 439. Links between *Kubla Khan* and Collins were discussed anonymously in the *Nation and Athenaeum* for January 28, 1922 (XXX, 664, 666). Cf. also Lowes, *op. cit.*, pp. 399–400, 593. As Lowes ignored the overt meaning of *Kubla Khan*, he failed to notice how the kinship of theme heightens the importance of verbal similarities.

31. *Miscellaneous Criticism*, p. 161.

32. Coleridge and Southey may have discussed Milton's extended simile of "Sabean Odours" in August or September, 1799, when they

injected a bit from this same book of *Paradise Lost* into *The Devil's Thoughts*. A number of the parallels between Book IV of *Paradise Lost* and *Kubla Khan* have been observed before. Professor Lane Cooper, I believe, was the first to draw attention to the general resemblances in "The Abyssinian Paradise in Coleridge and Milton," *Modern Philology*, III (1905–6), 327–32. Cf. also Lowes, *op. cit.*, pp. 374–76. Later, but independently, Dr. I. A. Richards called attention to a number of Milton's lines as an important source of Coleridge's imagery (*Principles of Literary Criticism* [London, 1925], pp. 30–31, 227). Like Lowes, he was thinking rather of scattered images than of the scenes as a whole. Thomas Copeland in *Review of English Studies*, XVII (1941), 87–90, drew attention to Milton's reference to the Book of Tobit as a probable source for Coleridge's "demon-lover" but was puzzled by the waning moon and the woman's desire, in Coleridge's version, instead of fear. The *Arabian Tales*, from which *Thalaba* sprang, provides an answer to Mr. Copeland's question if we must suppose a printed source for everything in Coleridge's poem—as, in fact, we apparently almost must.

33. Lowes assembled several accounts from ancient writers in which the Nile and the Alpheus are mentioned in the same passages. Some also include the Tigris. No doubt some of these Coleridge had read at one time or another. But to the English literary reader mention of the Alpheus almost automatically calls up the phrases of *Lycidas*.

34. *Lear*, IV, vi, 14–15; *Paradise Lost*, II, 636–37; *Osorio*, V, i, 39–41; letter of Coleridge to Thelwall, October, 1797, in which the "hanging wood" passage of *Osorio* was quoted, *Letters*, I, 229; "The Phenomena of the Wye, during the Winter of 1797–8" by "J. T.," *Monthly Magazine* for May, 1798 (published in June), V, 343 ff.; Wordsworth, Preface to the edition of 1815; *Hyperion*, I, 6–7. The article on the Wye, though signed only with initials, is easily traceable as Thelwall's. It was continued in the following issue. Might this description, I wonder (it was an exceptionally interesting one), have sent the Wordsworths off on that tour of the Wye that produced *Tintern Abbey* a few weeks later?

35. Quoted from the Wordsworth *Memoirs* (1851) in facsimile *Christabel*, pp. 16–17.

36. *Poems*, I, 94, 102–3, 94–96.

37. *Ibid.*, p. 98. It is surprising that Coleridge's use of these highly developed patterns has gone largely unnoticed. Saintsbury, while praising Coleridge along with other poets for "vowel-music," seems to have missed most of it, for he maintained that the "deliberate" use of such music practically began with Keats. Keats's at its best is more beautiful; but that of Coleridge preceded it and was certainly deliberate—as well as much fancier (George Saintsbury, *A History of English Prosody* [London, 1923], III, 542).

38. Marginalia in Warton's edition of *Poems upon Several Occasions*, printed in Coleridge's *Miscellaneous Criticism*, pp. 171–77 (174–75 especially). The annotations were made in 1823 or later, but those I have quoted probably record observations made much earlier. Italics are Coleridge's.

39. *Unpublished Letters*, I, 109.

40. *Biographia literaria*, II, 156.

41. Bodkin, *op. cit.*, p. 95.

42. *Laocoön*, trans. E. C. Beasley (London, 1853), chap. xxi, p. 149.

43. *Ibid.*, pp. 149–51.

44. *Ibid.*, chap. xvi, pp. 103–5.

45. The statements of Coleridge here and in later years do not conform entirely to Lessing's ideas. He took his own departures from them deliberately or else had not absorbed them fully. His remarks, for example, were in accord with the illustrations presented in chap. xvii of the *Laocoön*, but not with one or two of the accompanying generalizations, a distinction that, according to Crabb Robinson, Coleridge himself marked in later years: "He [Coleridge] spoke of Lessing's *Laocoön* as very unequal and in its parts contradictory, his examples destroying his theory" (*Miscellaneous Criticism*, p. 395).

46. *Miscellaneous Criticism*, pp. 162–65. Professor Raysor notes that this distinction was applied by Schiller, not to Milton, but to Klopstock, in the essay "On Naïve and Sentimental Poetry." Schiller as well as Lessing perhaps also entered into the definition of "high poetry" offered by Coleridge. Comparisons between Milton and Klopstock were of course a commonplace of German criticism.

47. *Miscellaneous Criticism*, p. 413. Cf. the observation in the lectures of 1818 on Spenser's functional use of time in description (*ibid.*, p. 35).

48. *Ibid.*, p. 162.

49. Letter to Southey, August 7, 1803, *Letters*, I, 427.

50. For an interesting account of the architectural and social history of the Royal Pavilion at Brighton, see Clifford Musgrave's *Royal Pavilion: A Study in the Romantic* (Brighton, 1951). In the final chapter, "Domes of Xanadu," Colderidge's poem and the Pavilion are represented as flowers from the same stalk of English orientalism. The celebrated orientalizing of the Pavilion, however, was not undertaken until after the latest possible date for the composition of *Kubla Khan*. The original building, before the series of alterations initiated in 1801, was Palladian, with French influence predominating in the interior. The shallow dome of this earlier structure, if one can judge from the pictures, was not a spectacular or even a very commanding feature.

51. Facsimile *Christabel*, p. 18.

APPENDIX I

1. *Monthly Magazine*, VIII (1799), 634.
2. *Ibid.*, pp. 952–53, 972–75.
3. *Ibid.*, IX (1800), 58.
4. *Historischen Werke* (Göttingen, 1821) I, xvi–xvii, xx–xxii, lxxvi; cf. *Allgemeine deutsche Biographie*, XI, 244–46. Hornemann, whose name was mentioned in the first communication from Heeren, was an actual traveler. He had been in distant parts for some time.
5. *Travels in the Interior Districts of Africa . . . with an Appendix . . . by Major* [James] *Rennell* (London, 1799), pp. 34–35, 188. An earlier version, also containing Rennell's appendix, had been published in 1798 from the *Proceedings of the African Association*. In the Gutch Memorandum Book Coleridge made the single notation (undatable), "Major Rennell." Lowes, however (pp. 33–34, 382), was no doubt correct in referring that entry to an earlier work of Rennell's, the *Memoir of a Map of Hindostan*.
6. *Thalaba*, notes to Book IV. Though ordinarily, by the standards of that day, a meticulous transcriber, Southey spelled the author's name "Heering." One might reason in either direction from this: (1) that Southey (and, by inference, Coleridge) could not have known anything of Heeren or he would not have made that mistake, or (2) that he *did* know an earlier version of a *nom de plume* in which the professor's name was not quite so daringly appropriated.
7. "The veracity and credibility of Herodotus have increased and increase with the increase of our discoveries. Several of his relations deemed fabulous, have been authenticated within the last thirty years from this present 1808" (*Coleridge's Miscellaneous Criticism*, p. 265). "Bruce a great and for a long time most ungratefully calumniated Man" (*Unpublished Letters*, II, 391).

Neither Coleridge nor his intimate friends in Germany seem to have recorded any acquaintance with Heeren. In the autobiographical preface to his *Werke*, Heeren mentions a certain Englishman, "W. Hamilton," among persons of attainment who had formerly attended his lectures or whom he had known (I, lxii). This may be the acquaintance "Hamilton, a Cambridge man," who took Coleridge to a meeting of the Saturday Club at Göttingen (*Letters*, I, 281). It is unlikely, however (for reasons too complicated to be worth recording here), that communications from Heeren would have reached the *Monthly Magazine* through either William Hamilton or William Taylor, who was the *Monthly's* main writer on German subjects.

8. *Poems*, I, 209–11.
9. VII, 536, 541.

10. *Letters*, I, 303-4; *Unpublished Lettters*, I, 123; Hanson, *Coleridge*, pp. 353-55.

11. VI (1798), 514, 517.

12. V, 507.

13. Cf. also the articles on Bristol discussed in chap. iv.

APPENDIX II

1. John Livingston Lowes, *The Road to Xanadu* (Boston, 1930), pp. 5, 451, 513. The notebook was published, with a good many errors, by Alois Brandl in Herrig's *Archiv*, XCVII (1896), 333-72. Through the kindness of Miss Coburn I have been able to use a microfilm of the original, which is in the British Museum.

2. Gutch, fol. *55b* (*Archiv*, p. 366). Here and later, I quote from Brandl's printed version except for a few material errors which I have corrected either from Lowes or from the microfilm of the MS (*Letters*, I, 316; Hanson, *Coleridge*, pp. 137-38).

3. *Wordsworth* (New York, 1916), I, 387.

4. Lowes, *op. cit.*, pp. 14-15, 457; Gutch, fol. *4b* (*Archiv*, p. 342).

5. *Common-Place Book*, IV, 520-21; letters to John May, August, 1799, from Stowey; to C. W. W. Wynn, August, probably from Stowey; to Humphry Davy, September (misdated "May 4") and October 18 from Exeter (*Life and Correspondence*, II, 23; Davy, *Fragmentary Remains*, ed. J. Davy [London, 1858], pp. 36, 40-41 [corrected from Curry]; Southey, *Letters*, ed. J. W. Warter [London, 1856], I, 79).

6. Milton, *Works* (New York, 1932), X, 4-5.

7. *Unpublished Letters*, I, 125; Milton, *op. cit.*, pp. 2-3; Chambers, *Coleridge* (London, 1938), p. 117. Southey had probably been reading Milton's *History*, as well as Geoffrey of Monmouth and Spenser (who gives the story in *Faerie Queene*, Book II, Canto X, ll. 7-9), for he still had *Madoc* in mind and was trying to connect Welsh with Peruvian and other South American legend (cf. also notes to *Thalaba*, Book IX). Southey and Coleridge did not transcribe the Diocletian material directly from each other; differences in details show that more than one version of the story was in use at this time.

8. Gutch, fol. *36b* (*Archiv*, p. 361); Coleridge, *Poems*, II, 993, 1056; Sotheby, *Oberon*, Book I, Stanzas 12-15; Wieland, *Werke* (Berlin, 1935), XIII, 10. Coleridge's poem was first printed in the *Morning Post* on December 21, 1799, and is thought to have been written during or after his visit to Sockburn in November (*Poems*, I, 330-31).

9. Gutch, fol. *25a* (*Archiv*, p. 354); *The Devil's Thoughts*, Stanza 12; *Poems*, I, 322-23. Lowes, *op. cit.* (2d ed.), p. 604a, dates the event itself from a Bristol newspaper of November 8, 1795. E. H. Coleridge in his

note to the stanza marked the reference and its connection with the Gutch note.

10. Fol. 24b (*Archiv*, p. 353). This repeated another entry on an earlier page (fol. 7a): "Burnet's theoria telluris translated into Blank Verse, the original at the bottom of the page." The list of twenty-seven topics seems to have been made in part from running through the rest of the notebook and culling topics already recorded, as well as adding new ones.

11. *Thalaba*, VII, 4 and notes; cf. *Life and Correspondence*, II, 16; *Common-Place Book*, IV, 2-3.

12. *Thalaba*, V, 27. In his notes to this passage Southey quoted a long account of this ghoulish material from Grose's *Provincial Glossary and Popular Superstitions*, which Lowes (*op. cit.*, pp. 555-58) wondered if Coleridge knew. Southey may have been led to this work by Coleridge, who used it, if at all, earlier in *The Ancient Mariner*.

13. Fol. 35a (*Archiv*, p. 360); *Thalaba*, V, 36. Cf. Lowes (*op. cit.*, pp. 10, 455), who recorded later parallels of this in *Omniana* and *Aids to Reflection* but missed its appearance in *Thalaba*.

14. Gutch, fol. 7b (*Archiv*, p. 344); Lowes, *op. cit.*, pp. 17, 462-63; Southey, *Life and Correspondence*, II, 34, 40; unpublished letters of August 2, 1799, and January 8, 1800 (Curry); Duppa, *Journal of the Most Remarkable Occurrences* [in Rome] ... *1798* (London, 1799), Preface; Curry in *Review of English Studies*, XIV (1938), 193-99.

15. Gutch, fol. 23a (*Archiv*, p. 353, incorrectly printed); Hanson, *op cit.*, pp. 41-46, 356, 433; Southey, unpublished letter of October 12, 1799 (Curry); *Letters*, I, 306. Writing from Exeter, Coleridge identified Hucks to Poole as "the man who toured with me in Wales and afterwards published his 'Tour,' " which rather suggests that there had been little or no contact between them since. Hucks carried out his promise, and his verses duly appeared in the *Anthology*.

16. Gutch, fols. 4a, 19a (*Archiv*, pp. 342, 350).

APPENDIX III

1. *Journals of Dorothy Wordsworth*, ed. E. de Selincourt (New York, 1941), I, 31.

2. *Ibid.*, p. 34. In a footnote to the word "Kubla," de Selincourt identified it as "presumably" a MS copy of Coleridge's poem.

3. For all that follows on the subject of Dorothy Wordsworth's journals I am greatly indebted to the kindness of two persons. Miss Helen Darbishire confirmed for me the printed reading of the word, gave me a useful description of the manuscripts, and arranged for photographs to be made of certain portions of the journals. Later, when

inspection of these and other circumstances had raised additional questions in my mind, Miss Kathleen Coburn furnished me with other useful information from her examination of the two German notebooks. Both she and Miss Darbishire, however, are quite free of any responsibility for the use to which I have put their kindness.

4. In the notebook the word is not underlined and several of the letters seem to me doubtful. But if it is not "Kubla," I do not know what else it might be; certainly it is not *Kuche(n)*.

5. The connection of the poem with Porlock, which I see no reason to doubt, discourages any such assumption, as do a number of other circumstances.

6. *Journals*, I, 22, 61, 167; II, 22, 409, 410.

7. *Unpublished Letters*, I, 128, 146–47, 161, 164; *Letters*, I, 317, 337, 349 (the dates range from late September, 1799, to March, 1801).

For an example of the kind of family projects of copying that went on later at Grasmere, see a passage quoted in de Selincourt's Preface to the *Journals* (I, xi), in which Dorothy tells of recopying her journal (that of 1803, a more ambitious and finished affair than the German one) for her niece, while Sara Hutchinson has been making a copy for Coleridge. In the retrospective conclusion of the German journal Dorothy used the word "fountain" immediately after "Kubla." This "fountain" might have helped produce a cross-current of associations and hence a slip of the pen if she had been hearing or thinking of the poem recently. The actual visible fountain as seen at the time, an artificial arrangement of water for drinking in a city market place, would hardly have done so; but the *word* might, especially if she were rewriting later from notes in which the word "fountain" already lay before her.

8. My account of this is based upon information supplied in part by Miss Darbishire and in part by Miss Coburn, except for most of the observations connected with Lessing's *Fables*, which photographs of the MSS enabled me to make.

9. *The Brothers* was founded on an incident Coleridge and Wordsworth heard of during their tour of the Lake District, reported in Coleridge's notebook on November 12. Wordsworth mentioned it ("the pastoral of Bowman") as "begun" when he wrote to Coleridge on Christmas Eve, 1799. It was completed by about February (*Early Letters*, p. 237; *Poetical Works*, II, 467; *The Prelude*, ed. de Selincourt, p. 512).

10. *Journals*, I, 107, 110, 114, 116–24 *passim*, 128. Shortly after her return from Germany Dorothy Wordsworth intended to improve her German sufficiently to make translations. This attempt of 1802 seems to have been the first serious effort to carry out the plan, though in his

Christmas Eve (1799) letter to Coleridge Wordsworth had written: "We shall be glad to receive the German books though it will be at least 3 weeks before D will have any leisure to begin" (*Early Letters*, p. 237). The work on Lessing in 1802 may have been a revival, however, of something begun two years earlier and abandoned (cf. *ibid.*, p. 253).

11. Cf. Harper's *Wordsworth* (New York, 1916), I, 253, for the dates of Wordsworth's Godwinism. Coleridge, it will be recalled, had written an attack on Godwinism on October 8, 1799, shortly before his visit to Wordsworth. Discussion of the subject at that time might have inspired Wordsworth's notes. For the dates of *The Prelude*, see the statement by de Selincourt in his edition of the poem (Introd., pp. xxxiv–xxxv) about the earliest-known manuscript of any considerable length. He does not mention this fragment. The spacing in the notebook suggests that the "Kubla" passage preceded the Lessing material, and Miss Coburn reports that different pen and ink appear to have been used for these two entries. That fact may mean a materially earlier date for the first entry, though in a literary household with much transcribing going on, the use of different pen and ink may signify little.

12. *Journals*, I, 31–32.

13. *Early Letters*, p. 202; *Journals*, I, 34. But the matter is more complicated. One manuscript of the journal, that in the notebook, mentions no hour of arrival; the fair copy, of which only fragments remain, gives the reading printed by de Selincourt—"between 5 and 6 in the evening." The letter too is something of a puzzle. The manuscript is not now known, and de Selincourt and Knight printed it from Christopher Wordsworth's *Memoirs*, where only fragments are given without date or even any indication that the extracts are from a single letter. Knight printed the matter as two letters, de Selincourt as one, with the conjecture that it was addressed to Mary Hutchinson. As far as one can judge from what survives, the beginning would seem to have been written soon after the Wordsworths' arrival at Goslar, the subsequent passages somewhat later.

14. The letter: "We quitted Hamburgh on Wednesday evening, at five o'clock, reached Luneburg to breakfast on Thursday, and arrived at Brunswick between three and four on Friday evening." The journal: "We quitted Hamburgh on Wednesday evening, October 3, at 5 o'clock, reached Luneburg at breakfast on Thursday," etc. In Notebook 2 the expression "at breakfast" was first written in the quainter idiom of the letter, "to breakfast." Then or later, Dorothy corrected "to" by writing "at" over it. This and the comment on diligences and the phrasing of the date, taken all together, establish, I think, quite certainly that the letter could not have been written after the journal or have been copied from it.

15. The letter: "There [at Brunswick] we dined. It is an old, silent, dull-looking place; the duke's palace a large white building, with no elegance in its external appearance." The journal: ". . . after we had dined. It is an old, silent, dull looking place. . . . The Duke's palace is a large white building. There is nothing of elegance in its external appearance, but the gardens seemed as if they would be very pleasant." The fragments of the letter printed by Christopher Wordsworth are very much chopped up; the correspondences may actually therefore have been much more extensive.

16. I do not think the difference in the time given grew out of an error in copying, for Dorothy Wordsworth was inclined to use "evening" for a part of the afternoon, as is still done in the southern United States. As the hour and word both are different, I think the discrepancy more likely one of memory.

17. *Journals*, I, 31, 33, 34. One or two other trivial circumstances strengthen my impression that the Hamburg-Goslar narrative in Notebook 2 is a copy rather than a first writing—for example, on the last page a canceled miswriting such as I think is rather more often an optical than a mental anticipation of a coming word.

18. *Journals*, I, 103, 104, 108-9.

19. (London, 1953), p. 49.

Index

Books and articles (with certain exceptions) are indexed only under the authors' names. References in the notes to standard editions of the works and letters of Coleridge and Southey are not indexed.